American Judaism in Transition

The Secularization of a Religious Community

Gerhard Falk

University Press of America, Inc.

Lanham • New York • London

Copyright © 1995 by
University Press of America,® Inc.
4720 Boston Way
Lanham, Maryland 20706

3 Henrietta Street
London, WC2E 8LU England

Library of Congress Cataloging-in-Publication Data

Falk, Gerhard
American Judaism in transition : the secularization of a religious
community / Gerhard Falk.
p.   cm.
1. Juddaism--United States--History--20th century. 2. Secularism--
United States. 3. Secularization (Theology)--History of doctrines. 4.
Jews--Cultural assimilation--United States.   I. Title.
BM205.F33   1995   296'.0973'0904--dc20   95-4926   CIP

ISBN 0-7618-0015-8 (cloth: alk ppr.)
ISBN 0-7618-0016-6 (pbk: alk ppr.)

ACKNOWLEDGEMENTS
AND DEDICATION

I want to thank my son, Clifford Falk, for the many hours he spent proofreading this manuscript and helping me in the use of the computer.

This book is dedicated to the government and people of the United States who gave me and my family, though marked for death, a second chance to live.

Contents

Preface

Secularization of Western Christianity is at least as old as the writings of the Jewish philosopher Baruch Spinoza (1634-1677).

Since then, and to our day, an enormous literature has developed concerning the secularization of Christianity. Some writers have also produced periodical literature concerning this phenomenon in Judaism. However, a full exploration of this trend in Judaism is yet to be achieved. Therefore this is an attempt to work towards that end.

An understanding of the secularization of the American Jewish community is somewhat easier to develop than is true of a similar work concerning American Christianity because the number of American Jews in so small. Such a small number lends itself better to a comprehensive study than would be true of a very large group. Thus, according to the National Jewish Population data of 1990 there are only 4.4 million Jews in the U.S.A.

Not so with Christianity which had about 150 million followers in the United States in 1995. This means that in addition to the six million followers of non-Christian religions, there are about 100 million Americans who have no religion.

Evidently then, secularization has made great inroads among all Americans, regardless of religious background or ethnic origins. Among Jewish Americans however, this tendency has become so pronounced that numerous observers now speak of the "Vanishing American Jew," a phrase first used by *LOOK* magazine in 1958.

While it is most unlikely that Judaism will disappear altogether from America it is evident that great changes have altered that ancient faith profoundly. It is the purpose of this book to describe the origin and the outcome of these changes.

Introduction

"Secularization refers to the decline of religion as a coherent identifiable system of beliefs and practices."[1] This definition of "secularization" is useful because it is a sociological definition in the sense that it defines the concept of secularization with reference to visible behavior. Thus, it can be reasonably assumed that a person who attends a house of worship and there engages in ritualistic conduct such as singing hymns, kneeling before icons, reciting prayers or eating or drinking specially designated foods such as "unleavened bread" is motivated to do so by beliefs associated with religion.

Marcus Tullius Cicero (106-43 B.C.E.) ("Before the Christian Era") explains in "De Natura Deorum" or "On the Nature of the Gods", that the word religion is derived from "relegere" meaning to "read again." He observes that believers read the same texts over and over again so as to influence the gods. Despite this explanation Cicero uses the word in that same book to also mean "to bind together" or "res ligare" hence, "the thing that binds." The English word league is of the same origin.[2] These Latin origins of the word religion are significant because both relate to behavior and interaction and recognize the sociological nature of religion.

It must be understood that some would dispute the trend towards secularization here discussed because they make no distinction between "religion" as an institution involving conduct and "the religious" which refers to subjective attitudes concerning personal beliefs as to the meaning of life, the nature of the universe, the existence of God, "life" after death and other so-called spiritual matters. It is however impossible to deal with "the religious" in the present context because the subjective feelings of millions of people cannot be observed. In short, any effort to discuss "the religious" must remain in the realm of speculation while a discussion of religion can rest on such visible facts as church attendance, financial contributions, baptisms, "bar mitzvah" celebrations, wedding ceremonies and a host of other events depending on observable behavior.[3]

Since it has long been established by numerous studies in the field of social psychology that what people say they think or feel does not accurately correspond to what people do, it is behavior which indicates far better than anything else to what extent a population adheres to religion.[4]

Now religion is one means of conferring identity on an individual or a group of individuals. Nationality is another means of identifying people as is family, economic status, occupation, education, club membership and a host of other measurements and criteria.

Prior to the seventeenth century religion was a more useful means of identifying various populations and individuals than is true today. The reason for this change is that philosophical and scientific changes have made religious identification irrelevant while nationality, education and its consequence, occupation, are very important in an age and in complex nation - states which depend on the division of labor for their existence. The evidence for this contention is found in every newspaper in America, where people are identified as "German business men," or "American baseball players," or "British actors" while the religion of the persons described is either not mentioned at all or given as an afterthought in a paragraph buried at the end of the news story.

Until the rise of science religion was a unifying force, as it still is in non-Western cultures such as the Moslem states. In Western cultures, however, religion cannot unify large populations. The dream of unifying all men in one church died with the advent of the Reformation which made it plain that religious consensus could never be achieved in Christian lands. Therefore nationality has been and is now the unifying force in all of Western culture where history is viewed as the experiences of nation - states in terms of wars, depressions, migrations and scientific achievements. Religion is seldom, if ever, part of the content of modern historical writing.

Now Martin has shown that historical events have a direct influence on social change and that the origins of secularization go much further back in time than the nineteenth century when the word *secularism* was first coined by the then popular writer George Holyoake (1817-1906) who defined *secularism* as "the improvement of life by material means".[5]

While Holyoake made no distinction between secularization and secularism it is the process of secularization which is of concern here. That process is summarized by noting that secularization occurs when large scale urban societies steadily absorb small, traditional societies holding a religious world view; that these societies are governed by rational, scientific rules and regulations which void supernatural ideas; that therefore religion becomes marginalized outside the dominant economic and familial concerns of most people and that religion ceases to be public and becomes entirely a private affair.[6]

These aspects of secularization in earlier centuries became much more visible in nineteenth century Europe than ever before and became particularly obvious with reference to the Jewish population of that continent. This means that the Jews of Germany in particular, but also the Jews of other European countries became or appeared to be the leaders in the secularization process then under way.

Because after the Reformation Christianity could no longer integrate Europe as evidenced by the religious hatred produced by Martin Luther and his numerous enemies, unity of the nation became the watchword of those who sought security in unity and certainty in uniformity.[7] Thus, the extremes of nationalism became the substitute for religious loyalty in most European countries and in particular in Germany, the leader in science, art and literature in the 19th century Western world.

This means that the process of secularization which had begun when Christianity was still dominant in the minds of most Western men could not be halted by appeals to religious unity. Now it turned out that appeals to nationalism were equally incapable of halting the progress of secularization. Fearing the progress of the secular, many nineteenth and early twentieth century Americans and Europeans clung to traditions which they hoped would save them from constant social change. In America this lead to Prohibition, quotas on immigration, revivalism among Protestants and isolationism.[8]

In Europe the fear of social change and the advent of secularization finally led to fascism and its most excessive manifestation, Nazism.

The reasons for this are easily enumerated. First, secularization meant that numerous privileged groups lost influence and power to people who were consulted by governments and others because of their expertise in science and technology. Thus, beginning with the nineteenth century, engineers or chemists or physicians, including Jewish experts, were asked for advice concerning public affairs while traditional elites whose influence and power rested on land holdings or family connections were ignored. As a consequence of this "democracy of expertise" demands for political democracy grew rapidly in nineteenth century Europe as it is growing in Asia and South America at the end of the 20th century.

This development then led traditional elites to promote the view that democracy is somehow foreign and selfish. Traditional elites then in Europe and now in Asia and in Iran, for example, decry individualism which always accompanies technological and scientific expertise, and point to the "old" values to which these elites like to appeal as "community" values. Such traditional elites consistently appeal to these "old traditions" in which they claim the community took precedence over the individual because they, the elites, benefit from so-called community values solely because of their birth and not because of their achievements. In short, secular, technological society rewards ability and personal achievement while traditional society rewards inherited status sanctioned by religion. Thus, the introduction of the right to choose one's life work, the development of free public education, the growth of large impersonal industries and the increase in financial accumulations by newly rich citizens of any origin has led to great fear and insecurity both for the European aristocracy and for all those ordinary citizens who could not or would not participate in these new developments and who could easily be led to believe that this "new world order" was caused by the illegitimate manipulations of Jews, Communists, Capitalists and a host of other "enemies."

Meanwhile it is obvious that European Jews, whose status had for centuries been no better than that of blacks in Mississippi before the civil rights movement, made every effort to emancipate themselves precisely by the means which were so resented by the conservatives among the traditional elites and the unsuccessful populations whom the aristocrats dominated.[9]

All this therefore led to great anxiety among the Jewish populations of Europe in earlier years and America now to make certain that individual achievement and not tradition or group association be the criteria for success. This is precisely the formula for success in secular America today and is the key for understanding the success of the American Jewish community at the end of the 20th century.

The trend towards secularization is of course visible in Europe as well as in America. In 1981 The European Values System Study Group conducted a survey in ten European countries. This survey, later repeated in several additional countries, aimed at obtaining representative samples of adults between the ages of eighteen and sixty five. Respondents were asked to answer four questions. These were: 1. "How important is God in your life?" 2. "Do you find you get comfort and strength from religion?" 3. "Do you take some moments for prayer, meditation or contemplation?" 4. "Independently of whether you go to church or not, would you say you are: a religious person, not a religious person, a convinced atheist? (Don't know)".

The outcome of this survey showed that only 3% of the people of Denmark, a Protestant country, attend church while in France, a Catholic country, only 12% attend church. Other countries such as Germany had a 22% attendance while Ulster, with a two thirds Protestant majority, had an attendance of 53%. Only Ireland exhibited an 82% church attendance rate that year. We see therefore that secularization has made great progress in Europe if we use church attendance as a criterion to provide us with a reason for drawing such a conclusion. Since the other three questions on the European Values Survey were subjective we will not analyze them here.[10]

A similar study has not been made in the United States. However, in 1990 the Council of Jewish Federations conducted a *Jewish Population Survey* in the United States. This survey clearly showed the extent of secularization which had overtaken the American Jewish community at that time and which has altered that groups leadership, practices, life styles and future orientation considerably from that of their immigrant ancestors.

What is true of the European community and the American Jewish community with reference to secularization is most probably also true of the Christian community in America. However, empirical evidence for making such a claim is now lacking. This is in part true because there are at least 150 million Christians in this country so that a study concerning them would be a massive and expensive undertaking. There are however only about 5.8 million persons in the United States who can in some sense be identified as Jews. Therefore the *Jewish Population Survey* was readily undertaken and published in 1991. Beginning with the meaning of that survey I shall show in these pages why and how secularization has made such great inroads into the Jewish group.[11]

Because Jews in Europe and America are a small minority in the Christian world I have reviewed the history of Christian secularization over the past four hundred years. This is absolutely necessary because the influence of Christian values and Christian philosophy and Christian actions upon Jews is profound.

In short, it is reasonable to contend that events in the Jewish community are directly influenced by events in the non-Jewish world surrounding the Jewish community. This does not suggest that Jewish influence upon Christian thinking is not also very great. On the contrary. The relationship is a close and reciprocal one as will be demonstrated in these pages.

We begin then with a survey of the status of American Jews in the census year of nineteen ninety.

NOTES

[1]Liana Giorgi, "Religious involvement in a secularist society etc." *The British Journal of Sociology*, Vol. 43, No. 4, December, 1992, p. 640.

[2]Marcus Tullius Cicero, *De Natura Deorum,* Cambridge, The Harvard University Press, (1933) 1961.

[3]David Martin, *The Religious and the Secular: Studies in Secularization,* London, Routledge and Keegan Paul, 1969.

[4]See for example: W. Warren and Marie Jahoda, *Attitudes,* Harmondsworth, Penguin Books, 1973.

[5]George Jacob Holyoake, *The Origin and Nature of Secularism,* London, Swan, Sonnenschein, 1886, p.51.

[6]Robert Wuthnow, *The Restructuring of American Religion: Society and Faith Since World War II,* Princeton N.J., Princeton University Press, 1988.

[7]Johannes Brosseder, *Luther's Stellung zu den Juden im Spiegel seiner Interpreten ,* Munich, Max Hueber Verlag, 1972.

[8]Selig Adler, *The Isolationist Impulse,* New York, Collier Books, 1961.

[9]Werner Jochmann, *Gesellschaftskrise und Judenfeindschaft in Deutschland 1870-1945,* Hamburg, Christians Verlag, 1991, pp. 39-40.

[10]S.G. Harding et. al., *Contrasting Values in Western Europe: Unity Diversity and Change,* Houndsmills, The Macmillan Press, 1986.

[11]Barry A.Kosmin, et al. , *Highlights of the CJF Jewish Population Survey,* New York, Council of Jewish Federations, 1991.

Part One

The Present Condition of Judaism In America

Chapter I

The American Jewish Community at the End of the Twentieth Century

I.

In 1966 the eminent Jewish scholar, Rabbi Robert Gordis, wrote: "It cannot be denied that there are major ills in the Jewish community which often serve to alienate from Judaism many young people, not to speak of their elders." [1]

These words were not only relevant to the Jewish community at the time they were written. They were also prophetic as the *National Jewish Population Survey of 1990* has shown.[2]

In addition, the work of Herbert Gans, Erich Rosenthal and others demonstrated in the 1950's that major intergenerational changes had already taken place in the Jewish community. It was then also anticipated that further changes in the third and fourth generation of American Jews would lead some to question whether Judaism would survive at all in the U.S. in the next, the 21st, century. Among those who believed then that the American Jew could vanish from American society altogether were such diverse publications as *Look* and *Commentary*.[3]

Between the comments of the *Look* editors in 1958 and the analysis of Edward Norden in 1991 was the Conference on Jewish Population, held in 1978. The proceedings of that conference plainly indicate that the participants knew at that time that "The Coming Shrinkage of American Jewry" could not be halted or averted by any strategy then known.[4]

It is therefore the purpose of the present study to discover the reasons for this shrinkage. Further, it is intended to sort out those factors in American society which govern this shrinkage and which are not under the control of the Jewish community. Principally, however, I shall discuss those aspects of the American Jewish experience which are under the control of the Jewish community and which contribute to the shrinkage of Jewish numbers as well. The purpose of that discussion will be to limit this shrinkage and to strengthen the remnant of Jews in America at a time when "most of the remaining Jews will no longer be in America but in Zion."[5]

II.

The demographic facts concerning the American Jewish community are best understood if we inspect the *National Jewish Population Survey of 1990.* Because of the excellent methodology used in conducting this survey and because of the sophisticated analysis given the results by the professionals who wrote the report derived from it, we can rely on the results obtained. These results we call demographic facts. These demographic facts may be interpreted in several ways. Nevertheless, some conclusions drawn from these facts can hardly be denied by anyone reading that study. These then are the facts derived from that survey:

1. In 1990 there were in the U.S.A. 4,210,000 persons who were born Jewish and whose religion was Judaism. Further, there were 185,000 persons in the U.S.A. that year who were not born Jewish but who had converted to Judaism. Together with these "Jews by Choice," there were then 4,395,000 adherents to Judaism in America.[6]

2. In 1990 there were 1,120,000 persons in the U.S.A. who were born Jews but at that time had no religion. If these secular Jews are counted as Jews because they consider themselves Jews then the grand total of Jews in America in 1990 was 5,515,000 or 2% of the American population of 254,105,000 persons estimated in 1992.[7]

This should be compared to the condition of the American Jewish population in 1937 when all Americans numbered about 131 million and Jews were 3.7% of all Americans and 1968 when that proportion had sunk to 2.9% and the country had about 200 million people. [8]

The "Survey" shows in detail that various other indicators of decline in the Jewish community reveal the same trend as the population count. For example, the age distribution of the Jewish population of the U.S. is such that it contains nearly one third more "elderly", i.e., people over sixty-five than is true in the whole American population. Similarly, the proportion of young Jews is smaller than is true in the general American population. Thus, only 18.9% of Jews are under age 15 while 20.4% of all Americans are under fifteen. A very significant indicator of Jewish decline in the U.S. is the birth rate. Thus, while the U.S. white population has a birth rate of 1.29 children per woman age 25 to 34 and 2 children per woman age 35 to 44, the number of children ever born to Jewish women in those age groups is only .87 and 1.57 for those who practice Judaism. It is yet lower for those who, although Jewish, have no religion. This means that Jews do not replace themselves from generation to generation and are indeed committing "endogenous genocide."[9]

The director of the earlier, 1970 *National Jewish Population Study*, Fred Massarik, reports that upon the conclusion of that study, the "leadership" of the Jewish community sought to deny the findings of that study to the effect that the Jewish community "had been losing Jewish population in massive numbers."[10] That study, conducted with all those methods then available, was nevertheless politicized by those who had the influence and the power to spend community money to repeat the work already done solely because they didn't like the outcome. Thus, "research design is unavoidably enmeshed in a social, political and economic matrix."[11] To avoid similar pitfalls, the 1990 *National Jewish Population Study* used phone calls rather than personal interviews to gain the data accumulated. The study thereby was more extensive than before. The findings are indeed reliable. The question the Jewish community must answer therefore is: "Do we *really* want to know?" What needs to be acknowledged by those interested in Jewish survival in America are then these inescapable conditions as uncovered by the *National Jewish Population Study of 1990*:

1. There is a core of Jews in America who identify themselves as Jews either in terms of religion or as secular Jews.

2. Since 1985, over half of born Jews chose a spouse who is not Jewish.

3. Of the 3,186,000 American households containing Jews, only 56.8% are entirely Jewish.

4. 700,000 children born to at least one Jewish parent are being raised in another religion.

5. The Jewish population is extensively dispersed across all of the United States so that major centers of Jewish life have been greatly weakened.

6. Since 91% of all American Jews are natives, and since immigration from Israel and Eastern Europe is small, the Jewish community is distinctly American.

7. Divorce has become relatively common among American Jews.

8. Non-Jewish religious practices are wide-spread among American Jews. Thus, 28% of Jewish households have a Christmas tree some times or every year, yet only 22% of Jews light Sabbath candles every week.

9. 72% of American Jews do not belong to any Jewish organization.

10. All this, and many other indicators, reflect a growing secularization of the American Jewish community.[12]

This secularization is best understood if we briefly review the relationship between religion and science and the effect of that quarrel upon the American Jewish community.

III.

The quarrel between science and religion, which is as old as the beginnings of knowledge and inquiry, took on a virulence and importance during the nineteenth century in Europe which it never possessed before and which of course influenced the European Jews as much as it did other Europeans and Americans. Then, when the European Jews began to come to this country in great numbers at the end of the 19th century and the beginning of the 20th century, they brought the consequences of that quarrel with them as did everyone else who came from Europe in those years.

At first, this quarrel was seen by its combatants as an "all or nothing" fight which both sides thought they had to win in order to save the world. Thus, the supporters of "science" as it was understood at the beginning of this century contended that religion would soon disappear, that science contained all knowledge and that only a "know-nothing" would support antiquated religious beliefs. The materialists attempted to show that all the world is only matter. However, this view has always had few followers because the average person, having some common sense, knows from experience that this is nonsense. Nevertheless, scientific thinking influenced many Europeans and Americans, Jews among them, to view with skepticism many of the claims of religion, particularly concerning rituals and ceremonies and their effect upon the material universe. In short, hardly anyone in the Western World was willing to take Scripture literally, although those who shouted that Darwin had disproved the Bible were seldom welcome.[13] The reason for this is, that the claims of science and its discovery had nothing to do with religion or belief in the supernatural. Science cannot and does not prove or negate religion. "No enquiry into the realm of the physical could produce results in the realm of the spiritual."[14] Those, however, who have little education in either religion or science, tend to believe extremes. Therefore some declare that science not only proves the absolute control man has over all things human, but that science also proves the utter futility of religion. Likewise, others insist that religion, not science, is the sole means of discovering the universe.

Even before the appearance of Charles Darwin's *Origin of Species* in 1859, a book which few of its opponents or proponents had ever read, numerous writers and lecturers had already incited the controversy concerning materialism based on new scientific knowledge.[15] It should be understood, however, that working scientists seldom participated in these debates because they knew then and know now that science is limited and uncertain. Among the semi-educated middle classes of Europe and America, however, there were those who rushed in and repeating crude slogans and poorly apprehended scientific information believed they had arrived at the final utopia, the establishment of the "scientific age" and the rule of utter materialism. Included in these middle class followers of the "new age" were a number of Jews simply because most Jews belong to the middle class and because a disproportionate number of Jews receive a higher education. Thus, while in 1987 13.2 percent of all American white men had a college education and 11.3 percent had at least some post graduate education, more than 20 percent of American Jewish men in 1990 were college graduates without post graduate education and more than 30 percent had at least some post graduate education. Among white women this discrepancy was just as great. Thus, nearly 25% of Jewish women are college graduates and a similar number hold graduate degrees. In the white American population only 11 percent of women are graduates of a college and a little more than 6 percent hold graduate degrees. Therefore Jewish women and men are much more likely to encounter anti-religious sentiments as expressed in many forums of higher education in America than would be true of non-Jewish people.

It is further of importance to note that Jews have shown an unsual degree of interest in the social sciences and that the number of Jews among sociology professors is exceptionally great. This is important because sociology from its beginning was founded on the assumption that religion is an antiquated form of institutionalized ignorance and superstition and that it was doomed to disappear shortly.[16] This belief, seldom examined or tested, is so entrenched in the social sciences and among some physical scientists that it is now a dogma seldom questioned and founded upon "a deep and abiding antagonism to religious belief and various expressions of organized religion."[17] This antagonism was part of the very reason for the existence of sociology founded by the French mathematician August Comte. Comte, a son of the French Revolution, viewed religion as a participant in all the oppression suffered by the French people at the hands of the old aristocracy. In this he was joined by almost all European sociologists who sought to establish a scientific religion as proposed by him.[18] Similar views were held by the most important sociologists in the United States, despite the fact that many sociologists were the children of the clergy or clergymen themselves.

In addition to the anti-religion bias encountered by college students, younger Jews of European birth and American Jews of the first generation had frequently become disillusioned with religion when they contrasted the freedom of and from religion in this country with the oppressive religious constraints they saw in Europe and in the orthodox families whence they came. In additon to the wish to escape the control of the rabbis in their own communities, Jews were particularly anxious to promote secularization and secularism because they had suffered so much from religious persecution in Europe and were by no means exempt from anti-Jewish bias here. Therefore many Jews believed that their problems would be alleviated if religion were weakened. All of these motives attracted Jewish students and other Jews, as well as many non-Jewish Americans to the doctrines of secularization. Hadden has summarized these doctrines in three propositions. These are: 1. "Once the world was filled with the sacred in thought, practice and institutional form. 2. After the Reformation and the Renaissance, the forces of modernization swept across the globe and secularization, ...loosened the dominance of the sacred. 3. In due course, the sacred shall disappear altogether..............[19] This has not happened nor is there any sign that it will happen. Instead, we find that in the United States secularization continues side by side with religion so that extreme positions concerning the advance of the secular are as untenable today as are the views of the extreme fundamentalists.

Thus, it can well be said that Alexander Pope had no better target for his phrase that "fools rush in where angels fear to tread" than the erstwhile and current support for extreme positions in the great debate between science and religion.[20] Indeed, many people were and are influenced by popular "scientific" thought, such as the belief that the universe has no purpose or that science is always successful. In fact, however, science nowhere attacks religion because it does not deal with religion, despite the indisputable evidence that some arguments by persons favoring religious explanations for the natural universe are untenable in the light of scientific evidence.

Those who are acquainted with the writings of the Jewish philosopher Baruch Spinoza (1632-1677) will recognize that Spinoza clearly distinguished between science and theology in his own century. Writing in his *Theologico-Political Treatise*, Spinoza demanded over three hundred years ago that theology be separated from reason.[21] "Those who know not that philosophy and reason are distinct, dispute whether Scripture should be made subservient to reason, or reason to Scripture: that is, whether the meaning of Scripture should be made to agree with reason; or whether reason should be made to agree with Scripture:..............Both parties are, as I have shown, utterly in the wrong, for either doctrine would require us to tamper with reason or Scripture. In short," said Spinoza, "one party will run wild with the aid of reason and the other will run wild without the aid of reason."[22] Spinoza was the first truly articulate secularist in Jewish philosophy although he did not subscribe to secularism, i.e., the doctrine that all things are human. Likewise, Moses Mendelssohn (1729-1786) was not a humanist but nevertheless a contributor to secularization among Jews. By translating the Torah (Old Testament) from Hebrew into German, Mendelssohn opened the doors of the Enlightenment to the Jewish population of German speaking lands. Nevertheless, he remained firmly within Judaism as demonstrated by his open letter to the theologian Lavater who had invited him to become a Christian. However, the translation of the Bible into German was meant to achieve the entrance of Jews into the German language and literature and to supply the still medieval Jews with an opportunity to adopt reason as their guide. There can be no doubt that Mendelssohn promoted secularization in Judaism as much in the 18th Century as Spinoza had in the seventeenth century.[23]

When the Zionist movement became popular in the Eastern European Jewish communities during the 19th century, secularization received additional prominence. The physician Leo Pinsker (1821-1891), an erstwhile assimilationist, recognized the need for Jewish "Auto-emancipation" in a stirring pamphlet published in 1882 calling upon Jews to establish their autonomy by building a national home based on political reality, not religion,[24] a sentiment echoed by the founder of political Zionism, Theodore Herzl (1860-1904). Herzl was far removed from the Jewish religion when he founded the Zionist movement as a response to anti-Jewish riots in France and elsewhere . His efforts were entirely secular as is still the case among the preponderance of his followers to this day (1995). [25]

In the United States, not only Zionism, but secularism in American life has led to the establishment of The Society for Humanist Judaism, The Congress of Secular Jewish Organizations and other groups seeking to secularize that ancient faith. [26]

Evidently, most Americans would agree with Spinoza concerning the failure of both extreme scientism and extreme secularism to sustain men's lives. Thus, anyone willing to ask will find that Americans are and have been in favor of "religion" for all of American history. While only 40% of Americans attend a house of worship once a week, and 68% are members of a religious body, 55% say that religion is very important.[27] This discrepancy in conduct and opinion is also a sign of secularization as is a respect for rational explanations of events, the right of people of different views to hold such views and, mainly, the wide spread opinion that religion is only one of several institutions, thus narrowing the functions religion is expected to fulfill.

The great disadvantage of these attitudes for many Americans has been that so many Americans have no transcendental hope and see no meaning in their lives. These two human needs cannot be met by science.[28] It is of course common knowledge that both the erstwhile Soviet Union and the "Thousand Year Reich" promoted ceremonies and rituals which took on the functions of religious rites because the followers of these political "cults" needed these spectacles in the absence of suspect religions which both dictatorships despised and which were discouraged and even persecuted by the bureaucracy in both police states.

In the United States, science created a problem for its followers which has sometimes been to the benefit of religion. That is the evidence that as scientific knowledge increases, ignorance increases as well. This increase is due to science because scientific findings raise more and more questions which cannot always be answered by scientific means. This increase of ignorance, brought about by science itself, makes the survival of religion possible. Nevertheless, secularization has triumphed in large measure in the United States of the 20th century and this is the principal reason for the decline in Judaism and Jewish affiliation.

Thus, the secularization of Judaism in America has been the inevitable outcome of the secularization of American society. American secularization in turn was and is a process that has continued for all of the history of mankind and has been defined as , "a process of decline in religious activities, beliefs, ways of thinking and institutions ......" .[29] A further description of secularization is : "the gradual deposition of religion from almost every structure and dimension of society, except perhaps, the most private and personal."[30]

We recognize, therefore, that the secularization of the Jewish community in America is in no sense unique, but that this phenomenon also affects the much larger, non- Jewish community. Thus, Max Weber has shown that Puritanism inevitably led to secularization because : " Puritan teaching encouraged wordly success..." and " ..... to the massive process of secularization, in the course of which utilitarian industriousness replaced the search for the Kingdom of God and created a specific bourgeois economic ethos."[31]

This occurred not only among Puritans but also among American Jews.

Not only Americans, but also other people have had to deal with secularization. Nevertheless, it is evident that the Jewish community in the United States has undergone a profound change in emphasis from a "sacred" to a "secular" community in less than one hundred years. This change among Jewish Americans has come about at a much faster rate than is true among Christian Americans.

One reason for this great change may be, as Nathan Glazer argues, that Jews lost their faith so easily because they had no faith to lose. This means that Jews have no doctrine, no collection of dogmas to which they could cling and with which they could resist argument.[32] Herein lies one of the true differences between the Christian and the Jewish view of conduct. While among Christians belief constitutes the basis for morality, among Jews practice, not belief supports the moral code.

Before we consider the consequences of secularization upon Jewish conduct in the United States further, it is necessary to recognize that there are some who object to this description of American Judaism. Four reasons have been listed for the proposition that Judaism in America is not tending toward the secular as much as is commonly assumed. These four arguments are first, that the abandonment of erstwhile orthodox practice in favor of a minimal practice by reform and conservative Jews does not constitute a decline in commitment to the supernatural but rather a restructuring of the emphasis in Jewish life from ritual to involvement in liberal causes. This involvement is seen as linking the practitioners of this kind of Judaism to the "prophetic tradition," as Reform Jews like to insist. Whether one wishes to accept this argument as valid depends on whether the "sacred" is seen as "any system of beliefs and practices anchored in ultimate concerns," or whether the sacred is viewed as synonymous with the "religious" which implies adherence to a system of beliefs and practices generally associated with orthodoxy.[33] The second argument denying the secularization of Judaism in America is that the numerous Jewish civic organizations, particularly the welfare federations, are evidence that the religion of American Jews may be found in the activity and ideology of the vast array of Jewish organizations which are typically thought of as secular.[34] A third argument, denying excessive secularization among American Jews, has been that Jews have become greatly involved in the "new religious movements." This argument, mainly advanced by Stark and Bainbridge, is based on their thesis that "*secularization is a self limiting process that leads not to irreligion but to a shift to the sources of religion.*" This argument seems quite weak when applied to Jews since those associated with any "new" religious movement are "a small proportion of those not affiliated with a synagogue."[35] Finally, it is argued by some that the emergence of private prayer circles among Jews, called "Chavurah," or "Chevrot," as well as an increase in the numbers of orthodox "chasidim" or "pious" Torah observers indicates a Jewish counter movement balancing the trend towards secularization. This too, however, is hardly tenable in view of the heavy trend towards secularization among American Jews visible in innumerable practices easily sufficient to neutralize these minor counter movements.[36]

IV.

There are a number of indices of secularization which have been uncovered in the extensive literature on that subject and which we may use to test the hypothesis that the American Jewish community has undergone extensive secularization over many years.

The first of these is the fact that religion has lost its social significance and has become "marginal to the operation of society." This means that rational and not supernatural forces control the American Jewish community at the end of the 20th century. [37]

This development was first discussed by Will Herberg in his 1955 analysis called *Protestant, Catholic, Jew.*[38] Here Herberg shows that the so-called "three major religions" in America have agreed to view participation in one of them as "alternative ways of being an American." Herberg argues that there is a common culture religion in America which may be expressed by belonging to one of the "three great faiths" and that all three have embraced a secularized form of interfaith religion which is seen as "the highest expression of religious coexistence."[39]   Thus, says Herberg, overt anti-religion is held as inconceivable and obnoxious in the U.S. while religiousness without religion is a well established way of life. It is this hollowed out kind of religion which has been called civic religion and which has distinct political overtones. The civic religion to which all are expected to subscribe identifies the American cause with the cause of God, however expressed. A good example of this attitude was the introduction of a religion theme into the Republican convention of 1992 which permitted even some evangelists to speak to the delegates and the nation.

A civic religion is one which has no sense of transcendence but rather is used to assure its followers that this American world is right and that this nation, this culture and the American himself is accepted by the Almighty.

American believers thus segregate religion from daily affairs and see no connection between their business and political affairs and their religion. Instead, the spirit of secularism prevails so that those who are affiliated with a religion in America are in agreement with the secularists who practice secularism and have nothing to do with any religion, that all things are either human or can be controlled by human intervention, even the Deity. This is as true among American Jews as it is among American Christians as all seek to rationalize their actions as much as possible.

Evidence for this effort to rationalize the structure and function of the American Jewish community is the personnel of the governing boards which supervise the operation of Jewish communal agencies in the U.S.. Almost all of the members of such boards are business men, lawyers, a few professors and on rare occasions a rabbi. Contrast this with the governance of the European Jewish community or the late 19th century Jewish community in America. "The world of the East European Jews," says Howe, "was colored throughout by religious emotion." Yet, even there "The closer the world came to modern life, the more did wealth challenge and usurp the position of learning."[40] In the United States, this challenge became at first a radical revolution against the encrusted rabbinate and its orthodoxy. Extremists even organized "Yom Kippur Balls," but failed to attract very many followers even as the challenge to established orthodoxy was taking hold among the masses of Jewish immigrants.[41] Already in the 1870's that challenge had split the Jewish community in America into orthodox and reform Jews only to be further segmented with the rise of conservative Judaism after the organization of the Jewish Theological Seminary in 1880.[42]   These developments changed the role of the rabbi in America drastically. While the European orthodox rabbis had the primary function of promoting Jewish scholarship, American conservative and reform rabbis are confronted with quite different roles, roles that have encroached upon the orthodox American rabbis as well. These roles are best understood as the expectations of the congregants when choosing a rabbi. Thus, these characteristics were listed by conservative congregations when asking the Jewish Theological seminary for candidates to fill their vacancies:

1. Scholarship 2. Youth 3. Pastoral activities 4. Sermons 5. Supportive wife 6. Experience 7. Educator 8. Executive leadership 9. Programming skills 10. Community involvement 11. Wife's involvement 12. Importance of age.[43]

Although this list of twelve attributes begins with scholarship, scholarship is generally defined as anything the rabbi may have learned while a student at the seminary. It is usually made clear by most congregations that what is not wanted is a rabbi who seeks to be a scholar now. It is therefore evident from a reading of the other eleven requirements that the role of the American rabbi has been radically changed from that of interpreter of the law to that of a minister in the Protestant sense. Very important is the repetition of the age factor in both the second and twelfth point of this list and the repetition of the "rebbetzin's" role in the fifth and eleventh items. Together with the need to sermonize, program and participate in communal affairs it is obvious that rational decision making has become all encompassing in the American rabbinate while appeals to God or supernatural forces are left to a few sermons in which the Deity is mentioned and to religious exercises generally labeled "services" in American Judaism. The principal reason for this change in rabbinical functions is the loss of social significance of religion in general. Therefore, rabbis are assigned tasks that could also be fulfilled by a person trained only in such secular occupations as social worker or recreational worker, provided such a secular professional had some knowledge of Jewish customs and ceremonies.   Indeed, there are numerous small Jewish congregations who have no rabbi and who employ, either with or without pay, some professional who has a fair Jewish background and who plays the role of   "pseudo-rabbi" on Saturdays, Holidays and at life cycle occasions. This has become possible because "religious symbols have lost their vibrancy and meaning." [44]

American orthodox rabbis are equally employed in secular activities. Earlier in the twentieth century, orthodox rabbis were greatly criticized and even held in contempt because they appeared to be the very epitome of religious fanaticism, defending a "relic doomed to disappear."[45] This most orthodox rabbis overcame in the latter part of this century by running the synagogue office, writing letters, supervising the Hebrew school, the nursery and the youth program and the building. The rabbi, whether orthodox or conservative or reform, must visit the sick, counsel bereaved and disturbed members and officiate at life cycle events.

"He assists with charitable causes within the community and beyond it; he participates in regional and national organizations in the larger Jewish community ....and he is at times an ambassador of good will to unaffiliated Jews, to the Gentile world, to other synagogues."[46] In short, the orthodox rabbi also participates in the widespread secularization of Judaism. The prestige or social honor accorded rabbis is far less in a secularized world than was true among the Jews of an earlier age. Here is a complaint by an immigrant orthodox rabbi which exemplifies in one man's words the great change which secularization has forced upon those still clinging to a world imbued with supernatural beliefs and practices: "A rabbi is good to be if you have the correct authority. The authority has been broken. A rabbi like in the old home, a rabbi for the town, we knew his word was law. We knew that the people must obey the rabbi.....etc." [47]

This reduction in the authority of the rabbi goes "hand in glove" with the development of secularization within religion itself. It is therefore important to understand that we are not discussing secularism. That concept refers to the denunciation of all matter supernatural and hence to atheism. Secularism is an ideology. Secularization is a process which can lead to secularism but usually does not. Instead, secularization ordinarily leads to the hollowing out of what appears to be religion because the symbols of religion continue to involve many citizens even when the substantive meaning has been lost. In these circumstances, such symbols as the Menorah, a seven or nine branched candelabrum, are merely decorative objects as are the Sabbath candle holders which only 22% of all American Jews light regularly. The Bible, or Torah, also becomes an unread symbol rather than an important lesson or guide to daily living. Thus, only 13% of Jews by religion consider the Torah or Bible the actual "Word of God."[48]

Religious actions have also declined in the Jewish community as secularization has increased. Only 61% of Jews by religion fast on Yom Kippur, only 59% attend a synagogue on the "High Holy Days", weekly synagogue attendance is only 11% and only 17% eat only kosher foods.[49]

An excellent means of calculating at least a minimum of participation in Jewish activities is the level of contributions given by Jews to Jewish philanthropies such as the United Jewish Appeal. It may seem amazing, but in 1974 Will Maslow reported that in New York City only 25% of all Jews contributed to the UJA. campaign. That percentage is somewhat higher in smaller and better organized Jewish communities such as Cleveland, Ohio where 80% of Jews made contributions to the United Jewish Appeal in the '70's.[50] The 1990 survey revealed that 62% of those who viewed themselves Jews by religion contributed to Jewish philanthropies at that time. Secular giving reached 67% within that same group. [51]

There is however one religious action which is widely observed in the Jewish community although it too has become utterly secularized in the hands of many American Jews. That is the observance of Bar Mitzvah and Bat Mitzvah. This is a *rite of passage* from childhood to adulthood. That phrase was invented by the Dutch-French anthropologist Arnold van Gennep who sought to show that in all societies these ceremonies seek to mark the transition from one status to another .[52]

Since 85% of born Jews who consider themselves Jewish by religion become Bar Mitzvah and since the same is true even of that 36% who say they have no religion, it is evident that the Bar Mitzvah rite plays a major role in maintaining the Jewish identity of most American Jewish adults. Bar Mitzvah has been called "the most clear cut rite of passage" by Jack E. Bynum and William E. Thompson, who argue in their book, *Juvenile Delinquency,* that delinquency is much lower among Jews than other Americans because of the "assumption of adult religious responsibilities and duties" by Jewish adolescents. Bynum and Thompson then suggest that all Americans "symbolize the rite of passage from childhood to adulthood ....".[53]

It is of course true that Bar Mitzvah, and to a lesser and more recent extent Bat Mitzvah, has had a salutary effect upon Jewish adolescents and provided them with all those benefits which rites of passage have always provided all mankind. Nevertheless, it can be easily demonstrated that the Bar/Bat Mitzvah ceremony has frequently become so secularized that it has lost its religious content almost entirely.

The origin of the Bar Mitzvah may be found in the "Mishnah". The Hebrew word "Mishnah" is derived from "shanah" to repeat. The "Mishnah" constitutes the first part of the Talmud which is a collection of scriptural interpretations first written in the 3rd century of the Common Era. In the 6th Division of that book, called "Tohoroth" in the subdivision called "Niddah" or vows, verse 6 deals with the validity of vows by children and holds that the vows of a boy age thirteen are valid and that the same holds true for girls at age twelve.[54] This interpretation then lead to the custom of instituting the Bar Mitzvah ceremony and designating the thirteen year old an adult. Usually these Hebrew/ Aramaic words are translated as "Son of the Commandment". This designation first came into use in the late Middle Ages. Prior to that time other labels were attached to a thirteen year old, such as "Godol" meaning big or adult or "Bar Onshin" meaning responsible. [55]

The great twelfth century Jewish scholar Maimonides commented upon this Mishnah in his explanation of the roles played by men at various ages. Said Maimonides: "At five years of age one is ready for the Bible; at ten years for the Mishnah, at thirteen years for the precepts etc."[56]

Bar Mitzvah was not known to the ancient Jews. This was true because minor children were permitted to participate in all religious ceremonies, including the reading of the Bible or Torah and used the "Tfillin." "Tfillin" are two boxes containing Scripture. These two boxes are attached to the forehead of a male congregant by a leather strap placed upon the skull and by another leather strap placed on the left forearm. The Greek word "phylactery" is sometimes used to designate these boxes, the word meaning "guards" in the sense that the words contained in the boxes are expected to guard the wearer from evil thoughts during prayer.

The two religious rights, witnessing the reading of Torah and using the "Tefillin", were restricted in the fourteenth and fifteenth century until participation in these religious observances became strictly a sign of adult status. That in turn made the "Bar Mitzvah" ceremony significant because a major status change was thereby initiated. It is the view of this author that this change became possible because life expectancy increased after the fifteenth century in Europe. Prior to that time death came so often to young children and life expectancy was so short that the community could not risk postponement of these duties to a later age. The history of childhood plainly shows that children were not much valued when there were many who died easily and seldom reached maturity. It was only in the 15th and 16th century "when people began to take increasing pleasure in them. New moral standards for the young began to appear in the 16th and 17th centuries as did a new emphasis upon parental responsibility for the welfare of children."[57]

Once the Bar Mitzvah ceremony had become generally accepted, the celebration of Bar Mitzvah was increasingly augmented both in the synagogue and in the home. In Germany and in Poland the Bar Mitzvah boy read portions of the Prophets as well as portions from the Bible or Torah. He also delivered a sermon and in some cases showed such scholarship and erudition that he was viewed a great scholar and "rebbe" even at a very young age. These customs continued in Europe until the 1940's when the Nazi killers wiped out the entire Jewish community there and America and Israel became the focus of Jewish life instead.

As we have already said, the Conservative movement was launched in this country. Together with its older branches, Reform and Orthodox Judaism, the Conservative movement became secularized and the Bar Mitzvah celebrations showed it. Today, some Bar Mitzvahs have become so ostentatious and so expensive that all sight is lost of the original intent of Bar Mitzvah and the religious and spiritual values previously associated with it have been voided.

It has become customary among some Jews to impose a sports theme upon Bar and Bat Mitzvah celebrations. Thus, a child may chose Football or Hockey as his theme. That done, table decorations at various elaborate meals during the Bar Miztvah weekend, carry football emblems. Sometimes, professional football players or hockey players or baseball players, who are seldom Jewish themselves, are invited to the Bar Mitzvah party to lend an authentic sports quality to the respective celebrations. Pictures of prominent athletes are often displayed at such Bat and Bar Mitzvahs. Occasionally fights develop in the hotels where Bar Mitzvahs are celebrated. The author is aquainted with a Bar Mitzvah party at which $3,000 worth of damage was done to a hotel in which the party took place as guests fought among each other, threw food into the wall and became totally drunk.

Often, the Bar Mitzvah boy and his family congratulate each other on the fact that at party time the actual Bar Mitzvah ceremony is over and the recently admitted "adult" can now forget the minimum of Hebrew and Jewish civilization he was forced to learn. It is rare that a Bat/Bar Mitzvah continues his Jewish education after the event so that the only memory a twelve or thirteen year old will have of the ceremony will be the party after the synagogue activities have been concluded.

While Bat and Bar Mitzvahs are generally held on Saturday because the Torah (Bible) is read that day, a few conduct the ceremony on a Monday or Thursday because the Torah is also read on those two days each week. This is not generally known but is derived from the ancient custom of the Israeli population to travel to Jerusalem on market days which were Monday and Thursday and then read the Torah so that farmers from outlying areas could hear the reading. There are now a number of American legal holidays on Mondays and a few, such as Thanksgiving, on Thursday. Therefore, some Jews have Bat or Bar Mitzvahs on those days. This then indicates that the Bar Mitzvah ceremony has become so strongly influenced by secular American society that the distance between the sacred and the profane has diminished to a minimum.

This reduction in the distance between secular and religious concerns is visible, not only in the Bar/Bat Mitzvah ceremony but also in the activities of religious congregations. While erstwhile religious activities consisted of prayer, study of sacred texts, participation in ceremonies and home observance of religious rites, the secularization process has translated these actions into fund raising and "good" works. Among the secularized Jews and others in late 20th century America, participation in political activities, money collection and active intervention in a variety of civic causes is very common. Thus, "good works," take the place of dogma, "liberal" politics became a substitute for ritual and financial contributions replace the promotion of scholarship.

Yet, it was Jewish scholarship which in addition to the rise of science and the secularization of the Christian world has led to the present condition of the American Jewish community. Beginning in the 17th century with the writings of the philosopher Baruch Spinoza and continuing in the 18th century with the works of Mendelssohn and in the 19th century with the efforts of Leo Pinsker and Theodor Herzl, secularization has reached an unsurpassed crescendo in the 20th century and now (1995) determines almost all of Jewish life. We therefore turn next to these writers and thereafter to the secularization of Christianity in which European and American Judaism has been embedded for so long.

NOTES

[1]Robert Gordis, *Judaism in a Christian World*, New York, McGraw Hill, 1966, p. 193.

[2]Barry A. Kosmin, Sidney Goldstein, Joseph Weksberg, Nava Lehrer, Ariella Keysar and Jeffrey Scheckner, *Highlights of the CJF 1990 Jewish Population Survey*, New York, Council of Jewish Federations, 1991.8

[3]Herbert J. Gans, "American Jewry: Present and Future," *Commentary*, Vol.21, No.5, May, 1956 pp.422-430 ; Herbert J. Gans, "The Future of American Jewry," *Commentary*, Vol. 21, No.6, June 1956,pp. 555-563. Erich Rosenthal, "Five Million American Jews," *Commentary*, Vol. 26, No.6, December 1958, pp.499-507. No author, "The Vanishing American Jew," *Look*, Vol.22, May 13, 1958, pp.74--78.

[4]Edward Norden, "Counting the Jews," *Commentary*, Vol.92, No.4, October 1991,pp.36-43. See also: Steven Cohen, "The Coming Shrinkage of American Jewry: A Review of Recent Research," in Judith A. Zimmerman and Barbara Trainin, Eds., *Jewish Population, Renascence or Oblivion*, New York, Commission on Synagogue Relations, Federation of Jewish Philanthropies, 1979, pp. 1-26.

[5]*Ibid.* p. 43.

[6]Barry Kosmin, et.al.,*op.cit.* p.4.

[7]*Information Please Almanac*, Boston, Houghton Mifflin & Co., 1993, p.3.

[8]*Ibid.* p.821 and H.J. Roberts, "Endogenous Jewish Genocide: The Impact of the ZPG Non-Parenthood Movement," in Zimmerman, *op.cit.* p. 235.

[9]Kosmin, et.al., pp. 11-15; Roberts, *ibid.*

[10]Fred Massarik, "Knowledge About U.S. Jewish Populations," *Journal of Jewish Communal Service*, Vol.68, No.4, Summer 1992, pp. 299-305.

[11]*Ibid.*, p. 302

[12]Sidney Goldstein, "Profile of American Jewry: Insights from the 1990 National Jewish Population Survey." *American Jewish Year Book, 1992,* Philadelphia, The Jewish Publication Society, 1992, pp.77-.

[13]Owen Chadwick, *The Secularization of the European Mind in the 20th Century,* Cambridge, England, The Cambridge Unversity Press, 1975, p. 162.

[14]*Ibid.,* p. 167..

[15]Charles Darwin, *The Origin of Species by Means of Natural Selection* or *The Preservation of Favored Races in the Struggle for Life,* New York, Macmillan, 1927.

[16]Gerhard Lenski, *The Religious Factor,* Doubleday, Garden City, N.Y., 1961.

[17]Jeffrey K. Hadden , "Desacralizing Secularization Theory," in *Secularization and Fundamentalism Reconsidered,* Jeffrey K. Hadden and Anson Shupe, eds., N.Y., Paragon House, 1989, p. 4.

[18]Auguste Comte, *Catechisme Positiviste,* Paris, Delmont, 1852.

[19]Hadden, *op.cit.,* p. 13.

[20]Alexander Pope, "An Essay On Criticism: Verse 625" in *Masters of English Literature,* Paul S. Wood and Evelyn M. Boyd, Eds., New York, The Macmillan Co., 1942, p. 960.

[21]R.H.M. Elwes, *The Chief Works of Benedict Spinoza,* New York, Dover Publications Inc., 1955, p. 182.

[22]*Ibid.* p. 190.

[23]Max L. Margolis and Alexander Marx, *A History of the Jewish People,* New York, Mediridan Books, Inc., 1960, p. 595. See also, Will and Ariel Durant, *Rousseau and Revolution,* New York, Simon and Schuster, 1967, p. 639.

[24]Leo Pinsker, "Auto-Emancipation," in Azriel Eisenberg, *Modern Jewish Life In Literature,* New York, The United Synagogue of America, 1957, pp. 153-155.

[25]Margolis and Marx, *op.cit.* pp. 703-712.

[26]Seth Kulick, "The Evolution of Secular Judiaism," *The Humanist,* Vol. 53, March/April, 1993, p.32.

[27]The *Gallup Report, #259,* April 1987.

[28]Peter I. Berger, *The Sacred Canopy, Garden City,* N.Y. , Doubleday, 1967.

[29]Bryan R. Wilson, "Secularization," in *The Encyclopedia of Religion, Vol. 13,* Mircea Eliades, Ed., New York, Macmillan Publishing Co., 1987, p. 159.

[30]Lawrence Barman, "Confronting Secularization: Origins of the London Society for the Study of Religion," *Church History,* Vol. 62, No. 1, March 1993, p.22.

[31]Reinhard Bendix, *Max Weber: An Intellectual Portrait,* Berkely, The University of California Press, 1977, p. 66.

[32]Nathan Glazer, *American Judaism,* Chicago, The University of Chicago Press, 1972, Chapter VI.

[33]Stephen Sharot, "Judaism and the Secularization Debate," *Sociological Analysis,* Vol. 52, No. 1, Spring 1991, p.262.

[34]Jonathan S. Woocher, *Sacred Survival: The Civil Religion of American Jews,* Bloomington, Indiana University Press, 1986, Chapter III.

[35]Rodney Stark and William S. Bainbridge, *The Future of Religion: Secularization, Revival and Cult Formation,* Berkely, University of California Press, 1985.

[36]Chaim I. Waxman, *America's Jews In Transition,* Philadelphia, Temple University Press, 1983, p. 124.

[37]*Ibid.* p.160.

[38]Will Herberg, *Protestant, Catholic, Jew,* New York, Doubleday & Co., 1955.

[39]Ibid. p.274.

[40]Mark Zborowski and Elizabeth Herzog, *Life Is With People,* New York, International Universities Press, 1952 ; see also: Irving Howe, *World of Our Fathers,* New York, Simon and Schuster, 1976, p. 9.

[41] *ibid.,* p. 106.

[42]Jacob Rader Marcus and Abraham J. Peck, *The American Rabbinate,* Hoboken, N.J., KTAV Publishing House, 1985, p. 104.

[43]*Ibid.,* pp. 103-104.

[44]Wilson, *op.cit.,* p. 159.

[45]Basil Herring, *The Rabbinate as Calling and Vocation,* Northvale, N.J., Jason Aronson, Inc., 1991,p.ix.

[46]*Ibid.* p. xi.

[47]Jerome E. Carlin and Saul H. Medelovitz, "The American Rabbi :Loss of Authority," in *Understanding American Judaism,* New York, KTAV Publishing House, 1975, p. 173.

[48]Kosmin, *op.cit.,* p.36.

[49]*Ibid.,* p.36.

[50]Will Maslow, *The Structure and Functioning of the American Jewish Community,* New York, American Jewish Congress, 1974, p. 16.

[51]Kosmin, *op.cit.* p. 36.

[52]Arnold van Gennep, *Les Rite de Passage,* Paris, No publisher, 1909.

[53]Jack E. Bynum and William E. Thompson, *Juvenile Delinquency: A Sociological Approach,* Boston, Allyn and Bacon, 1992, p.463.

[54]Herbert Danby, *The Mishnah,* Oxford, The Clarendon Press, 1933, pp. 750-751.

[55]Hayim Schauss, *The Lifetime of a Jew,* New York, Union of American Hebrew Congregations, 1976, p. 112.

[56]Moses Maimonides, *The Commentary to Mishnah Abbot,* Arthur David, Translator, New York, Bloch Publishing Co., 1968 p.121.

[57]Phillippe Aries, *Centuries of Childhood,* Robert Baldick, Trans., New York, Alfred A. Knopf, 1962, p. 48.

Part Two

The Development of Secularization
In the Western World

Chapter II

The Influence of Jewish Philosophers
on the Secularization of Judaism

I.

All the world knows that Baruch Spinoza was excommunicated from the Jewish community of Amsterdam for heresy (July 24, 1656).

The dramatic account of that excommunication has been repeated often and is without doubt as good an example of religious intolerance and fear of change as the murder of Bruno (1548-1600), the indictment of Galileo (1564-1642) and the excommunication from Islam of Salman Rushdie in our own day.

Having thereby been treated to more advertisement than they could ever have produced themselves, these thinkers developed a following quickly as their detractors and persecutors propelled their names around the world.

Accused of every crime, denounced from the pulpit of every faith, insulted, ridiculed and held in contempt, these thinkers and writers created the secular world we know today as they demonstrated in word and deed that the erstwhile conceptions of God and his universe were false and that their views based on reason, not superstition or faith, could withstand the rigors of debate and argument.

As we have already seen, however, the skeptics who were as certain of science as any believer have found after 350 years that THE

TRUTH does not reside in science and that man may be more ignorant of the "big questions" now than he was 350 years ago.

It is the great merit of Baruch Spinoza (1632-1677) that he recognized the limitations of both science and religion. Nevertheless, Spinoza contributed mightily to the secularization of Judaism and, to the extent that his work was known, to the secularization of the western world. Certainly, Christianity was influenced by this doubter who could see no purpose in arguments from authority or opinions derived from superstition.

Spinoza had been trained in synagogue ritual, in the Hebrew language and in the sacred books. But he had gone further than that. An outstanding student, he not only studied the Talmud but also the works of philosophers and thinkers who were not Jewish, who were Christians or who had no faith and who had, in earlier days, challenged established authorities and traditions.

This is not to say that Spinoza published his "heresies" in his life time. Indeed all but one of his books was published posthumously. However, Spinoza talked about his views and was therefore denounced to the elders of the Amsterdam synagogue. After his death, however, his works were read and translated into numerous languages. Most important of these for our purposes is *Tractatus theologico-politicus* or, *The Treatise on Theology and Politics.*[1] Here he argued that freedom of speech and thought must be upheld for the sake of the very piety demanded by his opponents. Spinoza was not an atheist but a supporter of religious beliefs. However, he critiqued the Bible severely and denied its divine origin. He pointed out contradictions in various Biblical passages and books and underscored the violent quarrels between theologians which these difficulties produced.

Spinoza attributed belief in Biblical miracles to the prejudices of the writers whom he considered human and fallible and he insisted that just and kind behavior, not dogma, were to be the province of religious believers.

Spinoza proposed that thought should be free and that faith and philosophy (meaning secular study) have nothing in common.

Principally, *The Treatise on Theology and Politics* seeks to teach in order to change and improve the order of things. Spinoza fights against superstition, prejudice and hypocrisy in order to establish truth and reason as the basis of piety. Thus, Spinoza promotes justice, free inquiry and freedom of expression and thought, not to eliminate religion but to support it. All this Spinoza writes with a good deal of anger and evident emotion in view of the humiliation he suffered at the hands of the Amsterdam synagogue.

The importance of Spinoza's criticism of religion lies in the consequences of his work. While his critique will seem old and trite to present day readers, it must be kept in mind that his views were far more radical and surprising in 1654 than they are now after having been repeated these three hundred years.

Spinoza was of course not the only writer to criticize religion. In this he was preceded by the Greek philosophers Democritus (460-374 B.C.E.) and Epicurus (342-270 B.C.E.), and numerous others in the ancient and medieval world such as Cicero (106-43 B.C.E.), Lucretius (94 B.C.E.-50 B.C.E.), Seneca (4 B.C.E. - 65 C.E.), Tacitus (55 - 117), Machiavelli (1469-1527) and, in his own century, Grotius (1583-1645), Isaac de la Peyrere and Thomas Hobbes (1588-1679) as well as Montaigne (1553-1592), Descarte (1596-1650) and Uriel da Costa. These thinkers provided Spinoza with writings he could not ignore and which supported with their doubts and arguments his skeptical views concerning religion.[2]

Da Costa, a contemporary of Spinoza, had been excommunicated from Judaism in 1618 for denying the immortality of the soul and retribution in the "World to Come". He also promoted disbelief in the Bible. Da Costa was a native of Amsterdam, and like Spinoza, had come of a "Marrano" family. The word "marrano" means "swine" and was applied by Christians to Jews who had converted to Christianity. A number of these "new Christians" moved to the Netherlands in the 16th and 17th century to escape the Spanish and Portuguese "Inquisition" into the sincerity of their Christian beliefs. Among these was the Da Costa family who had raised Uriel as a Catholic. Having renounced his Christianity, Uriel became a Jew but could not support these beliefs any more than the Christian dogmas in which he was raised. Instead, da Costa adopted a naturalistic religion, without dogma and without ritual.[3]

In 1655, Isaac de La Peyrere published two Latin works together. These books were *Prae Adamitae* and *Systema Theologicum or Before Adam* and *Systematic Theology*. Holding that there were men prior to Adam, La Peyrere cast doubt on the validity of Scripture and also proposed to prove from the words of the Bible itself that men existed before Adam was created. These beliefs eliminated Mosaic Law from the history of salvation leading to the historical critique of the Five Books of Moses thereafter.[4]

These views were also very much influenced by the earlier works of Laelius Socinus (1525-1562) and Faustus Socinus (1539-1604) who organized Unitarianism in Poland and Geneva respectively. Although Unitarianism did not succeed in gaining very many adherents among Christians, the views of the Socinians lived on because Socinus argued that belief in the Old Testament is not necessary and that Christians could dispense with the Old Testament or Torah. This argument opened the Five Books of Moses, the Prophets and the Writings to criticism as practiced by La Peyrere and others.[5]

La Peyrere argued that reason alone rules men, that divine law could not be known by men but that men know only the laws of nature. Believing in salvation through the elevation of man into a state of nature greater than this one, La Peyrere also promoted the re-establishment of a Jewish State so as to further this advance in the natural state of man. This "temporal salvation" of the Jews was to take place after the Jews "turned to Christ" for their spiritual salvation all with the help of the king of France and the Pope who would both be instrumental in the "inclusion of the Jews in Christendom."[6]

We come now to the writings of Thomas Hobbes (1588-1679) whose influence upon the mind and work of Spinoza cannot be overestimated. When Spinoza was 19 years old, in 1651, the great work of Hobbes, *The Leviathan,* was published.[7] "One of the landmarks in philosophy," this work was subtitled *The Matter, Form and Power of a Commonwealth, Ecclesiastical and Civil.*[8]

Hobbes was a deist and not an atheist. He viewed God as incomprehensible and as *The First Cause.* He granted the existence of God but could not believe that anyone can understand what God is. Hobbes critiqued the Bible, doubting Moses' authorship of the Pentateuch. He proposed that government permit public opinion to be freely expressed. That was precisely what happened to Hobbes book after it was published. Denounced by every clergyman in England and elsewhere he defended his views in yet more writing and died at 91 the most famous philosopher in Europe.[9]

Despite his protestations to the contrary, Hobbes' contemporaries considered him an atheist. Yet, Hobbes' argument that God is unknown to man and that we have no conception of God did not differ from the arguments of St. Thomas who doubted any value in any argument concerning the beginning of the universe in time.[10] Furthermore, Hobbes agreed with the scholastic view that words spoken by God and revealed in the Bible must be understood through the use of the faculty of reason. Thus, Hobbes argued, reason need not give way to belief nor belief to reason. Therefore Hobbes considered in detail when and by whom the various books of the Bible were written.[11]

Hobbes wrote that the laws of the Bible became valid only because a Christian sovereign sanctioned them. Only God's existence can be ascertained, said Hobbes. Other than that, Hobbes insisted that all things are material, that angels and other supernatural beings are the products of dreams and the imagination. Hobbes also held that the expression "The Kingdom of God", was to be understood as a real, earthly kingdom under the kingship of a returned Christ, however long such an event might take.

Hobbes thought that the authority of the monarchy must decide whether a prophet or any so-called wonders were true or merely efforts to swindle the public. Even the belief in transubstantiation as claimed by the Catholic church with reference to communion should be subject to the interpretation of the sovereign king, said Hobbes. Thereby Hobbes makes religious teachings dependent on the political power of a this-worldly monarch. Thus, Hobbes holds that the sovereign is simultaneously a priest and a teacher of theology but that priests and theologians are by no means sovereigns or kings.

Next Hobbes denies the right of the Pope to excommunicate a king. Furthermore, Hobbes disputes the right of the Pope to excommunicate a subject of any king who does not believe something which the law of the land will not permit.

Hobbes denies the Pope the right to appoint the clergy, a right Hobbes assigns to the king as well. In democratic societies, which have no king, the same authority devolves upon elected officials, argues Hobbes. Thus, heresy is a belief deviating from that of the law of the land, but not a belief deviating from the Pope whose authority Hobbes denies.

According to Hobbes, the claim that the church is identical to the kingdom of God on earth is a swindle. Hobbes teaches that such a belief is derived from the wish of priests and popes to gain advantages and power for themselves.

Having dealt with theology, Hobbes then proceeds to a discussion of religion. Like others before and after him, Hobbes wrote that religion is the outcome of fear of the unknown for which men seek some answer. This answer lies in the inescapable conclusion that a "First Mover" must exist since all causes have previous causes *ad infinitum* and that this first cause is called "God", says Hobbes.

Hobbes then proceeds to once more deny the existence of spirits and superhuman ghosts. He recognized that men everywhere attribute their fate to places, or persons or the speaking of certain words. He compares the attitudes of men towards human powers with the behavior, words and deeds of the religious towards their God or gods.

Four things promote the essence of religion, says Hobbes. These are the belief in ghosts, ignorance of secondary causes *i.e.* causes other than God, reverence for that which one fears and the belief that accidental conditions are viewed as signs of things to come.

Hobbes reviews primitive religions and their beliefs that various animals were viewed as gods while natural phenomena were interpreted as events having to do with human misfortunes. He shows that the Romans, Christians and others sought to teach that which was forbidden in any particular society was also displeasing to the God or gods.

The purpose of all this, according to Hobbes, was to promote peace and keep the populace from rebelling against the rulers. This, thought Hobbes, could be attained by blaming their misery on failure to perform this or that ceremony thus diverting attention from the rulers themselves.

Finally, Hobbes declares that all alterations in religion have been caused by the obnoxious conduct of priests and clergy of all denominations.[12]

In sum, Hobbes not only criticized the Church, Christianity and religion in general. He also assaulted theology and promoted the secularization of European religion with more vigor than anyone had done before him. When Spinoza published his "Theological - Political Treatise" in 1670, the "Leviathan" by Thomas Hobbes was already 19 years old. (1651).

Therefore it is not surprising that Spinoza and others were heavily influenced by the work of Hobbes. Writing in Latin, Hobbes used the vehicle of scholarly intercourse in his century and had little trouble being understood and misunderstood, at least noticed   everywhere including the Netherlands.

II.

The principal purpose of   Spinoza's "Theological-Political Treatise" is to elevate reason and rational conduct above superstition , prejudice and hypocrisy. In addition, this treatise promotes the right of everyone to believe what he pleases and to express his opinion on all issues.

"I have often wondered, that   persons who make a boast of confessing the Christian religion, namely, love, joy, peace, temperance and charity to all men should quarrel with such rancorous animosity, and display daily towards one another   such bitter hatred   that this, rather than the virtues they claim, is the readiest criterion of their faith."[13]

Spinoza goes on to say that he can see no difference between the life style of Jews, Christians or heathens (agnostics) but that they only differ in the clothes they wear, the opinions they pronounce and the teachings each supports. He views religion as a nonsense promoted mostly by those who hold reason in contempt. He sees the religious as wanting to hang on to their authority at any cost. He calls so-called "Holy Writ" or "Scriptures" human inventions and sides with the Protestants of his day when he denies the authority of the Pope to interpret religion." Thus, it is quite impossible to argue from the Jewish high priest's authority to interpret the laws of his country to the Pope's authority to interpret religion; on the contrary, it is easier to conclude from it that the authority to interpret religion rests with the individual."[14]

Spinoza now turns his attention to prophecy. He defines a prophet as someone who can reveal the will and the teachings of God by supernatural means in that he can perform miracles which confirm his authority to speak in the name of God. Spinoza denies that such authority exists and denounces as nonsense the ability to perform miracles. He also views books describing the deeds of the prophets as written by humans so as to manipulate others into believing that such books contain infallible truths. These books then are called "Holy Writ."[15]

Spinoza further shows how many of the writings of the prophets contradict one another, and that the nature of God differs depending on the experiences and interest of each prophet.

Yet, Spinoza denied the divinity of Jesus and declared him to be a human being equipped with some unusual gifts or "charisma" but not God. God, says Spinoza, is nature. The general laws of nature are seen by him as the essence of the divine and the decisions of God are contained in these laws of nature.[16]

Laws other than the laws of nature are attributed by Spinoza to human efforts to control the passions. These passions must be suppressed, says Spinoza, and that is done by attributing rewards and punishments for conduct that conforms to the rules of a particular place or time. Spinoza grants that there are divine laws. These however are seen as stemming from nature, i.e., from the nature of man. Thus, divine laws are the product of the nature of God and are eternal truths because they stem from the nature of things. Such laws, claims Spinoza, cannot be contradicted nor repealed.

There are also, according to Spinoza, many laws which are labeled divine but are in truth commandments given arbitrarily by the whim of nobility for their advantage and the disadvantage of others. These, however, are not divine as evidenced by the fact that these laws are and can be contradicted and denied and not obeyed.[17]

Spinoza points out that all the writers of the Old and New Testament were Hebrews who used that language and that therefore anyone who really wants to understand Scripture would have to learn Hebrew. Furthermore, says Spinoza, we need to know the fate of the books called "holy", how they first became included in the canon and which changes were made in them and by whom. Thus, he denies that the actual author of the Pentateuch, or Five Books, was Moses but asserts he was someone who lived much later than Moses. Spinoza also shows how various interpreters have tried to interpret contradictions in the many books of the Bible without succeeding in anything more than to deliver their authors to the contempt which emphasis on these contradictions produces.

The true scriptures of God, according to Spinoza, consist not of these human writings but of the impression God makes on the human spirit. Thus, Spinoza holds that *the entire content of the Bible consists of the need to love God and one's neighbor as one self.* This view is illustrated by a Jewish story concerning the first century Rabbi Hillel, who lived in Israel during the Roman occupation. It is told that Hillel was once confronted by a "heathen" who sought to become a Jew. The applicant objected to the requirement of spending years in learning numerous books to meet the usual requirements for conversion. Instead he insisted that he be taught the entire Torah while standing on one foot. So Hillel said: "Do not onto others what you would not have others do onto you. All the rest of the Torah is only commentary."[18] Evidently, Jewish tradition already understood the superiority of ethics as the essence of religion before Spinoza.

Spinoza now lists those fundamentals which he believes are the corner stone of Scriptural teachings. These, he says, are : 1. That God exists 2. that He foresees all things 3. that He is almighty 4. that by his decree the good prosper and the wicked come to naught and 5. that our salvation depends solely on His grace. Furthermore, Spinoza derives some universal moral doctrines from Biblical teachings which are to uphold justice, to do no murder and to covet no man's goods.[19]

Opinions, according to Spinoza, without respect to actions cannot be either pious or impious. Spinoza therefore becomes a forerunner of the sociology of religion in the sense that sociology deals only with that which is visibly done by reason of belief and never with belief itself.[20]

Obedience to God, says Spinoza, consists then of loving one's neighbor as oneself. Such an achievement makes the practitioner "blessed according to the law," while "he who hates or disregards him is rebellious and disobedient."[21]

Therefore, according to Spinoza, a sharp line can be drawn between philosophy and religion. Thus, philosophy must be derived from nature itself. The basis of philosophy are "notiones communes," or concepts held in common by everyone. The aim of philosophy is to reach the truth; the aim of theology to attain obedience. Therefore, theology cannot and does not wish to do anything contrary to reason. Instead, theology rests on moral certainty and therefore cannot be discarded only because it cannot be proved with mathematical certainty. Thus, Spinoza sees no real conflict between science and religion. For even as he defends theology against the accusation that it is of no use because it does not conform to the laws of mathematics, so he defends science on the grounds that it should not be and cannot be the subject of prejudice and emotion for, "....neither should be subservient to the other, but ...each should keep her unopposed dominion."[22]

Despite his efforts on behalf of reason, Spinoza thought that it "more reasonable to teach the multitude unreasonable beliefs than to despoil them of belief altogether."[23]

The influence of Spinoza upon the thought of western man and most assuredly Jewish thought has been continuous. There are therefore many who believe that the secularization of Judaism began with Spinoza. One such writer is the Israeli philosopher Yirmiyahu Yovel whose two volume study of Spinoza has caused some controversy among academics but is nevertheless an important contribution to our understanding of Spinoza's influence upon Jewish life and thought. Says Yovel: "(Spinoza) took the first step in the eventual secularization of Jewish life by examining it empirically as a natural phenomenon subject solely to the forces of secular history."[24]

Yovel rightly recognizes the great influence which the Marrano experience of his parents had upon Spinoza. Reviewing the work of other writers in this area Yovel recognized that Spinoza, although not himself persecuted in Spain, was a marginal man and that his writings reflect this. The term "marginal man" is not used by Yovel but it is plain that Yovel means exactly that when he shows that Spinoza wrote in an indirect fashion and used language designed to be acceptable to the public at large and protective of its author. The need to be deceptive in writing about religion was not only necessitated by the anxiety all dissenters from official beliefs felt in any part of Europe during the 17th century. It was also produced by the "Marrano" experience which Spinoza, a first generation Dutch citizen, could of course discern in his family and other Jews at that time. Such anxieties are also discernible among the children of Holocaust survivors today. Both the work by Yoval and the earlier volume by Leo Strauss, *Spinoza's Critique of Religion,* agree that ambivalence and anxiety made Spinoza, what Yoval called "A Marrano of Reason."[25]

Sociologists refer to the conflict which such migrants to a new society experience as "marginality" and view particularly the children of such immigrants as "marginal men." This term was first used by the Chicago scholar Robert E. Park who defined a marginal man as one "whom fate has condemned to live in two societies and in two not merely different but antagonistic cultures."[26] Evidently, Spinoza was a marginal man, not only because his family were immigrants but also because his family and he were Jews. Jews are marginal men everywhere outside of Israel. Like marginal men everywhere the Amsterdam Jews of Spinoza's day suffered all those characteristics which Park describes and which led them to excommunicate Spinoza, not only because of his "heretical" views but mainly because his views caused so much tension between the newly arrived Jews and their Christian hosts. Spinoza did indeed, in Parks' terms, create a "conflict of values and loyalties." Having been labeled a renegade by his own people, Spinoza, however, could not rely on support from the majority culture as do most marginal people rejected by their family of origin. Instead he lived alone among non-Jewish friends willing to take him in. These friends were in the main dissenters from established Calvinist orthodoxy. Although the Calvinists predominated in the Netherlands in the 17th century, and although the Dutch government showed some zeal in suppressing Catholics and other "heretics", numerous sects flourished in that country just the same. Lucianites, Pietists, Unitarians and Mennonites, including the Collegiants who befriended Spinoza, all managed to live in the Low Country and worship there in their own fashion. Dominated by the business classes, the Dutch reduced the influence of the clergy in favor of trade and commerce. "Refugees from other lands, contributing to the economy or the culture, demanded and received a limited religious freedom" and this benefited Spinoza as well.[27]

Yet, he had lost all contact with the Jewish community. He was also at odds with the dominant Calvinist community. This left Spinoza no choice but to associate with other heretics and/or people whose religious views were at odds with the majority. Thus he became a friend of Jan de Witt, at one time a leading politician and statesman in Holland whose views on religion were at least in part responsible for his fall from power and his eventual murder. Benedict Spinoza, as he called himself after his excommunication, therefore became "marginal" in three ways. He was of Spanish Marrano parentage. He was excommunicated and excluded from the Jewish community and he was excluded by the established, Calvinist Christian community. Surely, all the conflicts this situation had to produce in any man was reflected in his writings. The Marranos, forcibly living as Catholics while practicing a truncated Judaism, were "marginal people " *ipso facto.* They could not be anything else because they were not given any alternative. Obviously then, these conflicts within the greater community led to conflict within those who experienced these social forces and is reflected in their thoughts, beliefs and conduct. Therefore Spinoza wrote in a manner which has been called "indirect" .

Spinoza evidently believed that he needed to write in a protective manner so as to avoid the wrath of the clergy and the government. In fact, he published very little during his lifetime and left most of his books to be published *post mortem.* Most important among these books are the *Tractatus,* already discussed, and *On the Improvement of the Intellect,* and his *Ethics.*

All of these writings seek to show that man's ultimate salvation lies in his capacity to transcend his own finitude. Spinoza, like Buddha, seeks to "instruct man how to reach salvation by transcending his own finitude....and that he thought this could come about only by thinking about the true essence and causes of things."[28]

It is the view of Yovel, and we concur, that Spinoza was indeed the forerunner, in fact the founder, of the secular movement in Judaism which has become prominent in this century. Having left the religious doctrines behind, Spinoza and his present followers continue to be Jews in what Yovel calls "immanence," derived from the Latin "to remain" in this world, now and here. Thus, such Jews today can be interested in Jewish communal events, participate in fund raising and above all be Zionists without subscribing to any religious affiliation, Jewish or otherwise. Yovel believes that Judaism itself promotes such attitudes and that Jewish "heresy," whether in Spinoza or today fulfills the Jewish message to the world. The secular emphasis on Jewish thought and conduct has been distinguished from Judaism and has been called Jewishness. It is this attitude which continued long past Spinoza and found additional expression in the career of Moses Mendelssohn (1729-1786) who, in the next century, continued in Germany the intellectual tradition among Jews which Spinoza had precipitated a hundred years before.

III.

Moses Mendelssohn had three children. Two daughters, Dorothea and Henrietta who converted to Catholicism and a son, Abraham who induced his children to become Christians for he believed that "it (Christianity) is the conviction of most well-bred human beings."[29]

It is well known that Moses Mendelssohn's entire progeny left the Jewish fold because his famous grandson, the composer Felix Mendelssohn (1809-1847) was a nominal Christian as were so many successful German Jews during the nineteenth century and until the time of Hitler and his exterminators.[30]

Because this is so well known there are those who regard Moses Mendelssohn as an apostate and one who sought to renounce his Judaism for favors available from the Prussian government. The orthodox have accused him, the rationalist, of abandoning belief in the revelation of Judaism and equally resented his effort to connect the Bible to the German language; reformers resent his adherence to Jewish rituals; nationalists and Zionists cannot understand his rejection of a Jewish state.

Yet, Moses Mendelssohn, a "Torah true" Jew, became the object of considerable hostility from traditional Jews because he translated the Torah into German. Mendelssohn published this translation in Hebrew script. This means that the words were German but Hebrew letters were used to spell the German words thus making the translation accessible to the vast majority of German Jews who could not read the Gothic German then in use. Traditional rabbis feared that this translation would lead to the neglect of Hebrew studies thus leading to the abandonment of Judaism whether intended or not. That Mendelssohn did not intend the abandonment of Judaism is certain. That apostasy became frequent after his death is certain as well. The reason for this unintended outcome of Mendelssohn's efforts was that he had become admired by the German Christian upper classes and intelligentsia and had become a role model " .....and encouraged Jews to think that they too could achieve the status to which they aspired."[31]

Thus, it can well be said that Mendelssohn did indeed participate in the re-formation of Judaism in the sense that his contributions reflected the social trends of his time. It is however simplistic and devoid of sociological understanding to either credit or blame Medelssohn for the secularization of Judaism in the years following his life because "political, socio-economic and demographic factors," not one person or one writer, can ever be considered responsible for any major social movement.[32]

In fact, *Jerusalem,* Mendelssohn's defense of traditional Judaism, indicates without a doubt that he devoted his life to living in both the world of the "Enlightenment" and the world of Jewish orthodoxy.

Thus, *Jerusalem* has been called " ...a remarkable synthesis of Mendelssohn's twin commitments , to Judaism and to reason."[33]

It was this double commitment which distinguishes Mendelssohn's contribution to the advancement of secularization in the 18th century from Spinoza's teachings in the 17th century. For although Spinoza never claimed to be an atheist, his excommunication and his subsequent naturalism resulted in an attack on Judaism by him and his followers. Therefore, Mendelssohn was most concerned in distancing himself from Spinoza as shown by the famous controversy which erupted after the death of Mendelssohn's friend Lessing who was posthumously identified as a Spinozist, a label Mendelssohn would not accept either for himself or for Lessing.[34]

The reason for the vehemence with which Mendelssohn rejected the possibility that Lessing was a Spinozist was the belief among many people that Spinoza was an atheist, no matter his thin defense of revelation.

"Spinoza's philosophy stood for radical scientific naturalism......and the consequences of Spinoza's philosophy, if it were to delete its superfluous religious language, was atheism and fatalism."[35] Yet, even as Mendelssohn rejected atheism and tried to show how we could rationally conclude that there is a God, that there is immortality of the soul, that there is revelation and providence, Mendelssohn defended Spinoza's rationalism without permitting this attitude to lead him, like Spinoza, to reject religious beliefs as man-made. Thus, Mendelssohn recognized with Spinoza that the consistency and order of the universe is replicated by human reason even while he, Mendelssohn, held the Jewish ceremonial law as revealed and hence applicable in his own day and at all times.[36]

Unlike Spinoza, who held that the laws of nature were the only laws God had given man, Mendelssohn held that the rabbinic laws were revealed truth. Nothing illustrates Mendelssohn's devotion to traditional Judaism more than his principal work, *Morgenstunden* or Morning Hours. Candidly borrowing from Kant Mendelssohn argues that no object can be real unless it conforms to a concept. Here Mendelssohn also borrows from Descartes and agrees with that writer that "My own thoughts I know to be real while I myself, as the subject in which these thoughts occur, am real in an unqualified sense."[37]

The sum of Mendelssohn's metaphysical arguments are these: First that there is an external reality to which our senses testify; second, there is cognition consisting of experience, rational knowledge and reasoning; third, there is a close relationship between reason and common sense; fourth, there is a difference between imagination and objective reality so that we can be misled; five, external reality is an association of ideas reflecting cause and effect in accordance with the laws of nature (a Spinozian notion), sixth, that the difference between the ideal and the real is much narrower than usually assumed and seventh , that Kant's *Ding an sich,* the thing in itself, can only be explained by what a thing effects and how it is affected. This argument would no doubt be understood by sociologists today but falls short of the work of Kant who argued that since we know a thing only in its spatial relations it was quite legitimate to ask what it was in itself.[38] According to Mendelssohn, however, only God knows the "thing in itself." Thus, Mendelssohn held that the endless controversy between idealists and realists was only semantic and not a matter of substance. Mendelssohn also taught that the first source of knowledge is the study of man himself. Like Alexander Pope (1688-1744) before him he believed that "the proper study of mankind is man."[39]

From these preliminary statements Mendelssohn derives his proof of the existence of God. This, he said, is derived from the reality of a sensible world outside ourselves. Mendelssohn seeks then to root his beliefs in common sense. "Experience has taught me," he wrote, "that common sense is usually right." He thought that "what no thinking being conceives as possible is in fact not possible, and what no thinking being thinks is real is in fact not real."[40]

Then, as now, there were and are those who find Mendelssohn's adherence to Jewish law contradicts his rejection of ecclesiastical power and his commitment to the principles of the enlightenment. Mendelssohn insisted on supporting reason at all times but would not permit himself to conclude that such a Spinozist position bore within it the rejection of revealed religion. Instead he insisted that both reason and rabbinic Judaism could be supported even though most enlightened Christians held rabbinic Judaism to be an obstacle to the acceptance of Jews in Prussian and general European society. Mendelssohn argued that Jews, born to accept the Law, did not have the authority to abrogate it and that therefore rabbinic law was also revealed and permanent. Yet, he demanded the acceptance of Jews in European society even while observing the details of rabbinic Law. He had achieved this for himself. Now he insisted that his Jewish brethren be given the same privilege.[41]

Mendelssohn believed that acceptance of Jews would come first in Germany and he strove for the development of Jewish culture within the borders of Germany. Mendelssohn loved Germany and German civilization as did so many of his co-religionists who insisted on believing in the humaneness of their German brethren. Mendelssohn sought to develop "Jewish Prussians" rather than Prussian Jews and, for a short time after his death, succeeded. Thus, a limited amount of fraternity between Jews and Christians in the upper classes of German society did develop at the end of the eighteenth century particularly because there were some leading Christians who sought to facilitate the entrance of the Jews into German social life. Others, again, were vehemently opposed to such a possibility so that there was never a clear cut German attitude towards Mendelssohn's proposals. The dispute concerning the role of the Jews is best illustrated by the positions taken in this matter by Christian Wilhelm Dohm (1751-1820), a historian and superintendent of the Prussian archives who favored Jewish assimilation and Johann David Michaelis, a Gottingen professor who denounced the Jews despite his reputation as a rationalist in theology. In 1781 Dohm wrote a pamphlet entitled "Upon the Civil Amelioration of the Condition of the Jews". Avoiding religious controversy, Dohm dealt only with the political and economic aspects of Jewish life and denounced the disabilities borne by the Jews as unworthy of the "enlightenment of our times." He proposed that Jews be given equal rights with others in Prussia. He promoted the freedom for Jews to work in any occupation; the right of Jews to attend Christian schools or their own; the free exercise of religion and religious education and to admit them to other civil rights except the right to hold public office. Christians, however, greeted Dohm's proposals with great hostility. It seemed to the majority that Jews should not and could not ever be equals to Christians.

Led by the fulminations of Michaelis bigots of every class denounced Jews as "an incorrigible race." Michaelis thereby became an authority on the "Jewish Question" in Gemany and was cited again and again as a source of denunciation and hatred of Jews.

Nevertheless, and in spite of the negative attitude of the majority, some progress toward equality of rights for Jews was made in the 18th century.[42]

This trend, to permit the assimilation of the European Jews into Christian society, can best be illustrated by listing some of the 18th and 19th Century laws and decrees favoring Jewish liberation. Thus, "The Jew Act" was passed by the British Parliament in May of 1753. It granted English Jews British citizenship but was repealed in 1754. On February 11, 1812 the king of Prussia issued an edict allowing Jews to serve in the Prussian armed forces with the result that for one hundred years thereafter Jews from then and through the First World War became exceptional German patriots. Thus, despite the denials of German Nazis, the Jewish participation in the German war effort between 1914 and 1918 far exceeded the proportion of Christian participation. Although there were only 550,000 Jews in Germany in 1914, 100,000 served in the German armed forces and 12,000 were killed at the front. This did not prevent the vast majority of Germans to deny the patriotism of their Jewish "brethren", and to pretend that all Jews were "shirkers" who had not served the "fatherland" at all.[43]

In Austria, at the price of abandoning both Hebrew and Yiddish, the Emperor Joseph II offered to admit Jews to the universities and to allow them freedom of trade and commerce by an "Edict of Toleration" issued in 1782. This edict was shortly overshadowed by the "Declaration of the Rights of Man and of the Citizen" as adopted by the French Assembly on August 26, 1789. In article X of that declaration the assembly declared that "No person shall be molested for his opinions, even such as are religious ..." a view which was then reflected in the French constitution of 1791 which guaranteed "Liberty to every man to ....exercise the religious worship to which he is attached." Similar laws were passed in the Netherlands in 1796 and in Prussia in 1812. The "Edict Concerning the Civil Conditions of Jews in the Prussian State" in that year was indeed a model of toleration for that day and age. Nevertheless, the very word "toleration" implied an attitude foreign to the United States even then, as evidenced by the letter President Washington had sent to the Newport, Rhode Island Hebrew congregation on August 21, 1790. Therein Washington used this phrase: "It is now no more that toleration is spoken of, as if it was by the indulgence of one class of people, that another enjoyed the exercise of their inherent rights."[44] In Europe, however, this attitude was hardly visible. Instead, the Jews of that continent considered themselves fortunate that they were now "tolerated."

While the Prussian example of 1812 was the first in that century to favor Jewish liberation, other, similar decrees and laws followed all over that continent. In Denmark a "Decree on Civil Rights" was passed in 1814; in France the "Constitutional Charter" of June 4, 1814 once more guaranteed freedom of worship and the Congress of Viennna sought to maintain the rights of the Jews as first granted by the then defeated Emperor Napoleon. This did not mean that the German Jews truly enjoyed those rights. It only means that these rights existed "on paper." Similar rights were included in the laws or constitutions of England (1845), Greece (1830), Austria (1849), Sardinia (1848), Germany (1869), Italy (1870), Switzerland (1874), Poland (1921), and the Soviet Union (1936).[45]

Because of these events, Jews insisted on believing that they were gradually being accepted by Europeans as equals, particularly when the Jew Simon Kremser received the "Pour le Merite" order from the Prussian king in 1812 and, a century later, Wilhelm Frankl received the same from Kaiser William II in 1914.

Thus, Moses Mendelssohn's hope that someday there would be Jewish Germans seemed to be coming true. Had not the Prussian theologian Theodor von Hippel written this of the Prussian Jews during the "Wars of Liberation" early in the nineteenth century? "A number (of Jews) distinguished themselves by a show of courage and became officers or received medals and iron crosses. Therefore, some believed, there were no more Prussian Jews but only Jewish Prussians."[46]

Such an acceptance was of course never granted the German Jews. On the contrary. The very veterans who had fought at the front for the fatherland and had lost their limbs, their sight and their health there were gassed to death by the same "fatherland" only 25 years later. But all this, Moses Mendelssohn could not have expected. Instead he expected the impossible. Namely that the German Jews would maintain their religion and yet be Germans.

During the century following Mendelssohn's death in 1786 his efforts seemed to have advanced the cause of Jewish assimilation into German culture at least in part. Jews made great strides in economic terms during those one hundred years and at first appeared to gain political rights as well. Yet, by 1879 when Wilhelm Marr published the German best seller *The Victory of Judaism Over Teutonism,* the conduct of the German population announced that Mendelssohn's hope was shattered. It took the trains to Auschwitz to convince most of the German Jews of this.[47]

The efforts of Mendelssohn were two fold. He sought to defend traditional Judaism even while "subjecting it (Judaism) to the searching rationalism of the Englightenment."[48] The consequence of this effort was that in his own day Mendelssohn faced innumerable conflicts which he could not bridge and which produced ambivalent attitudes toward Judaism in numerous areas of thought and action. Thus, Mendelssohn himself recognized that Jews could not participate in the new world of the Enlightenment if they clung to a calcified tradition and made no allowances for change. Yet, he sought to preserve these traditions even as he urged his people to emancipate themselves from the ghetto which still bound them. From his day to the present (1995), the conflict has remained in the Jewish soul. The question was then and is now: "How can the Jews of Europe and America or any other country participate in the culture of their native land and yet preserve their Jewish identity?"

In his own day Mendelssohn was already challenged by Kant and other non-Jewish thinkers. In part, that criticism relied on the usual rationalists' and Deists' criticism of religion in general and hence of Judaism as well. However, in his book *Religion in the Limits of Reason Alone,* Kant accepted the basic rituals and tenets of Christianity as means of promoting the religion of reason, but damned Judaism as a mechanical form of ritualism devoid of ethics and only useful to prevent crime by blind acceptance of rigid laws. Kant viewed traditional Jews ineligible for citizenship in Prussia and used all those arguments against Jewish equality which had been the traditional Christian viewpoint. One consequence of Kant's contempt for Jews and Judaism was the repetition of these accusations in the writings of later German philosophers, including Hegel, and therefore Marx in whom these views turned into a malicious form of anti-Jewish hatred born of a wish to distance himself from his own Jewish parentage.[49]

In the century following Mendelssohn's death, the ambivalence of Mendelssohn's position resulted in open conflict within the Jewish community between the traditionalists, the Zionists and the assimilationists.

An example of the assimilationist trend in European Judaism in the nineteenth century was the French writer Bernard Lazare who argued that the Jews themselves were the cause of "anti-semitism" because of their failure to assimilate quickly enough and because of their distinctiveness and inability to fit into European society and culture. Lazare was not alone in this self-blaming attitude and alluded to the so-called financial and business finesse of Jews which he and others also saw as a "cause of anti-Jewish hatred." Thus, shortly before the Dreyfus trial there were those who believed that "anti-semitism" would disappear if only the Jews would give up their separateness.[50] The belief that Jews could only become equal citizens of Europe if they relinquished their Jewish existence by denying their history and their theology was as old as the French revolution. It was in the French Assembly that Clermont-Tonnerre first proposed what remained the slogan of Jews and non Jews from then to the rise of Hitler: "To the Jews as a Nation everything is to be denied, to the Jew as a human being everything is to be granted."[51]

The assimilationists were in the majority among those who sought to end Jewish disabilities at the end of the nineteenth century. However, they were not the only voices in Judaism at the time. There were still many traditionalists who continued to seek their salvation in religious exercises and beliefs. In addition there were also the Zionists and among the Zionists was Leon Pinsker (1821-1891).

The son of Simha Pinsker, a distinguished Hebrew scholar, Leon Pinsker was a physician in his native Odessa. He had promoted the assimilation of the Russian Jews only to discover with others that the non-Jewish world would no more welcome an assimilated Jew than one who remained faithful to the traditions of his forbears. It was this disappointment which led Pinsker to write his pamphlet "Auto-Emancipation", one of the most important documents in the development of Jewish secularization and Zionism.

IV.

"Auto-emanzipation," written in German, was and is an exciting essay in any language. Written by Leon Pinsker in 1882, this pamphlet was published anonymously and was attributed only to "A Russian Jew." The principal thesis of this book is the view that the Jew cannot be assimilated and that the only solution to "The Jewish Problem" would be the establishment of a Jewish homeland. Written at the end of the nineteenth century, this book subtitled "*Ein Mahnruf an seine Stammesgenossen von einem russischen Juden,*" or "*A Warning Call to his People by a Russian Jew,"* Pinsker not only rejected the efforts of European Jews to assimilate in the countries of their residence but attacked both the orthodox view that Jews must suffer in silence until the arrival of the Messiah and the "diploma chasers" in the western world who sought to rationalize Jewish disabilities by viewing the Jewish dispersion as a "mission."[52] Having at one time promoted assimilation himself, and having become a physician by graduating from the University of Moscow, Pinsker knew both the orthodox views of his famous father, the scholar Simha Pinsker and the "diploma chasers " very well.

Said Pinsker: " The essence of the problem......................lies in the fact that, in the midst of the nations among whom the Jews reside, they form a distinctive element which cannot be assimilated. etc...". His principal arguments then were these: 1. Jews are everywhere despised because they are everywhere aliens. 2. The civil and political emancipation of the Jews will not raise them in the estimation of the people. 3. Only the establishment of a Jewish nation in its own homeland will alleviate this problem. It is this which Pinsker calls "auto-emancipation." 4. Neither humanity nor enlightenment will ever remedy the misery of the Jews. 5. Lack of self-respect and lack of self confidence prevent the national Jewish rebirth. 6. The permanent Jewish exile and wandering can only come to an end when Jews have a land of their own. 7. The present is the time to take action. 8. The plan to acquire a Jewish homeland will develop slowly and must be carried out by successive generations. 9. A "congress" of important Jews must be held to "open the national regeneration." 10. Because the Jews are everywhere in danger, no sacrifice can be too great to reach the goal of a national Jewish home. 11. The finances for this enterprise are available and 12. God helps them who help themselves.[53]

In the main, these proposals were reflections of Pinsker's and other Jews' belief in Free Will and self help, ideas which are found in the Torah and which had been ignored by generations of Jews before the "Haskalah" or enlightenment. These ideas can be found in Deuteronomy 31: 6,7 and 23 and in Joshuah 1: 6 . In all of these verses the phrase "Be strong and of good courage" is repeated with reference to the conquest of the Holy Land and was therefore taken as a tradition in Judaism to be emulated in the 19th century.[54]

Thus, although Pinsker was a secularist and one who promoted a secular answer to the Jewish dilemma, he drew upon Torah tradition

for his inspiration. There are of course innumerable references in the
Torah concerning self help. Isaiah 52: 1 reads: "Awake, awake, put on
thy strength, O Zion, etc." and in Isaiah 52: 2 the prophet continues
with: "Shake thyself from the dust; arise and sit down Jerusalem;
Loose thyself from the bands of thy neck, captive daughter of Zion."[55]
Self - emancipation is therefore a Biblical, Jewish tradition while
reliance on others is foreign to Judaism. This is not to say that Jews
have not looked for help from others and have not at times become
almost fatalistic in their outlook. However, Pinsker's appeal to self -
help struck a chord in the Jews of his day and of ours precisely because
self-help is at the very core of what it means to be Jewish.

Having witnessed anti-Jewish riots in Odessa in 1881 and 1882
Pinsker became convinced that hatred of Jews would never cease and
that nothing could eradicate the hatred for the Jewish people within
the Christian psyche. Therefore, Pinsker became the first Jewish writer
to define the Jewish problem, not in terms of what others might do or
learn or how they might eventually practice   brotherhood and
acceptance, but rather what Jews themselves could do even in the
absence of an eventual change of mind by their Christian neighbors.
Thus, Pinsker focused not on the causes of anti-semitism but on the
solution, namely, self - emancipation through the acquisition of a
Jewish state. This was Pinsker's great achievement for by proclaiming
"Auto-emancipation" as the only answer to the Jewish problem he
simultaneously rejected the other wordly orthodoxies of the Jewish
religious leadership and the efforts of the assimilationists to become
more Russian than the Russians and more German than the
Germans.[56]

Pinsker was of course not alone in seeking to promote a Jewish
state. In the 18th century the orthodox rabbinic scholar Zevi Hirsch
Kalischer (1795-1874) demanded of the immensely wealthy Meyer
Rothschild that he buy all of Eretz Israel, The Land of Israel, from the
Turks and thereby achieve "the ingathering of the exiles.". Despite his
orthodoxy he had evidently given up the belief in a miraculous
solution to the Jewish "problem," and concluded that human
intervention was now necessary. This became so acute during the life
time of Kalischer because he was a contemporary of the Russian
Empress Catherine II, (1762-1796) and her successors, Czars Paul
(1796-1801) and Alexander I (1801-1825). All three monarchs did
improve the legal standing of the Russian and Polish Jews in several

ways. Nevertheless, these efforts at reform by the monarchy failed because the Russian and Polish populations protested these reforms and undermined them at every opportunity. In addition, theses reforms were short lived for as soon as Nicholas II ascended the Russian throne the most primitive persecutions returned to Russia such as forced baptism, increased taxes and lengthy conscriptions into the Russian army. All this convinced the Russian and Polish Jews that they could never hope to gain equality in their native lands any more than the German Jews could have hoped for acceptance despite the efforts of the German Jews to "cover up" their civil disabilities.[57]

Moses Hess (1812-1875) was a German Jew who was by no means orthodox. In his book *Rome and Jerusalem*, he stressed the view that Jews will never be accepted in non-Jewish society and that the only solution to the Jewish dilemma would be the "reconstruction of a national life in the ancient homeland." Hess was a socialist who had abandoned Judaism and wrote, not from the Jewish tradition, but in response to the nationalism he witnessed all around him, particularly the dramatic reunification of Italy in 1859. Hess called the Jewish cause "The Last National Problem".[58]

Hess thus became the first, but surely not the last, of the Zionists who did not come from the Jewish tradition. He was soon followed by Theodor Herzl who was equally ignorant of Jewish culture and Jewish history but who could plainly see that a Jewish state would be the only solution to the Jewish problem. Therefore Herzl published *Der Judenstaat* or *The Jew State* in 1896. It is significant that Herzl did not call his book *The Jewish State* as is commonly claimed by translators. In German that would have been *Der Jüdische Staat.* Instead, Herzl deliberately used a term which carries with it an opprobrium invented by both anti-Jewish hate mongers and their self denigrating Jewish counterparts, the assimilationists, who used such circumlocutions as "Hebrew" and "Israelite" to describe themselves.[59]

Herzl had come to the conclusion that a Jewish state would be the only answer to the Jewish problem in Europe after first considering the possibility of leading all the world's Jews into baptism. This was by no means a far fetched idea at the end of the nineteenth century since it had so many precedents and current examples as well. Seeking to divorce themselves once and for all from the hatred and contempt their Jewishness earned them, large numbers of German, Austrian and other Jews sought to escape into the majority culture by not only discarding the ancient theology of their ancestors but by adopting the theology of their enemies. Thus, the secularized Jews in both Western and Eastern Europe pretended to become Christians for the sake of escaping the disabilities their Judaism had provoked. Yet, they were no more interested in the Christian religion than they had been in their own. What they wanted was escape from persecution but that was not granted them. With the advent of "anti-semitism", a phrase first invented by Wilhelm Marr in 1873, conversion no longer served the purpose of altering the status of the Jews. As the Nazi doggerel would have it, "Was der Jude glaubt ist einerlei; in der Rasse liegt die Schweinerei" or, "What the Jew believes is all the same; in the race resides the filth and shame."[60]

Thus, racial anti-semitism made no distinction between Jews who had formally adopted another religion and those who adhered to Judaism. All, including their children's children, were regarded as Jews and consigned to the gas ovens. Hence the lesson taught by the Nazi movement was that neither adherence to religious observance nor secularization could save the Jew. Furthermore it was obvious to European Christians, although not to the Jews, that a secularist who had renounced his own Jewish religion would be no more a Christian than he had been a Jew. The European Jewish assimilationists deluded themselves into believing or pretending to believe that they would be accepted as a mere sect among the Germans or the French or the Russians. The second secularist delusion was that Jews must earn their freedom from European oppression by divesting themselves of their own culture and adopting the culture of others.

Neither of these efforts succeeded. Yet, these two delusions drove the early Reform movement among the German Jews to embrace the view that Jews were mere "Staatsbürger jüdischen Glaubens", i.e., "Citizens of the Jewish faith" and that Jews needed to reform themselves into Germans by repudiating their own history and culture.

Theodor Herzl understood this. He recognized, even before the Dreyfus affair, that Jews could not solve their problem by attempting to adopt the culture of the haters but that they must define their own society and their own political state in their own land. It did not take the Dreyfus case to demonstrate this. In his short life time (1860-1904), Herzl witnessed the convening of the International anti-Jewish Congress at Dresden in Germany in 1882; the founding of "The League of Anti-Semites" in 1879; the inclusion of "anti-semitism" in the platform of the German Social Reform Party in 1880; the bloody "pogroms" against the Russian Jews in 1881; the great success of the book *The Jews, Kings of Our Time*, by Bockel in 1884 and the spectacular success of the Jew-haters in the political arena where they increased their vote from 47,000 in the German elections of 1890 to 263,000 in 1893.[61]

All of this and in addition the trial of Alfred Dreyfus made it plain to Herzl that a political solution of the Jewish problem was the only one possible and that all other proposals would fail. Herzl therefore insisted that the Zionist movement concern itself with the political solution of the Jewish problem and did not spend its energies on such issues as cultural revival, religious reform or emancipation of the Jew in the lands of his birth. Herzl, like Pinsker, rejected all of these formulas. Herzl understood: "that accommodation to Gentile standards, whether of the *ancien regime*, the bourgeois or the "classless society" was not a satisfactory basis for solving the Jewish problem;".[62]

Thus, Herzl's Zionism was practical and secularist and contributed a great deal to the overall secularization of Judiasm everywhere. Nothing demonstrated the need for self help and secular methods of achieving Jewish liberation more than Zionism. Despite the fact that some Zionists were and are orthodox in religious outlook, Zionism did not wait for the Messiah. Zionism created its own "Moshiach." This then gave the secularists a great boost, particularly because Zionism succeeded dramatically in 1948 when Israel re-established itself and gained its independence by human effort, not divine intervention.

Such a view was also held by Asher Ginzberg (1856-1927), who used the pen name Achad Haam or One of the People. Achad Haam promoted the doctrine of spiritual and cultural nationalism in the Diaspora, in the Exile, by arousing in the Jews outside of the Jewish state a Jewish consciousness. This did not mean, however, that Achad Haam or his followers were ideologically separated from the Zionists. On the contrary. Both the proponents of Jewish cultural autonomy in the Diaspora and the Zionists viewed the assimilationists with contempt.[63]

Thus, the views of Achad Haam became the cornerstone of the work of Rabbi Mordechai Kaplan, an American scholar and founder of the Society for the Advancement of Judaism generally called the Reconstructionist movement. It is the Reconstructionist movement and its influence on American Judaism which illustrates the secularization of Judaism in America more than any other although it can be said emphatically that all branches of Judaism became thoroughly secularized in America not only because of the influence of the general American culture but also because the immigrants, Jewish and Christian, to this country brought secularization with them from the "Old Country".

Yet, it was not always so. On the contrary. At the turn of the century America was largely a Protestant country. Religion was taken seriously. The "separation of church and state" in Jefferson's phrase was hardly understood. Public institutions were assumed to be Protestant and the new immigrants from Eastern and Southern Europe, Catholic and Jewish, were looked upon with suspicion by that vast number of Americans who felt the newcomers threatened every value and every conviction of the White, Anglo-Saxon, Protestant majority.

NOTES

[1]Baruch Spinoza, *Tractatus Theologico-Politicus,* in: *The Chief Works of Benedict de Spinoza,* Translated from the Latin by R.H.M. Elwes, New York, Dover Publications, Inc., 1951.

[2]Leo Straus, *Spinoza's Critique of Religion,* New York, Schocken Books, 1965, p. 52.
Originally published in Berlin in 1930 and translated from the German by E.M. Sinclair.

[3]Max Margolis and Alexander Marx, *History of the Jewish People,* New York, Meridian Books, Inc., 1956. p. 496.

[4]*Ibid.* p. 73.

[5]Straus, *op.cit.,* p.66.

[6]*Ibid.,*pp. 80-81.

[7]Thomas Hobbes, *Leviathan,* Richard Tuck, Ed., New York, Cambridge University Press, 1991, pp. 75-86; pp. 333-388 and Chapter XXX.

[8]Will and Ariel Durant, *The Age of Louis the XIV,* New York, Simon and Schuster, 1961, p.549.

[9]*Ibid.* 560

[10]A.E. Taylor, *Philosophy, Its Scope and Method,* Vol. XIII, London, A. Constable & Co., 1908, pp. 27-54.

[11]John P. Plamenatz, *Man and Society,* London, Longmans, 1963, p. 154.

[12]Hobbes, *op. cit.*

[13]Spinoza, *op.cit.,* p. 6.

[14]"Longe igitur abest ut ex autoritate pontificis Hebraeorum ad leges patriae interpretandum posset concludi Romani pontificis authoritas ad interpretandum religionem; com contra hanc unumquemque maxime habere facilius ex illa concludatur." See: Benedict de Spinoza, *The Political Works,* A.G. Wernham, Translator, Oxford, The Clarendon Press, 1965, p. 108.

[15]Spinoza, *Tractatus etc.,* Chapter VIII.

[16]*Ibid.* Chapter X.

[17]*Ibid.* Chapter XII.

[18]Deborah Pessin, *The Jewish People*, New York, The United Synagogue, 1952, p. 121.

[19]Spinoza, Elwis translation, *op.cit., p.172.*

[20]*Ibid., p. 180.*

[21]Quare nemo etiam negare potest quod is qui ex Dei mandato proximum tanquam se ipsum diligit revera est obediens, et secundum legem beatus; et qui contra odium habet , vel negligit , rebellis est et contumax.

[22]Baruch Spinoza, Elwis translation, *op.cit.,*p. 200.

[23]Michael L. Morgan, "Spinoza In History," *Judaism, Vol.40, No.2,* Spring 1991, p. 40.

[24]Yirmiyahu Yovel, *Spinoza and Other Heretics: The Marrano of Reason and The Adventures of Im manence (2 vols.)* Princeton, N.J. , Princeton University Press, 1989, p.199.

[25] Yovel, *op.cit.,*pp. 1-127.

[26] Robert E. Park, "Human Migration and the Marginal Man," *American Journal of Sociology,* Vol. 33, May, 1928, p. 891. See also: Everett V.Stonequist, *The Marginal Man,* New York, Scribner, 1937.

[27] Will and Ariel Durant, *The Age of Louis the IVX,* New York, Simon and Schuster, 1963, p. 167.

[28] Morgan, *op.cit.,* p. 41.

[29] Bertha Badt-Strauss, *Moses Mendelssohn, Der Mensch und das Werk,* Berlin, Welt Verlag, 1929, pp. XXII - XXIII.

[30] Gerhard Falk and Vern Bullough, "Achievement Among German Jews Born During the Years 1785-1885. *Mankind Quarterly,* Vol. XXVII, No 3., Spring 1987, pp.337-365.

[31] W. Gunther Plaut, "Emancipation The Challenge of Living In Two Worlds," *Judaism,* Vol., 38, No., 4
p. 441.

[32] *Ibid.,* p. 443.

[33] Michael L. Morgan, " Mendelssohn's Defense of Reason in 'Jerusalem' , *Judaism,* Vol. 38, No.4, Fall, 1989, p. 449.

[34]*Ibid.,* p. 451.

[35] Frederich C. Beiser, *The Fate of Reason: German Philosophy from Kant to Fichte,* Cambridge, The Harvard University Press, 1987, pp. 65-68; see also: Morgan, op.cit., p. 451.

[36] Klaus Werner Segreff, *Moses Mendelssohn und die Aufklarungasthetik im 18ten Jahrhundert,* Bonn, Bovier Verlag, 1984, p. 5.

[37] Alexander Altmann, *Moses Mendelssohn - A Biographical Study,* University, Ala., The University of Alabama Press, 1973, p. 676.

[38] *Ibid.,* p.672.

[39] Segreff. *op.cit.,* p. 9.

[40] *Ibid.,* p. 684.

[41] Edward Breuer, "Politics, Tradition, History: Rabbinic Judaism and the Eighteenth Century Struggle for Civil Equality, " *Harvard Theological Review,* Vol. 85, No. 3, July 1992, p. 9.

[42] Heinrich Graetz, *History of the Jews, Vol 5,* Philadelphia, The Jewish Publication Society, 1895, pp. 350-365.

[43] Ruth Gay, *The Jews of Germany,* New Haven, Yale University Press, 1992, p. 243.

[44] Charles C. Haynes, *Religion In American History,* Alexandria , Va., Association for Supervision and Curriculum Development, 1990, p. 30.

[45] Raphael Mahler, *Jewish Emancipation*, New York, The American Jewish Committee, 1941.

[46] Otto Zarek in : Moritz Brasch, Editor, *Moses Mendelssohn's Schriften zur Metaphysik und Ethik sowie zur Religionsphilosophie,* Leipzig, Leopold Voss Verlag, 1880, p. 385.

[47] Gerhard Falk, *The Jew In Christian Theology,* Jefferson, N.C. and London, McFarland & Co., 1992, p.50.

[48] *Encyclopedia Judaica,* Vol. 2, The Macmillan Co., New York, 1971, pp. 1329-1341.

[49] Immanuel Kant, *Die Religion Innerhalb der Grenzen der Blossen Vernunft,* Hamburg, Felix Meiner Verlag, 1956. See also: Hegel, *On Christianity,* New York, Harper, Row, Inc., 1948, pp. 182-205.

[50] Bernard Lazare, *L'Antisemitisme: Son Histoire et Ses Causes,* Paries, Le Puits et le Pendule, 1982, pp. 11-56.

[51]Ludwig Lewissohn, *Theodore Herzl,* New York, The World Publishing Co., 1955. p.22.

[52]*Encylcopedia Judaica, Vol. 13,* New York, The Macmillan Co., 1971, p. 546.

[53]Leon Pinsker, *Auto-emancipation,* New York, Masada, 1935.

[54]Deuteronomy 31: 6,7,23 and Joshuah 1: 6.

54Isaiah, 52, 1 and 2.

55Nachum Sokolow, *History of Zionism, v. 1,* London, Longmans, Green and Co., 1919, pp. 217-227.

56Jacob Katz, *Forerunners of Zionism,* Jerusalem, Keter Books, 1973, p. 8.

[57]Jacob S. Raisin, *The Haskalah Movement in Russia,* Philadelphia, The Jewish Publication Society of America, 1913, pp.110-120.

57*Ibid.,* p. 25.

58 Lewissohn, *op.cit.,*p. 29.

59 Marjorie Lamberti, *Jewish Activism In Imperial Germany,* New Haven, Yale Univrsity Press, 1978,
p.36.

60 Lewisohn, *op.cit.,* p.29.

61. Claude R. Foster, "Historical Antecedents: Why the Holocaust?" *The Annals of the American Academy of Political and Social Science,* Vol. 40, No. 7, 1980, p. 3.

62. Ben Halpern, *The Idea of the Jewish State,* Cambridge, The Harvard University Press, 1961, p. 80.

63. *Ibid.,* p. 93.

Chapter III

The Influence of Christian and Other Philosophers on the Secularization of the Western World

I.

The influence of Christian civilization upon the Jews and Judaism is so immense because the vast preponderance of the world's Jews lived in Europe from the fourth century, when the Roman emperor Constantine made Christianity the state religion (325 C.E. Common Era), until 1945 when most of them had been murdered by the European Christians.[1]

Therefore it is necessary and reasonable to now show how the secularization of Christianity proceeded almost from the day that Christianity became so favored. This must be done because Jewish secularization began far later than was true of Christian "free thinking", a phrase first used in English literature at the end of the 17th century.[2]

In fact, the European Jews did not emerge from the Ghetto until the end of the eighteenth and the beginning of the nineteenth century and therefore did not take part in major European developments until the French revolution and the ascendancy of Napoleon. This is true despite the fact that Spinoza, Mendelssohn and others wrote their treatises long before 1789.[3]

Therefore, the impact of the secularization of the Christian world in which they lived was not felt among the European Jews until the early nineteenth century. Nevertheless, that impact was considerable and accelerated as the Jews of Europe, and later of the United States, attained the learning and scholarship to become acquainted with such writers as Spencer in England, Comte in France and Lessing in Germany.

In short, a discussion of secularization must focus on the secularization of Christianity because it, and not Judaism, is the preponderant religion of the Western World, thereby influencing developments inside Judaism profoundly. While it is undoubtedly true that Christianity cannot be understood without reference to its Jewish origins, it is equally evident that developments in Western Judaism are so intertwined with the Christian world that both must be presented to comprehend either one.

II.

Christianity was challenged almost from its inception by heretics, unbelievers and doubters. This was true because the ancient Jews, the ancient Greeks and the Romans all included "secularists" who weakened the religious convictions of their readers. Since Christianity owes as much to its Jewish roots as it does to its origins in the Greco-Roman culture the writings of these ancient unbelievers were very much available to the educated Christian of any day and at any time. Therefore it is not surprising that "secularization" was part and parcel of the Christian experience for all of its existence since the doubters and the questioners preceded the arrival of Christianity in the Roman Empire by hundreds of years. In ancient Israel and in ancient Greece these doubters and "secularizers" challenged established beliefs, denied accepted orthodoxies and delivered their writings into the literature of the new religion.

It is claimed by some that both Job and Ecclesiastes, i.e, Koheleth, are examples of "secularization" in ancient Judaism in that both books appear to challenge the notion of the immortality of the soul as taught in Judaism and in Christianity.[4]

If that is the case, then Judaism itself may well contain the seeds of such "free thought" although there is hardly any evidence that such attitudes had much of a following among the Jews of Europe during the Christian era from the fourth to the twentieth century. Such notions may well be implicit in these books, depending on who reads them.

The book of Job implies that reward and punishment do not follow good deeds and sin as taught in Judaism and Christianity but are applied arbitrarily. It also shows the limits of human understanding and therefore denies or at least questions the need for religion. For if as pious a man as Job can be allowed to suffer so much, then piety has no meaning and religion no purpose.[5]

Likewise, Koheleth or Ecclesiastes, points to the futility of any human effort which may be the most profound heresy of them all.[6] It is of course possible to interpret "Koheleth," i.e. "Ecclesiastes" in yet another way. Thus, Carlebach holds that "Koheleth" seeks to teach that individual misfortune is not to be taken as exceedingly important. Because all suffer some misfortunes and because no man can determine for himself to have things go only his way, optimism and pessimism are possible. Carlebach argues that if we could decide to have only good fortune and no setbacks, then the difference between optimism and pessimism would not exist. "We exaggerate the meaning of each event without knowing its ranking. Therefore one must look directly into the eye of the truth so that one does not founder upon her."[7]

In Greek scholarship "free thought" was explicit as is true among the Greek philosophers beginning with Socrates (469-399 B.C.E), Plato (427-347 B.C.E.) and Aristotle(384-322 B.C.E.) (The abbreviation, B.C.E., means Before the Common Era).

The influence of Socrates on Christianity is no doubt minimal and indirect. Nevertheless, even this indirect influence continues to this day as there is hardly any fairly educated person who has not read his ideas as reflected in his intellectual progeniture.

Thus, "the orthodox in religion considered him to be the most dangerous of the Sophists (scholars), for while he observed the amenities of the ancient faith he rejected tradition, wished to subject every rule to the scrutiny of reason, founded morality in the individual conscience rather than in social good or the unchanging decrees of heaven, and ended with a skepticism that left reason itself in a mental confusion unsettling to every custom and belief."[8]

This may be too harsh an indictment. For like Mendelssohn, so many years later, Socrates wanted to rationalize conduct without rationalizing belief. That means that Socrates, according to one of the

Platonic dialogues, "is made to say he holds by the ordinary versions of all the myths, on the grounds that it is an endless task to find rational explanations for them." Of course, Socrates was most unpopular because he constantly cross examined every popular opinion. Socrates is not depicted as an atheist. On the contrary. He is described as one who believes, not only in the gods of Athens, but in other gods. In fact, the charges brought against him which led to his death were that he would not recognize the city's gods but strange gods.[9]

Plato, the student of Socrates, advised that those who would not believe in the gods were to be imprisoned or executed. This made Plato most unusual among Socrates' students even as he also held that the gods could not be propitiated, a view shared by Thucydides, the historian, who was a rationalist and whose work reveals him to have been an atheist as well.[10]

Finally Aristotle, without doubt an unbeliever, denied the usefulness of prayer and sacrifice. Aristotle has been described as a monotheist without a religion.

Numerous other students of Socrates were also "freethinkers," or atheists or at least denied that the gods, if they did exist, did anything or had any interest in humans or this world. This was particularly true of Epicurus and his followers who may be called forerunners of the theists of the past three hundred years. Epicurus lived a simple life and was in no manner an "epicurean" as commonly depicted. However, his name became synonymous with apostasy as the Rabbis called Jews who followed his teaching "Apikorase".[11]

It is certain that Jefferson, Emerson, Thoreau and many other American writers and thinkers held a theistic view of the universe and were therefore latter day followers of Epicurus. It is this failure to attribute any action or involvement of God in the affairs of men that distinguishes the secularist from the religious person even if the secularist does not deny the existence of a deity or a God.[12]

Thus, the cynics, the hedonics and others set religion aside entirely despite the fact that some were exiled and others executed for holding such beliefs and making such statements.

The consequences of these writings and teachings were best seen by looking at the influence these writers had on Rome and on Roman thought. It is surely reasonable to hold that Roman civilization owes so much to Greece that the Latin speakers could not escape the Greek influence which had penetrated their language as well as their art, their philosophy and their daily lives.

III.

The best example of the great influence of the Greek secularists upon Roman writers is the work of Lucretius (145 B.C.E.-30 B.C.E.). In his best known work, *On the Nature of Things,* Lucretius uses the famous phrase *"To so many evils has religion persuaded"* and, like Epicurus before him denies that the gods have any interest in men. *"Nothing exists but atoms and the void,"* says Lucretius and all things are physical and material. Lucretius denies the immortality of the soul, denies the *Hereafter* and asserts that virtue lies in living a life of reason.[13]

Somewhat less direct in his criticism of religion was the great scholar and orator Marcus Tullius Cicero (106 B.C.E.-43 B.C.E.). In his books, *On the Nature of the Gods* and *On Divination*, he exhibited an obvious contempt for popular orthodoxies and an utter disbelief in the recognized religious practices of the day. In this, Cicero resembled most of the prominent men of Rome, including his contemporary, Julius Caesar. Cicero was an accomplished orator and used religion to attack his enemies. This is particularly visible in his orations *Against Cataline*. Nevertheless, this public display of religiosity was no more than an effort by Cicero to meet the needs of political expediency for his writings clearly show that he saw religion only as a means of supporting his political opportunism.[14] Numerous other Roman writers, including Horace (65 - 8 B.C.E.) and Ovid (43 B.C.E. - 17 C.E.) protested against the assumption that the sacrifices of the rich were more important than good conduct.[15]

IV.

Christianity had hardly entered the Roman world when its doctrines became subject to the challenge of Arius. Labeled the "Arian Heresy," the views of the Alexandrian priest Arius (280 -336 C.E.) challenged the very substance of Christian theology and led to the first ecumenical (world) council of Christian bishops called by the Emperor Constantine at Nicaea in 325. This resulted in the original Nicene Creed formulated in an effort to preserve the unity of the Christian church thereby laying the foundation for the so called Middle Ages in which religion was to be uniform, unified and absolute.

This was, of course, not to be. On the contrary. As soon as one "heresy" had been condemned by the Church another arose. Thus, in the fifth century the monks Pelagius and Caelestius taught that the doctrine of original sin was mistaken and that there was no "fall of man." This included the denial that Adam's sin was inherited; the assertion that death is strictly natural and not a punishment for Adam's sin; denial that children and virtuous adults who die unbaptized are damned; assertion that the will is free and that good deeds are the outcome of good will.[16]

The Monophysites argued that Christ had only one divine nature; Nestorius, the bishop of Constantinople was excommunicated for holding that Mary was the mother of the human but not the divine side of Christ.

Rationalists of every persuasion argued against Christian beliefs incessantly. Among these was Lucian who doubted the Greek religion as much as the new religion (Christianity) so that life appeared to him "a ridiculous confusion" and that efforts to understand "origins and ends" are nonesense and useless. Thus, Lucian became the epitome of skepticism.[17]

V.

"It would be an error ....to suppose that even in the Dark Ages,..the spirit of critical reason was wholly absent from...Christendom." So says Robertson, and we concur.[18] For example, the Italian monk Jovinian denounced celibacy in the fourth century and a number of Christians and in particular the emperor Leo III opposed the use of statues and pictures. Leo III the Isaurian, so named because he was born in southern Turkey which was then called Isauria, became known to history as Leo the Iconoclast which means "Image Breaker". Leo and his followers sought to rid the churches of icons. An icon, in the Greek churches, is any picture, mosaic or carving depicting a religious scene or persons. Leo launched a campaign against such icons in 726 by a decree against images. The emperor Constantine V continued this campaign by calling a Council in 753 which ruled that "there shall be rejected and removed and cursed out of the Christian church any likeness which is made of any material whatever by the evil art of painters."[19]

Although the empress Irene (780-802) revived the use of pictures and mosaics and denounced those who called these works of art icons, the emperor Leo V continued the iconoclastic campaign. This effort was again defeated by yet another empress, Theodora (841-855), who restored the use of images to their former position in the church. None of this affected the Western or Roman Catholic church where the iconoclastic movement did not appear until the days of Erasmus (1469-1536) and Luther (1483-1546), that is in the 16th century, and became in part responsible for the Protestant reformation.

Nevertheless, the persecution of the iconoclasts promoted by Theodora, led to their movement into Bulgaria where they succeeded in finding many converts to their view. Subsequently the Bogomilians of Bulgaria brought these ideas into Western Europe leading directly to two more heresies, those of the Albigenses and the Waldenses.[20]

The Albigensian heresy was so called because it was mainly espoused in the diocese of Albi in the part of France called Provence and Languedoc.

These "heretics" held that an evil god, Jehovah of the "old" testament, was responsible for all the evil in the world. He existed, they explained, in opposition to the good god of the "new" testament . They viewed the evil god as having as his province of concern this material world while the good god, in their judgment, presided over things spiritual. They also predicted that the good god would eventually win the struggle with the evil god. Furthermore, the Albigensians identified the church with the evil god and called the church "the synagogue (assembly) of Satan." They therefore sought to abolish the church and taught their followers that they were the only road to salvation and eternal bliss.

The Albigensians also called themselves "Cathari", a Greek word meaning "pure." They were pacifists who not only opposed war but also capital punishment and crusades. They would not eat meat or any animal product such as eggs or milk. They ate only vegetables. Dividing their followers into two classes, that is, the perfect and the believers, they succeeded in gathering a large following of those who as mere believers needed only to support these doctrines without living the life style only lived by the "perfect."[21] This entire "heresy" was of course persecuted by the church and the state in the Albigensian crusade until these believers were entirely wiped out.[22]

Likewise, the Waldensian heresy became anathema to the orthodox church. Founded by an erstwhile rich merchant, Peter Waldo, who gave up his wealth in order to live a life of purity, similar to the Buddha, the Waldensians were also known as "the poor men of Lyon". Although they taught nothing "heretical" these "poor men" taught the Gospel in the local language without permission from the local authorities as required by the Pope. Thus, solely because they would not ask for permission to preach, and not because of any deviation from orthodox belief, the Waldensians were lumped with the Albigensians by the church and the state and equally persecuted.

Persecution, as always, led these believers to more exteme positions than they had earlier proposed so that it cannot be doubted that these "heretics" and many others became the forerunners of the Protestants of the 16th century.

Before making brief reference to the heresies of the renaissance it is necessary to mention the greatest scientist of the Middle Ages, the Englishman Roger Bacon (1214-1292), who was imprisoned for teaching "heresies", despite his membership in the Franciscan order. Bacon had severely criticized the "Holy See" that is, the papal court, the curia and the religious orders and in addition the princes and governments of his time.

It was not Bacon, but the scholar John Wyclif (1320-1384) who may be regarded however as the first of the English reformers. His theology, based on predestination, created Protestantism even though that word was not used until Luther's time and even though Wyclif lived and died a Roman Catholic. Wyclif anticipated Luther, proposed that the English church sever its relationship to the Roman Catholic church, preached that salvation and damnation were decided by God long before anyone is born and, with the help of Hereford and Purfey translated the Bible into English from the Latin version of Jerome.[23]

A more radical heretic than Wyclif was the Welshman Reginald Peacock (1395-1460) who "alientated every section of theological opinion in England" by denying the authenticity of the Apostels' Creed as he supported reason against scriptualism.[24]

VI.

The word "renaissance" or rebirth was first used in France to describe the great production of letters and arts in the fourteenth, fifteenth and sixteenth centuries in Italy and in France.[25]

This rebirth referred to the recovery of classic Greek and Roman literature but was in reality a new departure involving not only ancient but also modern expression and thought. Nevertheless, such freethinkers or secularists as Epicurus received a new influence which led to additional "heretical" writings beginning with Durante Alighieri or Dante (1265-1321), Franceso Petrarca or Petrach (1304-1374), and Giovanni Boccacio (1313-1375). Many others participated in the great effort to rid Western thought of the stifling limits imposed upon it for so long. Anti-clerical and rational in many of its pronouncements, this literature was condemned by the Church but to no avail. On the contrary. Rebellion against the established orthodoxies became a flood after the fourteenth and fifteenth centuries. Gabriele de Salo wrote in 1497 that Jesus was not the son of God but a charlatan who had died on the cross for crimes he had committed. He had been preceded by Galeotto Marcio who wrote that any man who lived a decent life would go to heaven no matter what his religion. These heretics kept the Inquisition busy so that Giorgio da Novara was burned in 1500 at Bologna for denying the divinity of Jesus.[26]

The best known rebel against established Christian orthodoxy in Italy at the end of the fifteenth and beginning of the sixteenth century was Niccolo Machiavelli (1469-1527). Some thought that Machiavelli was an atheist. In any event, he blamed Christianity for the failure of men to live a humble and decent life. He was joined in his criticisms by Pietro Pomponazzi (1462-1525), who wrote "On the Immortality of the Soul" in which he denied immortality and instead insisted that the mind or soul could only exist in a body and not at all in a disembodied state. Pomponazzi also doubted miracles and supernatural causes of all kinds and insisted on natural and reasonable origins of all phenomena.

Numerous other writers produced a consderable body of "heretical" literature which eventually led to the Reformation, itself seen as a "heresy" by the established European catholicism of its day. However, the Reformation, once established, continued to pursue additonal heresies against its power and privileges as neither Luther nor Calvin "dreamt of toleration" but hoped to establish for themselves a tyranny at least as repressive as the one they had abandoned.[27] The reason for this was that the Reformation was a political and commercial rebellion so that the continuation of "freethought" and secularism occurred outside of its sphere and therefore in Catholic Italy.[28]

VII.

Although Michael Servetus was burned at the stake by the Calvinists in 1553 at the instigation of the Catholic Inquisition, "heresy" continued unabated within Christian lands. In fact, it was in Switzerland where Servetus died that deism was born. The deists rejected all "revealed" religion, but seeking to distance themselves from atheism called themselves deists. Deism, atheism and innumerable variations thereof may have been common in the Europe of the 16th century. However, the extreme repression in both Catholic and Protestant lands of dissent and opinion culminated in the persecution for "heresy" of Giordano Bruno (1548-1600). Bruno called Reformers, Deformers and told his persecutors that he believed in an infinite universe consisting of innumerable worlds which he thought were like our own. Calling universal law "Providence" he held that everything lives, grows and attains perfection in accordance with this law which is supported by the "Divine Being" whose attributes Bruno held to be mind or the source of general existence, intellect or the source of particular or distinct existence and love or the harmony between these two.

In sum, Bruno denied the trinity and other Christian orthodoxies and was burnt at the stake for these opinions in the year 1600. Bruno wrote that the intellect should be free and that no man has the right to compel another to think as he does and that every man ought to tolerate with patience the beliefs of his neighbors.

It was for this reason that Bruno was also unwilling to submit uncritically to the opinions of humanism which he believed was another tyranny even if it had begun as a promoter of free thought and tolerance. In seeing this danger Bruno became a modern thinker and a man of honor and consistency. As we shall see, the great problem for the followers of modern humanism is their inablity to permit others a viewpoint not to their liking and different from that generally approved by the "politically correct" at the end of the 20th century.[29]

Deism is implied in Bruno's writings. In Vanini it found full expression. Cesare Lucilio Vanini (1585-1619) questioned the existence of a personal god. Like Bruno before him, Vanini believed God to be Nature and nature to be god. Although Vanini knew no more about science than his century allowed, his efforts to promote nature and reason above theology and bigotry led to his execution in 1619. Yet, his views live on in the insistence on freedom of inquiry of our own day. The great contribution of Vanini to human freedom, at the cost of his life, was his skepticism born of a study of nature.[30]

We cannot leave this period in the development of human reason without mentioning Galileo Galilei (1564-1642). Although an orthodox Catholic in all repsects save his assertion that the earth moved about the sun, he was condemned as a heretic but not punished. It was not until 1990 that the Pope finally admitted the error of that condemnation.

VIII.

"De Omnibus dubitandum" "Doubt everything!" So wrote Rene Descartes (1596-1650) and thereby became the founder of modern science and philosophy. Yet, he too needed to find one fact, one condition men could consider certain, one anchor in a sea of uncertainty. This one truth Descartes found in himself as he wrote the most famous sentence in philosophy, i.e, *Cogito Ergo Sum,* "I think, therefore, I am."[31]

Descartes holds that "it seems to me that I may adopt it as a general rule, that all things which I conceive very clearly and distinctly are true."[32] Relating this observation to the possible existence of God, Descartes argues from First Cause and proposes that unless God has created him, he must have created himself. That however, Descartes holds for impossible, since anyone who created himself would have given himself immortality and perfection, two categories in which all men are lacking.

Despite Descartes' effort to prove the existence of God, an evident religious exercise, Descartes nevertherless promoted the "Age of Reason" and the use of rational arguments because he sought to demonstrate the existence of God and of things certainly known by the use of mathematics. "Just as it follows from the essence of a triangle that the sum of its angles are equal to two right angles, so it follows from the nature of God that he exists".[33]   Descartes then lists some "eternal truths" among which he considers that: 1.Nothing can originate from nothing 2. It is impossible that the same thing should at the same time exist and not exist   3. Whatever is done cannot be undone   4. He who thinks cannot be nonexistent as long as he thinks. These proposals are all included in Descartes' great work *Principles of Philosophy* which is, however, more a scientific than philosophical treatise because its aim is to discuss the principles of human knowledge and the principles of material things, the visible world and the earth.   Thus, *Principles of Philosophy* placed scientific truths and methods ahead of speculation, religion and belief and for that reason became important in the development of the secular in the present Western world.[34]*

IX.

David Hume was born in 1711 and lived until 1776, thus traversing almost the entire 18th Century. A Calvinist, or Presbyterian, by upbringing, Hume devastated orthodox religion so that his very name became synonymous with skepticism.

The principle contribution of Hume to the continuation of empirical thinking is his discussion of the origin and meaning of the fundamental concepts of substance and causality. Thus, to Hume an object   remains the same even when its characteristics change and causality, he argues, is the fact that the first phenomenon is the condition from which the second phenomenon arises. This means, according to Hume, that we derive our knowledge of causality only through experience. Since the effect is entirely different from the cause it cannot be learned except through experience. Therefore, Hume argues, one cannot reason from empirical data to that which is transcendent, like God or immortality, since these concepts cannot be known by experience.

It is this argument which, perhaps more than any other, gave secularism an immense impetus and continues to hold great fascination for those who are not only skeptics, like Hume, but humanists, agnostics and atheists.

In his essay on miracles Hume seeks to destroy belief in miracles altogether. Here Hume wrote "that no testimony is sufficient to establish a miracle, unless the testimony would be more miraculous than the fact which it endeavors to establish; and that in that case there is a mutual destruction of arguments." This means that since it is contrary to experience that a miracle should be performed, but not contrary to experience that men speak lies and deceive one another, it is reasonable to reject any testimony but not reasonable to credit a miracle.[35]

John Locke (1632-1704) is regarded by some "the most influential philosopher of his age." His *Essay Concerning Human Understanding* was instrumental in founding the "Age of Reason." It was however Locke's three *"Letters Concerning Toleration"* which laid the groundwork for the return of the Jews to England in 1649, i.e., in Cromwell's day, after an absence of 350 years. Locke wrote this: "Neither pagan, nor Mahometan nor Jew, ought to be excluded from the civil rights of the commonwealth because of his religion."[36]

X.

On the surface Immanuel Kant (1724-1804) does not appear as an enemy of orthodox religion nor a proponent of secularism or humanism. Yet, in his most important work on religion, *Religion Within the Limits of Mere Reason,* "is expressed his reduction of religion to the moral consciousness." It is well to take a look at the original German name Kant gave this book, *"Religion innerhalb der blossen Vernunft."* The word "blossen" means unaided or unassisted. This is very significant because it means that Kant looked for religion to be unassisted by supernatural revelation. This made Kant a deist precisely because a deist is defined as one who acknowledges the existence of God but rejects religion and its exercises. For example, Edward Stillingfleet, Bishop of Worcester, described a deist as: "a particular person who owned the Being and Providence of God , but expressed mean esteem of the Scriptures and the Christian religion."[37]

Thus, Kant taught philosophical ethics as a substitute for religion. Kant claimed to believe in Christian miracles and supernatural events but also held that religion is needed for the masses of people in the sense that a police department is also needed to insure good behavior. Kant promoted moral conduct apart from religious services designed to propitiate God or court favor with Him. The truly religious spirit, argues Kant, is that which recognizes all our duties as divine commands. This leads Kant to teach in *The Critique of Practical*

Reason, the famous *Categorical Imperative*, which is expressed in English as *"Act so that the maxim of thy will can likewise be valid at all times as the principle of a universal legislation."* The meaning here is clear. If men's actions were based on the proposition that what anyone is about to do would then become universal law, then hardly anyone would do anything which would harm the whole community and himself thereafter.[38]

Furthermore, Kant holds that a "supreme intelligence" or God must exist. He even accords organized religion, or churches, some value in that he proposed that for almost all men religious ritual and ceremony are needed to live a moral existence. However, he looked forward to the development of true religion, that is, "the supremacy of purely religious faith" without "mock services and priestcraft."[39] It is precisely this position which has led to widespread secularization of the Western World. Innumerable people in Europe, America and elsewhere have argued for years that they have no interest in organized religion but are nevertheless "religious" in the sense of holding religious faith outside of churches, synagogues and other institutions. The argument between those who continue to hold to organized religion and those who do not centers upon the issue of human nature. Kant believed that no society can be founded on the basis of pure religious faith alone. Therefore he recognized the need, for most men, to adhere to organized religion and ritual. Yet, Kant also taught, in *The Critique of the Faculty of Judgment,* that the pursuit of moral duties is a universal law for all, outside of religious doctrine or ritual. Kant thought that these moral duties relate to ends such as one's own perfection and others' happiness, including our duties to ourselves and our duties to others. Thus, a 'perfect duty' to ourselves would be the law prohibiting suicide; an 'imperfect duty' to ourselves would be a command forbidding slothfulness in the use of our talents. Among 'perfect duties' to others would be abstinence from falsehood and deceit while an 'imperfect duty' , according to Kant, is positive care for others.

Thus, Kant taught a moral system hardly reached by many men. If it could be reached, then indeed the need for religion based on fears of the supernatural might well be obviated. Yet, as we have seen, Kant recognized that without organized religion a society could hardly hold together. Thus, Kant, whether with or without his will and belief, may well be categorized as a deist and thereby became a major contributor to the secularization of Western man.

XI.

For English speaking students the influence of German, French and other writers could hardly have been as great as the influence of the English writers Hobbes and Hume and the deists whose literature begins with the work of Lord Herbert of Cherbury (1583-1648) at the beginning of the seventeenth century and continued to the days of George Washington, Thomas Jefferson, Thomas Paine and Benjamin Franklin, all leaders of the American revolution and all very influential in shaping the American mind in favor of that attitude.[40]

Herbert was not the only nor the first writer to attack the notion that truth is divinely revealed. Other enemies of revelation and authority, like Bacon, argued from the viewpoint of science and sought to demolish the authoritarian obstacles to scientific inquiry which revealed religion represents. Herbert, however, was not a scientist. His philosophical objections to revelation was that he could not agree that something that definitely conflicts with reason can be true. The merit of Herbert's work lies not in presenting readers with yet another example of truth as promoted by yet another philosopher, but in "inquiring how the fallible human mind might attain some reasonably accurate notion of what the truth actually was."[41]

From this notion Herbert proceeds to the Doctrine of the Five Common Notions concerning religion which he thought were universal and understood by all men. These five "common notions" are: 1. there is some supreme divinity. 2. It is agreed, according to Herbert, that this divinity is to be worshipped. 3. Virtue joined with piety leads ultimately to eternal happiness. 4. All peoples always have had a sense of sin and have believed that crime and sin can be expiated by penitence 5. all agree that there is a reward and punishment in an afterlife.[42]

Herbert does not argue that religion is useless. He does however insist that religious ceremony not be confused with the essence of religion.

We have already seen that Hobbes (1588-1679) was either a deist or atheist depending on the view a reader might wish to take concerning his writings. Hobbes rejected prayer, ritual and ceremony and defined religion as: "Fear of power invisible, feigned by the mind or imagined from *tales publicly allowed,* RELIGION; *not allowed,* SUPERSTITION." In contrast to Descartes who at least gave lip service to the clergy, Hobbes sarcastically assailed all clergy and showed them an unusual degree of intellectual hostility.

This hostility to the clergy and established religion evidently took on considerable proportions in 17th century England since the government of the City of London felt it necessary to ask Parliament to prohibit all private meetings because of the immense increase in "heresies and blasphemies" then in evidence. Numerous sects or groups had banded together to demand religious toleration. The Levelers not only demanded that all religions be tolerated but even insisted that the State should leave religion alone altogether. Atheists abounded and were called "monsters" by theists of all kinds. The impact these writers must have had on England in the 1600's is best understood by recognizing that a flood of pamphlets, books and lectures favoring religion and Christian belief appeared after 1685, all designed to refute the numerous unbelievers who were gaining new adherents every day. In 1696 Parliament even passed a Blasphemy Law which was somewhat effective in limiting the manner, but not the substance, of the trend to publish deistic and atheistic literature.

The Trinity was now also criticized and Unitarianism came into vogue.[43] With it came Deism as described by William Stephens, an Anglican country preacher, who wrote *An Account of the Growth of Deism in England* in 1696. According to Stephens, "Deism is a denial of all revealed religion."[44]

Three causes of deism are listed by Stephens. First, he mentions "Men of loose and sensual lives," meaning Hobbes and Spinoza. He calls them "practical atheists" rather than deists because these writers and their followers deny both miracles and revelation. The second cause of deism, according to Stephens, is foreign travel. He calls this the external cause and refers to the *Grand Tour* undertaken by the English upper class and which always included Italy, France and Germany and often other countries. This travel, Stephens claims, lead to a "crash course" in comparative religion as Englishmen returned home with " a more discerning and critical eye."

Finally, Stephens blames the priests of the Anglican church for the rise of deism in that he accuses them of the same pretensions and political selfishness as the Catholics whom he despised. He wrote: "The old Deists, tell those of their Pupils, who never traveled abroad, that there is now no need of going over the Water, to discover that the name Church signifieth only a self interested Party and that the Clergy have no Godliness but Gain."[45]

Deism, and hence secularism, thus received considerable impetus in 17th century England particularly because of the "Glorious Revolution" of 1688 which led many to "merging the republicanism of the English revolution with religious and philosophical radicalism."[46] As the 17th century closed, other writers, such as John Toland, continued the attack on Christianity in favor of Deism with his book *Christianity Not Mysterious* in 1696.[47]

By then, however, Deism had become respectable. In the succeeding, 18th century, however, Anthony Collins introduced a new controversy into England with his *Discourse on Freethinking*. This book contains attacks on prophecy and the authenticity of the Bible. Similarly, Matthew Tindal's *Christianity as Old as Creation*, published in 1730, presents a theistic view and attacks the clergy. Numerous other English theists published their view during the eighteenth century. Among these were Thomas Woolston, Conyers Middleton and the politician Henry Bolingbroke (1678-1751) who fled to France in 1715, in part because he had scorned Christian theology and promoted Deism. [48]

If Bolingbroke had been a Prussian, and particularly had he lived at the court of Frederick II (1712-1786), he would not have been forced to flee. But Bolingbroke lived too soon and Prussia was the only "enlightened" state in all of Europe.

XII.

Frederick II of Prussia wrote thirty one volumes on politics, history, government, military strategy, poetry, philosophy and religion. His correspondence was immense and he also composed music. Seldom, in the long history of despotism, had there been so intellectual a ruler on the throne of any country.

Although Frederick did not conduct his affairs according to the theory of "enlightened despotism" as taught by the French *philosophes,* he nevertheless resembled the ideal proposed by them in that he held it important that his actions benefit the state rather than himself, personally. [49]

Frederick was a "freethinker" influenced immensely by the French philosopher Voltaire who lived at his court briefly.

In addition to Mendelssohn and Kant, both permitted to write on religion with greater freedom than had hitherto been possible anywhere in Europe, Prussia during the rule of Frederick the Great, attracted numerous other enlightened writers of whom Johann Christian Friedrich Schiller (1759-1805) and Johann Wolfgang von Goethe (1749-1832), Germany's greatest poets and dramatists were foremost.

Schiller, under the influence of Kant and the *philosophes* accepted the current view that reason, not religion was the road to salvation. Rejecting all churches he believed in an impersonal god and wrote to Goethe that he accepted no religion because of religion.[50]

Goethe was an atheist in his youth and a deist in his age. His work is undoubtedly among the greatest ever produced in literature. He ranks with Dante and Shakespeare as one of the immortals of human achievers. Goethe's greatest drama is *Faust.* This ancient story of the philosopher willing to make a pact with the devil in order to recapture his youth refers to Goethe himself.

Goethe's religion was Spinozan. He adored nature and rejected the supernatural. He did not consider himself a Christian and viewed the story of the virgin birth as nonsense. He viewed the Protestant as well as the Catholic religion as unfulfilling but nevertheless hoped for an after life. As he aged, Goethe's views became somewhat more conservative. Yet, the *Prologue In Heaven,* which introduces *Faust,* gives theology scant credit for teaching anything at all. Said Goethe: *"Habe nun, ach! Philosophie, Juristerie und Medizin, und leider auch Theologie , Durchaus studiert mit heissem Bemüh'n; Da steh ich nun ich armer Tor! Und bin so klug als wie zuvor"* or *"Alas, with every effort I studied Philosophy, Law and unfortunately even Theology - Yet, here I stand, a fool galore; and am no wiser than before."*[51]

XIII.

His name was Charles Louis de Secondat, but he is known to history by his title, Baron de La Brede et de Montesquieu. His fame rested squarely on *The Spirit of the Laws,* which he published in his later years. His *Persian Letters,* published in 1721, revealed his heresies. These *Letters* sought to critique French society and the French government. Religion, however, also received a considerable criticism.

Montesquieu recognized that to blacks, God is black and perhaps, the devil white. The church is severely criticized in the *Letters* as always taking and never giving. Montesquieu taught relativism and appreciation of the view of other cultures and other attitudes. In this he was undoubtedly a precursor of the great German poet Gotthold Ephraim Lessing, whom we have already met as a contemporary of Moses Mendelssohn.

That Montesquieu and Goethe were original thinkers and artists cannot be denied. Nevertheless, like all great minds of the eighteenth century they were influenced by one man whose very name means enlightenment and the humanitarian developments of the eighteenth and nineteenth century. That man was Voltaire.

XIV.

Voltaire was the pen name of Francois Marie Arouet (1694-1778). His life and his work are the prime example of the victory of secularization over Christianity in Europe despite the evident fact that Christianity continues to have millions of adherents three hundred years after Voltaire's birth.

This "victory" was not a victory in the sense of annihilating the"enemy" but rather a victory in the sense that the thinking and the attitude of almost all who have lived in a "Christian" environment since then have lived in a secular world as well. The truth is, that Voltaire and "The Prophets of Paris" secularized the Western World, a condition which is dominant even today (1995).[52]

Nothing that Voltaire said about Christianity had not been said before by those we have briefly reviewed, and by thousands of others not here mentioned. The significance of Voltaire lies, therefore, not in his originality, but in the manner in which his words were accepted by millions previously loyal to Christian doctrine and orthodoxy. The fact is that at the beginning of the eighteenth century secularization had won important victories in the minds of men so that at the end of the eighteenth century the French revolution sealed what Voltaire had begun.

Voltaire was not an atheist although, like other deists, he was charged with atheism by his enemies. There is also no doubt that in Voltaire culminated the drive for free expression and the freedom from superstition which had dominated mankind for so long. The consequences of Voltaire's teaching were not only the French revolution of 1789 but, more important, the introduction of free speech, freedom of religion and a free press into the American constitution. The intellectual and artistic freedom of the 19th century and the achievements of the 20th century in Western civilization could not have taken place without the contributions of the *philosophes* led by Voltaire because these ideas spread to all parts of Europe and to America and have now become the liberal tradition embodied in the concept of civil rights and human rights by which the world measures the progress of civilization.

Voltaire had the advantage that he could draw upon information from all parts of the earth inasmuch as technology had advanced enough in his day to make that possible. Therefore he, and many of his contemporaries, were impressed by "the relativity of custom" from which they derived the view that no religion could have a monopoly of truth. Instead, Voltaire and his contemporary intellectual brethren believed that God was a watchmaker who had created the universe and then left it to its natural laws, a view we have already encountered in Spinoza.

Here is an example of Voltaire's view:

> "*Consider that the eternal wisdom of the most high has with his hand engraved natural religion in the bottom of your heart; believe that the simple candour of your mind will not be the object of his immortal hatred; believe that before his throne, always, everywhere, the heart of just man is precious; believe that a modest bonze, a charitable dervish, find grace in his eyes rather than a merciless Jansenist or an ambitious pontiff. ....A god has no need of our assiduous attentions: if he can be offended, it is only by injustice; he judges by our virtues, and not by our sacrifices.*"

The sum of Voltaire's arguments against Christianity was that the Christian god is a   monster and not the god of nature. This argument was particularly aimed at the Jansenists, followers of Cornelius Jansen, a Dutch theologian who, although a Catholic, sided with the Calvinists in proclaiming the doctrine of predestination as derived from St. Augustine. Voltaire was a skeptic. "*Incredulity is the basis of all wisdom*" is the opening sentence of his biography of Charles the XII of Sweden. His researches included a publication of the views of the physicist Newton, numerous plays, especially *Candide* which ridicules religion and his vigorous defense of a family unjustly accused of murdering one of their own members. Voltaire was also a contributor to the great *Dictionnaire Philosophique (1751)*, edited by Diderot. This dictionary, roundly condemned by every church in Europe, was instrumental in distributing the anti-clerical attitude of its contributors throughout France and can be understood as one of the precipitating causes of the revolution of 1789.[53]

The *Encyclopedie,* although containing what appeared to be orthodox articles on religion, Christianity and clergy, used a surreptitious approach to criticize and ridicule all of these concepts. Denis Diderot (1713-1784), the editor of the *Encyclopedie,* was a deist like Voltaire. In his hands the *Encyclopedie* promoted the interests of science and reason, criticized scholasticism and separated philosophy from theology as Diderot wrote: "*Reason is for the Philosopher what grace is for the Christian.* "[54] Technology and mechanics were given a great deal of space in the *Encyclopedie.* Thus, Diederot and his co-authors became major contributors to the enlightenment and the distribution of its ideas throughout the educated world. Included in their encyclopedia were, however, all the errors and all the shortcomings with which agnosticism, rationalism and scientific humanism have been saddled since then. In their anxiety to discredit religion they overlooked the contributions of religion to art and music, to morals and philosophy and to social solidarity. Distributed in Germany, Switzerland and Italy as well as Russia this encyclopedia was read widely among the intellectual leadership in Europe and America. It had a profound effect on deism in the United States where its ideas and those of Montesquieu where written into the Constitution by Jefferson and Madison and where these views form the basis of our freedoms to this day.

NOTES

[1]Max Margolis and Alexander Marx, *A History of the Jewish People,* New York, Meridian, 1958, p. 229; Martin Gilbert, *The Holocaust,* New York, Hill and Wang, 1979.

[2]J.M. Robertson, *A Short History of Free Thought*, New York, Russell and Russell, 1957, p. 1.

[3]Cecil Roth, *History of the Jews*, New York, Schocken Books (1st paperback edition), 1963, p. 320.

[4]Stephen Mitchell, *The Book of Job,* San Francisco, North Point Press, 1987, pp. xxx-xxxi.

[5]*Ibid.*

[6]Robert Gordis, *Koheleth-The Man and His World: A Study of Ecclesiastes,* Schocken Books, N.Y. 1968
p. 4.

[7]Joseph Carlebach, *Das Buch Koheleth*, Frankfurt, a.M., Hermon Verlag, 1936, p. 8. Translated from the German by G. Falk.

[8]R. Nicol Cross, *Socrates, The Man and His Mission,* Freeport, N.Y., Books for Libraries Press, 1970, p. 242.

[9]Gordon H. Clark, *Hellenistic Philosophy,* New York, Appleton-Century Crofts, 1940, pp. 1-8.

[10]*Ibid,* p. 8.

[11]*Ibid.*

[12]Ralph Waldo Emerson, "The Over-Soul", in *The Social Philosophers,* Saxe Commins and Robert N. Linscott, Eds., New York, Random House, 1947, pp. 409-426. See also: Daniel Boorstin, *The Lost World of Thomas Jefferson*, New York, Holt, 1948.

[13]Lucretius, *De Rerum Natura, "Tantum religion potuit suadere malorum,"*; Thomas Jackson, Translator, Basil Blackwell, Publisher in Clark, *op. cit.* pp. 8-49.

[14]Marcus Tullius Cicero, *De Natura Deorum and De Divinatione,* London, The Loeb Library, 1948.

[15]Robertson, *op. cit.,* p. 142.

[16]Adolf Harnack, *Outlines of the History of Dogma,* Ed Knox Mitchell, Translator, London, Hodder and Stoughton, 1893.

[17]Will Durant, *The Life of Greece*, New York, Simon and Schuster, 1939, pp. 494-495.

[18]Robertson, *op.cit, .*p.195

[19]James W. Thompson and Edgar N. Johnson, *An Introduction to Medieval Europe 300-1500,* New York, W.W. Norton & Co., Inc., 1937.

[20]Robertson, *op.cit.,* p.198.

[21]Thompson and Johnson, *op.cit.,*p.626.

[22]Will Durant, *The Renaissance,* New York, Simon and Schuster, 1953 p. 67.

[23]Friedrich Ueberweg, *The History of Philosophy from Thales to the Present Time,* George S. Morris, Translator.,New York, Charles Scribner's Sons, 1890, *pp.133-147.*

[24]Will Durant, *The Reformation,* New York, Simon and Schuster, 1957, pp. 30-35.

[25]Robertson, *op.cit.,* pp. 238-239.

[26]John Owen, *Skeptics of the Italian Renaissance,* New York, The Macmillan Co, 1908, pp. 147-160.

[27]*Ibid.,* p. 208.

[28]Jim Herrick, *Against the Faith: Essays on Deists, Skeptics and Atheists,* Buffalo, N.Y., Prometheus Press, 1985, pp. 56-70.

[29]Robertson, *op.cit.,* p. 259.

[30]Owen, *op.cit.,* p. 320.

[31]*Ibid.*p.326.

[32]Owen, *op.cit.,*p.327.

[33]*Ibid.,* pp.369-370; Robertson, *op.cit.,* pp.290-291 and Will and Ariel Durant, *The Age of Reason Begins,* New York, Simon and Schuster, 1961, p. 624.

[34]Ueberweg, *op. cit.,* pp. 48-54.

*See also Will and Ariel Durant, *The Age of Voltaire:* "Descarte, ... and many others ... invent hypotheses and evasions...etc. (p.616).

[35] Wilhelm Wundt, *Einleitung in die Philosophie,* Leipzig, Verlag von Wilhelm Engelmann, 1901, pp. 241-244.

[36]John Locke, *A Letter Concerning Toleration,* Mario Muntori, Ed., The Hague, Martinus Nijhoff, 1963.

[37]Allen W. Wood, "Kant's Deism," in *Kant's Philosophy of Religion Reconsidered* Phillip J. Rossi and Michael Wreen, Eds. , Bloomington, Indiana University Press, 1991, p. 2.

[38]Ueberweg, *op.cit.* p.189. See also: Immanuel Kant, *Religion Innerhalb der Grenzen der blossen Vernunft,* Robertson, *op.cit.,* p. 370.

[39]*Ibid.,*p. 187

[40]Harold R. Hutcheson, *Lord Herbert of Cherbury's "De Religione Laici",* New Haven, Yale University Press, 1944.

[41]*Ibid.,* p. v

[42]*Ibid.*p. 29 - 40.

[43]Robinson, *op.cit.,* pp. 305-307.

[44]William Stephens, *An Account of the Growth of Deism in England,* Los Angeles, The University of California , 1990 p.iv. (This is a reprint of the original which was published in 1696.)

[45]*Ibid.,* p. 10.

[46]Margaret Jacob, *The Newtonians and the English Revolution, 1689-1720,* Ithaca, N.Y., Cornell Univeristy Press, 1976, p. 202.

[47]Robertson, *op.cit.,* p. 308.

[48]Will and Ariel Durant, *The Age of Voltaire,* New York, Simon and Schuster, 1965, p.90.

[49]John E. Rhodes, *Germany: A History,* New York, Holt, Rienhart and Winston, 1964, p.234.

[50]Will and Ariel Durant, *Rousseau and Revolution,* New York, Simon and Schuster, 1967, p. 595.

[51]Goethe, Johann Wolfgang, *Faust Part I,* R.M.S. Heffner, Helmut Rehder and W.F. Twaddell, Edtrs., Madison, Wis; The University of Wisconsin Press, 1956, p.179.

[52]Frank E. Manuel, *The Prophets of Paris,* New York, Torch Books, 1962.

[53]Herrick, *op.cit.* , p. 59.

[54]Durant, *The Age of Voltaire, op.cit.,*pp. 644-645.

CHAPTER IV

The Secularization of the U.S. before 1900

I.

"At the time of the War of Independence the leading statesmen of the American colonies were Deists." This statement has some validity because among these Deists were Benjamin Franklin, Thomas Paine and Thomas Jefferson.[1] Whether George Washington was also a deist is hard to determine and by no means certain. However, because of their prominence in American history it is sometimes believed that these men founded Deism in the colonies or in the United States.

Yet, deism had already made considerable inroads in Colonial America because, as we have seen, this point of view was wide spread in England whence most of the colonists had come. Furthermore, the physical universe was explained by the work of Isaac Newton (1642-1727) as a machine, created and then abandoned, by its Creator. This ruled out miracles altogether and also raised the question of whether it is reasonable to believe that a God who acts according to general principles would reveal himself to one particular group of humans and not to others. This, together with numerous attacks upon the Puritan and Anglican clergy in America led to a great rise in deistic and anti-Christian literature both in England and in the colonies.[2]

A leader in the writing of such deist literature was Benjamin Franklin, as was John Adams, later to become President of the United

States. William Livingston, editor of *The Independent Reflector,* "aroused the enmity of the clergy" with this magazine as did Cadwallader Colden, a prolific writer who denied the need of a "First Cause" . That these writers had considerable success in spreading their ideas in the British colonies is evident not only because the number of churches had declined a great deal by the end of the eighteenth century but also because so many Christian clergy made strenuous efforts to convert deists to religion as they preached sermons, wrote tracts and books and published Christian magazines.[3]

It is therefore not surprising that the American revolutionary leadership was filled with deist ideas. It should be understood however, that many people, such as George Washington (1732-1799), were not totally wedded to the deist viewpoint. An examination of Washington's letters and speeches reveals that he did indeed view himself a Christian in that he was always a member of the Episcopal church although he evidently did not participate in communion and avoided writing or speaking of religion unless absolutely necessary.[4] There is however one document which President Washington signed on November 4, 1796 which some would interpret to include Washington among the deists and which others view only as an expression of his religious tolerance and willingness to let others believe as they please. That document is a treaty between the United States and the government of Tripoli which read in part: *"As the government of the United States is not in any sense founded on the Christian religion etc.".* This phrase undoubtedly refers to the right of Americans to be free of government interference in their religious activities and that non-Christians could expect to enjoy the same rights as Christians. It does not, however, mean that the signer was therefore a deist.

Hence, it would be unreasonable to assume that Washington was a deist. In fact, his biographers show that Washington was "always serious and attentive in church, but never knelt."[5] In addition to attending church regularly, Washington also mentions religion favorably in his Farewell Address. Thus he wrote that religion and morality were both "great pillars of human happiness," and were indispensable to "private and public felicity".

Moreover, Washington's Farewell Address was quoted liberally in churches and became a part of the Rev. William Lynn's "Proclamation Sermon" in 1798. Likewise, Washington attended Episcopal services on Independence Day in 1799 and listened to a sermon by the Rev. Dr. Davis.[6]

There is however no doubt that Washington was anxious to promote religious freedom in the United States and that he was even capable of understanding the difference between mere toleration of another's religion and the right of any man to religious liberty *ipso facto*. An excellent example of this attitude is the letter he wrote to the Jewish congregation of Newport, R.I., on the occasion of his visit to that city in 1790. "The citizens of the United States of America," wrote George Washington, "have a right to applaud themselves for having given to mankind examples of an enlarged and liberal policy : a policy worthy of imitation. All possess alike liberty of conscience and immunities of citizenship. It is now no more that toleration is spoken of as if it was by the indulgence of one class of people, that another enjoyed the exercise of their *inherent natural rights*. For happily the Government of the United States, which gives to bigotry no sanction, to persecution no assistance, requires only that they who live under its protection, should demean themselves as good citizens, in giving it on all occasions their effectual support."[7]

Thus, while Washington was without doubt an early and strong supporter of religious liberty, we look to the writings of Thomas Jefferson (1743-1826) to find an example of colonial and early American deism. For example, the Constitution of the United States does not once mention God or any deity. This omission was principally associated with the influence of Jefferson and reflects the impact of Jefferson's beliefs upon that most important document .[8]

It ought to be understood, however, that deism does not guaranty freedom from bigotry. Thus, unlike Washington, Jefferson repeated all those anti-Jewish clichés which were common in his day and continue to be recited in our days as unexamined "truths" in a manner similar to the medieval and ancient opinion that the earth is flat. Both beliefs were assumed to be matters of fact needing no further explanation or comment. Here is Jefferson's view of the Jewish minority. Said he: "Jews: 1. Their system was Deism; that is, the belief of one only God. But their ideas of him & of his attributes were degrading & injurious. 2. Their Ethics were not only imperfect , but often irreconcilable with the sound dictates of reason & morality, as they respect intercourse with those around us; & repulsive and anti-social respecting other nations........."[9]

Despite his evident bigotry, or because of it, Jefferson was undoubtedly a Deist. His deism rested not only on his desire to act from reason alone, but also on his anger at the established religions of his day, notably Calvinism. Wrote Jefferson: " .....the demoralizing dogmas of Calvin (are these): 1. That there are three Gods 2. That good works, or the love of our neighbor , are nothing 3. That faith is everything , and the more incomprehensible the proposition, the more merit in its faith. 4. That reason in religion is of unlawful use 5. that God, from the beginning , elected certain individuals to be saved, and certain others to be damned; and that no crimes of the former can damn them; no virtues of the latter save." Jefferson claimed that established religions : " are mere usurpers of the Christian name." and " false shepherds". Jefferson believed that the "doctrine of one God" will become so popular that " there is not one young man now living in the United States who will not die an Unitarian."[10]

Although Thomas Jefferson rejected supernaturalism of any kind and wrote that :"The question of his (Jesus) being a member of the Godhead , or in direct communication with it ....is foreign to the present view..." Jefferson thought that only fragments of Jesus' teachings had been preserved and that these fragments were disfigured by: "the corruption of schismatising followers, who have found an interest in sophisticating & perverting the simple doctrines he taught by engrafting on them the mysticisms of a Grecian sophist, frittering them into subtleties, & obscuring them with jargon , until they have caused good men to reject the whole in disgust, & to view Jesus himself as an impostor......" [11]

We have said that Jefferson was a Deist. Yet, he said of himself : "I am a real Christian, that is to say, a disciple of the doctrines of Jesus , very different from the Platonists, who call me infidel and themselves Christians and preachers of the gospel, while they draw all their characteristic dogmas from what its author never said or saw. ." Jefferson goes on to claim that the "great reformer" (Jesus) would never recognize one feature of the system of belief Jefferson claims was "compounded from heathen mysteries" and "beyond the comprehension of man." It serves no useful purpose to argue here whether or not Jefferson was a Christian. It is however certain that he rejected all dogma and would not participate in organized religion and that he defined his own religion as one that "is known to my God and myself alone." [12]

Jefferson's contempt for the clergy knew no limits. It can be said that he truly hated the clergy. An example of his attitude toward "men of the cloth" is the following letter he wrote in 1816: "You judge truly that I am not afraid of the priests. They have tried upon me all their various batteries, of pious whining, hypocritical canting, lying & slandering, without being able to give me one moment of pain. I have contemplated their order from the Magid of the East to the Saints of the West, and I have found no difference of character , but of more or less caution, in proportion to their information or ignorance of those on whom their interested duperies were to be paid off. Their sway in New England is indeed formidable. No mind beyond mediocrity dares there to develop itself. If it does, they excite against it the public opinion which they command & by little, but incessant but teasing persecution, drive it from among them. Their present emigrations to the Western country are real flights from persecution, religious & political, but the abandonment of the country by those who wish to enjoy freedom of opinion leaves the despotism over the residue more intense, more oppressive. They are now looking to the fleshpots of the South and aiming at foothold there by their missionary teachers. They have lately come forward boldly with their plan to establish "*a qualified religious instructor* over every thousand souls in the U.S. And they seem to consider none as qualified as their own sect.".[13]

Jefferson was the author of *The Virginia Statute of Religious Freedom.* This he regarded as one of the three greatest achievements of his life.[14] Although introduced into the Virginia Legislature by Jefferson in 1779 it was not passed until 1786. Therein Jefferson denounced the practice of forcing anyone to contribute money "for the propagation of opinions which he disbelieves," and even denied government the right to force anyone to support a religion in which a citizen does believe. "Our civil rights," said Jefferson, "have no dependence on our religious opinion," and then went on to support the view that holding public office should in no way be dependent on membership in any religious sect.[15]

These and many other writings on religious liberty establish Jefferson as a foremost defender of freedom of conscience. Together with his undoubted devotion to deism he set the course of American interest in that movement for the past two hundred years despite the reverence he showed on every occasion to the teachings of Jesus as he understood them. This concession to Christianity was not always present among the principal deists of Jefferson's day. Most certainly it was absent from the writings of Thomas Paine (1737-1809), although he too was not an atheist but one who assumed the existence of God in all of his many letters, pamphlets and books.

II.

Thomas Paine (1737-1809) was so exciting a writer that over a million copies of his *Rights of Man* were sold in England alone when it was published in 1791-1792. Outlawed from the country of his birth for treason because he had written this pamphlet, he returned to America where he had participated in the revolution as a soldier, secretary of the congressional Committee on Foreign Affairs and clerk of the Pennsylvania Assembly.

In 1792, Paine went to France, participated in the French Revolution, was imprisoned by the French but later freed by the American ambassador, James Monroe, in whose house he finished *Age of Reason*. Ostracized for his criticism of the Bible when he returned to America in 1802, he was nevertheless voted $3,000.- by Congress and received a 300 acre farm from New York State where he died in 1809.[16]

Determined to cast off "the trammels of authoritative religious teaching", Paine sought to reform "the evil religious institutions that had brought disharmony to man's private and social life."[17]

Paine held the usual deistic view that God is the creator and first cause of the world but that God was not concerned with His creation thereafter. The deists deny the Christian doctrines, such as the Trinity, the Incarnation, the divinity of Christ, future reward and punishment and the immortality of the soul. As a rationalist, Paine, together with other deists, accepted only those views which he and they thought could be proved empirically.

We have already seen that some deists, notably Thomas Jefferson, compromised with public opinion and upheld the moral teachings of the Gospels and the Bible even while attacking the churches and organized religion. Thomas Paine, however, was much more radical and attacked the Bible in his *Age of Reason*. He evidently believed that if he could destroy belief in the Bible he could thereby undermine and destroy the influence of organized religion. For example, Paine wrote this: "As to the Bible, whether true or fabulous, it is a history, and history is not a revelation........As to the expression so often used in the Bible that *the word of the Lord* came to such an one, or such an one, it was the fashion of speaking in those times like the expression used by a Quaker, that *the spirit moveth him*, ...".[18] It should be noted here that Paine was raised a Quaker by his father although his mother was an Anglican. [19]

Further, Paine criticized the Bible by writing that " ..if we admit the supposition that God would condescend to reveal Himself in words, we ought not to believe it would be in such idle and profligate stories as are in the Bible; and it is for this reason among others which our reverence for God inspires, that the Deists deny that the book called the Bible is the Word of God, or that it is revealed religion."

Paine ridiculed and criticized numerous Bible stories and concluded that the Bible could not be true because it contains so many contradictions. As a Deist he maintained however, that "every person, of whatever religious denomination he may be, is a Deist....." and "the creation is the Bible of the true believer in God. Everything in this vast volume inspires him with sublime ideas of the Creator. The little paltry, and often obscene, tales of the Bible sink into wretchedness when put in comparison with this mighty work." [20]

Nothing indicates better the impact of Paine's work than the criticism it provoked. There were of course innumerable "refutations" of Paine's writings. An excellent example of such a refutation was the two volume book by the Rev. Azalea Ogden. Published in Newark, N.J. in 1795, this book was as abusive as it was calumnious and claimed to know that Deists are drunks, and "men of libertine conduct." Ogden thought that Paine had become *"a lunatick". " With a mind besotted with liquor; replete with prejudice against christianity;"* wrote Ogden, *"grossly ignorant of its nature; under the domination of vice, and encircled by deistical companions, it is probable he will drag out the remainder of his days in infidelity, guilt and wretchedness, and leave the world, either in stupid insensibility, or in a state of horror without the least rational hope of happiness."*

Two critics of Paine who were far more reasonable and sophisticated than Ogden were David Levi, a Jewish theologian and writer and Elias Boudinot, first director of the U.S. mint and a Christian who was preparing for the Second Advent.

Levi was trying at that time to save the English speaking Jews from the freethinkers in London and in America. He published an answer to

Paine and published it in London, Philadelphia and New York between 1796 and 1798. He did so by claiming that a series of prophecies by Moses had been exactly fulfilled. This was important to him because Paine denied that Moses could have been the author of the "Pentateuch" i.e., the Five Books which bear his name. Thus, Levi asked how Moses could have foreseen the expulsion of the Jews from their homeland; how could he have known about the persecutions the Jews then suffered and above all, how could he have known that the Jews would not abandon their religion despite all persecutions but survive nonetheless. In our own day, 1995, Levi might have asked how it was possible for the Jews to return to Israel after 1878 years and once more inhabit an independent Jewish state there. Thus, Levi insisted that the Jews had lived a unique history which proved the truth of his convictions and the falsity of Paine's arguments. This point of view was also in accord with the views of Christian millinarians. Thus, Bishops Thomas Newton and Robert Clayton were convinced that Jewish history proved the accuracy of the Bible as were many other Christians such as Isaac Newton, Joseph Priestley and Elias Boudinot.

Boudinot believed that the native Americans, called "Indians", were the so-called "Lost Tribes of Israel", that the biblical injunction to "Love Your Neighbor as Yourself" was being fulfilled in America and that the Jews would be returned to "their own land." Thus, Boudinot contributed a good deal to Christian "fundamentalism" as he combined with David Levi in their attack on Paine's work.[21]

In sum, Paine was received with the same hostility by organized religion as Spinoza had been one hundred and fifty years earlier. For in Paine, Hobbes and Spinoza once more found a voice declaiming their teachings and promoting their cause.[22]

Benjamin Franklin (1706-1790), sometimes called "The Oldest Revolutionary" and "the American Voltaire," was one of the most influential deists in America. Franklin saw Reason "as the experience through which God is discovered and known." Greatly influenced by Newton's physics (Isaac Newton 1642-1727), Franklin, at age 22, wrote out his "Articles of Belief and Acts of Religion." These included belief in "one supreme, most perfect Being". Franklin thought that in view of the vastness of the universe and its unknown size and infinite worlds, "this little Ball on which we move seems, even in my narrow Imagination, to be almost Nothing, and myself less than nothing and of no sort of Consequence."[23] Franklin therefore concluded that religion and its ceremonies serve no purpose since he believed that *the Infinite Father* is far above requiring any worship of praise from men who are, in Franklin's words, *inconsiderable Nothings.*

At a younger age, 19, during his stay in London, England, Franklin worked as a printer for a London printing establishment and there wrote a pamphlet entitled : *A Dissertation on Liberty and Necessity, Pleasure and Pain.*" The gist of this pamphlet is that there are no future rewards or punishments because all creatures and all things are equally good and esteemed by God. Furthermore, there is no reason to believe in a future life nor is there reason to believe that man is any better than "the brutes." Franklin also denied all religion.[24] Franklin returned to this theme thirty one years later in his *On the Providence of God in the Government of the World,* published in 1732.

Franklin was a polytheist. That is, he thought that a hierarchy of lesser gods exists below the Supreme God and above man and that these gods, either immortal or changeable after many years, each govern a separate system within the universe.

Whatever Franklin wrote about his own beliefs, it is evident that he was not a Christian but a Deist but one willing to let others believe as they saw fit. In fact, he went further than that. He helped the Catholic community by writing to the Pope in 1784 asking for the appointment of a Catholic bishop in America. In this he succeeded and Bishop John Carol was appointed "Superior" of the Catholic clergy in the U.S.. Franklin also helped the only Jewish congregation in Philadelphia when the first synagogue ever built there was almost delivered to the auction block. Franklin led a list of subscribers in raising the funds to maintain that house of worship.[25]

The significance of Franklin for American deism lies in the manner in which he represented all Americans of his day and in which he represents, even now, the "ideal type" of an American. A scientist, a humanist, one willing to live a democratic life and give others the same, he represented the new American man in the 18th century and became a role model for those who followed him. Franklin was a scientist who believed that Reason was and is the principle that should guide the American. In promoting that view, even before the American Revolution, he laid the foundation for that which was to follow. For surely it is evident, that in 1995, as in 1795, Reason predominates decision making in this country and Deism is its undoubted ally.[26]

III.

Ralph Waldo Emerson (1803-1882) represents American thought in the nineteenth century as much as Franklin and Jefferson did in the eighteenth century. In fact, there is a direct   connection between Franklin and Emerson. Thus, we have already seen that Franklin regarded mankind and himself with skepticism and believed that all men were "negligible finite in face of a glorious incomprehensibility."[27]

Franklin then relied on Nature and as a scientist maintained an aloof and disinterested attitude towards human affairs which rested on Reason. This is what Emerson continued in his "Essay on Self - Reliance" which became the very epitome of the American point of view prior to Franklin Roosevelt. Thus, Franklin equated virtue with happiness and happiness with material success. This then is a demonstration of secularization as we know it today, at the end of the 20th century, and as Emerson also knew it.

The significance of Emerson as a deist and secularizer can easily be overlooked not only because he had been a clergyman and Pastor of the Second Unitarian Church in Boston, but also because he was one of the founders of "Transcendentalism". Thus, Emerson rejected form for substance and taught a Transcendental philosophy which holds that the outer world of objects is only a representation of the inner world of man which should be governed by Self Reliance. "..the highest merit was ascribed to Moses, Plato and Milton," says Emerson," because ," they set at naught books and traditions, and spoke not what men, but what *they* thought." Thus, Emerson looks to man and not religion for support. It is in fact self reliance which is the very core of secularization. It is also significant that when the Great Depression of 1929-1939 seriously threatened the tradition of self reliance in America, it was government, not religion which was sought as the savior of the common man in the United States.

"God will not have his work made manifest by cowards," says Emerson, but "Trust thyself." Also, "Whoso would be a man must be a nonconconformist." For "nothing is at last sacred but the integrity of your own mind."[28]

"What I must do is all that concerns me, not what the people think." Thus, both Franklin and Emerson held that "work, virtue, salvation and enjoyment of the world are functions of one another."[29]

Emerson taught that the pursuit of wealth is consistent with the natural order of things and like Franklin in his *Autobiography,* was willing to dispense with revelation. [30] In fact, after a life long search for a religious identity "Emerson replaced the God of denominational religion with the God of nature itself."[31]

Transcendentalism, the word used by Emerson and the New England minister Theodore Parker to describe their religion, sought to encompass the teachings of all the major religions thus transcending or "climbing over" any written set of dogma or tenets. Thus, the transcendentalists founded the Free Religious Association. "Its members took literally the idea of free inquiry and pushed it to its furthermost bounds. In this spirit they demolished ....every traditionally held religious view."

The Free Religious Association first organized in 1867 included not only Ralph Waldo Emerson, but also the renowned scholar Charles Eliot Norton (1827-1908), who had published Emerson's books; Lucretia Mott (1793-1880), the Quaker minister and social reformer, anti-slavery agitator and feminist and Isaac Meyer Wise (1819-1900), rabbi and founder of American Reform Judaism. These and many other American intellectuals saw in this new movement a reflection of their own rebellion against religious orthodoxy.[32]

Despite the fact that Emerson, Mott and Wise and others were ordained clergy they adopted the following views for their organization:

> *"The purpose of the Association shall be the advocacy of a rational religion without a priesthood; a moral code without a theology; a God without a dogmatic system; a religion of liberty, recognizing no limits of thought; a religion of reason submitting all things to its decision; a religion of action, holding the chief good to be man's humanity to man; a religion of equality, acknowledging in its most comprehensive sense human brotherhood; a religion of love, yielding obedience to it as the great fundamental law of moral agency."[33]*

Members of the association attacked Christianity and other established religions, proselytized others, published pamphlets and books to promote their ideas and made every effort to change the thinking of Americans concerning religion. In that they were quite successful, despite the fact that few joined them. Their success then and now was visible, not in the number who openly subscribed to the ideas of the Free Religious Association, but in the number of Christians and Jews in America who subscribe to their views.

It is of course evident, that the Free Religious Association was more a consequence than a cause of the secularization of America. For that process was and is the outcome of philosophy and history as already discussed in this chapter, but also the rise of science, the subsequent communication revolution and the development of liberal social and political ideas, all of which undermined superstition and freed Americans and others from the yoke of dogma.[34]

Now it is significant that by the end of the eighteenth century Thomas Paine and his teachings had become anathema to most Americans and certainly to the political establishment. This was true despite the fact that secularization had become widespread in the United States at that time. The reason for this apparent paradox, i.e., widespread secularization and almost universal approval for religion in the United States, is that religion itself was becoming secularized in the U.S. at the end of the nineteenth century so that most Americans could "have their cake and eat it too." This means that since the 1860's and to this day (1995) Americans have succeeded in absorbing the views of the Free Religious Association while also participating or at least giving "lip service" to organized religion. The consequence of this dual need to be rational, scientific and objective and also adhere to a religion has been that religion has adopted a secular mode and has ceased to operate only in the spiritual or supernatural realm.

Thus, Thomas Paine, although denounced from every pulpit for a hundred years, survived nevertheless so that by 1897 Moses Coit Tyler, an established Cornell University historian included a whole chapter on Paine in his book *The Literary History of the American Revolution*[35]. Since then a whole literature on Paine has been written and accepted by the American public without protest whatever. In fact, it would seem bizarre to the average American today if the clergy were to rail against Tom Paine now, in 1995. "Thus," writes Warren, " by a gradual process of reinterpretation, Thomas Paine achieved a respectability which would have horrified his own contemporaries." [36]

IV.

That the United States had become a thoroughly secular country is best illustrated by the fact that the Free Religious Association and other groups devoted to the elimination of Christian orthodoxy from American life had few followers. In fact, none of the humanist, atheist, agnostic and other groups ever developed a large membership in America precisely because their aims were already available to anyone living in the United States. Religious liberty, the "separation between church and state", freedom to worship or not to participate in any religion have been so much taken for granted in the U.S. that few would care to enter into a battle that need not be fought or even a war whose outcome is already known.

The contributors to these assumptions were however not all Americans. In Western civilization the writers and thinkers of Europe had a great deal of influence upon American understanding and upon American expectations. Chief among those who so influenced Americans were the early French sociologists and particularly the founder of that science, August Comte (1798-1857).

We have seen earlier that sociology in particular promoted the views of the "freethinkers" and deists and that the development of that science in the hands of Americans was immensely successful in inducing many students to a world view which excluded organized religion. Therefore we are now called upon to briefly outline the views of August Comte and his teachings.

As can be seen by considering his date of birth, August Comte was born during the French revolution and grew up in the decade of Napoleon. (1804-1815). Therefore the dramatic events which greeted him on his advent in this world became principal catalysts in his thinking and contributed a great deal to the rise of sociology and in particular the attitude of Comte and his followers to religion. The French revolution was of course a revolution against the entire French establishment, including the Church, and therefore disestablished Roman Catholicism as the state religion in that country.

"The most violent revolutionaries, ...pressed for total 'dechristianization.' " This campaign against established religion led the revolutionaries to close all churches, celebrate "The Feast of Liberty and Reason" at Notre Dame in November 1793 and to establish a new religion by decree. Accordingly, the worship of a Supreme Being was now taught. This deism sought to seek legitimacy by promoting both morality and patriotism. The "Father of the Universe" was addressed as the supreme intelligence by the adherents of this new religion which even included the invention of a new calendar.[37]

Although this new religion was discarded by Napoleon Bonaparte who signed a concordat with the Vatican in 1801 and restored the rights of the Church to conduct its rites in France, religion now became subject to the state which recognized non-Catholic rights as well and permitted all religions to function equally in France.[38]

August Comte was a mathematician. Trained in a science based on assumptions derived from human reason, Comte now proposed that reason also be used to discover the basic laws of society which Comte thought could be applied to the benefit of man in a manner similar to the application of scientific knowledge concerning the physical universe to the benefit of all men.

To effect the necessary changes in human social life from reliance on theology to reliance on scientific thinking, Comte founded a new religion based on his "Positive Philosophy." This religion was to be directed by a caste of sociologist-priests whose superior knowledge, Comte believed, would be used to educate men in the Religion of Humanity as envisioned by Comte. Comte thought that a reign of his followers who had a scientific or positive understanding of good and evil would lead to "harmony, justice, rectitude and equity." Comte believed that human relations could be totally objectified and therefore lead to an ultimate altruism in which everyone lived for others. Thus, Comte considered himself not only a social scientist but founder of a new religion promising this-wordly salvation or solutions to all human needs here and now.[39]

Comte believed that he had found the basic law of society. This Law of Human Development, Comte thought, could be found in all human societies and that mathematics, physics, astronomy, chemistry and biology were the forerunners of a Science of Society which he called Sociology. He called his method Positivism and attracted to his views men like John Stuart Mill and Herbert Spencer who made his work accessible to the English speaking world.

"The law," (of Human Development) said Comte, " is this: -that each of our leading conceptions , -each branch of our knowledge,- passes successively through three different theoretical conditions: the Theological, or fictitious; the Metaphysical, or abstract; and the Scientific, or positive."

Comte thought that all human knowledge travels through each of these stages and, most important, that "the constitution of the new system cannot take place before the destruction of the old."[40] This belief, for which there is no evidence, nevertheless is most influential in promoting deism because it relegates established supernaturalism to the past in face of the presence of scientific achievements of all kinds. The truth is that in the midst of scientific secularism there exists fundamentalism in religion. It is therefore evident, that 150 years after Comte, science has not supplanted religion but has altered religion so that religion itself has become secularized and that a secular religion has, for some people, supplanted traditional religions.

It is further to be noted that Comte, in his lifetime, sought to substitute one religion for another and demanded adherence to his religion, i.e., positivism. His religion inlcuded a High Priest of Humanity who, like the Pope, would institute a reign of scientific objectivity leading to justice, virtuous conduct and salvation for all of mankind.

The lives of August Comte and Emile Durkheim (1858-1917) extended through the entire nineteenth century as Durkheim was born of a Jewish family one year after Comte died. Durkheim was the father of the sociology of religion. Like Comte before him, Durkheim was confronted with the abandonment of traditional Christianity in favor of "The Religion of Reason" and "The Religion of Humanity" and other schemes, none of which could answer the essential question of "how public and private morality could be maintained without religious sanctions."

To answer this question, Durkheim studied the work of W. Robertson Smith, the great student of semitics, and then proceeded to define religious phenomena as: "...obligatory beliefs united with definite practices which relate to the objects given in the beliefs."[41] Here Durkheim sought to show that religion differs from other beliefs such as patriotism, or democracy or scientific thinking in that it unites thought and action inseparably. Since Durkheim considered all religious beliefs and practices obligatory and viewed all that is obligatory to be of social origin, he concluded that religion is of social origin and is in fact the worship of society.[42]

Rites and dogmas, said Durkheim, are the creation of society. Therefore, men worship the power of society because the power of society so transcends that of any individual that men give it a sacred meaning and set it apart from the secular which they can understand. Since Durkheim lived in an age when established religion was being abandoned by masses of people and criticism of religion had become commonplace, Durkheim urged that men observe a civic morality because society elevates each man in a manner which the older religions had assumed were the outcome of theological and supernatural conditions and events. In his book, *The Elementary Forms of the Religious Life,* devoted mainly to a study of primitive religion, Durkheim lists the functions of religion which he describes as discipline, cohesion, vitalization and euphoria.

Discipline, Durkheim thought, is promoted by religious ritual; religious ceremonies he saw as means of promoting cohesion as they give people a sense of belonging to a common bond; religious observance, Durkheim believed, revitalizes the group and transmits the religion from one generation to the next and religious euphoria was seen as giving the believer a feeling that the moral order of the world continues to be maintained.[43]

Durkheim's central thesis then is that religion is socially determined; that it will continue and be a universal and permanent part of the human experience because of its functions but that religion will also give up its cognitive stance because science explains far better than religion the most important relationships between man and the universe. Durkheim predicted that social relations, heretofore also explained by religion, would become the province of sociology.

Durkheim taught that the only legitimate approach to a comprehension of the nature of the social order is by an examination of morality. "But if there is one fact that history has irrefutably demonstrated," said Durkheim, "it is that the morality of each people *is directly related to the social structure of the people practicing it.*"[44] Hence, the power of the moral order, which is closely tied to religion, "elevates it above any single individual."

Thus, to Durkheim, religion is a primitive form of sociology and an interpretation of the social order. Society is god, Durkheim taught, because it is the power of society which overwhelms each person and which is worshipped by the group.

This explanation of the supernatural constitutes a form of agnosticism, if not atheism, much further apart from traditional religion than deism. Yet, it became the basis for the explanation of religion as understood and taught by American sociologists in the 20th century. Therefore it is reasonable to hold that sociology contributed more than any other science to the growth of deism, agnosticism and atheism among Americans, particularly college educated Americans.

V.

It is not possible to discuss the rise of secularism in the world without viewing the contributions of Karl Marx (1818-1883) to this development.

Perhaps the most famous phrase attributed to Marx with reference to religion is the phrase "Religion is the opium of the people." This phrase was never written in this form. Instead, Marx wrote this: "Religion is the sigh of the oppressed creature, the heart of a heartless world, the soul of a soulless environment. It is the opium of the people."[45]

It is very important to consider this entire sentence. For in this sentence lies the sentiment of a European Jew who had just come out of the ghetto after centuries of oppression and who faced even worse in the century yet to come. Thus, Marx and a number of other 19th century writers, attacked religion which had been for so long the source of their misery. Among these writers were Moses Hess, Bruno Bauer, Ludwig Feuerbach and Friedrich Engels, Marx's eventual collaborator.

The literature concerning Karl Marx is so immense that it has been said that there are at least 100,000 books about Karl Marx in the libraries of the United States. This serves to recognize that Marx was one of the true intellectual giants of the nineteenth century whose influence has been so immense that even today (1995), a billion Chinese live by his teaching.

It is unclear whether or not Marx was an atheist. Early in his career he published literature promoting atheism. Yet, he criticized atheists because he viewed the denial of God's existence as a negative recognition of God. Marx would not deal with the relationship of man to the supernatural and ignored this issue. In other words, for Marx, God and the supernatural were not worthy of mention.

Marx did however discuss religion. That institution, he recognized, has a number of functions. Marx granted that religion makes life meaningful; that it offers an antidote to man's natural fears, and that it is "an antidote for man's inhumanity to man." In addition, Marx thought that religion has a social control function in so far as the state uses religion to suppress its subjects or citizens for the purpose of maintaining power.[46]

Marx also believed that man makes religion because he cannot live without it as long as society is "sick" and badly ordered. Marx held that religion makes the unbearable endurable and that therefore religion would persist as long a society continues in its innate conflict between the state and society. Thus, religion was seen by Marx as the outer manifestation of this conflict and therefore could not be seen as a source of brotherhood but as a source of divisiveness.[47] Marx, like Durkheim, thought that social being determines consciousness and that the origin of religion lies in the social structure. Durkheim, however, viewed religion as functional while Marx ascribed conflict to religion and thought of religion as a deformation of reality. Marx also saw religion as a lower class phenomenon which would disappear as the class struggle would inevitably bring about socialism and hence the end of alienation as well as the end of religion which would simply not be needed any more. For Marx, then, religion serves through inculcation by the ruling class to maintain the rulers' privileges. Thus, religion was seen as an instrument of class domination and churches were given no importance except as they constituted a financial power, or "Kapitalmacht", to use Marx's own expression.[48]

Religious institutions, churches, synagogues, mosques and others are viewed by Marxists as representatives of class division and of the usefulness of these institutions to the perpetuation of economic and political power by the ruling classes. Marx, raised as a Christian, admired the Christian god and drew a distinction between the revolutionary teachings of Jesus, as Marx saw it, and organized religion. Because both of Marx's parents had been Jewish converts to Christianity, anti- Marxist writers who also hate Judaism like to portray him as a Jew. Marxists, however, also imbued with anti-Jewish sentiment, call him a German and make no mention of his Jewish origins. Marx never thought of himself as a Jew but on the contrary criticized the religion of his ancestors as well as all religions severely.

Thus, he separated religious feelings from religious institutions so that, in that respect his views resembled the opinions of Jefferson who used the well known motto: "Resistance to tyranny is obedience to God."[49]

So far we have discussed Marx's attitude toward the Christian religion. When it came to Judaism, however, a religion which he did not know very well but which had been the religion of his grandparents, Marx relied on all the canards which were endlessly repeated by innumerable authors including his predecessors Kant, Hegel and Feuerbach. Thus Kant denounced Judaism for enslaving its followers to the Law, Hegel claimed that Judaism induced its followers to be abject materialists, Feuerbach wrote that Jews are utter egoists and Marx added that Judaism enslaves its followers to be interested only in money. Marx argued therefore for the dissolution of Judaism in the same sense that he argued for the abolition of labor. He did not mean, as some have claimed, that Jews should be slaughtered as was done by the followers of the Nazi cult. Marx wanted to abolish Jewish law which he viewed as an invitation to hypocrisy. To Marx, Judaism was not a religion but a commercial and industrial practice or a money system. Judaism, wrote Marx, was selfish need and egoism which was "Judaizing" Christianity in the sense that the feudal order had given way to capitalism which, according to Marx, was also selfish and egoistic and Jewish to the core.[50]

This analysis of Judaism by Marx led in part to the disparagement of Jews and Judaism in the former Soviet Union and was even used by the Nazi party to promote their hateful programs. Nevertheless, and despite the fact that Marxist socialism has failed in the Soviet Union, it cannot be denied that Marxian analysis of religion has had the beneficial effect of leading the sociology of religion to concern itself with the relationship of religion to economic and political institutions and interests. Marxism then holds, with other writers already reviewed, that reason must eventually triumph over religion because reason coincides with reality and religion does not. However, Marx did not promote the persecution of religion, nor did he hope for the forcible abolition of religion. He believed that religion would disappear of its own accord because "communism will produce a world that is reasonable and controllable and therefore a world in which religion, being unnecessary, will disappear.[51]

The influence of Karl Marx upon social thought cannot be exaggerated. Similarly, his influence on the rise of socialism and socialist parties in Europe is crucial. Nevertheless, the opposition to religion which Marx taught was not included in most nineteenth century socialist programs. Thus, in Germany and in other European countries, socialist parties were founded as a consequence of Marxian analysis. These parties almost always included an anti-clerical theme without calling for the diappearance of religion.

In Germany, the rise of socialism after the unification of that country in 1871 was seen as a threat by the repressive government, particularly after two attempts were made to kill the emperor William I. Although neither of the would-be assassins succeeded, and although neither was in any way associated with the German Social Democratic Party founded in 1869, the German government outlawed that party, blaming them for these assassination attempts. It was precisely this persecution of the socialists which increased their membership and spread their ideas further. After the anti-socialist law was lifted in 1891, the German socialists met in Erfurt and drafted a program which resembled precisely the teachings of Karl Marx. The "class struggle" was described therein as the great theme in history. The collapse of capitalism was predicted. Universal suffrage was demanded and innumerable affiliated organizations were created which gave the workers and union members who chose that party an entire social life and became so intertwined with it that union members provided the socialist party with most of its votes.[52]

In France, the anti-clericalism was fueled by the Dreyfus affair, which revived many of the anti-clerical attitudes first developed during the French revolution of 1789. This finally led to legislation which in 1905 separated church and state in France. In addition, the Dreyfus affair propelled some of the most radical socialists to power after 1899.

In Italy the socialists had made considerable progress. By 1903 they had thirty three members in the Chamber of Deputies, owned a number of newspapers but were divided among themselves into Marxists, British style laborites and French syndicalists. Nevertheless, all of them agreed on a secular agenda and ant-clericalism.[53]

In Russia the socialist movement may be traced to the activities of Alexander Herzen who founded the Russian language paper "The

Bell" while an emigre in London in 1847. If this influential paper was the beginning of socialist thought in Russia, then it was Nikolai Chernyshevsky who became the first radical socialist writer on Russian soil. These, and many other writers had inspired Russians to promote the "Go to the People" movement which became the vehicle for the distribution of Karl Marx's *Capital* after its translation into Russian in 1872. It was the merger of the indigenous Russian effort to change the Russian Czarist tyranny, together with the Marx inspired socialism mainly centered on Germany as well as numerous other events, such as the persecution of the Russian Jews, which led not only to the Russian Revolution and all its anti-clericalism, secularism and anti-semitism, but also to the large scale immigration of radical Europeans to the United States. The principal anti-clericalism came from Germany. These immigrants found, however, that there was in the United States a considerable anti-clericalism and an indigenous secularism. The Europeans, heavily influenced by Marx, derived their views from the scientific rationalism of the enlightenment already discussed. American anti-clericalism and secularism, however, was mainly influenced by the trade union struggle in this country particularly because the middle and upper class churches were hostile to that movement.

These nineteenth century American trade unionists were not anti-Christian. They were opposed to churches and organized religion because they believed that religion had betrayed them. Hence there developed in 19th Century America a "social gospel" movement which sought to liberalize theology and reform the churches in favor of the working man. In addition to the Marxists and the Christian socialists, there also developed in this country the Brotherhood of the Cooperative Commonwealth, organized by Eugene Debs and devoted to: "Ushering in a union of socialists in the world.........or the Kingdom of God here and now."[54]

VI.

This review of American and European social thought in the 18th and 19th centuries serves to show how the influence of these major writers created the secularization of the United States and Europe in the 20th century. Obviously the influence of academic and intellectual work upon the majority of citizens takes a long time. Such an influence can however become accelerated by reason of the migration of large numbers of people from the places where ideas originate to a new land where such ideas can then be brought to fruition. This is precisely what happened to the United States of America when millions of European immigrants came here between 1880 and 1920. Most of these immigrants came from central and eastern Europe and brought with them the secular views taught by the French philosophers and by writers of other nationalities, such as Karl Marx. Together with the native American secularists here reviewed these new Americans transformed this country from a Protestant, Christian motivated society to a secular society in which religion has not been abolished because it too has become as secular as all the other American institutions.

At the end of the nineteenth century this transformation was not yet visible in the United States. However, by 1914, when the first World War shook the foundations of the "old order" in Europe, the Protestant Establishment in America felt severly threatened by the millions of newcomers to this country. These migrants from the Old Country were mostly Catholic, Jewish or agnostic. Their attitudes, beliefs, behavior and political agenda seemed to constitute a severe threat to established, native Americans who decided therefore to defend themselves against those who appeared to take from them that essence of Americanism celebrated in Protestant churches and protected by orderly government which was Protestant as well. They did this mainly through the establishment of immigration quotas and the introduction of the 18th Amendment to the Constitution, usually called "Prohibition."[55]

Among the immigrants who came in such vast numbers at the outset of the century, were some who sought to explain the misery and suffering of ghetto life by communist or socialist theories. It was for that reason that these parties, always small in America, gained their principal adherents from the immigrants of the early 20th century. Yet, socialism and communism, despite its appeal to the poorest of the poor, never grew much in the United States. The reason for this was that the United States did provide the children, if not the immigrants, with opportunities not available in Europe or Asia. While upward mobility often took three generations, nevertheless, the opportunity to eventually leave the ghetto decreased the appeal to radical politics in this country. However, the secularization of America remained and became even more pronounced as the children and grandchildren of the Eastern and Southern European immigrants improved their economic conditions later in the 20th century. This was true not only because socialism and communism as taught to the immigrants was opposed to religion, but also because the economic opportunities available to immigrants in the United States could be achieved without any religious sanctions whatever. Religion among the newcomers was therefore relegated to special occasions, like Christmas, or Easter, or Passover or "The High Holy Days," but it did not play a vital part in the lives of those who sought to make a great deal of money in a society which had long ago decided to separate the church from the state and the individual from other-wordly salvation.

Thus, religion, well established in the United States at the beginning of the 20th century remained and will remain a symbol of respectability and Americanism. The change in attitude towards religion may be understood by this comment: "Whereas 75 percent of the children of the Bronx during the thirties were receiving no Jewish training, in the suburbs of the fifties, 75 percent report attendance at Sunday School."[56] This means then, that the radical immigrants of the early 20th century sought to abandon religion for the reasons already cited. Their children and particularly their grandchildren and their later progeniture succeeded in making Catholicism and Judaism respectable religions in America's triple melting pot even as the dominance of science and business hollowed out traditional beliefs and produced in America both secular religion and religious secularization.

It will therefore be the task of the next chapter to trace the development of scientific thinking since Francis Bacon (1561-1626) because that intellectual movement is the second foundation upon which the secularization of Judaism and the Western world now rests.

NOTES

[1]J.M. Robertson, *A Short History of Free Thought,* New York, Russell and Russell, 1957, pp. 376-382.

[2]Herbert M. Morais, *Deism in Eighteenth Century America,* New York, Russell and Russell, 1960, pp.54-84.

[3]*Ibid.,* p. 80.

[4]Douglas S. Freeman, *George Washington: A Biography,* New York, Scribner's , 1957.

[5]John A. Carroll and Mary W. Ashworth, *George Washington, vol.7,* New York, Scribner's Sons, 1957, p. 235.

[6]*Ibid.,*pp.405-581.

[7]Solomon Grayzel, *A History of the Jews,* Philadelphia, The Jewish Publication Society of America, 1947, p. 563.

[8]*The Constitution of the United States,* in : Ralph V. Harlow, *The United States,* New York, Henry Holt and Co., 1959, pp. 871-884.

[9]James Trulow Adams, *Jeffersonian Principles,* Boston, Little Brown & Co., 1928, p. 130.

[10]Thomas Jefferson, Letter to Dr. Benjamin Waterhouse, June 26, 1822 in : *Ibid.,* p. 128.

[11]Thomas Jefferson, *Syllabus of an Estimate of the Merits of the Doctrines of Jesus , Compared with Those of Others,* April 1803. In : Adams, *op.cit.,* p. 133.

[12]*Ibid.*p.135.

[13]Thomas Jefferson, Letter to Horatio Gates Spafford , January 10, 1816. Adams, *op.cit.*pp.139-140.

[14]Jennings B. Sanders, *The United States,* Evanston, Ill., Row, Peterson, 1962, p. 322.

[15]Thomas Jefferson, *A Bill Establishing Religious Freedom,* Adams, *op.cit.,* 142.

[16]Dominic Elder, *The Life of Thomas Paine,* Notre Dame, Ind., The University of Notre Dame, 1951, pp. 35-37.

[17]Robert Falk, "Thomas Paine: Deist or Quaker?" *Pennsylvania Magazine of History and Biography,*
Vol. 62, 1938, pp. 52-63.
[18]Daniel E. Wheeler, *The Life and Writings of Thomas Paine,* New York, Vincent Parke & Co., 1908,
p. 2.
[19] Elder, *op.cit.,* pp. 48-49.
[20]Paine in :Wheeler, *op.cit., p. 123.*
[21]Richard H. Popkin, "The Ageof Reason," versus "The Age of Revelation," in: *Deism, Masonry, and the Enlightenment,* J.A. Leo Lemay, Editor, Newark , The University of Delaware Press, 1987, pp. 158-170.
[22]G. Alfred Koch, *Republican Religion,* New York, Henry Holt and Co., 1933, p. 250.
[23]Frank L. Mott and Chester E. Jorgenson, *Benjamin Franklin,* New York, American Book Co., 1936, p. 131.
[24]John Bach McMaster, *Benjamin Franklin as a Man of Letters,*Boston, Houghton, Mifflin & Co., 1887, p.40.
[25]Richard Amacher, *Benjamin Franklin,* New York, Twayne Publishers, Inc., 1962, p. 155.
[26]J.A. Leo Lemay, *The Oldest Revolutionary,* Philadelphia,, The University of Pennsylvania Press, 1976.
[27]Perry Miller, "Benjamin Franklin, 1706-1790" in *Major Writers of America,* New York, Harcourt, Brace and World, 1962, Vol.1, pp.95-97.
[28]Ralph Waldo Emerson, "Self Reliance," in Saxe Commins and Robert N. Linscott, *The Social Philosophers,* New York, Random House, 1947, pp. 383-408.
[29]Lemay, *op.cit.*p. 149.
[30]*Ibid.,* p. 150; See also : Benjamin Franklin, *Autobiography,* in Mott and Jergenson, *op.cit.,* pp. 3-96.
[31]Donald L. Gelpi, *Endless Seeker: The Religious Quest of Ralph Waldo Emerson,* New York, University Press of America, 1991, p.152.
[32]Sidney Warren, *American Freethought 1860-1914,* New York, Gordian Press, Inc., 1966, p. 97.
[33]*Ibid.,* p.101.
[34]*Ibid.,* p.103.

[35]Moses Coit Tyler, *The Literary History of the American Revolution, 1763-1783,* New York, G.P. Putnam and Sons, 1897.

[36]Warren, *op.cit.*p. 116.

[37]Lucien Romier, *A History of France,* London, Macmillan & Co., 1962, p. 336.

[38]*Ibid.,* p.355.

[39]Lewis A. Coser, *Masters of Sociological Thought,* New York, Harcourt Brace Jovanovitch, Inc., 1971, pp. 12-13.

[40]August Comte, "The Positive Philosophy" in : *The Philosophers of Science,* Saxe Commins and Robert N. Linscott, Eds., New York, Random House,1947, pp. 218-219.

[41]Steven Lukes, *Emile Durkheim, His Life and Work: A Historical and Critical Study,* New York, Penguin Books, 1973, p. 241.

[42]Coser, *op.cit.,* p. 137.

[43]Harry Alpert, *Emile Durkheim and His Sociology,* New York, Columbia University Press, 1939, pp.198-203.

[44]Ray P. Cuzzort and Edith W. King, *20th Century Social Thought,* New York, Holt, Rinehart and Winston, 1980, p. 62.

[45]Owen Chadwick, *The Secularization of the European Mind in the Nineteenth Century,* New York, Cambridge University Press, 1977, p. 49.

[46]Julius Carlebach, *Karl Marx and the Radical Critique of Judaism,* London, Routledge & Keegan Paul , 1978, p. 150.

[47]*Ibid.,* p.57.

[48]David Mc Clellan, *Marxism and Religion,* London, The Macmillan Press, Ltd., 1987, pp. 166-167.

[49]Herbert Aptheker, *Marxism and Christianity,* New York, The Humanities Press, 1968, p. 32.

[50]Carlebach, *op.cit.*pp. 151-153.

[51]Aptheker, *op.cit.,* p.39.

[52]Hajo Holborn, *A History of Modern Germany,* New York, Alfred A. Knopf, 1969, pp. 354-360.

[53]Paul H. Beik and Laurence LaFore, *Modern Europe,* New York, Henry Holt and Co., 1959, pp. 441-443; 626-629; 672,788 and 803.

[54]Catherine R. Harris, "Religion and the Socialist Movement in the United States," in Aptheker, *op.cit.,*

pp. 217-220.
[55]E. Digby Baltzell, *The Protestant Establishment,* New York, Random House, 1964, p. 48.
[56]Baltzell, *op.cit.,* p. 53.

Chapter V

The Influence of Scientific Thinking on the Secularization Process

I.

"Secularization is the organization of life as if God did not exist." So said Georgia Harkness in her book *The Modern Rival of the Christian Faith* in 1952. This definition is still useful forty three years later not because very many Americans are atheists but, as we have seen, are deists.[1]

Numerous surveys over a number of years have concluded that Americans are overwhelmingly willing to say that they believe in the existence of God or a Supreme Being or a Creator. In fact, between World War II and 1990, the percentage of adult Americans who said they believe in God has never gone below 90% while 40% have said throughout that time that they attend religious services.[2] Nevertheless, fifty percent of Americans who also say they believe in God attend to no religious ceremony and contribute nothing to any denomination. Nevertheless, those who view themselves as Christians and those who see themselves as Jews, with a similar outlook, believe the words Jew or Christians to mean "a good person" or one who lives morally or one who has attended Sunday school in the past. Others consider such a label to mean that they support the teachings of Judaism or Christianity to the extent that they think they know it even if they have not entered a house of worship in years and have no intention of doing so.[3]

Literally used, the word *saeculum* means generation or age and therefore reveals the common bias to the effect that one's own age is always less religious, less pious, more rebellious and wordly than all previous generations and ages. We have already seen that no age and no epoch has ever been free of secularism and the efforts of secularizers. It is however also evident that philosophy, and as we shall see, science, have made a direct attack upon religion unnecessary since science has succeeded in simply by-passing religion and making it largely irrelevant in the every day lives of Americans.

This irrelevance is fostered by scientific advances because science can explain many phenomena which were at one time the province of religion. In addition, however, the rise of the health industry, welfare and social work, education and political life in democracies make it possible for many citizens to do philanthropic work, devote their time to meaningful pursuits and fulfill their lives in satisfying efforts without participating in any religious activity. Furthermore, the erstwhile "warfare of science with theology" has no more meaning at the end of the 20th century as almost all Americans have accepted science as the norm to which they adjust their behavior while religion in America has adapted itself to that norm by either agreeing with scientific thinking or avoiding the issue.[4]

It is easy to show that science is by no means the only way of knowing. Nevertheless, Americans, and Western man generally, are so accustomed to accepting "scientific" explanations and holding the opinions of "scientists" in awe that the very word "science" is given as much weight and authority as did other ways of knowing, such as religious or supernatural ways, in other ages and in other places.

Therefore, all religions are suspect in Western Civilization. Belief in religious dogma is based on popular opinion in Western countries and not on study of religious texts or theological treatises.

The methods of science, the pronouncements of scientifically educated persons, are given credence and prestige in America and the Western world. There is of course good reason for this. Comparison of life in America to life in Africa, South America, Asia or any other non-Western part of the world easily demonstrates that extreme poverty, disease, ignorance and misery are far more common in the non-scientific parts of the world than in the science oriented areas of the earth.

Entertainment, excitement, travel, communication of every kind and scientific solutions to a multiplicity of problems are available to Western man. Therefore it has become difficult for many people to believe in any religious system since all apparently fail to measure up to the expectations which science has met for so long and so often.[5]

The great intellectual revolution which has brought about the predominance of science in the minds of men, not only in the Western world, but also in other parts of the earth, began as early as the writings of the ancients in Greece and Rome.

Nevertheless, the seventeenth century in Europe was the century which gave the primary impetus to the secularization of the Western world as it is known at the end of the 20th century.

II.

Among those who were mainly responsible for the intellectual revolution then begun was the British philosopher Francis Bacon (1561-1626). Although trained as a lawyer and active in politics Bacon is known today for his efforts to maintain religious beliefs in the face of ever advancing scientific challenges. What Mendelssohn was to attempt for the Jews a century later, Bacon sought to promote in the 17th century. He tried to reconcile both faith in Christianity and the interests of science by writing that the practical benefits to be derived from science would restore man's dominion over nature which had been lost by Adam's transgression. Bacon also taught that Christian humility, piety and submission would result from the use of the experimental method in physics because these experiments would show man that God, who could have made any world he chose, made this world as revealed by a study of physics. This argument, favoring a theological explanation for the physical universe, was also made by other writers in the seventeenth century such as the French priest Marin Mersenne (1588-1648) and the English physician Thomas Browne (1606-1682).

Thus, Mersenne attacked Aristotle and Kepler on the grounds that they and others had spoken of a natural place for created objects. Mersenne argued that there were no natural places for anything because God could have freely chosen to put any object he created anywhere at all. Thus, Mersenne rejected the notion that the planets moved according to preconceived geometrical criteria.[6]

Likewise, Browne, who wrote a treatise entitled *Pseudodoxia Epidemica (False Beliefs among People) or Vulgar Errors,* nevertheless supported the belief in witchcraft even to the extent of testifying in court against suspected witches. Thus, Mersenne and Browne and Bacon and a host of others looked to the new sciences even while clinging to the old religion.[7]

In his *Advancement of Learning,* Francis Bacon sought to enlist the help of the English king, James I, and the help of other prominent persons of his era in inaugurating Englishmen into the new sciences of his day. Aware that the religious leadership viewed science with suspicion, he argued that the common accusation that a knowledge of science leads to heresy is unfounded. The Creator, argued Bacon, has set "bounds and limitations whereby human knowledge is confined and circumscribed." Bacon thought that there were then three limitations to human knowledge. These were, first, that we remember our mortality even if we place great trust in knowledge; second, that knowledge be used to make life easier and "we give ourselves repose and contentment" and third, that we do not arrogantly imagine we can comprehend "the mysteries of God."[8]

"The singular advantage," says Bacon, "which the Christian religion has (over pagan religions) towards the furtherance of true knowledge is that it excludes and interdicts human reason ....from examining or discussing of the mysteries and principles of faith."

Thus, Bacon sought to separate revelation from reason, not only because he needed to remain faithful to his Calvinist upbringing but also because he may have wanted to avoid the wrath of the ecclesiastical authorities. It is undoubtedly difficult for Americans at the end of the 20th century to appreciate or understand the strictures which 17th century writers faced both in Europe and in America (the colonies) in face of the political power of churches and clergy of various denominations.[9]

Bacon sought to limit the power of "divines", i.e., the clergy. He believed that scientific knowledge should indeed be limited by religion but should not be exterminated by it. Thus, he ranked "The Word of God" as first in man's considerations but "natural philosophy", limited by religion, he ranked as next important in revealing the works which God had created. This importance, Bacon believed, lies in the ability of science to ease man's burden on this earth "for the relief of man's estate."[10]

Although other authors, like Hobbes and Spinoza, were again and again accused of atheism, this never happened to Bacon despite the fact that it was common in his day to be very much absorbed with theological discussions. Either Bacon knew how to temporarily satisfy those who demanded conformity from him or he truly believed that revelation is a way of knowing in itself. Bacon did not, like Spinoza, believe that God's nature could be found by studying the world. Neither a rational mind nor a divine mind can be found in nature, according to Bacon. Bacon would not concede that nature exhibited any divine attributes in either its structure or function. Instead, Bacon held, contrary to those who taught pantheism, theism, immanence or transcendentalism that God or Cause lies altogether outside of nature. Thus, Bacon viewed science as utterly independent of religious speculation and held that theology should never enter into inquiry about nature. This argument may well be the origin of the doctrine of "the separation of church and state," although Bacon always used language protective of religion and pleasing to Christian authorities.[11]

Bacon began his work by writing *The Proficience and Advancement of Learning* between 1603 and 1605. This was written in English. To reach a wider intellectual audience however, he translated this into Latin as *De augmentis scientarum* and then wrote *Instauratio Magna* or *The Great Renewal* in Latin. His most important work however he called *Novum Organum* or *The New Instrument*. He used that name because for two thousand years the logial treatises of Aristotle had been called *Organon* and Bacon wanted to show that Aristotle's work would now be superseded by his work.

Since Bacon lived until 1626, he wrote at a time which represented the passage from the belief that truth could best be found by looking at the writings of ancient philosophers such as Aristotle and the time, most certainly arrived after 1700, when Western man sought to find truth by reason and experiment.

Some have called this era "The Great Intellectual Revolution." It was marked by an increasing use of mathematics, the language of nature; as well as an increase in the use of the inductive method which derives general principles from a large number of instances. This is in direct contradiction of the deductive method used until then and which sought to derive laws of nature from so called unquestionable truths.[12]

It is of course understood that this intellectual revolution had even by 1700 affected only a few learned men in a few countries and was utterly unknown to most of mankind. That however is true even today, in 1995, when few understand the leading edge of science or have even heard of those events in the scientific establishment which have been taken for granted there for the past fifty years.

Nevertheless, our most profound and "deep seated assumptions" today are governed by the discoveries and inventions of the seventeenth century and all the additional work done by scholars for nearly four hundred years since the days of Francis Bacon who, willingly or not, inaugurated the scientific age and promoted that secular view of the world which in this century dominates the thinking of Western man.

III.

Innumerable and famous scientists, philosophers and scholars could be listed here to illustrate the march of science and the consequent secularization of the Western world. For our purposes, however, it will suffice to discuss only a small number of such contributors, beginning with Sir Isaac Newton (1642-1727) who was the very pinnacle of scientific success in the 17th and the early 18th century.

> "Nature and Nature's laws lay hid in night;
> God said, Let Newton be! and all was light."

So wrote the poet Alexander Pope (1688-1744) at Newton's death in 1727.[13]

There was of course good reason for Pope to write those two dramatic lines. For surely, until the advent of Albert Einstein (1879-1955), the achievements of Newton in physics were not equaled.

Newton's fame rests mainly on his invention of the calculus and his discoveries concerning gravitation. Since the German mathematician Gottfried Wilhelm von Leibniz (1646-1716) also invented the calculus at about the same time there are those who believed that Leibniz or Newton might have "stolen" the idea from the other man. The fact is, however, that the calculus, like so many human inventions, was the product of many people's efforts and can truly be said to have been produced as a result of the culture base then achieved. This means that the work of many mathematicians, including Archimedes, Kepler, Fermat, Cavalieri, Torricelli, Pascal, Barrow and Gregory all contributed to the invention of the calculus.[14]

Newton also discovered the mysteries of light by making a reflecting telescope. By that means he found that white light consists of seven colors. No doubt Newton's discoveries concerning light had "cosmic consequences for astronomy."[15]

Gravitation had been studied for centuries before Newton. But it was he who discovered that the force of attraction which holds the planets in their orbits varies inversely with the square of their distance from the sun, thus confirming by mathematics what had already been observed by astronomers.

As every school child knows, Newton also formulated three laws of motion. Here he met objections from religious believers and sought to placate them by writing that the initial source of all motion must be God. Newton, as a professor of mathematics at Cambridge, was obliged to adhere to the Anglican faith. This does not mean, however, that he was adverse to religion. On the contrary, Newton studied the Bible and left considerable theological writings at his death. He evidently believed in such books as Daniel and Revelation as literal truth.[16]

Newton's problem as one who sought to cling to religion even while explaining the universe in mechanical terms was however quite severe. On the one hand, the belief that the universe runs like clockwork implies that God has no role in this. On the other hand, the argument that God has the power and therefore does move matter directly as we move our hands or feet implies pantheism.

Newton solved his dilemma by first proposing that divine attributes could be read in the book of nature. Newton believed that nature revealed evidence of choice, not chance, a view also expressed by Albert Einstein whose oft repeated comment was: "The Lord does not throw dice."[17] Thus, Newton did not separate science from religion, but instead fused them. This was true of a number of other 17th century scientists although the outcome of their work was the separation of science from organized religion and the strengthening of deism. Our argument is that deism, not atheism or even agnosticism, is the principle consequence of the intellectual revolution in philosophy, science and literature among Western men since the 17th century.

In any event, Newton included God in his speculations. Thus, he wrote: "*There exists an infinite and omnipresent spirit in which matter is moved according to mathematical laws.*"[18]

Newton even used scriptural passages in his famous *Principia*. Newton taught that the solar system suffers decay and instability and that from time to time it would need reformation. This he also attributed to God.

Newton attempted to correctly interpret the Bible and therefore listed fifteen rules which could achieve this. The ninth of these rules holds that: "It is the perfection of God's works that they are done with the greatest simplicity.....etc."

Newton thought that a correct understanding of nature would confirm the contents of the Bible; that science and mathematics proved Biblical claims and that even belief in ghosts, spirits and magic could be interpreted by an examination of nature.

Nevertheless, Newton critiqued Christian beliefs and declared that some theologians had corrupted Christianity. Thus he was unable to accept the doctrine that the father and the son of the trinity were co-equal and hence sided with the Fourth Century Christian bishop Arius who preached that the son is inferior to the father. For this and other heresies Arius had been excommunicated by the Council of Nicea in 325.

Newton thus was an Arian, i.e. a follower of Arius. Newton also doubted many of the miracles of the "Old Testament".[19]   There was therefore a considerable gap between Newton's beliefs and the doctrines of the Church of England. An example of his Arianism is this: "We are therefore to acknowledge one God........................and to have no other Gods but him. We must love and fear him, honor him, trust him etc...............And this is the first and principal part of religion. This always was and always will be the religion of Gods' people, from the beginning to the end of the world. .....*These things we must do not to any mediators between him and us but to him alone etc.*"[20]

Newton thought that obedience to God's commandments was the best way to worship Him. He was opposed to religious enthusiasm and to atheism. The work of Descartes as well as his own work had already given some the notion that all belief in any deity could now be abandoned. He opposed this vehemently but he also thought that Christianity is a form of polytheism because he could not reconcile himself to the doctrine of the Trinity. He railed against Roman Catholicism because he believed religion to appeal only to.less inquisitive heads. He regarded Roman Catholicism with hatred and fear believing that the downfall of the papal power would come about the year 2000. Such bigotries are appalling in the U.S. at the end of the 20th century. We need to remember, however, that Newton lived in the shadow of the Reformation begun by Luther in the early years of the 16th century. Together with the "counter - Reformation", the founding of the Society of Jesus (Jesuits), the Inquisition, which was still active in Newton's day, and many other influences, religion was a major theme in Newton's life time and motivated men as much then as economic interests motivate men in Europe and America at the end of the 20th century.[21]

Newton was a monotheist. He thought that the Second Coming would prove him right by showing that Christ was not God. Newton also insisted on the freedom of the divine will. He thought that science and his philosophy proved this as did his arguments that prophecy is fulfilled in numerous respects. Newton was known to his friends as a Unitarian, a denier of the Trinity and a Baptist. While this was not known publicly it needs to be kept in mind that such beliefs not only would have led to Newton's dismissal from his academic career but that such views were also against the law and punishable by imprisonment in England.[22]

Despite all of these theological concerns, Newton nevertheless was a forerunner of deism as it emerged in the next generation. Newton at least implied that after the world had been formed it would continue to run by the laws of nature for ever. Nevertheless, Newton also tried to show that the Laws of Nature are the will of God who could repeal them at will. [23]

Newton wrote a chronology of world history assuming that the world began in 4004 B.C. as proposed by Bishop Usher. From this and the assumption that accurate information concerning the historical accuracy of the Bible is available in that book Newton constructed geological tables showing the year of the Deluge and the ages of the Patriarchs.

Thus, it would appear that Newton's interest in religion would make him a bulwark against deism and agnosticism despite his much feared heterodoxy in his own day. The fact is, however, that Newton's work in theology has no impact on present thinking at all. It is his scientific work which Newton thought would be a basis for theological convictions which became a basis for attacks upon the Christian religion by scientists who had no interest in Newton's theology because they recognized only matter, time and space.[24]

IV.

The immensity of the universe was not really appreciated by anyone until the German born astronomer William Herschel (1738-1822) gave some estimates of its size which he had calculated. Born in Germany, he represented a generation of scientists who came after Newton and were therefore able to benefit from Newton's influence. Herschel moved to England where he was knighted by King George III for his creation of a telescope with a seven foot mirror which permitted him to discover the planet Uranus.

Herschel held a view of religion which was typical for scientists in the eighteenth century. He was in effect a deist, although he formally belonged to the Church of England. He believed that the Universe was established by a divine creator and that science reveals more and more of the Creator's works through describing the operations of nature. Herschel made no concessions to the biblical account of creation but instead promoted the view that the universe evolved slowly. Those who then held that the universe was in fact created all at once and in six days were offended by Herschel's views, but by the end of the eighteenth century it was too late to suppress the consequences of scientific inquiries.

Doctrines were foreign to Herschel's thought. Hence the entire Christian theology was ignored by him except to hold that Christianity had a moral and an ethical mission to which he was willing to subscribe. He even urged his son to become a clergyman, not because he was a subscriber to any theological viewpoint but because he thought the clergy afforded its practitioners "time for the attainment of the more elegant branches of literature, for poetry, for music, for drawing, for natural history, for mathematics, for astronomy, for metaphysics, and for being an author upon any one subject in which his most advantageous and respectable situation has qualified him to excel."[25]

In short, Herschel, although an unbeliever, thought it convenient to use the church as a means of attaining a comfortable livelihood because it allowed the incumbent time to be a "scholar and a gentleman."[26]

His son, John Herschel, continued William Herschel's work of cataloguing thousands of nebulae and clusters of stars.

Michael Faraday (1791-1867), like Newton and Herschel before him, sought to cling to revealed theology even as his work in chemistry and physics undermined the Biblical account of creation to which he clung so fiercely.

Faraday's great achievements included the liquifidation of chlorine, the discovery of benzene, and the laws of electrolysis. He also discovered electromagnetic induction, made the first generator and built a primitive electric motor. Numerous other achievements were also to his credit.[27]

Faraday was a follower of the Sandemanian sect which believed that the present-day physical world was created by God according to the narrative in Genesis. He also held with others, and with Einstein who lived in the succeeding century, that God did not act arbitrarily but with design and purpose. He thought that the laws of physics were willed by the Creator at the creation in a self sustaining system. He had an antipathy towards the notion of void space. Faraday believed that all events were ordered by divine providence and that nature worked according to God's plan.

Thus, Faraday's understanding of the physical world was theistic. He thought that the Bible told him how the physical world, which he examined in the laboratory, came into existence. He subscribed to an understanding of geology which was also in accord with the biblical account of creation although in his own day a secular approach to the geology of the earth became dominant.[28]

V.

It was left to the great scientists of the nineteenth century to give a lethal blow to the religious orthodoxies which eighteenth century scientists tried to maintain alongside their scientific endeavors. This was true despite the fact that those early scientists also called themselves philosophers while philosophers engaged in scientific research. The distinction between the two concepts had not been made at the end of the eighteenth and the beginning of the nineteenth century although the two branches of thought embodied an inherent contradiction. Evidently, its practitioners were not aware of the twofold movement which they themselves exemplified.[29]

Thus, there can be no doubt that nineteenth century research into nature and the consequent understanding of natural processes thereby uncovered altered radically the entire conception of the world as theretofore conceived even if those who contributed to these changes were not aware of the eventual consequences of their work.

In politics the rise of democracy constituted an unprecedented revolution brought on by the developments in philosophy already discussed. Reason, which dominated the motives of Jewish and Christian philosophers alike, also gave rise to the scientific revolution begun in the eighteenth century and continued to our day, the end of the twentieth century.

A limited list of the scientific achievements of the nineteenth century beginning in the year 1800 shows at once how immense the revolution in knowledge became after that year.

In physics, it is reasonable to mention the work of Galvani who lived to the end of the 18th century (1737-1798) and whose discoveries bear his name. He was succeeded by Faraday and Andre-Marie Ampere (1775-1836) who developed means of current measurements still in use. The century progressed with the discovery of the theory of polarization and the wave theory of light by Augustin Fresnel (1788-1827). In turn Georg Simon Ohm (1787-1854) and Karl Friedrich Gauss (1777-1855) contributed greatly to our understanding of electricity.

Gauss was a child prodigy and leading mathematician of his day. Gauss was a member of the Lutheran church but nevertheless rejected most Christian dogmas. Called a deist by a faculty colleague at the University of Göttingen, he was careful not to offend believers. He thought it unjustified to disturb the faith of others who needed religion as a means of gaining consolation for earthly suffering and misfortunes. Because of his independence from dogma Gauss developed a strong tolerance for those who believed otherwise. He viewed science as a means of "exposing the immortal nucleus of the human soul."

While Gauss found no consolation in creeds he sought to live his creed without reciting it. Thus, for him, religion was not a matter of literature but of life. Thus, Gauss rejected "tablets of stone and sacred parchments." He did however, believe in the immortality of the soul and said:

> *"In this world there is a pleasure of the intellect, which is satisfied in science, and a pleasure of the heart, which consists principally of the fact that human beings mutually ease the troubles and burdens of life....................................One is ...forced to the view, for which there is so much evidence even though without rigorous scientific basis, that besides this material world another, second, purely spiritual world order exists, with just as many diversities as that in which we live-we are to participate in it.*"[30]

Gauss told his friend Rudolf Wagner, a professor of biology at Göttingen University, that he did not believe in the Bible but that he had meditated a great deal on the future of the human soul and speculated on the possibility of the soul being reincarnated on another planet.

Evidently, Gauss was a Deist with a good deal of skepticism concerning religion but incorporating a great deal of philosophical interests in the Big Questions, that is. the immortality of the soul, the afterlife and the meaning of man's existence.

It was however in the area of biology, and particularly in zoology, that the greatest impetus toward a deistic world view developed in the 19th century. The work of Jean Baptiste de Monet, Chevalier de Lamarck (1744-1829) and his contemporary Georges, Baron de Cuvier (1769-1832) led to the greatest revolution in the view of man concerning man and the role of mankind in nature when Charles Darwin (1809-1882) continued the efforts begun by Lamarck.

At the end of the 20th century Lamarck and his theories appear quaint, if not foolish. It is however certain that the influence of Lamarck upon evolutionary theory was so great during the 19th century that the development of evolutionary theory as understood today depended on Lamarckism.

In sum, Lamarckism was the view that acquired characteristics can be inherited. As late as the 1950's such a view was still held by the Russian biologist Lysenko and became part of Soviet doctrine during the Stalin era.

In his book *Philosophie zoologique,* Lamarck maintained that changes in the needs of an organism lead to changes in habits which in turn become part of the animal's inheritance, that is, they are transmitted through the genes.

Such a view is rejected today. Nevertheless, the achievements of Lamarck cannot be minimized for in that book Lamarck showed the need for viewing biology as a body of principles thus making theory a precondition for scientific investigation.

Now we must remember that Newton, Faraday and others were still very much under the influence of theological considerations in their investigation of nature and its mysteries. In Lamarck however, we see a true effort to deal with the contradictions theology imposes on science.

Lamarck no longer speaks of "The Creator" as had other scientists before him. Lamarck's greatest problem was to avoid the label "atheist" while nevertheless rejecting the notion of a simultaneous creation of all the worlds living things as told in Genesis. Lamarck tried to convince his readers that God could have created all the universe over a long period of time and not in only six days. Lamarck then proposes that there is a progressive genealogy of living beings despite the brevity of life of each individual and an undeniable permanence of types.

To get around the contradiction between creationism and the observations he had made, Lamarck took the approach that God is not accessible to human investigation but that nature is, and that therefore there is a difference between the execution of God's plan, that is nature, and the originator of the plan.

By these arguments Lamarck removed the natural from the supernatural and science from religion. Lamarck admits that there is "a power without limits" which is responsible for the orderly progression of the universe. God has transferred some of his power to nature, argued Lamarck, and this natural power becomes "mechanical" for it does not include decision making. Lamarck defines nature in these terms: "Nature is an order of things extraneous to matter, ascertained by the observation of bodies, and the whole of which constitutes a power inalterable in its essence, subject in all of its acts and constantly acting in all parts of the universe."[31]

Lamarck held that nature is immutable and unalterable. Such a definition of course contrasts with the complete freedom of God. Life is in turn defined by Lamarck as an "invisible power dependent on the power of nature." Lamarck also excluded final causes from his consideration because he saw that this is a principle upon which scientific objectivity must rest.

> *"In the creation of His works,"* wrote Lamarck, *"and especially those we can observe, this omnipotent Being has undoubtedly been the ruling power in pursuing the method which has pleased him, namely his will has been:*
>
> *Either to create instantaneously and separately every particular living being observed by us, to personally care for and watch over them in all their changes, their movements or their actions, to unremittingly care for each one separately , and by the exercise of his supreme will to regulate all their life;*
>
> *Or to reduce his creations to a small number, and among these, to institute an order of things general and continuous, pervaded by ceaseless activity (movement) especially subject to laws by means of which all the organisms of whatever nature, all the changes they undergo, all the peculiarities they present, and all the phenomena that many of them exhibit, may be produced.*
>
> *In regard to these two modes of execution, if observation taught us nothing we could not form any opinion which would be well grounded. But it is not so; we distinctly see that there exists an order of things truly created (veritablement cree), as unchangeable as its author allows, acting on matter alone and which possesses the power of producing all visible beings , of executing all the changes, all the modifications, even the extinctions, so also the renewals or recreations that we observe among them. It is to this order of things that we have given the name of nature. <u>The Supreme Author of all that exists is, then, the immediate creator of matter as also of nature, but he is only indirectly the creator of what nature can produce.</u>*[32]

Thus, Lamarck, without being an atheist, removed God from immediate involvement in scientific considerations to opening remarks, prefaces and introductions. Hence, according to Lamarck, nature is evidence of God and divine power does indeed act through nature but nature itself has neither a soul nor any intention nor any final outcome.

Dealing with the biblical account of creation, Lamarck conceived of the idea of regarding days in Genesis as lengthy periods. This made it possible for him to promote his theory of "transformism." According to that view, one species could transform into another, for example reptiles into birds, by circumstances. This then led him to the erroneous conclusion that acquired characteristics can be inherited. It is significant however, for the development of deism and secularism, that transformism denies creationism, in fact, makes creationism impossible.

Transformism therefore holds that 1) God is indirectly present to His creation through a distinction between His creative act and the modality of His act and 2) the transformation of species are made possible by the productive activity which nature holds from God.[33]

The outcome of Lamarck's research and speculations was the firm entrenchment of evolution in the minds of nineteenth century intellectuals and their followers thus leading directly to the great work of Charles Darwin.

Before discussing the contributions of Darwin to secularization it is necessary to mention the experiences of the great chemist Joseph Priestley (1733 - 1804), an Englishman, and the French paleontologist George Cuvier.

Priestley began his scientific publications by writing a *History of Electricity,* followed by *Familiar Introduction to the Study of Electricity* in 1768. He also wrote *Familiar Introduction to the Theory and Practice of Perspective* and his most important *An Account of the Discoveries relating to Vision, Light and Colors.* All this work was done before he conducted his experiments on air leading to his six volume work on that subject. These six volumes established his great fame as a chemist despite the fact that he included in them all his errors and all his failures.[34]

Without describing in detail all of Priestley's writings and assumptions about religion it is necessary to reveal that Priestley, like Newton before him, also wrote on theology. Unlike Newton however, Priestley was attacked both verbally and physically because of his religious views. He was believed to have denied immortality and of being a "materialist." In the popular mind "materialism" was viewed the same as "atheism" a charge utterly false and contrary to Priestley's opinions. [35]

Nevertheless, Priestley was so labeled. When Priestley moved to Birmingham in 1780 he there joined the "Lunar Society" which also included both grandfathers of Charles Darwin, i.e, Erasmus Darwin and Josiah Wedgwood. Erasmus Darwin had already published *Botanic Garden* and *Zoonomia* and anticipated his grandson by inferring the origin of species from a common ancestor.

In Birmingham Priestley proclaimed his belief that the doctrine of the Trinity is a "corruption" for he could not believe this. He published *History of the Corruption of Christianity* and *History of the Early Opinions of Jesus Christ.* In these books he asserted that reason must be the foundation of religious belief and he denounced the contradictions inherent in some theological assumptions. He also denied the need to believe anything simply because an apostle said so. Priestley was not an atheist but denounced that stance as well. Nevertheless, his views were very unpopular so that in July of 1791 a crowd of citizens burned down his house when they could not find him at home. They had come to physically abuse him on the grounds that he was not a Christian. Branded a heretic in Parliament, Priestley emigrated to America in 1794 when he was already sixty one years old. He was forced to do so for he was shunned in England by former friends and even his Fellows in the Royal Society.[36]

Georges Leopold Cretien Frederic Dagobert Baron de Cuvier (1769-1832) was professor of comparative anatomy at the College de France. He founded paleontology and classified fossils for the firs time. His conclusions, however, were unlike those of Lamarck as he rejected the gradual evolution of species and adopted a theory of catastrophic changes.

Cuvier sought to discover the laws of nature which determine the behavior of animals. Cuvier, although interested in "the reign of virtue" and "love of peace" was not interested in religious ritual but in moral action. Greatly influenced by Kant and his emphasis on sentiment in the religious experience, de Cuvier held that religion could not rest on reason but must rest on belief, a view taught by his Lutheran church and by the Protestant Ethic, that much discussed philosophical attitude which reputedly led to worldliness, utilitarianism, and *the questioning of authority*. Such an attitude is of course congenial to scientific thinking and to the view that each person must fulfill "his calling" in life.

Therefore, de Cuvier would not accept the Bible as an authentic history nor a text leading to an understanding of the present physical world despite his willingness to cling to the "social gospel" , that is the explanation of the relationship of man to man. Meanwhile, the battle between science and religion was developing in de Cuvier's life time as most scientists and philosophers came to identify God with nature while Christians and Jews sought to demonstrate God's existence by means of geology and biology. [37]

The views of Gauss, Lamarck, Priestley and de Cuvier concerning religious orthodoxy are of course only four examples of the gradual distance which developed between science and religion in the 19th century and contributed heavily to the secularization of the whole Western world in the 20th century. Significant is that educated women and men, and particularly those who received a higher education in the 20th century, could not escape the philosophers or the scientists who challenged orthodox beliefs by their writings. Since 85% of Jewish people of college age receive a higher education in the U.S. at the end of the 20th century it is evident that Jews more than anyone are exposed to a secular world view. This became even more pronounced with the work of Charles Darwin (1802-1892) and the spread of his findings and opinions as the nineteenth century ended and the 20th century began.

VI.

The work of Charles Darwin cannot be viewed as isolated or utterly new in the history of science. On the contrary, his grandfather Erasmus Darwin, as we have already seen, supported the work of Lamarck and others concerning the probability of evolution. However, when Charles Darwin wrote *On the Origins of the Species by Means of Natural Selection* in 1859, he published the most influential book of the 19th century because he thereby revolutionized the biological sciences and philosophy at the same time. His views led to the famous Scopes trial in Tennessee, a state which had prohibited the teaching of evolution in the public schools because fundamentalist believers viewed Darwin's work as a challenge to their religion and morality in general.

Nevertheless, Charles Darwin remains vital to the growth of science and the philosophical consequences of scientific thought because he used empirical research and not speculation to undergird his opinions.

In 1831, Darwin had traveled as "naturalist" on the government owned ship *Beagle* and recorded his findings along the South American coast. There he noticed the great diversity of animal variations and set out to study their causes. Nature, according to Darwin, selected for perpetuation the best adapted and rejected the least adapted. Heavily influenced by the work of Alexander Humboldt who had already explored South America before him, Darwin provoked the most consistent and vigorous attacks upon scientific thought by proponents of religious orthodoxy ever undertaken. To this day, 1995, there are still some who reject the theory of natural selection as well as evolution although in America at least, such rejectionists are generally viewed as outlandish and peculiar like the wide brimmed black hats and long beards worn by some orthodox Jews and Amish fundamentalists.

The reasons for the storm of protest which the publication and dissemination of *The Origin of Species* caused are easily understood. For it seemed evident to proponents of religious orthodoxy that the views there expressed undermined the entire structure of Jewish and Christian teachings and would lead to doubts and even rejection of the Bible or Tora.[38]

There are many accounts of the public meetings, angry exchanges and vitriolic attacks upon Darwin and his supporters. Despite these, however, the *Origins* became more and more influential each year. Not only in Great Britain, but in all counties of the Western World, Natural Selection gradually became, not a theory, but a fact. In the U.S.A. and other English speaking countries the work of Darwin could be read at once. Darwin published his 6th and final edition in 1872, the others having appeared in 1859, 1860, 1861, 1866 and 1869. By then, there had been three American and three Russian editions. Four editions had been published in French, five in German and at least one each in Italian, Dutch and Swedish. In that year Darwin made these comments concerning the acceptance of his great work : ".....I formerly spoke to very many naturalists on the subject of evolution, and never once met with any sympathetic agreement. .....Now things are wholly changed, and almost every naturalist admits the great principle of evolution.."

Six years later, in 1878, he wrote: "Now there is almost complete unanimity among Biologists about Evolution , etc."[39]

Disputing the views of Lamarck, Darwin held that "*natura non facit saltum*" or *nature cannot take a sudden leap.*"

Darwin had from the beginning used the term "Natural Selection" which the biologist Alfred Russel Wallace (1823-1913), explained as "the continuous adjustment of the organic to the inorganic world." Wallace had discovered the principle of natural selection independently and simultaneously with Darwin. The two men thereafter cooperated in presenting these ideas to the scientific community.

Since there were some who charged that Darwin had theological intentions in using the term "natural selection" he wrote that he wished he had used "natural preservation" or "survival of the fittest" as first promoted by the sociologist Herbert Spencer.[40]

Now one of the consequences of Charles Darwin's great work had been its use by politicians and others to justify aggression and cruelty of every kind. While Darwin sought to teach the truth as nature revealed it to him, others have used Darwin's work to substitute a form of mechanistic materialism for any considerations of human kindness or compassion. It is in this area that the teaching of natural selection and survival has challenged traditional religion and its appeal to moral law and the rights of the weak and powerless.

Followers of Darwin have argued that his work has taught us that "might is right", that cheating and swindling are also right and that the aggressive wars and persecutions marking the history of bloodshed in this century must be attributed to Darwin and his discoveries. This social interpretation of Darwin's work was mainly taught by Herbert Spencer (1820-1913), a British sociologist who observed the brutal conditions of English industrial and economic life and interpreted the terrible struggle of the English workers to maintain themselves in the sweat shops of the early industrial age as a human example of natural selection. He taught that society is analogous to a biological organism and that the economically weak had no more right to live than the weak who lost the struggle for survival in nature.[41] The consequences of this belief directly contradicted the views of religious believers and their assessment of the need to support and help the poor, the weak and the disadvantaged. In the view of Spencer and his followers, unsuccessful individuals were "unfit" to survive and should be left to fend for themselves. It was and is feared by these "social Darwinists" that if government were to help the needy, then the efforts of the successful will be wasted since without such interference the fate of society is governed by the same laws of nature which govern animals. The view here is that if no one interferes with the laws of nature then all problems will correct themselves and society will not only survive but also become better.[42]

When Darwin's book first appeared in 1859 the curriculum of every school in England and America was fashioned according to assumptions far removed from natural selection and other Darwinian propositions. Although science was gradually appearing in the curriculae of some schools, elementary schools continued to teach the "Three R's" and advanced schools taught bookkeeping and mathematics.

In 1878 however, an eminent geologist, Alexander Winchell, a professor at Vanderbilt University, taught his students evolution and the existence of "pre-Adamite" man. The board of trustees of that university thereupon abolished his "chair" on the grounds that his ideas were contrary to "the plan of redemption."

By 1884, six years later, the English had adjusted their curriculum to the teachings of Darwin and the English church or the "Anglican Communion" had made no objection to these views. It was in that year, however, that the Rev. Dr. James Woodrow was brought to trial and convicted of "heresy" because he chose to teach evolution at the South Carolina College and Theological Seminary "with undue sympathy for the Darwinian school."

It was however the Scopes trial in 1925 which became a *"cause celebre"* when John Thomas Scopes, a teacher in Rhea County, Tennessee was arrested for teaching the theory of evolution and found guilty of violating the law in that state. Although the shallow arguments of the anti-evolutionists had long been exposed as non-sense by the American Association for the Advancement of Science and other groups, the evangelical Protestant fundamentalism of the nineteenth century defeated these efforts for some time as Prohibition, quotas against immigrants and other zealous causes dominated the thinking of many Americans.[43]

Nevertheless, Darwinian views became the dominant force in American education in the 20th century. As we shall see, John Dewey, as well as the philosophers James and Peirce introduced evolution and

all its philosophical consequences into American education and altered
it radically.

Now, any discussion of Darwin and his contributions to science
must include the influence of Thomas Henry Huxley (1825-1895) upon
the progress of scientific thought. Huxley was a biologist but he was
also the leading proponent of both Darwinism and agnosticism in the
nineteenth century. A naval surgeon, Huxley carried out his own
studies leading him to support evolution by publishing *Evolution and
Ethics* in 1893. Prior to that date however, Huxley had become
involved in a debate with the English politician William Gladstone
(1809-1898) as to the veracity of the Bible. Such a debate would not
occur at the end of the 20th century as only a small number of
"fundamentalists" would even be willing to engage in such a public
discourse. In the middle of the nineteenth century however, Huxley
was viewed with alarm by many when he said that it was degrading
that men of the nineteenth century should accept the "demonology" of
the first century and then proceeded to question the credibility of the
Gospels.[44]

During Huxley's early years fundamentalism had gripped England
and was so popular that he called it "the evangelical flood." Disgusted
with fundamentalist preaching Huxley determined to make war upon
theology and to expose ecclesiastic pretenses to the scrutiny of reason.
He debated bishops and other clergy and wrote critical essays
concerning biblical accounts of such "events" as creation, the deluge
and other stories he considered mythology.

In *Evolution of Theology,* published in 1886, he analyzed the
relationship between morality and supernaturalism and found the
latter unnecessary. Huxley was so convinced of his anti-religious
position that some called him "Pope Huxley" because he was evidently
as dogmatic in his pronouncements against all religious positions as
were some churchmen on the other side.

Huxley invented the word "agnostic" and meant by that, that all
conclusions concerning anything supernatural were not subject to
verification and could therefore neither be accepted nor rejected. In his
day Huxley was seen as a "Godless materialist", "infidel" and a
promoter of a "libertine" lifestyle despite the fact that he was much
more the Puritan in his personal conduct than many who criticized his
views.

In fact, Huxley was not opposed to the ethical teachings of religion. He was opposed to supernaturalism. Thus he wrote in 1892: ".....the only religion that appeals to me is prophetic Judaism. Add to it something from the best Stoics, and something from Spinoza and something from Goethe, and there is a religion for men."[45]

Huxley, like Hume before him, "struck horror in the breasts of the orthodox." But Huxley lived over a century later than Hume and by then there were even churchmen, particularly within the church of England, who were as opposed to "bibliolatry" as he was. His efforts to show that miracles were hardly believable and his insistence that the Bible was hardly history were already taken for granted by many in the later part of the nineteenth century. Nevertheless, Huxley was a major contributor to the secularization of the Western world and remains so, as anyone gaining a higher education at the end of the 20th century can hardly ignore him.

VII.

Darwin, Huxley and the English scientists were of course not the only contributors to the ever advancing march toward the secularization of the Western world. After Darwin, innumerable scientists were willing to insist that reason and experiment should be the sole means of deciding the nature of reality and they therefore rejected traditional beliefs and religious teachings as inadequate. This is not to say that all held the same view. For example, the great French chemist and founder of microbiology, Louis Pasteur (1822-1895) was a practicing Roman Catholic all his life. This was possible for Pasteur because he was not interested in promoting a philosophical doctrine. Instead he held that Creation is far greater than can be understood by us even when using scientific instruments or methods. He thought that men disagreed so profoundly because they could see only a small segment of reality. Thus, Pasteur relied on the experimental method but never sought to explain the origin of the universe or elaborate on the Great Questions.[46]

Despite the efforts of many scientists in the nineteenth and 20th century to hold on to their religious ties even while making important advances in science, these experimenters and scientific contributors also advanced the cause of secularization willingly or not. This was however even more true of Alfred North Whitehead (1861-1947) a mathematician and philosopher and Lord Bertrand A. Russell, his student (1872-1970).

Whitehead sought to establish a whole system of scientific cosmology by combining his interest in mathematics with his interest in morals and esthetics which he published in 1929 in his book *Process and Reality.*[47]

Whitehead is so important to the secularization of the western world in the 20th century precisely because he was not an atheist but because he included the concept of God in his system without surrendering to any religious denomination or theology. Whitehead was then a deist as were most of the other great contributors to philosophy and science in the three centuries since Newton. It is this view, deism, which is now at the end of the 20th century most popular not only among scientists, not only among the educated but also among a vast number of other Europeans and Americans.

We have already seen how this came about before the 20th century. We will see now how this point of view became universal in this century. To that end the example of Whitehead, his student Russell, and the views of Albert Einstein will illustrate our contention.

Whitehead speaks of "a system of ideas which bring the aesthetic, moral and religious interests into relation with those concepts of the world which have their origin in natural science." [48]

This effort to construct a metaphysical system is of course a direct challenge to established religion, whether Christian, Jewish or other, because religions are themselves cosmological systems. Let us take a look at some of Whitehead's contentions, not because we seek to make any attempt at explaining his philosophy but only to show that in the 20th century science and philosophy have moved so far away from the Judeo-Christian explanation of the universe, or the Judeo-Christian cosmology that a student, a reader, anyone who comes in contact with the views of Whitehead and others will see therein a challenge to the traditional world view proposed by traditional religions to this day.

Whitehead argues that the universe is a self-creative process of which God is the "principle of origination and order." Whitehead held that God "is the originator of all the subjective aims of actual entities" and the source of order and value in the world. Whitehead's God is infinite, eternal and unchanging, but nevertheless, His "feelings" are lacking because his "feelings" are purely conceptual.[49]

Whitehead also believed that God is dependent on the world even as the world is dependent on him. God is therefore not wholly independent and omnipotent. God, according to Whitehead, involves time and change. He experiences the world as objects, is related to the world but not part of it. God is not identical to the world nor does he include it but he transcends it. That belief is of course *deism,* although Whitehead's deism differs somewhat from the deism already discussed. Thus, Whitehead criticizes popular supernaturalism as supporting the view that God has or uses arbitrary power. Together with other deists Whitehead believed that God responds to the changing world. Whitehead also questioned the idea of a "personal" God but thought of God as impersonal and therefore again agreed with the deists or theists we have already met. Yet, even as Whitehead makes these statements he also talks of God as showing "wisdom", "love" and "purpose."[50]

Whitehead showed a good deal of piety toward creation and hence nature. He criticized "scientific naturalism" and the technological exploitation of nature. Whitehead believed that the religious and moral concern for final causes are compatible with science because man is part of nature because man depends upon his body and upon other creatures and is a product of the evolutionary process himself. Thus Whitehead stresses the unity of man with nature and uses this realization to support his deism.[51]

Not all of the leading minds of the early 20th century were deists. A major exception to this rule was Bertrand Russell (1872-1970), Whitehead's student and co-author with Whitehead of *Principia Mathematica.*

Russell was an agnostic, that is, someone who held that "it is impossible to know the truth in matters such as God and the future of life with which Christianity and other religions are concerned. Or, if not impossible, impossible at the present time."[52]

Russell popularized his views on repeated occasions and thereby became one of the major contributors to secularization in both Europe and America. His views as expressed in 1953 are undoubtedly the best example of the widespread views held by innumerable agnostics everywhere.[53]

Russell rejected atheism. He viewed that belief as akin to any dogma, Christian or otherwise, because he would not concede that we can or cannot know the existence of a God but that we must suspend judgment on this until it can be known.

Russell further shows that an agnostic does not accept any authority in the religious sense but that everyone must deal with questions of conduct himself. Referring to various contradictions in the Bible he rejected that source of authority entirely and excoriated in particular the contention regarding "sin" which he viewed as "belief in vindictive punishment." He defended the ethics of agnostics who rejected Christian and other beliefs in supernatural events and personages. He held agnostics to be as ethical as anyone and perhaps more than some who uphold religion. He viewed the word "soul" as ill defined and without meaning while the "afterlife" seemed to him unproved and therefore without evidence one way or another.

As to the argument that nature is harmonious and beautiful he denied both pointing to the endless conflict in nature and the ugly aspects of it such as the tapeworm or the cruelty of killing between animals which exists everywhere.

While Russell acknowledged that individual human beings have purposes he denied that life in general has a purpose. He did not defend the view that reason alone could answer all questions. On the contrary, Russell shows that many purposes and ends are based on faith and not reason such as the belief that someone undertaking a journey will find the town he intends to visit to be still there when he arrives.

In 1927 Russell delivered a lecture to the National Secular Society in London, England. The lecture was called "Why I Am Not a Christian." Here he defined a Christian as one who at least believes in God, immortality and Christ all concepts which he rejected.

Russell then proceeds to demolish the standard arguments of religious believers beginning with the argument from Natural Law which, as we have seen, was held valid by Isaac Newton.

His prime contention here is that so many things thought to be "Natural Law" are only human conventions and not law at all. He showed also that many so-called laws are only a matter of statistical averages emerging from chance.

The "Argument from Design" Russell treats as so much antiquated non-sense because evolution has shown that living creatures adapt themselves to their environment, not the other way around. Russell cites Voltaire's sarcasm that "the nose was designed to fit spectacles."[54]

As to the "Moral Argument" for deity, Russell is willing to agree with some Gnostics who said that this world was made by the devil when God was not looking. The belief that God must exist lest there be no justice in the world seems a fantasy to Russell who not only points out how much injustice this world suffers at all times but also because the very concept is difficult to define.

In addition to all of these arguments Russell wrote on the defects in Christ's teachings, in particular the threat that those who would not agree would go to hell.

In the end, Russell insists that we look to science to teach us to not look for imaginary support, to stop "inventing allies in the sky" but to look to ourselves and our own efforts to make the world a fit place to live.[55]

VIII.

At the end of the 20th century it would appear to some that if there ever was a conflict between science and religion then science has won. It is however also evident now that while traditional religion and its cosmology has been entirely defeated in the minds of Western men, religion outside of traditional ritual is very much alive and will no doubt remain so. Nothing suggests that classical, traditional mythology will have a great comeback and yet defeat the forces of secularization. Everything suggests however, that despite the great victory of the secular world view now commonly espoused in Europe and America, religion in its secular form is here to stay.

The reason for this was well expressed by Norbert Wiener (1894-1964), the founder of cybernetics.

"I have said that science is impossible without faith," said Wiener. "What I say about the need for faith in science is equally true for a purely causative world and for one in which probability rules. No amount of purely objective and disconnected observation can show that probability is a valid notion. To put the same statement in other language, the laws of induction in logic cannot be established inductively. Inductive logic , the logic of Bacon , is rather something on which we can act than something we can prove, and to act on it is a supreme assertion of faith. It is in this connection that I must say that Einstein's dictum concerning the directness of God is itself a

statement of faith. Science is a way of life which can only flourish when men are free to have faith. "[56]

Here Wiener shows that while logical reasoning plays a crucial role in science such descriptions of science as "rational activity" or "organized common sense" are wholly inadequate.

Wiener repeatedly discussed the need for faith in the building and organization of great projects which far outlast any one lifetime. His contributions were of course an excellent example of his comment that: ".....*what the great scholars.....of the present day will do that will affect the human race centuries from now, is something that we cannot see with our own eyes.*" In this, other great scientists of the 20th century agreed with him as would any thinking person.

Surely Albert Einstein (1879-1955) was the epitome of a thinking person in the 20th century. No scientist in his generation and since has achieved such fame nor had such influence in revolutionizing science and contributing to the world view of Western man.

The life of Einstein clearly shows that he had no use for traditional religion, did not participate in his Jewish heritage and would not support supernaturalism or ritual of any kind. Yet, on April 25, 1929 he told the New York Times: "*I believe in Spinoza's God who reveals himself in the harmony of what exists.*" [57]

Thus, Einstein not only had a tremendous influence on physics, but also on metaphysics, i.e, philosophy. The reason for this influence is that Einstein presented mankind with an entirely new view of the universe which challenged the most ingrained fundamental ideas concerning the structure of the physical world and the concepts of space and time.[58]

Newton had taught that there was absolute time and absolute space. Einstein saw both as an integrated whole involving the abstract concept of a "field". Because of this view Einstein made a principal philosophical discovery which led to our understanding that space and time are united in one single entity observable through the use of geometry, not physics. Thus, Einstein was not a positivist for that theory "confines itself to the description and prediction of experimental results."[59]

Instead, Einstein was a theorist who explained the laws of nature in terms of mathematics but also in terms of an explorer gradually uncovering the mysteries of the universe. Einstein viewed nature as

God and God as nature as had been taught by Spinoza. He viewed the world with wonder and despite his rejection of organized religion admired most "the comprehensible world."

In 1952, three years before his death, he wrote this:

> *"Now, a priori, one should, after all, expect a chaotic world that is in no way graspable through thinking. One could (even should) expect that the world turns out to be lawful only in so far as we make an ordering intervention. It would be the kind of ordering like putting into alphabetical order the words of a language. On the other hand, the kind of order which, for example, was created through the discovery of Newton's theory of gravitation is of a quite different character. Even if the axioms of the theory are put forward by human agents, the success of such an enterprise does suppose a high degree of order in the objective world, which one has no justification whatever to expect a priori. Here lies the sense of wonder which increases ever more with the development of our knowledge".*[60]

And here lies the weak point for the positivists and professional atheists. ....What Einstein meant to discover is why the world is thus and not otherwise. Like Spinoza, Einstein was certain that for every action there must exist a cause. Hence he was a determinist. He rejected "freethinking" as much as he rejected superstition and sought to define the legitimate roles of both science and religion. Again, he did not mean ritualistic or dogmatic teachings. He meant "true religion has been ennobled by science and made more profound by scientific knowledge."

Again we see that Nature was Einstein's God in Spinoza's words *Deus Sive Natura.* Einstein described himself as a *"deeply religious non-believer"* because he rejected miracles and myths but he also rejected atheism and the popular notions of success and called the ideal of ease and comfort the "ideal of a pigsty."[61]

IX.

We have now briefly shown how scientists since Francis Bacon secularized the Western world by means of rational and scientific explanations for many phenomena at one time only explained by religious dogmas. Thus, "there was a time in the history of mankind when it was considered blasphemy to make any kind of inquiry into the workings of the natural law.....But the inquisitive mind could not be put to sleep. .....the time came when the scientific mind emancipated itself completely from the clutches of theological thinking."[62]

Thereafter, during the Age of Reason and later rationalism and experimentation became the dogma of the educated world and the rejection of all religion or supernaturalism went with it.

Today, few advanced thinkers would be solely rationalists and experimenters. Einstein showed that there is design and order in the universe and in nature and that this is cause to view nature with reverence because "God does not play dice with the universe."

The secularization of the Western World was thus the currency of educated men after the middle of the 20th century, if not before. Yet, even as that had been achieved, religion did not disappear. Not only did it continue as always among the least educated, but it took new hold on scientists and their followers albeit in a form different than heretofore. A new kind of religion became evident with Albert Einstein and others. A secular religion. A universal religion which merges science with philosophy for the continued edification of all men.

NOTES

[1]Georgia Harkness, *The Modern Rival of the Christian Faith*, N.Y. Abbingdon-Cokesbury, 1952.

[2]Mark Chaves, "Interorganizational Power and Internal Secularization in Protestant Denomenations,"
The American Journal of Sociology, Vol. 99, No.1, July 1993, p. 4.

[3]Georgia Harkness, *op.cit.*, p. 11.

[4]Andrew Dickson White, *A History of the Warfare of Science with Theology in Christendom*, New York,
The Free Press, 1965.

[5]*Ibid.* pp.16-17.

[6]John Hedley Brooke, "Science and Religion" in R. C. Olby, G.N. Cantor, J.R.R. Christie and M.J.S. Hodge, eds., *Companion to the History of Modern Science*, London, Routledge, 1990, pp. 766-767.

[7]J. F. West, *The Great Intellectual Revolution*, London, Cox and Wyman Ltd., 1965, pp. 114-115.

[8]*Ibid.* p. 2.

[9]Fulton Henry Adamson, *The Philosophy of Francis Bacon*, Chicago, The University of Chicago Press, 1948, p.18.

[10]*Ibid.*, p.96.

[11]Charles Whiteny, *Francis Bacon and Modernity*, New Haven, The Yale University Press, 1986, p.30.

[12]J.G. Crowther, *Francis Bacon*, London, The Cresset Press, 1960, pp. 24-25, 58-61 and 87-89.

[13]Alexander Pope, *Collected Poems, Epistles and Satires*, New York, Everyman's Library, 1959.

[14]Abraham Wolf, *A History of Science, Technology and Philosophy in the 16th and 17th Century*, New York, Harper, 1959.

[15]*Ibid.*

[16]Frank Manuel, *The Religion of Isaac Newton*, Oxford, Clarendon Press, 1974.

[17]Cornelius Lanczos, *Albert Einstein and the Cosmic World Order*, New York, Interscience Publishers, 1965, p. 116.

[18]John Brooke, "The God of Isaac Newton," in *Let Newton Be!*, New York, The Oxford University Press, 1988, p. 172.

[19]Louis T. More, *Isaac Newton: A Biography*, New York, Dover Publshing Inc, 1934, p. 622.

[20]William H. Austin, "Isaac Newton on Science and Religion," *Journal of the History of Ideas*, vol. 31, Nol 1, 1970, pp. 521-1940.

[21]H.D. Anthony, *Sir Isaac Newton*, New York, Abelard-Schuman, 1960, p. 156.

[22]More, *op.cit.*, p. 629.

[23]*Ibid.* pp. 173-183.

[24] More, *op.cit.*, p. 616.

[25]Angus Armitage, *William Herschel*, Garden City, N.Y., Doubleday & Co., 1963, pp. 35-36.

[26]*Ibid.*, p.36.

[27]James Mitchell and Jess Stein, Eds., *The Random House Encyclopedia*, New York, Random House,1990, p.2181.

[28]*Ibid.*, p. 162.

[29]Madeleine Barthelemy Madaule, *Lamarck, The Mythical Precursor*, Cambridge, The MIT Press, 1982, p. 22.

[30]G. Waldo Dunnington, *Carl Friedrich Gauss: Titan of Science*, New York, Expository Press, 1955, p. 301.

[31]Barthelemy-Madaule, *op.cit.*, pp.26-29.

[32]Alpheus S. Packard, *Lamarck*, New York, Arno Press, 1980, pp. 376-377.

[33]Barthelemy-Madaule, *op.cit..*,p. 40.

[34]Anne Holt, *A Life of Joseph Priestley*, Westport , Conn., Greenwood Press, 1970 (Originally published by Oxford University Press in 1931).

[35]*Ibid.* p.174.

[36] Wolf, *op.cit.*, p. 353.

[37]William Coleman, *George Cuvier: Zoologist*, Cambridge, Mass., Harvard University Press, 1964. pp.176-177.

[38]Geoffrey West, *Charles Darwin*, New Haven, Yale University Press, 1938, pp 78-79.

[39]*Ibid.*, p. 262.

[40]*Ibid., p. 263.*

[41]Stephen K. Sanderson, *Macrosociology*, New York, Harper & Row, 1988, p. 422.

42 AlexThio, *Sociology: An Introduction,* New York, Harper & Row, 1989, p. 10.

43 Paul R. Sears, "Faith and Learning" in *Charles Darwin,* Charles Scribner's Sons, New York, 1950, p. 97.

44 Albert Ashforth, *Thomas Henry Huxley,* N.Y., Twayne Publishers Inc., 1969, p. 132.

45 *Ibid.,* p. 138.

46 Rene Dubos, *Louis Pasteur: Free Lance of Science,* Boston, Little, Brown and Co., 1950, p. 399. See also: Rene Dubos, *Louis Pateur,* Boston, Little, Brown and Co., 1976, pp. 385-399.

47 Alfred N. Whitehead, *Process and Reality: An Essay in Cosmology,* New York, Harper Torchbooks, 1960 (Macmillan 1929).

48 *Ibid.* p. vi.

49 Lawrence T. Wilmot, *Whitehead and God: Prologomena to Theological Reconstruction,* Waterloo, Ontario, The Wilfred Laurier University Press, 1979, pp.19-29; pp.41-51.

50 *Ibid,* pp. 171-181.

51 *Ibid,* pp. 171-181.

52 Alan Wood, *Bertrand Russell: The Passionate Skeptic, A Biography,* New York, Simon and Schuster, 1958, p.569.

53 Bertrand Russell, "What Is An Agnostic?" in: Leo Rosten, *The Religions of America,* N.Y., Simon and Schuster, 1955.

54 Bertand Russell, "Why I am Not a Christian," London, Allen & Unwin, 1957.

55 *Ibid.,* p. 596.

56 P. R. Masani, *Norbert Wiener,* Basel, Birhauser Verlag, 1990, p. 318.

57 The New York Times, April 25, 1929, p.60, column 4.

58 Andrew Ushenko, "Einstein's Influence on Contemporary Philosophy," in *Albert Einstein,* Paul A. Schlipp, Ed., London, Cambridge Unversity Press, 1970, pp. 609-641.

59 Cornelius Lanczos, *op.cit,* pp. 107-119.

60 Janice Sayen, *Einstein In America,* New York, Crown Publishing, 1985, p.154.

61 *Ibid.* p. 155.

62 Lanczos, *op.cit.,* p. 111.

CHAPTER VI

The Influence of Some European and American Writers on the Secularization Process

I.

We have seen that philosophy and science greatly influenced the secularization of the Western World. In fact, there was no sharp difference between science and philosophy until the nineteenth century and even then and even now, the difference is not always discernible.

Similarly, literature cannot always be distinguished from philosophy particularly since many practitioners of the writing craft operate in both areas. Such writers were the French poet, historian and philosopher Francois Marie Arouet who called himself Voltaire (1694-1778) and the German poet, scientist and philosopher Johann Wolfgang von Goethe (1749-1832). We have met Voltaire and Goethe before in their role as philosophers.[1]

Now it is unlikely that an American who seeks a higher education would meet very many writers, novelists or poets who wrote in any language other than English. There are nevertheless a few giants of the written word, such as Voltaire and Goethe who are presented to English speaking students in translation because their influence cannot be overlooked.

Voltaire viewed himself as "the statesman and field commander of the French and the European 'freethinkers.' "[2] This may seem as an exaggeration to an American reader of Voltaire at the end of the 20th century. However, in 1734 the French government actually burned his *Lettres anglaise* and ordered a police investigation concerning him. Only two years later he was again in trouble with the law because of his poem *le Mondain.* Therefore Voltaire lived at the court of Frederick of Prussia from 1750-1753. Since Frederick was also a "freethinker" he offered Voltaire asylum from the interference of the church in his work.

Thereafter, Voltaire moved to Switzerland so as to evade the insecurity of a French agnostic writer in a Catholic country.

Yet even in Ferney near Geneva Voltaire aroused the opposition of the "authorities."

For now he published *Candide* (1759), a book which was burned in Switzerland but was widely read in France. Yet, he could not live in France and visited Paris only a few weeks before his death where all but the government recognized him because of his writings.

Voltaire's purpose was to teach humanity tolerance and intellectual freedom. His methods were often sarcasm and ridicule. However, his wish to teach men reason and liberty were sincere. He had lived in England and had studied with Newton, Locke and Shaftesbury and learned the need for equality before the law. Here he also learned to be suspicious of Catholicism then dominant in France.

Voltaire was therefore a good representative of English deism of the 17th and 18th century. This is visible in the articles he wrote for the French Encyclopedia on atheism. Here he was a good deal less skeptical concerning the existence of God than had been true of others. Voltaire agreed with Pascal whose "wager" bet that it is better to acknowledge that a God exists since nothing is lost if that turned out to be false.

Voltaire also held that it is better to believe in a God since such a belief prevents the worst immorality and appears to punish evil and reward good. He also thought that the belief in God has a policing function . Voltaire rejected atheism but viewed religious fanaticism as yet worse. Voltaire made no distinction between deism and theism but viewed the English believers in that point of view as having a religion.

We have already seen that Voltaire taught tolerance for those who think otherwise. The very word "tolerance" is now obnoxious since no one has the right to "tolerate" anyone else. However, two hundred years ago, the idea of tolerance was regarded as sensational since deists or theists were viewed as atheists by the churches.

The number of publications by Voltaire designed to spread deism everywhere are innumerable. In poems and in letters, in histories and in essays Voltaire exhibited a profound hatred for the Christian religion as best illustrated by his essay *Epitre aux Romains*. This was a call for revolution against Papal authority in Italy on the grounds that the Catholic church is guilty of nine forgeries. We need not recite the nature of these alleged forgeries. Suffice it that Voltaire compares the divinity of Jesus to the manner in which Bacchus, Perseus, Herakles or Romulus were deified by the ancients.

In sum, Voltaire firmly believed that deism would become the religion of all reasonable men and that it would be "erected over the ruins of superstition."[3]

We now turn once more to Goethe who was undoubtedly a follower of Spinoza and therefore not an atheist. Goethe used the word "God" frequently in his published work. However, he understood this to mean "Wie einer ist; so ist sein Gott" or "How someone is, so is his God." This implies that Goethe evidently knew that each human group, each culture creates God in its own image.

Goethe's attitude toward theology is well known because he recorded a number of his conversations with his friend Eckerman. Here he said on February 20, 1831: "I pray to the one who has introduced so great a power of creation in this world, that if only a millionth part thereof produces life the world swarms with creatures so that neither war, pestilence, water and fire can assail it. That is my God." Further, Goethe made these remarks: "I do not ask whether this highest Being has understanding or reason: I feel that it is understanding, it is reason itself."[4]

He also viewed religion as man made and calculated to deal with the needs of masses of people whose needs religion satisfied. He argued that if religion were made by God then no one could understand it. Since, however, religion is man made it cannot speak of the unexplainable.

In sum, Goethe was a decided enemy of organized religion and especially Christianity.[5]

Now nothing would be further from the truth than to equate the positions of Voltaire and Goethe towards religion. For although both were opponents of Christian dogma, Voltaire had no relationship towards religion, although he sometimes made references to the deity as a means of protecting himself against the interference of church authorities. Goethe, however, exhibited a real need for religious experience outside organized religion as shown by his most famous work, Faust. Here he said: "Whoever possesses science and art also possesses religion," a view evidently derived from Spinoza.[6]

Freedom was of great importance to Goethe. Both in "Faust" and in "Götz von Berlichingen", Goethe has his protagonists speak of freedom as their last words before dying. Said Faust: "Das ist der Weisheit letzter Schluss: Nur der verdient sich Freiheit wie das Leben, der täglich sie erobern muss" or, "That is wisdom's last conclusion, that only he earns freedom and his life, who needs to gain it daily with determined strife."[7]

Although "Faust" is the Goethe play most often taught in English translation in American universities, his *Götz von Berlichingen, The Sorrows of Young Werther, Iphigenie on Tauris, Egmont* and others all contribute to a secular view of the world which every reader of that literature must confront.

II.

There can be no doubt that the influence of literature on Americans must come almost entirely from English speaking writers, whether American or British. Indeed there are writers from other English speaking countries who may on occasion be read in American schools and colleges. However, the standard fare of all literature readers in America are first, British writers and then Americans in sequence.

Let us therefore take a look at a few major British writers and estimate their influence on the secularization of the English speaking world. It is of course understood that a thorough going review of all such British or American writers is neither necessary or useful here because our only purpose is to exhibit some examples of some of the curriculum a student in higher education would meet at the end of the twentieth century.

The biting sarcasm of Alexander Pope (1688-1744) together with jealousy concerning his immense talent caused him much enmity in his time and endless criticism to this day. A Catholic all his life, he nevertheless contributed greatly to deism and a secular attitude by his writings. The best example of Pope's attitude concerning religion is no doubt his *Essay on Man* which lends itself easily to a pantheistic or deistic interpretation.

The purpose of this long poem is to illustrate that man is a part of creation and part of the general order of the universe as planned by God. Pope, despite his Catholicism, was a Deist. He denied that man is the final triumph of creation. In fact, he called such an attitude a form of conceit and held that reason alone supersedes all other faculties.

"*Presumptious man! the reason wouldst thou find , why formed so weak , so little and so blind? (Essay on Man, verse 35.)* "   In verse 49 Pope wrote: "*And all the question (wrangle e'er so long) Is only this-if God has placed him wrong. Respecting man whatever wrong we call may, must be right, relative to all.* Reason is celebrated by Pope as well when he wrote: *Without this just gradation could they be subjected, these to those, or all to thee? The pow'rs of all subdued by thee alone, Is not they reason all these pow'rs in one?* (Verse 230) and also *Two principles in human nature reign, self love to urge, and reason to restrain.(Verse 53).* In verse 195 Pope then writes: *Thus Nature gives us (let it check our pride) the virtue nearest to our vice allied : Reason the bias turns to good from ill, and Nero reigns a Titus if he will.*" Pope believed that man must submit himself to Providence and is a fool for questioning God's dispensation. The implication is obvious. Religious observance can do man little good for it will not influence the providence that rules us nor change the fate that awaits us.

Perhaps the most pronounced enemy of Christianity among 18th century writers in the English language was Edward Gibbon (1737-1794) truly a master of expression. Author of *A History of the Decline and Fall of the Roman Empire* which appeared in seven volumes between 1776 and 1788. Gibbon held Christianity responsible for the *Decline* and in describing how Christianity had affected the Roman Empire Gibbon revealed his own antagonism to Christianity as well as Judaism.[8]

Gibbon viewed Christianity as a disrupting force. He cites the "zeal and enthusiasm" of the Christians, which he claimed they had gotten from the Jews, and stigmatizes this behavior. Gibbon believed that zeal and enthusiasm caused intolerance on the part of both religions as both taught that only one religion can be true. A lover of freedom, Gibbon condemned bigotry and gave numerous examples of extreme conduct derived from religious disputes. He discusses the religious hatred between Christian sects and the terrible fighting and bloodshed which came about in the fifth century over the issue as to whether the words "who was crucified for us" should be added to another prayer frequently repeated in synagogues and churches. Gibbon discusses various church councils which declared a belief to be true or heretical because of one vote. He shows that the word "heretic" has been considered more odious to a Christian than the word "barbarian" and that a "saint" or an "orthodox" person is one who sides with the winning faction in a religious dispute.

Discussing the Middle Ages, Gibbon showed that Christians, in their zeal to reach the Holy Land during the crusades, slaughtered thousands of Jews while calling themselves "servants of the Prince of Peace."[9]

Gibbon significantly devoted three chapters of his history to the life and reign of the Emperor Julian, although he ruled Rome for only two years. However, Julian "The Apostate" restored pagan temples and permitted all religions to freely practice. Says Gibbon: "He extended to all the inhabitants of the Roman world the benefits of a free and equal toleration; and the only hardship which he inflicted on the Christians, was to deprive them of the power of tormenting their fellow subjects......"[10]

The clergy of all religions were the target of Gibbon's extensive criticism as "always the enemy of reason."[11] He goes on to heap scorn on Christian martyrs and claims that Christians committed far greater atrocities upon one another than were ever inflicted on them by the Roman "pagans." Likewise, Gibbon viewed "miracles" as fraud and described theology as superstition and "intellectual bondage." He questioned the doctrine of the immortality of the soul and viewed Jesus as human as Socrates. He also derided prayer but accepted the view that there is a God or Supreme Deity. Thus, he rejected atheism as yet another form of bigotry and held with Xenophanes that "if lions were to formulate their idea of God, they would think of him as a lion."[12]

In sum, then, Gibbon was a deist as were so many other writers, scientists and philosophers of his day and later years so that he contributed as much as anyone to the secularization of the modern world.

Somewhat younger than Gibbon was the poet William Blake (1757-1827). Inspired by both the American and French revolutions, Blake saw theologians as enemies of virtue. He believed that he could speak to angels and prophets and heavenly messengers. However, he rejected religious orthodoxy but sought to teach the need for love and freedom as the only important values. His religion of imagination had two commandments: be free and love all things. Even more astonishing was Blake's willingness to accept non-Christian believers as worthy of human interest. Indeed he taught ecumenism long before it became popular and at a time when a positive regard for another's religion was viewed as blasphemy by the established churches. Here is an example of Blake's "The Divine Image" written in 1789.[13]

> *Mercy, Pity, Peace and Love all pray in their distress;*
> *And to these virtues of delight Return their thankfulness.*
> *For Mercy , Pity, Peace and Love Is God our Father dear;*
> *And Mercy , Pity, Peace and Love Is Man his child and care.*
> *For Mercy has a human heart, Pity a human face;*
> *And Love, the human form divine and Peace the human dress;*
> *Then every man of every clime, that prays in his distress*
> *Prays to the human form divine, Love, Mercy, Pity, Peace.*
> *And all must love the human form, in heathen, Turk or Jew;*
> *Where Mercy, Love and Pity dwell, There God is dwelling too.*

Clearly Blake had no room for sectarian dogmas but accused established religion of fearing liberty, supporting restrictive laws and imposing punishments.

In *Holy Thursday* he denounces the hypocrisy of allowing the poor to live in misery and in *The Garden of Love* rejects the pretensions of organized religion who turn a garden into a cemetery where *..priests in black gowns were walking their rounds, and binding with briars my joys and desires"* and in *Jerusalem* devotes this poem "To the Deists."[14]

Another outstanding example of deism and in nineteenth century English literature was the great poet Percy Bysshe Shelley (1792-1822). Although he began his career as an atheist who was expelled from Oxford University because he distributed atheistic propaganda, he became a follower of Spinoza in his later years. Thus he believed in a Soul of the Universe and thought that the liberation of mankind from all evil could be achieved through love and faith. Since Shelley died at age 30 he was young all his life. Yet, his views changed somewhat after leaving Oxford. Shelley hated senseless conventions and therefore deserted his wife and children so as to live with Mary Godwin.[15]

His poetry was extensive and conveyed the belief that the liberation of mankind would be achieved by love and faith, not by ritual and obedience. At the close of his great poem *Prometheus Unbound* Shelley wrote:

> *To suffer woes which Hope thinks infinite; to forgive wrongs darker than death or night;*
> *To defy power which seems omnipotent; to love and bear; to hope till Hope creates from its own wreck the thing it contemplates; neither to change, nor falter nor repent; this like thy glory, Titan, is to be Good, great and joyous, beautiful and free; this is alone Life, Joy, Empire and Victory.*

This poem "celebrated the freeing of the human mind from the trammels of outmoded religious belief."[16]

Robert Burns (1759-1796), Scotland's greatest poet, kept up the attack on religious orthodoxy and hypocrisy. In "Holy Willie's Prayer", and in "Address to the Unco Guide or the Rigidly Righteous" he lambasted religious hypocrisy in part as follows: "O ye wha are sae guid yoursel, sae pious and sae holy, You've nought to do but mark and tell your neighbour's fauts and folly."[17]

Samuel Butler (1835-1902) lived through most of the nineteenth and into the twentieth century and used those years to make a severe attack upon organized religion. Son of a Church of England clergyman, Butler wrote "*The Evidence for the Resurrection of Jesus Christ .....Critically Examined,*" wherein he concluded that Jesus had not died on the cross. Best known for his autobiographical novel, *The Way of All Flesh*, Butler also found time to write a number of essays including *God and the Devil*.

In this irreverent essay Butler writes:

> "*God's merits are so transcendent that it is not surprising his faults should be in reasonable proportion. The faults are, indeed, on such a scale that, when looked at without relation to the merits with which they are interwoven, they become so appalling that people shrink from ascribing them to the Deity and have invented the Devil, without*

seeing that there would be more excuse for God's killing the Devil, and so getting rid of evil, than there can be for his failing to be everything that he would like to be."[18]

Subsequently, Matthew Arnold (1822-1888) attacked priests and piety in this poem : *"Man is blind because of sin, Revelation makes him sure; Without that, who looks within, looks in vain, for all's obscure. Nay, look closer into man! Tell me, can you find indeed Nothing sure, no moral plan clear prescribed without your creed? 'No I nothing can perceive! Without that all's dark for men. That or nothing I believe' -- For God's sake, believe it then!* [19]

In a similar manner wrote Algernon Swinburne (1837-1909) a British aristocrat, poet and essayist in *"God by god flits past in thunder, till his glories turn to shades; God to god bears wondering witness how his gospel flames and fades..........Dead are all of these, and man survives who made them while he dreamed."*

And in "The Altar of Righteousness" Swinbourne skewers the clergy in these words: *"Priests gazed upon God in the eyes of a babe new-born, and therein beheld not heaven, and the wise glad secret of love, but sin, accursed of heaven, and baptized with the baptism of hatred and hell."* There follows a long indictment of hypocrisy and lies and the sins of clergy contrasted with the pure religion Swinbourne saw in love and truth.[20]

Swinbourne became the object of derision and denunciation upon the publication of this and other poems in *Poems and Ballads* in 1866. And yet, this storm of protest was mild compared to the anger with which the great novelist and poet Thomas Hardy (1840-1928) was treated thirty years later. In 1891 Hardy had published his great novel *Tess of the D' Urbervilles* and in 1896 followed *Jude the Obscure.* Both books were denounced as pornographic and obscene. Yet, the thrust of these books was the frustration derived from injustice. Hardy became disgusted with the publication of novels which brought him not only fame but also vehement criticism and therefore he turned to poetry after publishing fourteen novels. A deist, but not an atheist, a mechanist but not a rationalist, Hardy refused to be included in the *Dictionary of Rationalists.*[21]

An example of his attitude towards the supernatural is found in this poem, called "The Impercipient": *"That with this bright believing band I have no right to be, That faiths by which my comrades stand seem fantasies to me, and mirage-mists their Shining Land, is a strange destiny.*[22]

Thus, at the beginning of the 20th century, when Alfred E. Housman (1859-1936) wrote *Laws,* secular writing and antagonism to religion had become so widespread and popular that these lines hardly raised any eyebrows or led to any protests. In fact, some lines from this poem have become so familiar to English speaking readers that they are quoted often even by those who do not know their origin and have never heard Housman's name.

Laws

The laws of God, the laws of man, he may keep that will and can;
Not I: let God and man decree laws for themselves and not for me:
and if my ways are not as theirs, let them mind their own affairs.
Their deeds I judge and much condemn, yet when did I make laws for them?
Please yourselves say I, and they need only look the other way.
But no, they will not; they must still wrest their neighbors to their will,
and make me dance as they desire with jail and gallows and hell fire.
And how am I to face the odds of man's bedevilment and God's?
I, a stranger and afraid in a world I never made.
They will be master, right or wrong; Though both are foolish, both are strong.
And since, my soul, we cannot fly to Saturn or to Mercury,
Keep we must, if keep we can, these foreign laws of God and man."[23]

Houseman lived well into the 20th century and expressed a view that was by then one hundred and fifty years old. Developed in England and popular by the end of the 1920's. English deism and agnosticism came across the ocean in the eighteenth century but was not then popular but the province of some intellectuals only. In the nineteenth century, philosophy, science and literature continued the crusade for deism not only in Europe but also in the U.S.A. where American writers perpetuated the attack on religiosity and superstition and helped mightily in creating the secular culture of the end of this century. This secular culture has of course affected all

Americans, not only Jewish Americans. An excellent example of this drive towards secularization of religion itself was the result of the telephone survey of American Catholics on April 21-23, 1994 which revealed that Marcel Dumestre, director of the Institute for Ministry at Loyola University of New Orleans, had good cause to say: "We are a church at risk."[24]

III.

We turn now to some major American writers who promoted deism and secularism in the United States. First among these is Nathaniel Hawthorne (1804-1864) whose description of Puritan life in both *The Scarlet Letter* and *The House of the Seven Gables* is an assault upon that fundamentalist life style even though no explicit criticism is made. Yet, the description of the practices of the Puritans and their need to persecute anyone with a different view can only be taken as a confrontation with the remnant of Puritanism still visible in America in Hawthorne's day and as late as 1995. Hawthorne's principal message in these and other books was to convey to the reader an understanding of the sin of pride and arrogance.[25]

Far more direct in his criticism of religion and his proclamation of agnosticism was the great American poet Edgar Allen Poe (1809-1849).

Shortly before his death, Poe published a long essay in 1848 called *Eureka*. This essay seeks to describe the material and spiritual universe and discusses Poe's doctrine of immortality. According to Poe, "God is but the perfection of matter". Poe evidently knew that many of his "scientific" theories were not true and could not be proved. Therefore he wrote at the end the preface to *Eureka* that "It is as a poem only that I wish this work to be judged after I am dead."[26] By writing *Eureka* Poe "proves himself an entirely non-Christian deist."[27]

This work contains many foolish notions which would not be viewed with approval by any 1990's scientists. Despite the numerous scientific errors made by Poe he nevertheless succeeded in conveying his undoubted agnostic views to the reader. Again we find that Poe was also a deist, that he rejected the Christian trinity, that he was nevertheless not an atheist. "In the beginning," writes Poe, "we can admit, indeed we can comprehend but one *First Cause*, the truly ultimate principle, the volition of God."[28]

The American novelist William Dean Howells (1837-1920) describes several nineteenth century American writers in his *Literary Friends and Acquaintance*. First published in 1900, this volume gives the reader a good deal of insight into the religious beliefs of some of the writers Howells describes and is therefore a particularly good source for viewing the attitudes of these writers because Howells was himself an important literary man.[29]

The poet James Russell Lowell (1819-1891) was well known to Howells as they were neighbors in Cambridge, Mass. Said Howells of Lowell: "As we were passing Longfellow's house, in mid-street, he came as near the declaration of his religious faith as he ever did in my presence." Howells shows that Lowell had liberated himself from all creeds and that "all religious formulation bored him." Thus, although Lowell had written some poems which seemed to assert a belief in providence and even a God who "declares vengeance His and will repay men for their evil deeds and will right the weak against the strong." Despite these assertions, Lowell was evidently uncertain as to any "moral government of the universe" and rejected the notion of life after death.[30]

Samuel Clemens (1835-1910), who used the "pen name" Mark Twain, was an agnostic. Howells describes Clemens at length in his essay "My Mark Twain" and shows that Clemens declared that "Christianity had done nothing to improve morals and conditions." Clemens thought that the world was as well off under the pagan civilizations of the past as under Christians and that Clemens was happy to have "broken the shackles of belief worn for so long." Clemens admired Robert Ingersoll (1833-1899) who was undoubtedly the most prolific and influential promoter of "free thought" in the nineteenth century and with him denied the existence of "hell", leading to a controversy which was carried in the newspapers of that day. Although Clemens attended a church for some years he later ceased to be a formal Christian and denied immortality of the soul. "All his expressions to me," says Howells, "were of a courageous renunciation of any hope of living again or elsewhere seeing those he had lost."

Clemens did assert that the universe could not have come about by chance but he never subscribed to the existence of a divinity and left that issue to speculation.[31]

IV.

In the course of the early nineteenth century there developed in America a literary movement called "transcendentalism." This view, as we have already seen, was taught by Immanuel Kant in that he held that ultimate reality can never be known to humans.

In the view of its practitioners and followers there is an essential unity between nature and God reminiscent of the teachings of Spinoza. Those American authors, such as Emerson and Thoreau, Alcott, Melville and Whitman, who wrote from the transcendental point of view, encouraged individualism and self-expression. Some of these writers participated in the publication of a journal called "Dial" and in the operation of "Brook Farm" where they sought to combine work with thinking while practicing an egalitarian economics.[32]

Although this experiment failed for financial reasons, it is important to this discussion that transcendental writers promoted "the secular and equalitarian ideology of the (American) revolution." The outcome of this kind of writing was the encouragement of such reforms as free public education, local autonomy, universal suffrage. "Transcendentalism" teaches that morals cannot be derived only from personal habit or private whim but must be derived from a higher ethic. Nevertheless, "transcendentalist" writers reduced God to a universal human principle and held that each individual needs to judge for himself what his actual obligations may be in any given situation. All this was sustained by the belief that secular reason as developed by natural science must be the final arbiter of human action. The eventual outcome of all this, according to the writers in this tradition, was the hoped for control of nature itself for the satisfaction of human needs.[33]

In sum, we have here the most developed argument for a secular society in America, an argument which persists to the end of the twentieth century and has permeated American thinking for 150 years.

Thus, "Self- reliance" became the motto of individualism in America as Emerson wrote in his essay by that name: "It is easy in the world to live after the world's opinion; it is easy in solitude to live after our own, but the great man is he who, in the midst of the crowd, keeps with perfect sweetness the independence of solitude."[34]

After Emerson and his followers, innumerable American writers continued to produce literature in that tradition so that the consequences of the "transcendentalist" movement for American secularization cannot be overestimated.

It is of course a fact that throughout the nineteenth century and at least the first quarter of the twentieth century the vast majority of Americans had either not read nor heard of these writers or viewed them as "atheists" and in a negative light. This was the case because Americans were mainly small town Calvinist Protestant natives or they belonged to that huge wave of immigrants who came here after the Civil War and who were principally traditional Catholics or orthodox Jews.

There was however one man who was very well known to almost anyone who could read anything. That man was Robert Green Ingersoll, a lawyer and public orator who was born in 1833 and died in 1899. Undoubtedly the most vehement proponent of agnosticism in America he not only called attention to his cause during his life time which covered the nineteenth century but he also left behind twelve volumes of lectures, discussions, interviews as well as political and legal documents. All this was published in 1900 and in 1911 a biography of Ingersoll was added to these volumes which are influential to this day, the end of the twentieth century, not because they contain very many original or new ideas but because they popularized the secularist point of view as no other literature has done. The interest in the work of Ingersoll has continued far beyond his death as evidenced by a 1969 bibliography concerning not only the works of Ingersoll himself but articles, books and pamphlets about Ingersoll. At that time this list numbered 631 items.[35]

Ingersoll, the son of a Protestant minister, became famous because of the speech he gave at the Republican convention in 1876 nominating James G. Blaine for the presidency. Thereafter he lectured throughout the country on such topics as "The Truth About the Holy Bible," "Bible Idolatry," "Blasphemy," "The Clergy and Common Sense," "The Christian Religion," and others.

The principle message Ingersoll sought to convey in speeches and in writing were a plea for absolute freedom of thought, that religion must relinquish its dominant position to science and that he merely expressed the ideas of thousands of people not as articulate as he was. In that claim he was undoubtedly right, for as we shall see, the developments of the 20th century provide sufficient proof for this thesis.

Ingersoll became the principle American proponent of Darwin's ideas so that Walt Whitman commented that the Englishman Huxley and the American Ingersoll could together "unhorse the whole Christian giant."[36]

It was Darwin, the theory of evolution and a host of other scientific discoveries which led Ingersoll to write: "....the Garden of Eden is an ignorant myth." In this view he was supported by at least three quarters of the Harvard faculty which subscribed to "The Apostate's Creed" in these terms:

> *"I believe in a chaotic Nebula, self-existent, evolver of heaven and earth, and in the differentiation of the original homogeneous mass, its first-begotten product, which was self formed into separate worlds, divided into land and water, self organized into plants and animals, reproduced into like species, rationalized and perfected in man. He descended from the monkey, ascended to the philosopher, and sitteth down in the rights and customs of civilization under the laws of developing sociology. From thence he shall come again by the disintegration of the heterogenized cosmos back to the original homogeneousness of chaos.*
>
> *I believe in the wholly impersonal absolute, the wholly uncatholic church, the disunion of saints, the survival of the fittest, the persistency of force, the dispersion of the body and in death everlasting."*[37]

Subscribers to this creed pointed to the evidence Darwin had accumulated concerning the utter neutrality of nature. Nature, it had been shown, has no feelings but operates according to inexorable laws. Said Ingersoll: *"They point to the sunshine, to the flowers, to the April rain, and to all there is of beauty and of use in the world. Did it occur to them that a cancer is as beautiful in its development as is the reddest nose?"*

Ingersoll never tired of listing the innumerable scientific achievements the nineteenth century had produced and insisted that science and religion could not exist in the same society nor in the same mind. "An honest God is the noblest work of Man," said Ingersoll and horrified believers in an Absolute God by this paraphrase from Pope. Ingersoll was as convinced of the truth of his message that science is the salvation of man as were the religionists of his day and of our day.

At the end of the twentieth century, however, the evidence is that science is not only a great contributor to the happiness of man but also a great destroyer. This is an aspect of science which Ingersoll did not understand in part because he did not live long enough to see the horrors of the First World War, let alone the atomic bomb and other nightmares invented in scientific laboratories.

There were of course innumerable other writers in the second half of the nineteenth century and in the twentieth century in America who followed Ingersoll. A bibliography of such writers would include hundreds of books, pamphlets, newspaper accounts, journal articles and speeches. It would   include Paul Blanchard and Harry Elmer Barnes, Madelyn Murray O'Hair and Clarence Darrow, William Floyd and Corliss Lamont. As the agnostic movement gained momentum various organizations   published journals such as *The Humanist* to promote the cause of secularization.[38]

Among novelists Herman Melville (1819-1891) can hardly be ignored as a contributor to the secularization of American literature. He was a slightly older contemporary of Robert Ingersoll and his life also spanned most of the 19th century. Melville is without doubt one of the most important and best known American authors. His most famous novel is *Moby Dick,* although his other works, such as *Billy Budd, Omoo* and *Typee* are masterpieces of writing as well. In all of these books Melville exhibits the influence of his early education in Christianity. However, in all of his books he also shows his disappointment with the teachings of established churches, a disappointment which becomes severe criticism of religion in *Pierre or the Ambiguities* which he wrote in 1851-1852. In his earlier novels, *Typee* and *Omoo,* Melville had already unleashed some criticism of Christian missionaries. In *Moby Dick* there is a denial of the goodness of God.[39]

In *Pierre* Melville first portrays his *"contempt for the spinelessness of the clergy."* Melville even reviews the commandment requiring that men honor their father and their mother and asks:..........*should I honor my father if I knew him to be a seducer.?* Melville also argued that no man would try to live by heavenly standards and that it can be dangerous for man to be guided only by spiritual standards.[40]

Melville had been a Christian in his youth and continued to be one from his point of view. However, he reduced the divine commandments found in the Bible to what he called "virtuous expediency" and claimed that God required no more of man than that. Turning to the history of Christianity, Melville wrote:

> *"But if any man say that such a doctrine as I lay down is false, is impious; I would charitably refer that man to the history of Christendom for the last 1800 years; and ask him, whether, in spite of all the maxims of Christ, that history is not just as full of blood, violence, wrong and iniquity of every kind, as any previous portion of the world's story? Therefore, it follows, that so far as practical results are concerned-regarded in a purely earthly light- the only great original moral doctrine of Christianity ....gratuitous return of good for evil ....has been found a false one; because after 1800 years inculcation from tens of thousands of pulpits, it has proved entirely impracticable.* "[41]

Thus, Melville contributed mightily to the ever rising crescendo of deism in America. The evidence for that is not only his literary legacy. It is also that the public was very much displeased with Melville and that his reviewers called him *"immoral, irreligious and even insane.* "[42]

It was however the American author Sinclair Lewis (1885-1951), who won the Nobel Prize in 1930, who succeeded in finally emancipating American literature. His successors in American literature were such great and famous writers as Eugene O'Neill, Theodore Dreiser, Pearl S. Buck, T.S. Eliot, William Faulkner, Ernest Hemingway, John Steinbeck, Saul Bellow and Isaac Bashevich Singer. This means that since literature reflects social conditions and the beliefs of millions who do not write, it can well be said that Americans in general achieved a degree of emancipation from puritan strictures in the twentieth century which are reflected in the works of those just listed and a host of others such as Thornton Wilder, Sherwood Anderson, Michael Gold, John Dos Passos, William Faulkner and Thomas Wolfe. Among the lyricists of the age who had an equal influence and equally reflect this emancipation are Carl Sandburg, Robert Frost, William Carlos Williams, Ezra Pound and T.S. Eliot. Clifford Odets, John Howard Lawson, Maxwell Anderson and Elmer Rice should be added as representatives of the dramatic art.

Since novelists and short story writers have always dominated American literature it is important to pay attention to such authors and Sinclair Lewis and Theodore Dreiser who wrote after the First World War and participated in the end of isolationism. Particularly Lewis and Dreiser were the first to criticize American traditions and *taboos* by exposing the life styles and feelings of exactly those Americans who had heretofore always been seen as the supporters of *The American Way of Life*. Sinclair Lewis dealt with the American middle class whose entire life was concentrated upon business and the chase after *the almighty dollar*.

This theme becomes visible in *The Man from Main Street* but finds final expression in *Babbitt*, a word which is not only the title of Sinclair Lewis's book but which has become a concept in the American language. Already in *Main Street* Lewis concludes that the dollar sign has replaced the crucifix everywhere. In *Babbitt* Lewis describes a small town he calls *Zenith*. Here the dollar is the measurement of all things. The dollar rules over human relations and even the inner life of everyone. Material possessions are signs of power, influence and prestige for Babbitt and his fellow citizens. Even religion is a business in Zenith as Lewis displays the minister who describes his religion as: "Sort of Christianity Incorporated, you might say."[43]

The type of car a driver can afford becomes the surest sign of wealth as in the twentieth century, according to Lewis, the social position of an American family is determined by their car. "In the city of Zenith, in the barbarous twentieth century, a family's motor indicated its social rank as precisely as the grades of the peerage determined the rank of an English family -indeed more precisely"[44]

Lewis also shows how the very middle class *Babbitts*, pride themselves as the protectors of American rights and freedoms, and yet are utterly incapable of dealing with any outsider or non-conformist. "I know of no American novel," wrote H.L. Mencken, "that more accurately presents the real America. It is a social document of a higher order."[45]

While *Babbitt* earned Lewis a few compliments from a few Americans it led to a stream of angry attacks upon him from almost every source. He was called a traitor, his work was called a lie and he was defamed in every conceivable fashion. Yet, even these attacks were mild if compared to the outburst which greeted Lewis upon publication of his novel *Elmer Gantry* in 1927. These threats even included a threat to lynch him. This novel displays a revival preacher who becomes ever more successful as he becomes more corrupt, hypocritical and cynical. Religion is displayed as outstandingly bad and intolerable. The "faithful" are shown as fools as Lewis held them in unconstrained contempt. Thus, the book begins with the sentence: "Elmer Gantry was drunk" and continues with a portrait of religion as popular in the America of the 1920's as in the America of the 1990's. This is not to say that Lewis does not also portray other types of clergy besides the hypocrite Gantry.

However, the conclusion is inescapable. Lewis meant to deliver a blow to organized religion and he succeeded as no other American novelist had done before him unless it was Theodore Dreiser (1871-1945), his older contemporary whose book *Sister Carrie* was censored and withdrawn from circulation.[46]

Theodore Dreiser was a professed agnostic. The word *profess* is used deliberately here because it is derived directly from the Latin words for declaring something in public.

Theodore Dreiser was the twelfth of thirteen children of a Catholic family. In the course of his career he wrote several auto-biographical books, including *A Traveler at Forty*, *A Hoosier Holiday*, *A Book About Myself* and *Dawn*. In 1943 he also wrote an essay entitled *"The Salve Called Religion"* which he defined several times and which he viewed with great skepticism despite his Catholic heritage.

"It, (Religion) is a dread of dissolution and a desire for continuance , with the dream and even hope of some method of achieving it. It has allied with itself structures, forms codes, vestments, and unsubstantiated assertions, all based on the above reactions. And all slowly either vanishing or being transformed into their proper qualities of values or lack of values by the progress of exact and unbiased science."

Elsewhere, Dreiser writes: *"In all times and in all places religion must be entirely freed of ulterior and extraneous aims. It should not pile up wealth. Its ministers and priests should by no means live luxuriously. There is no need of dogma or special revelation ...."*[47]

Dreiser was of course severely criticized by those whose interests were religious orthodoxy. In addition however, Dreiser's book *The Genius* was cited by the New York Society for the Suppression of Vice and became a hotly debated issue after its publication in 1913. The "Genius" is autobiographical as are others of Dreiser's works. This book deals with a bad marriage and includes some sexual material which evidently offended the censors of the early century. It was however Dreiser's earlier novel, *Jennie Gerhardt,* which contains his most outspoken belief in fate as the principal determinant of man's life. Here one of his characters says: "*It isn't myself that's important in this transaction apparently; the individual doesn't count much in the situation. I don't know whether you see what I'm driving at, but all of us are more or less pawns. We're moved about like chessmen by circumstances over which we have no control.* "[48] Fatalism is of course the enemy of religion. For who needs rituals, prayers and a clergy if fate has already decided the lives of men. This is an age-old dispute and dilemma which has no resolution. However, a novelist who supports fate supports secularism and agnosticism and even atheism despite the evidence that Americans have, at the end of the 20th century, embraced agnostic deism coupled with a big dosage of individualism and entrepreneurial initiative. Americans are seldom fatalists. But fatalists must be irreligious by the very definition of that attitude.

Although *An American Tragedy* is a murder story, Dreiser uses that novel as a means of showing how the "American Dream" creates crime. The crux of the story is that a young man is driven to murder precisely because American society demands that one succeeds financially and socially. Hence this very demand creates the pressure to do anything at all to gain advancement, be that sharp dealings in business, marriage to someone in a higher social class or anything else. In effect, Dreiser uses a different vehicle than Lewis to exhibit the hypocrisy of blocked opportunities and "stifling moralism."[49] Thus, Dreiser teaches that American society has no standards and no values other than wealth, ease and social position. If that is true, and many indicators support this view, then materialism is the sole measure of all things American and crime, poverty, mental illness, divorce, alcoholism, drug addiction, delinquency, suicide and cruelty the price Americans have agreed to pay for the goods the god Mammon can provide.

Sister Carrie, another of Dreiser's novels, earned the criticism of the moralists when it was published in 1902 as did almost everything Dreiser ever wrote.

There is at the University of Pennsylvania library an unpublished manuscript by Dreiser called *A Confession of Faith.* Here Dreiser lists nine beliefs which guided his life. It is obvious from these nine statements that Dreiser had repudiated religion and become a thoroughgoing secularist, naturalist, realist and agnostic. Nature had become his god as he spoke of a "Creative Force" and his respect for it.

In 1945 Dreiser joined the Communist Party in a letter reprinted in the *Daily Worker* of July 30 that year. Thus he confirmed in his life and in his writings that for him, at least, the supernatural was no more and that *man had become the measure of all things.* [50]

V.

Jewish-American literature is now only about one century old if we include that literature which was written in Yiddish by immigrants between 1885 and 1935. That, however, would have little bearing on our subject, i.e., the secularization of the American Jewish community, because Yiddish is hardly used in America at the end of the 20th century so that anything foreign except some of the works of Goethe and Voltaire has no influence on the American Jew simply because he cannot read it.

That is not to say that Yiddish writers were not radicals and secularists. On the contrary. From the time of the first volume of Yiddish poetry published in America in 1877 to the end of the Yiddish era in about 1975, Jewish-American writers always exhibited a strong interest in radical and hence secular ideas. Yiddish writers expressed themselves in poetry, in the theater, in novels, in newspapers and in intellectual books, papers and pamphlets. Throughout these five media ran, for the most part, a secular attitude most visible in the novel.

The first Jewish novels written in America were written by immigrants. This was true, not because there were no Jews here before the last two decades of the nineteenth century, but because those Jews who had come here before 1881 were very few, had arrived in the 17th century from Spain and Portugal and in the nineteenth century from Germany and had rapidly assimilated the majority American culture. However, 1881 marked a major turning point in Jewish history. On March 1 of that year the Russian Czar, Alexander II, was assassinated. When his son, Alexander III, ascended the Russian throne persecution of the Jews became the policy of the Russian government and led to the prompt immigration of millions of Jews to America. These millions of Jews spoke Yiddish so that it is not at all surprising that the first American Jewish writers included in that migration wrote in that language.[51]

Thus, the Jewish writers of that day brought European Jewishness to America. Among these was Morris Winshevsky who promoted socialism but had very little Jewish content in his poetry. Instead, Winshevsky was a follower of the Jewish enlightenment, called *Haskalah,* a movement with a distinct secular emphasis. In fact, Winshevsky represented the revolt against religion at the end of the 19th century when he wrote: "*For me....my disbelief and hatred toward all faiths reached a high point of fanaticism.....My greatest delight was to prove that Moses did not write the Pentateuch, that Joshuah did not cause the heavens to stand still.*"

There were of course innumerable other authors but only a few stand out as major contributors to Yiddish writing in the U.S.A. There was Morris Rosenfeld, prime representative of the so-called "sweatshop" poets, who reflected the Jewish radicalism of his day. That radicalism was the reaction to the misery of living in immigrant slums, of the exploitation of the Jewish workers, and the desperation of the Jewish masses. It was a radicalism which rejected the religion of Europe and sought to rely on the politics of this world instead. Although Rosenfeld was translated into English, his following in the English language was only temporary so that his fame rests finally on the Yiddish following he was able to attract. He too was an agnostic.[52]

The most important Yiddish writer of the early twentieth century however, was Abraham Cahan. Although he spoke Yiddish better than English, Cahan succeeded in publishing *The Chosen People* and *The Rise of David Levinsky* in English in 1917. This book has been called "*the most important novel written by a Jewish immigrant*". In it Levinsky becomes an American millionaire at the cost of his Jewish heritage and upon first becoming a thoroughgoing secularist. "Spencer and Darwin replace the Torah, Dickens and Thackeray the Talmud." Cahan depicts the emptiness of Levinsky's life despite his rise to money and fame.[53]

Other American Jewish writers who wrote in the Yiddish or the English idiom were Sidney Nyburg, Anzela Yezierska, James Oppenheim, Samuel Ornitz and Ludwig Lewisohn who was born in the United States, the son of German Jewish immigrants. All these dealt with the fate of the immigrants. All of these rejected religion and sought to show how pragmatism and realism were far superior in solving man's problems than belief in anything supernatural.

During the depression of the 1930's American Jewish writers, now mostly born in the U.S.A., were very much affected by the discontinuity of European Judaism with American Judaism. Except for the 1978 Nobel prize winner in literature Isaac Bashevich Singer, who was born in Poland in 1904, these writers all wrote in English. Singer, although he wrote in Yiddish, was published in English so that his work is known to almost all Americans in the latter idiom.

Except for Ludwig Lewisohn and Meyer Levin, who defended Jewishness if not Judaism, these writers all rejected Jewish tradition. Instead, these writers leaned toward the political "left" and viewed their Jewishness as a secular condition. Nelson Algren in *Somebody in Boots,* Albert Halper in *The Foundry*, Isadore Schneider in *From the Kingdom of Necessity* and many others viewed socialism as the answer to the Jewish problem both here and abroad and disdained religion entirely. Demanding a future free of tradition writers such as Michael Gold in *Jews Without Money,* or Charles Reznikoff in *By the Waters of Manhattan* all believe that Marxism, not Judaism, is the inevitable answer to the degradations and hardships of the immigrant slums.

The writer Paul Goodman, whom the historian Irving Howe called a "Jewish intellectual alienated to the point of complete reduction," thought that the fellowship of all humans is enhanced by the Jewish tradition and that the fully Jewish is regarded as the fully human. Judaism as a religion or as a separate experience is hardly credited by Goodman.

Added to these novelists there were in the first part of the 20th century Jewish theologians who also strove to distance theology from the European tradition. Kaufman Kohler, a reform Rabbi wrote *Jewish Theology Systematically and Historically Considered* in 1918 and in 1934 Rabbi Mordecai Kaplan, a representative of the conservative movement in Judaism published his monumental *Judaism as a Civilization.*

Not only did these rabbis disconnect American Judaism from European Judaism, they also redefined the God concept. Thus, Kaplan presents God as "a chronologically variable social idea," or as a "struggling ordering force of nature."[54]

Thus, after the second world war, i.e., after 1945, a vast number of Jewish - American writers inundated the literature of the United States and have kept this up until the end of the century.

A list of all the American - Jewish writers who have contributed to American literature since 1945 cannot be presented here. It is far too long and would involve a discussion of a whole social movement with far reaching consequences for American culture. Some of the most prominent names among American-Jewish fiction writers are of course Saul Bellow, Bernard Malamud, Tillie Olson, Grace Paley, Cynthia Ozick, Herbert Gold, Joseph Heller, E.L. Doctorow, Stanley Elkin, Hugh Nissensen and Phillip Roth.

The works of Phillip Roth are undoubtedly excellent examples of the rejection of traditional Judaism already exhibited by the Yiddish writers a generation earlier. Like their non-Jewish contemporaries and predecessors, Jewish writers in the last half of the 20th century have contributed a great deal to the secularization of America and Jewish life as well as they created a distinction between Judaism and Jewishness which their grandparents never knew and which has become the Great Divide within the Jewish community in the twentieth century.

In 1933, when Phillip Roth was born, mass immigration to the United States had come to an end and Jewish immigration, mostly from Germany, was small and involved many newcomers already secularized by their German environment. Numerous Yiddish writers and the philosophical, scientific and literary world in America had secularized at least the academic world and in particular such institutions as the University of Chicago, where Roth was a student and where American sociology was created.

Like thousands of other Jews who came of age in the '30's, Roth entered into the world of higher education where the challenges to Judaism or any religion were already embedded in the curriculum. And since, as we have seen, over eighty percent of Jews of college age attend an institution of higher education and have done so for half a century, they, like Roth, found every reason to divorce Judaism from Jewishness and discard "the faith of our fathers."

Many of the Jewish writers with Roth in the forefront now opposed their Jewish heritage and treated it with contempt, disdain and calumny. In fact, since Roth wrote *Good-Bye, Columbus* in 1959 "there are those who still grit their teeth, hoping that the irreverent, satirical Mr. Roth will go away."[55]

Roth, of course, did to the Jewish world what non-Jewish writers had already done to the Christian world for a century. He secularized the sacred. He ridiculed the divine. He insulted the tradition and he vulgarized his "in-group." Thus, Roth, and so many other Jewish - American writers, contributed mightily, not only to the secularization of Judaism and America in general, but also to the de-mystification of the Jewish tradition. This means that both for non-Jews and for Americans of Jewish origins who had left the tradition behind, Roth provides insight into 20th century Jewish life as it is lived each day. He explains what is important to contemporary American Jews. He shows that Judaism is not one of the important ideas in the lives of American Jews but that Jews have substituted membership in clubs and organizations for membership in synagogues. Roth further claims that synagogues and rabbis are themselves secular institutions at the end of the century, that Jewish ritual emphasizes financial display as in Bar Mitzvahs and weddings and that the Jewish community in America is governed by the same type of business interests which Sinclair Lewis described governing the Christian community exhibited and shown over and over again in *Babbitt.*[56]

No doubt it is *Portnoy's Complaint,* however, which Roth wrote in 1969, that led to the accusations that Roth is a Jewish anti-semite, a self hater and a self promoter. This book, which attacks the stereotypical Jewish mother, recites at length and in detail the sexual problems of the protoganist. It has been labeled "pornographic" for good reason and was truly "shocking" on first coming to public attention. Now, at the end of the century, nothing else will shock anyone any more. Dreiser and Lewis and their companions also shocked Americans. But by the time Roth began to write, the only means of gaining the readers' attention among all the competing writers was to do something yet more extreme than what had already been done before the second world war. Merely proclaiming ones disbelief in orthodox theology was no longer necessary since, as we have seen, innumerable writers in philosophy, science and literature had already made secularization a most popular attitude. Roth and his contemporaries, particularly his Jewish companions, sought to now attack the core of Jewishness as they understood it. This Jewishness, in the hands of these writers, consists of being "raving hysterics", nagging "Jewish mothers," and female shrews of every variety. Thus, the popular Jewish writers in the tradition of Roth were accused of being Jewish "anti-semites", producers of filth and self - hatred and conveyors of the same calumnies which the Jews of the old world endured for so long.

Roth has rejected all of these complaints in an essay he wrote for *Commentary* in 1963. Roth argues there that his Jewish characters who are inevitably less than admirable, are never meant to represent all Jews or even a large number. To Roth, each story he wrote, refers only to the one person described and without any further implications. Yet, Roth himself quotes a letter he received after the publication of his story "Defenders of the Faith," which says in part.".......With your one story, 'Defenders of the Faith', you have done as much harm as all the organized anti-Semitic organizations have done to make people believe that all Jews are cheats, liars and connivers." Roth writes that he was even accused of legitimizing the murder of six million European Jews by stories which, he does not deny,. vilify Jews. Yet, his argument is that those who see these things in his stories do not understand them and that it is submission to anti-Semitism to *not* write about subjects which depict Jews as human beings, i.e., sinners, fools, adulterers, cowards and connivers.

Now Roth has always argued that fiction and reality are different. He did so again in 1987 in *The Counterlife* and seeks thereby to escape responsibility for what are clearly attacks on Jewishness and Judaism. To Roth Jewish identity cannot be taken for granted. It is always in question as seen once more in his latest effort called *Operation Shylock (1993).*

Roth holds that it is "timidity and paranoia" for American Jews to object to his stories about Jewish failure and Jewish moral weakness. He will not accede to the common Jewish view that a Jew must never talk about negative Jewish traits to non-Jews. Roth rejects that anti-Jewish conduct can result from his negative stories about Jews. Referring to a complaining rabbi, Roth writes: "Can he actually believe that on the basis of my story anyone is going to start a pogrom, or keep a Jew out of medical school, or even call a Jewish school child a 'kike'?"[57]

Although it is indeed true that one author cannot provoke a "pogrom" it is also true that those who like to set quotas on Jews in medical schools or call children ethnic names can easily feel themselves justified in that kind of persecution by using a story by Roth.

More important is that Roth and his followers have legitimized the distancing of Jews from Judaism and the Jewish tradition and have in that sense contributed immensely to the secularization of Judaism in the United Sates.[58]

This may be said of Roth despite the fact that in "Eli the Fanatic" Roth exposes the boorishness of many modern American Jews who find even the survivors of the Holocaust irrelevant in their anxiety to avoid being identified with Jews dressed in the black garb of the Chassidim and speaking with a distinct accent.

VI.

This then leads us to consider one more aspect to American -Jewish writing which is unique to Jews and has been very influential in promoting secularization in the Jewish community at the end of the twentieth century. That is the fiction and the historiography of the holocaust. This writing has led to the phenomenon in the Jewish community of literally substituting holocaust memorial activities for Judaism so that for many otherwise utterly secular Jews ceremony and ritual surrounding the holocaust has become their religion. This phenomenon was instigated by holocaust writers, both fictional and non -fictional. The second way in which holocaust literature has influenced secularization is raised by those who question whether a God can exist in a world which permits such horrors.[59]

Foremost among these writers is Elie Wiesel. Although of a Yiddish speaking background Wiesel has made a name for himself in both French and English. When "Night" was first translated from the French and published in America in 1960 it opened the door to a wide range of such literature thereafter.[60]

It is true that Chaim Grade had already published "My Quarrel With Hersh Rasseyner" in 1951, but that book was written in Yiddish and only later became available in English. Grade deals with one question in his book. The question is: "How can one believe in God after the Holocaust?" Grade renounces religion and belief in God. Saul Bellow, however, in *Mr. Sammler's Planet* describes in detail the horrors of the Holocaust experience but reaches the conclusion that God does exist and "*nihilism is denied.*"[61]

Many Jews have answered Grade's question by renouncing traditional religion and placing their emotions into "holocausting" which refers not only to attendance at various commemorative events, but also refers to financial contributions to the Washington D.C. holocaust museum, the Los Angeles based "Wiesenthal Center," and other such efforts to remember the mass murders of the second world war. This means in practice that it is much easier for commemorative organizations to raise money concerning the past than it is for Jewish educational institutions to raise funds for the propagation of Judaism among the young.

Jerzy Kosinski in *The Painted Bird,* Bernard Malamud in *The Fixer,* and Saul Bellow's *Mr Sammler's Planet* all deal with the issue of how the immigrant survivor can deal with his past and his future.

There are many additional Jewish-American fiction writers who have concerned themselves with the Holocaust. The work of Cynthis Ozick, Hugh Nissenson, Richard Elman, Zdena Berger, Norma Rosen, Isaac B. Singer, Joshuah Singer and Daniel Stern are only a small example of all that has been written and is still being produced concerning that heinous crime.

There is also an ever growing non-fiction literature concerning the Holocaust. Best known among these is Lucy Dawidowicz who has received the most attention among historians for her book *The War Against the Jews, 1933-1945* (1975) although Nora Levin, writing in *The Holocaust* in 1968 was far more detailed in her description of the events collectively so labeled than was Dawidowicz. There is also the book by Hilberg called *The Destruction of the European Jews* and more recently *The Holocaust* by Gilbert.

In addition to these major histories there are innumerable other works dealing with the holocaust such as oral histories, psycho-social analyses, memoirs and diaries. This literature is increasing as the years since that crime go on. Each of these many publications raises the questions anew. Is there a God? Is religion meaningless? Can one be a Jew by showing an interest in that terrible Jewish experience? The memorializing of the holocaust has yet one more dimension for the vast majority of American Jews who never experienced those horrors. It gives the native American Jewish population a pseudo-martyr status. American Jews, fortunately ignorant of what is really meant by the word "Holocaust" and not really willing to listen to the first hand accounts of survivors, enjoy the victim status some assume when these nightmares are discussed in public. This kind of stance is evident during the large Holocaust commemorations which secular American Jewish "leaders" like to stage in full view of television cameras and other media coverage. These events are generally chaired by some one known as a "great contributor." Such a personage addresses the crowd and the cameras and creates the impression, at least in his eyes, that he is somehow a victim. In the victim oriented American society at the end of the 20th century, this stance is sought after and prestigious and achieved by making large financial contributions. All that in face of living holocaust survivors who, by reason of their general poverty, are often ignored because they have neither the education nor the finesse to make a convincing television appearance. Thus, even the Holocaust and all that implies, has become banal and absurd in the hands of those who cannot understand that such overused phrases as "the Jews went to their deaths like sheep", are false and nonsense. Even worse is the effort on the part of some native American Jews, and a good number of non-Jews, to trivialize the Holocaust by comparing it to the bombing of Dresden, the use of the atomic bomb on Hiroshima and Nagasaki or the innumerable slaughters that have taken place since 1945 in every part of the world. All of that is the consequence of the perceived need to compete for victim status in a world so secularized that even the most incomprehensible of human experiences is categorized as an occasion to gain status and prestige.[62]

VII.

It is neither possible nor necessary to review the preponderance of philosophy, scientific thought or western Literature here in order to show how all of these developments have influenced American and hence Jewish-American secularization in this century. It suffices to show by the foregoing examples that at the end of the 20th century the secular point of view is most popular in the United States.

We now need to show what institutional developments followed the philosophical, scientific and literary abstractions which were known to a few at the end of the nineteenth century but are the common assumption of Americans, Christian, Jewish or agnostic at the end of the twentieth century. The next chapter will serve that purpose.

NOTES

[1]Voltaire was born as Francois Marie Arouet.
[2]Fritz Mauthner, *Der Atheismus und seine Geschichte im Abendlande,* Stuttgart, Deutsche Verlags Anstalt, 1923, Vol. 3, p. 44.
[3]*Ibid.,* pp. 44-57.
[4]Mauthner, *op.cit.,* p. 48.
[5]Mauthner, *op.cit.* vol. 4, p.78. "Ich aber bete den an , der eine solche Produktionskraft in die Welt gelegt hat, dass, wenn nur der millionste Teil davon ins Leben tritt, die Welt von Geschöpfen wimmelt, so dass Krieg, Pest, Wasser und Brand ihr nichts anzuhaben vermögen. Das ist mein Gott."
[6]*Ibid.* p.79 "Wer Wissenschaft und Kunst besitzt, der hat auch Religion."
[7]English translation and paraphrasing by the author.
[8]Edward Gibbon, *The History of the Decline and Fall of the Roman Empire*, London, Methuen & Co., 1896-1902.
[9]*Ibid.,* Vol. II, p. 469.
[10]Shelley T. McCloy, *Gibbon's Antagonism to Christianity,* Chapel Hill, The University of North Carolina Press,1933 p.23.
[11]Gibbon, *op.cit.,* Vol. II, p. 92.
[12]McCloy, *op.cit.,*pp.35-32.
[13]Gordon H. Gerould, Richard Foster Jones and Ernest Bernbaum, eds. *Romantic Literature,* New York, The Ronald Press Co., 1943, pp. 14-15.
[14]*Ibid.,* pp.17-20.
[15]*op.cit. p.490.*
[16]"Introduction " in Percy Bysshe Shelley, *The Necessity of Atheism,* Buffalo, Prometheus Books, 1993, p. vi.
[17]Clarence Darrow and Wallace Rice, *Infidels and Heretics,* Boston, Mass., The Stratford Co., Publishers, 1929, pp. 130-132.
[18]Stanley J. Kunitz and Howard Haycraft, *British Authors of the Nineteenth Century,* New York, The H. W. Wilson Co., 1936, pp. 101-103.

[19]Darrow and Rice, *op.cit.,* p.109

[20]From: *The Storms of Time, Ibid,* p. 114.

[21]Kunitz and Haycraft, *op.cit.,* pp. 275-278.

[22]Darrow and Rice, *op.cit.,* p. 115.

[23]*Ibid.,* p.42.

[24]Peter Steinfels, "Picture of Faith Worries Catholic Leaders," *The New York Times,* June 1, 1994, pp. A 1 and B 8.

[25]George P. Lathrope, Ed., *The Complete Works of Nathaniel Hawthorne,* Boston, Riverside Edition, 1893.

[26] Robert E. Spiller ed., *Literary History of the United States,* New York, The Macmillan Co., 1963, p.336

[27]John M. Robertson, *A Short History of Freethought,* New York, Russell and Russell, 1957, p. 413.

[28]Harvey Allen, ed., *The Works of Edgar Allan Poe,* New York, P. F. Collier and Son, 1927, p. 848.

[29]William Dean Howells, *Literary Friends and Acquaintances,* Bloomington and London, Indiana University Press, 1968.

[30]*Ibid.,* p. 192.

[31]Howells, *op.cit.,* p. 274.

[32]Thomas A. Bailey, *The American Pageant,* Boston, D.C. Heath and Co., 1961, p. 346.

[33]Spiller, *op.cit.,* p348.

[34]Arthur Hobson Quinn, *The Literature of the American People,* New York, Appleton- Century- Crofts, 1951, p.284.

[35]Marshall G. Brown and Gordon Stein, *Freethought In the United States: A Descriptive Bibliography,* Westport, Conn., The Greenwood Press, pp. 50 and 64.

[36]C.H. Cramer, *Royal Bob: The Life of Robert G. Ingersoll,* New York, The Bob Merrill Co., 1952, p.124.

[37]*Ibid.,* pp.127-128

[38]Brown and Stein, *op.cit.pp..65-67.*

[39]Herman Melville, *Typee: A Peep at Polynesian Life, (1846); Omoo: A Narrative of Adventures in the South Sea,* (1847); *Pierre, or The Ambiguities, (1853);* Evanston, Ill, Northwestern University Press, 1968 and 1971. Also: *Moby Dick or The Whale,* New York, The Heritage Press, 1943 (1851).

[40]William Braswell, *Melville's Religious Thought: An Essay In Interpretation,* New York, Pageant Books, 1959, pp. 74-85.

[41]Melville, *op.cit. Pierre,* p.215.

[42]Braswell, *op.cit.,* p.85.

[43]Sinclair Lewis, *Babbitt,* New York, Harcourt, Brace & World, Inc., 1950, p. 212.

[44]*Ibid,* p.42

[45]H.L. Mencken," *Portrait of an American Citizen,"* in : Martin Bucco, Ed., *Critical Essays on Sinclair Lewis,* Boston, G.K. Hall & Co., 1986, pp.37-39.

[46]Sinclair Lewis, *Elmer Gantry,* New York, Harcourt, Brace and Co., 1927. See also: Charles F. Ferguson, *"Sinclair Lewis and Blasphemy,"* in: Martin Bucco, *op.cit.,* pp.47-48.

[47]Theodore Dreiser, *Notes on Life,* University, Alabama, The University of Alabama Press, 1974, pp.277-285.

[48]Donald Pizer, *The Novels of Theodore Dreiser: A Critical Study,* Minneapolis, The University of Minnesota Press, 1976, p. 119.

[49]*Ibid.,* p.219.

[50]*ibid., pp. 181, 262, 327 and 330.*

[51]Jesse D. Clarkson, *A History of Russia,* New York, Random House, 1961, p.338; Max L. Margolis and Alexander Marx, *A History of the Jewish People,* New York, The Jewish Publication Society of America, 1961, p. 691-701.

[52]Irving Howe, *World of Our Fathers,* New York, Simon and Schuster, 1976, p. 422.

[53]Lewis Fried, *Handbook of American-Jewish Literature* ,New York, Greenwood Press, 1988, p.16.

[54]*Ibid.,* p.37.

[55]Sanford Pinsker, "Introduction," , in *Critical Essays on Phillip Roth,* Boston, G.K. Hall & Co., 1982, p.1.

[56]Lewis, *op.cit.,* p. 212.

[57]Phillip Roth, "Writing about Jews," in: *Esssays on Jewish Life in America: The Ghetto and Beyond,* Peter I. Rose, Ed., New York, Random House, 1969, pp. 449-463.

[58]*Ibid.,* p. 464.

[59]Dorothy Seidman Bilik, "The Fiction of the Holocaust," in: Fried, *op.cit.,* pp.315-440.

[60]Elie Wiesel, *Night,* New York, Hill and Wang, 1960.
[61]Bonnie K. Lyones, "American-Jewish Fiction Since 1945", in: Friedman *op.cit.,* p.77.
[62]Saul Friedman, "The Holocaust and Its Historiography," in: Fried, *op.cit.,* p.p.441-469.

CHAPTER VII

The Secularization of the United States in the 20th Century

I.

In the decade 1901 - 1910, the first decade of the twentieth century, the population of the United States grew from 75,994,575 to 91,972,266. During that same period 9,803,295 aliens entered this country. Thus, eleven percent of the population were recent arrivals in 1910 even though over one million of these had not been granted immigrant status.[1]

If immigrants had arrived in this country in the same proportions between 1985 and 1995 then over 28 million would have been allowed to enter here considering that the population of the United States was about 255 million in 1994. In fact, however, the rate of immigration into the United States during those years was less than 1% annually.[2]

Among the nearly ten million who came here during the first decade of this century and during the ten years before, there were at least one million Jews. During the second decade of the 1900's another million Jews came to the big cities of the American east coast, a few settling inland. Even the years between 1921 to 1924 when the quota law finally reduced immigration to a minimum saw another 250,000 Jews enter the United States. Since a quarter of a million Jews were already in the United States before the great migration of the late nineteenth century began, there were 2.5 million Jews in America by 1925.[3]

Almost all of the other immigrants who came during those years and who were not Jewish, were Catholics. Moreover, these Jewish and Catholic immigrants came from Eastern and Southern Europe unlike the ancestors of the European population already here who were of English, German, Irish or Scandinavian descent.

These immigration trends are well illustrated by comparing the immigration from Western Europe to that of Southern and Eastern Europe and the whole world as it stood in 1891, 1901 and the peak immigration years 1906 and 1907. Thus, the total who came in 1891 was 560,319. Of these 97.5% came from Europe. In turn, Europeans who came in that year came mostly from Western Europe, i.e., about 58% and only the remaining 42% came from Eastern and Southern Europe. Prior to the end of the nineteenth century the imbalance was even more severe.

By 1901, however, the balance had shifted in favor of the Eastern and Southern European immigrants. In that year, 487,918 persons migrated to the U.S. Only 4% were not Europeans. That, however, nearly doubled the non - European population who had come here in 1891. Of the 96% who came from Europe, only 24% were from a Western European country and fully 76% came from Eastern or Southern Europe and in the peak immigration years, 1906 and 1907, the trend in favor of Eastern and Southern Europeans became even greater. In those two years over one million immigrants arrived here each year constituting a level of immigration repeated only in 1913 and 1914.

Thus, in 1906 the immigrants from Southern and Eastern Europe numbered 802,550 while those from Western Europe only numbered 215,815.[4]

Clearly then, the United States was accepting vast numbers of people who not only differed in language and culture from the predominantly Protestant, Western European and white population, but who also differed in religion.

The immigrants looked terrible to the Protestant establishment who had been native here for so many generations. These people spoke Yiddish, a language written with Hebrew characters. Others spoke Polish or Russian, many of whom used the Cyrillic alphabet if they could read and write at all. Latin was used in all Catholic churches and Greek was used among the Eastern Orthodox Christian believers while Jews prayed and read the Bible in Hebrew.

All of this seemed extremely threatening to the natives who not only revived many of the groups who had fought the Catholic Irish immigrants in the mid-eighteen hundreds but who also placed a great deal of pressure on Congress to keep out foreigners, meaning particularly, Eastern and Southern Europeans.[5] This agitation finally led to the Emergency Quota Act of 1921. That temporary law permitted 3% of any nationality living here as of 1910 to enter the country in any one year. This law was replaced by Congress with the Immigration Act of 1924. That new version of the law required that the number of immigrants who could come into the country could not, in any one year, exceed 2% of the number among the American population of any national origin as of 1890. Since the number of Southern and Eastern Europeans living here in 1890 was quite small, this law effectively "froze" the ethnic composition of the country and reduced immigration to a trickle. In fact, in 1931, more people left the United States than arrived.[6]

Since then the immigration policy of the United States has changed considerably. Jewish immigration into the United States, however, had reached major proportions after the institution of organized persecution of Jews following the assassination of Czar Alexander II in 1881. With the Immigration Act of 1924 it ceased almost entirely, except for the admission of a few German Jews who came as a result of the Nazi horrors in the 1930's. After the second World War the United States received between 100,000 and four hundred thousand immigrants each year. However, there were hardly any Jews among them since six million Jews had been murdered in the European gas ovens and almost all of the others had migrated to Israel. Therefore it is not surprising that in 1995 almost the entire American Jewish community is native born and of Eastern European, mainly Russian or Polish descent. It ought to be remembered that Poland was not an independent country until 1914 and that therefore "Russian descent" often means Polish origin because Poland had been a Russian province since 1793.[7]

The ancestors of the American Jews who had come here after 1881 had lived in Eastern Europe for centuries. Some were the descendants of the Khazars who had adopted Judaism in the ninth century. The majority, however, descended from German Jews who had been invited to settle in Poland/Lithuania in the 13th century and thereafter. They came with the many Germans who settled in those lands as well and they spoke the medieval German language.[8]

This medieval German, spoken amidst a vast majority of Slavic speaking peoples, became Yiddish or Jewish. It was spoken by eleven million Jews in Europe before the Nazi Holocaust and, as a form of German, is so recognized by the world's linguists who include Yiddish in the German section of their professional meetings.

Now the Jews who came to the United States in such large numbers at the end of the 19th century and at the beginning of the 20th century had lived distinct from the Slavic population surrounding them. "They were set apart, not only by their religion and by the special judicial and fiscal regime, but by language, dress, and cultural traditions."

In Europe they were forced to live in special sections of each city (Ghettos); they had to wear distinctive clothing so that they could easily be recognized; they wore beards and earlocks to accommodate their beliefs; they had their own schools where boys, not girls, were taught the Scriptures and the Talmud, i.e., learning and scholarship based on Rabbinical exegesis. Secular learning was rare among the Eastern European Jews. Restricted by law to a limited territory within Russian ruled lands the Jews were allowed only a few occupations such as money lending and trading.[9]

The same conditions which faced the Jews in Russia were also enforced in non-Russian territories, such as the Balkans, Austria and the Baltic states.

Thus, when the Jewish masses arrived in the United States they were, with few exceptions, orthodox in religion, paternalistic in the management of their families, limited in knowledge of the non-Jewish world and extremely poor.

Yet, within less than a century, the grandchildren of these immigrants built here, in the United States, a magnificent edifice to American democracy. For while at the beginning of the century and even as late as the 1930's most American Jews were still living a ghetto like existence, their children and grandchildren at the end of the century have risen to the highest social positions in American life. Thus, American Jews have ranked highest in terms of income among all American religious denominations since 1989.[10] They have also contributed enormously to American culture and society, have adopted American attitudes and lifestyles and have truly become "a light onto the nation," if not "the nations." In the course of that success however, American Jews also adopted the secular attitudes of most of their countrymen , attitudes which were barely discernible when these Jews came but which were, at the end of the 20th century the main stream thinking of most Americans.

II.

Since most Americans were and are of the Protestant tradition, how did it come about that Protestant America, Christian America, became a secular nation at the end of the 20th century?

We have already seen that three major influences contributed to this great change. The first the developments in philosophy, the second scientific thinking and the third the consequences of both of these trends as reflected in literature.

It is of course understood that the writings we have reviewed, and the many other advances in all these areas of human concern which influenced secularization later in the 20th century, seemed to have little influence upon the Protestant Establishment and its numerous followers at the beginning of the century. This was also true of the Catholic and Jewish newcomers who were then, for the most part, populating the large cities of the U.S.. The reasons for this apparent lack of influence upon the general thinking in the U.S. by secularists of any stripe was that established religions were still functional in that they seemed to sufficiently explain the relationship of man to man and man to the universe. Furthermore, most Americans, whether natives or not, whether Christians or Jews, had little formal education. Few, if any, attended school for long. Therefore, hardly anyone had ever read any of the books, articles or pamphlets produced by philosophers, scientists and literary people.

When the huge wave of European immigrants came to the United States between 1881 and 1921 everything that was public in America was also considered Protestant. Thus, at the beginning of the Twentieth Century, when a number of states had adopted compulsory education laws, the King James version of the Bible was read in those schools every day. Textbooks even included anti-Catholic material. Because many Catholics stayed away from these schools and because a "school war" broke out in almost all large American cities, a compromise was attempted in the early years of this century whereby the Douay version of the Bible was read in heavily Catholic wards in New York while all other schools remained Protestant.[11]

This left out the Jews and other smaller religious groups. Furthermore, this did not satisfy the Catholic community who built their own school system after the First World War. In addition to religious differences schools also had other problems. Because the immigrants crowded into large cities, these city schools were soon very overcrowded so that ill trained teachers had to teach 100 students at a time. Therefore many schools operated two shifts, i.e., morning and afternoon. Together with the need of immigrant families to send their children to work so as to earn part or all of their own keep, these schools were rejected by many of the immigrants as centers of religious bias, poor teaching and overcrowding. In addition, all schools were only in English so that many of the immigrant children could neither understand nor speak the language in use.

Hence the early immigrants learned very little about the scientific, philosophical and literary achievements of their contemporaries or their intellectual ancestors for they either did not go to school at all or they attended ethnic schools where their language was used.

Among Jews that language was Yiddish and there were indeed Jews who sent their sons, and sometimes their daughters, to Yiddish speaking schools dealing entirely with the teaching of Torah and Talmud. There were also parents who sent their children to non-religious, but Yiddish speaking schools.

Unlike most immigrants, however, the Jews of New York, where about two thirds of all immigrant Jews remained, and the Jews in other areas sent their sons to the public schools. Thus, secular occupations, and in particular the medical profession, became the high status object of parental ambition in America. This was decidedly not the case among the Jews of Eastern Europe.[12]

There talmudic scholars were held in highest esteem. Hence, the attitude concerning the occupation of sons, and occasionally daughters, among American Jews was largely the outcome of conditions imposed upon Jews in Europe but unknown in America.[13]

Thus, the struggle for a livelihood, "unending and rarely successful," had to occupy much of the Jews' time. Learning and study, however, were given great weight because absorption in the Holy Books permitted the scholars and their followers to emotionally escape and to survive the unending hostility, persecution and intermittent bloodshed to which European Jews had been subject for a thousand years.[14]

The schools which the Eastern European Jews attended were by no means comparable to American schools at any time. Here is an example of a Jewish school in Vilna, Lithuania as it appeared in 1894:

> *"Our Talmud Torahs are filthy rooms, crowded from nine in the morning until nine in the evening with pale, starved children. These remain in this contaminated atmosphere for twelve hours at a time and see only their bent, exhausted teachers..........Their faces are pale and sickly, and their bodies evidently not strong. In parties of twenty or thirty, and at times more, they all repeat some lesson aloud after their instructor. He who has not listened to the almost absurd commentaries of the ignorant melamed (teacher) cannot even imagine how little the children gain from such instruction."*

Such schools were in part duplicated in New York and other American cities. However, they had little appeal. Thus, by 1918 only 24,000 out of 275,000 New York City Jewish school age children were being taught in a so-called *Cheder,* similar to the one described.[15]

There were of course no persecutions of Jews in America and the schools, compared to the foregoing, were far better. Jews in America did find, however, that there was then a good deal of anti-Jewish bigotry in education and in employment opportunities. This bigotry and the great rewards available to the educated led many to view the independent professions as a means of attaining high social status, a good income and individual freedom. Therefore, medicine, law, pharmacy, accounting and other educated professions were viewed as the panaceas for immigrants and particularly their children.

The whole Jewish family gloried in the achievements of their children and measured their own success by the attainments of the next generation. The accomplishments of outstanding Jews were constantly repeated by parents to their children and Jewish children were taught that success would come to those who studied and learned.[16]

What was true for Jews was also true for other immigrants who settled mainly in cities. There is good reason to believe that the hostility which the immigrants of the 1881-1921 period engendered among native Americans was not only due to their religion, speech, manners and customs but also because most Americans, even in 1920, were rural people who either lived on farms or in small towns. Thus, in 1900 only 40% of the American population were described as "urban", a number which in 1920 had risen to 50%.[17]

This hostility was illustrated by the symbol of 19th century American education called "the little red schoolhouse." Such anti-Catholic, anti-Jewish and anti-black organizations as "The American Protective Association," featured "the little red schoolhouse" on the masthead of their publications and the Ku Klax Klan used the symbol in their successful campaign to bring about the immigration quotas of the 1920's.

Thus, "the little red schoolhouse" idea *"symbolized values associated chiefly with rural, small town, homogeneous, white and Protestant America even as the country, irrevocably moved into the industrial age with its large, urban, heterogeneous, ethnically diverse, secular culture."*[18]

America was never uniform in religion. As Hammond has shown, religious harmony in the American colonies was *"secured not by finding a common religious outlook but by recourse to government."* Furthermore, emotional religious fervor de-emphasized doctrine, ritual, religious instruction and even denomination. Consequently American clergy lost authority and religious pluralism and the doctrine of brotherhood became central to American religious values, instead of an orthodoxy of any kind. This did not take place in one or two years. It took many years so that Christian holidays and ceremonies were still taken for granted in the schools of the 1950's and even in the 1990's. Nevertheless, religion, in Hammond's words, has become *"privatized"*, meaning that Americans can believe anything they like but also keep it to themselves. This goes so far that even a member of any denomination would not ordinarily be asked by that denomination's clergy to announce what he believes or does not believe. Therefore, says Hammond, *".....one belief is,.....as good as another as far as the law is concerned."*[19] Thus, America has four, not three, major religious orientations including those who abstain from any religion and who are usually called "secular humanists." The consequence of this situation is what Bellah has called "civil religion", referring to religious neutrality on the part of government and of a major segment of the American population. This he illustrates, among many other examples, with the observation that almost all official

American statements, whether oral or written, avoid the term "Christ" even when affirming the existence of God.[20]

"The most important consequence was the establishment of the voluntary principle with respect to the more formal aspect of religious obligation, notably church membership." This privatization of religion led to the development of religious toleration and to a denominational pluralistic society. Parsons argues that: *"the roots of the civil religion in America lie in the attempt to validate the legitimacy of the Puritan claim to have achieved a measure of success".* This he sees in the clear focus of Protestantism on worldly concerns. This also means that emphasis on God is uncommon in the U.S.A. at the end of the 20th century so that the United States is today "non-theistic" but not "atheistic."[21]

III.

There were a number of Jews and other children of immigrants who, in addition to the so-called "free" professions, entered teaching in the early part of the century. Here, Jews particularly were faced with a great deal of hostility and prejudice, a condition which was most evident in higher education. In fact, a study of the faculties of American colleges and universities revealed that almost all faculty in American institutions of higher education before the Second World War were Protestants, a condition which was even true in New York City which, by 1940, had absorbed nearly two million Jews and over four million Catholics.[22]

Before the Second World War the prestige colleges in this country, and many others, would take an entering class with an average aptitude score of only 500, making certain however, that the freshmen had "adequate scholastic preparation and good character," meaning that they were not Jewish. In fact, quotas were used at most colleges to keep Jews from entering in greater numbers than their share of the population. It was therefore not at all surprising that there were so few Jewish faculty members in any American university before 1945.[23]

In any event, both the attainment of an education in the sciences, in medicine, in the law and the profession of education attracted numerous young Jews at the beginning of this century and contributed mightily to the secularization of that religious community.[24]

Now it can easily be demonstrated that all of the beliefs and views associated with secular humanism which we have so far discussed crystallized around the person of John Dewey. He was undoubtedly the thinker and writer with more impact on American education than anyone before him.

John Dewey was born in Burlington, Vt. in 1859. His ancestor, Thomas Dewey who had settled there in 1630, also became the progenitor of the author of the library decimal system bearing his name, as well as the admiral George Dewey of Manila Bay fame and the governor of New York, Thomas Dewey.

In 1970, the following recollections concerning John Dewey were published:

> *"Dewey was an avid reader of detective stories, which he swallowed, one after the other at an amazing clip. Dr. Barnes banteringly insisted that he must be skipping pages, to which Dewey responded by offering to pickup the story from any place in one of the books that Dr. Barnes, (his travel companion) might select. Dr. Barnes opened a book to a random page, and read the beginning of a sentence aloud, which Dewey then proceeded to complete almost verbatim."*[25]

> *"When I was in the Far East....I found that Professor Dewey's name is highly venerated in Japan and Thailand especially. Their educational system is really based on his theories of progressive education. I visited....Bangkok and found that Professor Dewey is their patron saint."*[26]

> *" Professor Dewey ....has always carried his simplicity of manner , his dread of show or self -advertisement almost to the point of extravagance. In all his psychology there is no room for the psychology of prestige. His democracy seems almost to take that extreme form of refusing to take one's self or one's ideas to the attention of others."*[27]

> *" ....the quality that impressed me most was that, in spite of the many significant problems that occupied his (Dewey's) mind, he was always most willing to listen to any question or thoughts you might have............he never made one feel inferior ..."*[28]

John Dewey represented an aspect of the Protestant ethic which became pronounced in twentieth century American education even though Dewey was indeed a nineteenth century man. However, he lived so long that he also saw more than half of the twentieth century so that he was in the unique position of seeing his own ideas *"swept through American, and to some extent world, thinking during Dewey's own lifetime."*[29]

Dewey expressed these ideas in more than 50 books and at least 200 contributions to encyclopedias and over 750 articles in academic and other journals.[30]

There are some who believe that these ideas were utterly original with Dewey. It is however evident from reading the preceding chapters of this book that secular humanism, as developed over decades and centuries in philosophy, science and literature coalesced in the thinking of Dewey and permitted him to introduce these ideas into American education. That does not diminish in the least the great impact of this great thinker upon American life. Dewey came to maturity at about the same time as the Jewish and other non-Protestant immigrants first arrived in this country in great numbers. Because these Jews and others attended public schools then already under the influence of Dewey and his following, those immigrants who came to the American public schools in the 1920's and thereafter were at once in the grip of Deweys's ideas and therefore subject to the secular humanist message.

"Dewey spent a life time seeking a balance between individual freedom and institutional forms." However, he favored direct democracy and was criticized for giving institutionalized democracy short shrift.[31]

Dewey believed that "democracy and the one, ultimate, ethical ideal of humanity are to my mind synonymous."

Contrary to some uninformed critics, John Dewey did not promote "child-centered" schooling to the detriment of the whole society. On the contrary. Dewey was very much concerned with social life and the need to maintain a society. He was opposed to extreme permissiveness and to the lack of curriculum design practiced in some "progressive" schools.

Dewey was also action oriented. He wanted to teach ethics which were visible and the product of action, not inner guilt, or belief or introspection. As his life progressed Dewey began to view democracy as his religion and therefore discarded or at least ignored organized religion and the idea of an immanent God. He came to view the democratic social process itself as the highest ideal of mankind and he therefore abandoned religion.[32]

It was this attitude which appealed to many Jewish young people then in school because Judaism teaches that action is more important than belief. This may not seem to be the case if one were to judge Judaism only from the vantage point of an observer looking at the conduct of the ultra-orthodox as they existed in the big city ghettos of the late 19th and early 20th century. Nevertheless, it is Jewish not to insist on dogma but on deeds.

Whether or not John Dewey was a deist is not clear. His work reflects a good deal of ambiguity concerning the existence of a god. For example, in 1897, speaking of "My Pedagogic Creed," Dewey wrote: "*I believe ....that the teacher always is the prophet of the true God and the usherer in of the true kingdom of God.*[33] In *A Common Faith*, first published in 1934, he used the term God and the word divine. Yet, one year earlier he had published *The Humanist Manifesto*, which rejects deism, theism, personal immortality and all supernaturalism.[34] These are the fifteen propositions of the *Humanist Manifesto*:

1. *The universe is self existing and not created.*

2. *Man is part of nature and the result of a continuous process.*

3. *There is no dualism of mind and body.*

4. *Religion is the outcome of human culture in time and place.*

5. *Supernaturalism is rejected in favor of science.*

6. *Theism, "deism," and modernism are also rejected.*

7. *There is no difference between the sacred and the secular.*

8. *The "complete realization " of the human personality is the end of man's life.*

9. *A co-operative effort of social well being , not prayer and worship, are religious emotions worth promoting.*

10. *Religious emotions associated with the supernatural are unacceptable.*

11. *Humanism rejects wishful thinking relative to the crises of life. Instead it supports reasonable and "manly" attitudes.*

12. *Religious humanism supports achievement and creativity.*

13. *Institutions and associations exist to fulfill human life.*

14. *Humanists demand a shared life in a shared world and denounces profit seeking at the expense of the equal distribution of resources.*

15. Humanism seeks to establish a satisfactory life for all, not only for the few.[35]

Dewey drew a clear distinction between his conception of *Religion* and *The Religious*. Thus, he wrote that *religion* is a form of institutionalized entity while the "*adjective religious denotes nothing in the way of a specifiable entity, either institutional or as a system of belief.*" He also taught that religion is only a form which is discarded as social life changes and religion is incapable of changing as well. Thus, he thought that new forms of religion must be found as the old forms become useless and outdated.[36]

Dewey presents his readers with a choice. The choice between believing in a supernatural God who already exists or faith in the process of scientific discovery and the uncovering of nature's secrets. Dewey emphasized ethics and a naturalistic humanism which gave rise to the Ethical Culture Society, founded, not only on the basis of the philosophy of Dewey but also of Freud's student, the psychoanalyst Alfred Adler.

Now Dewey sought to bring his ideas into the schools as he shared with many Americans the view that education was and is essential as a guarantee of the continuation of democracy. Dewey and his followers became known as "The Progressives" in education as they sought to change the then existing school system by promoting the findings of psychology and of education.

From his position as professor of philosophy and education at the University of Chicago Dewey argued for a child-centered curriculum, active methods of teaching and gentler discipline. The progressives also introduced industrial education and vocational education into the school systems around the country. They also sought to take politics out of the school system in the U.S. by demanding that the schools be independent of politics and that they be run by "scientifically trained professionals."[37]

Dewey and his followers were and are relativists. Opposed to any fixed value system in education or anywhere else Dewey would not agree that there is any form of final truth. Instead, dynamic ideas, dynamic beliefs and processes were and are featured by Dewey and his followers and these processes are seen as *"instruments by which the purposes of life can be achieved."*[38]

Such beliefs and practices, which are of course utterly foreign to religious education and practice, have been taught in the vast majority of American public schools for at least fifty years and were already visible and influential at the beginning of this century when the huge waves of immigrants came from Europe and settled in America's cities. Thus, the native population and the immigrants, their children and their grandchildren, together learned in school to segregate religion and supernatural beliefs from education. The ends of public education were based on John Dewey's view that schools should teach liberal democratic values and that preparation for citizenship and encouragement of personal autonomy were to be the most important outcomes of education. In addition, naturalism and rational, scientific thinking was emphasized in the public school curriculum as the century progressed and this in turn had a tremendous influence on the secularization of the United States in this, the 20th century.[39]

IV.

It would of course be naive to believe that those who held and continue to hold supernatural beliefs ever abandoned the American public schools to the naturalists, humanists and Deweists. On the contrary. As schools became more humanist in outlook, as science and rational thinking became more and more the substance of public education, parents and others became more and more vociferous in insisting that the schools not abandon such practices as school prayer, Bible reading, the singing of religious hymns, the teaching of denominational theology during school hours, the use of schools for religious purposes and a host of other demands. Since religion had had its way in the American schools and in public functions for three centuries it seemed to those who had taken the presence of religion in the schools for granted as absolutely unacceptable that legislatures were beginning to remove religious practices from schools while refusing more and more to fund schools founded by religious groups. Yet, the courts have generally supported the secularists in bringing about religion neutral public education, except that the celebration of Easter and Christmas is now (1995) almost universal in the public schools in America, despite the court rulings about to be reviewed. These rulings did not come about in isolation or at the whim of the courts. Rather, these rulings must be understood as the ratification by law of the existing situation concerning the separation of church and state in America.

There have been numerous decisions of the U.S. Supreme Court that have dealt with the issue of religion. One of the earliest was *Pierce vs. Society of Sisters* decided in 1925. This decision favored the right of parents to send their children to a religion controlled school in Oregon after that state had passed The Oregon Compulsory Education Act mandating only public education. What is significant here is, that even at that time, Catholics at least felt uncomfortable in the public schools which were both Protestant and more and more secular all at the same time.[40] As secular humanism became more and more evident in the public schools, various religious groups either removed their children from the public schools or attempted to introduce their views into the public curriculum. In both cases, numerous law suits arose dealing with the disputes concerning resources to be allocated to the religion controlled schools. These decisions became confusing to Americans because in some instances the court ruled in favor of supporting some aspects of religious education while refusing such support in other cases. For example, in both *Cochran vs. Louisiana State Board of Education*[41] and in *Everson vs. Board of Education* the Supreme Court ruled that Louisiana could distribute textbooks to parochial school children and that such children could be transported to a religion controlled school by school bus at public expense.

Nevertheless, *Everson* was very important in laying the ground work for the secularization of American public education through the courts because it gave the Supreme Court an opportunity to make a statement concerning the court's interpretation of the First Amendment language concerning religion. Writing for the majority, which permitted the practice of Ewing Township, N.J. reimbursing parents for money spent on bus transportation of their children in attending both public and church controlled schools, Justice Hugo Black wrote this:

> *"The 'establishment of religion clause' of the First Amendment means at least this: Neither a state nor the Federal Government can set up a church. Neither can pass laws which aid one religion, aid all religions, or prefer one religion over another. .....No tax of any amount, large or small can be levied to support any religious activities or institutions whatever they may be called, or whatever form they may*

adopt to teach or practice religion.....In the words of Thomas Jefferson, the clause against establishment of religion by law was intended to erect "a wall of separation between church and state."[42]

Additionally, in *Mueller vs. Allen* the court ruled in 1983 that parents could deduct school expenses from the Minnesota Income Tax even if their children attend a religion controlled school. Decisions of this kind made it possible for parents who want their children to have a religion controlled, rather than a secular education to provide a religious atmosphere for their children. This became necessary for those seeking to maintain religion in the schools or at least in their schools because the courts became more and more aggressive in removing religion from public schools beginning with the late 1940's.[43]

In 1948 the U.S. Supreme Court decided in *Illinois ex rel. McCollum v. Board of Education* religious instruction could not occur inside a public school building but that "release time" could be given children whose parents wanted their children to receive a religious education during the school day. Prior to that decision it was customary for clergy of all denominations to come to the public schools at a given hour and instruct the children of their faith in classrooms designated for that purpose within the public school building. The court found this unacceptable not only because the schools were furnishing religious establishments tax supported access to the rooms, the utilities, the maintenance service and the supervision needed to keep the building open, but also because these practices tended to shame children who either had no religion or were members of minorities whose clergy were not available or willing to furnish this type of instruction. It was in this case that the Supreme Court once more employed the phrase first used by Thomas Jefferson as they held that the First Amendment to the U.S. Constitution *"erected a wall between church and state which must be kept high and impregnable."*[44]

No Supreme Court decision aroused more anger and demands for a constitutional amendment to lower that wall than the *Engel vs. Vitale* decision of 1962. This decision prohibited the conduct of prayers in a tax supported school building during school hours. The case concerned New York which at that time began each school day with a non-denominational prayer composed by the board of Regents, the governing board of New York public schools. This was the prayer then in use in all New York public schools: *"Almighty God, we acknowledge our dependence upon Thee, and we beg Thy blessings upon us, our parents, our teachers and our country."* It must be remembered that prior to the adoption of this non-denominational prayer, schools in New York and other states had always begun the school day with a prayer which was usually Protestant in nature. The Supreme Court decided, however, that "In this country it is not part of the business of government to compose official prayers for any group of the American people to recite as a part of the religious program carried on by government." Justice Black commented *"that New York has adopted a practice wholly inconsistent with the Establishment clause."*[45]

That the court would not change in this respect was emphasized again when twenty three years later, in 1985, the Supreme Court agreed with Dallas, Tex., school officials who had denied prayer requests to students in the Dallas schools.[46]

The same logic was applied to the case of *Abbington School District vs. Schempp* and to *Sherbert vs. Verner.* In those 1963 cases the Court prohibited the reading of 10 verses from the Bible as part of a religious exercise prescribed by Pennsylvania law.[47]

In Arkansas, the legislature made it a crime in 1968 to teach Darwin's theory of evolution in any public school either by word of mouth or by the use of a book. This law was promptly struck down by the Supreme Court in *Epperson vs. Arkansas* on the grounds that this law violated the establishment clause and *"resulted from fundamentalist sectarian conviction."*

Ever since *Epperson* fundamentalists have attempted by various means to get around that decision. They have claimed since then that the teaching of evolution is an aspect of the religion of "secular humanism" and that therefore their doctrines, now called "creationism" or "creation science" should be given equal time in the schools. Both Louisiana and Arkansas agreed to this view and introduced "creation science" into their curriculum.[48]

In 1971, the Supreme Court ruled that state salary supplements to religious school teachers *"unduly enmesh state authorities in monitoring to prevent inculcation of religious beliefs."* It was in this, the *Lemon vs. Kurtzman* decision, that then Chief Justice Warren Burger promoted a three part test for determining the constitutionality of government action concerning the establishment clause. This test holds, first, that the act have a secular purpose, second that the act neither advances nor inhibits religion and third   that "*excessive entanglement is avoided.*"[49]

The controversy concerning Bible reading in the public schools did not end with the *Schempp* decision. It continued into the 1980's because groups devoted to religious doctrines sought to read the Bible or meet for religious purposes on school grounds and in classrooms, but after the end of each school day. The argument here is that students belonging to religious groups ought to have the same right as other students to meet in classrooms, after school hours, to participate in "extra-curricular" activities which in their case consists of Bible reading and other religious exercises.

Because the First Amendment guarantees both free speech and also speaks of the right to freely exercise one's religion, there are those who believe that religious groups must be given the right to use school facilities, before and after hours, to discuss their religious views.

In 1980, the Supreme Court tried to deal with this issue and ruled in *Brandon vs. Board of Education,* that the school board did not have to grant the right to use classrooms for religious purposes because of the establishment clause. Even the posting of the Ten Commandments in Kentucky classrooms was prohibited by the Supreme Court in 1987.[50] Three years earlier, however, Congress passed   with an overwhelming majority the "Equal Access Act" of 1984. That act prohibits a public high school with a forum for non-curricular student activities to deny equal access to groups wishing to meet *"for religious, political, philosophical or other speech purposes."*

Note that this law affected high schools but not the lower grades. The law was meant to extend to high school students the same rights favored for college students by the *Widmar vs. Vincent* decision of 1981 which ruled that the University of Missouri could not deny religious groups the same access allowed nearly one hundred other groups at that university. Evidently, confusion concerning the rights of religious groups continued into the eighties.[51]

As the century progressed the U.S. Supreme Court became more and more involved in decisions affecting religion and religious practice in the U.S. Thus, of the thirty four cases involving religion which came before the U.S. Supreme Court in all of our history, only one was decided in the nineteenth century, and thirty three were decided in the 20th century, so far. Of these, six were decided in the 1940's, one in the 1950's, seven in the sixties, six more in the seventies and 12 in the eighties. One case has been decided in the 1990's.

Almost all of these cases favored a secularist interpretation of the constitution. Nevertheless, these decisions were not made in a social vacuum. On the contrary. The decisions of the Supreme Court concerning religion reflect the wish of most Americans to separate the state from the church but also to favor the right of religions to exist as long as that right does not impinge on the non-theistic nature of American society. For example, in 1985 Alabama was told by the court to discontinue the practice of having school children observe one minute of silence for meditation or individual prayer. The court called this practice *"entirely motivated by a purpose to advance religion."*[52] In 1965 Congress had passed *The Elementary and Secondary Education Act."* The purpose of that Act had been to distribute federal financial aid to schools for the needs of educationally deprived children. The court held, however, that this law does not apply to schools controlled by religious organizations because it *"inevitably results in the excessive entanglement of church and state."*[53] This decision was reinforced when the Court ruled adversely against New York State in the *Kiryas Yoel* case in 1994. This case was decided by a 6:3 majority and held that the State of New York had violated the Constitution when it set up a special public school district for Hasidic Jews in Kiryas Joel located in Orange Country N.Y. with a view of helping disabled students in that community. Once more using the three part test already in use since *Lemon vs. Kurtzman* in 1971, the court found that the State could not give 200 disabled students in that town special instruction at the expense of the tax payer. Instead, children in all religion controlled schools will have to continue to be bussed elsewhere for remedial education.[54] While the solution of bussing Catholic and other Christian children to remedial education outside the denominational schools is feasible for them, this does not apply to non-Christians. Jews, whether orthodox or not, find it very difficult to be involved in Easter and Christmas celebrations during the weeks preceding these holy days. Jewish children cannot in good conscience sing songs which refer to "....the king of Israel," involve class singing of Christian hymns and prepare Christmas gifts. "The Resurrection", although a noble Christian motif, appears to be an assault upon the sensibilities of Jewish parents and children, as well as families from other minority traditions. Yet, this too is foisted upon minority children in American classrooms each year without giving such children any choice but to participate or be viewed as outsiders. It is for this reason that in many American communities Jews have sought to live in the same neighborhood so that their children would gain some support from other Jewish children during those four weeks in the school year which cause them so much discomfort. Therefore, two issues have confronted the courts in dealing with the exercise of religion in the schools. One is, whether or not religious material may be taught in public schools in either a direct or symbolic fashion, and the other is whether those who view the schools as inadequate to teach religious values may separate themselves from the public schools, learn in their own schools and still gain public support. While there is still a great deal of ambiguity concerning these issues even at the end of this century, there is nevertheless a clear trend towards the exclusion of religion from public schools both directly and symbolically. Furthermore, non-public, religion controlled schools have been partially accommodated in that they can refuse to participate in public education if they wish to do so and in that they can expect some support for their position at the expense of the taxpayer in the form of bussing, book distribution and other functions not likely to be influenced by dogmatic teachings. It is therefore not true, as some would have us believe, that the courts have unduly befriended the "secular humanist" position. On the contrary. Numerous Supreme Court decisions have favored religious groups even as the court prevented those same groups from unduly influencing the public school curriculum or public school practices. In addition to some of those cases already mentioned, we can list *Zorach vs. Clauson,* which allowed religious instruction to take place during the school day provided it did not occur in a public building; *Walz vs. Tax Commission,* allowing tax exemption for religious organizations; *McDaniel v. Paty* invalidating a Tennessee law which would have prohibited clergy to run for public office; *Lynch v. Donnelly,* which permits the display of religious symbols on public property provided secular symbols are given equal space and *Mergens v. Board of Education,* which told the Omaha Board of Education that after school Bible study clubs had to be allowed in the school buildings if other clubs had the same privilege. The sum of the religious situation facing all Americans at the end of the twentieth century , and as inaugurated at the beginning of the twentieth century, is that America is no longer a Christian nation in the theological sense of that phrase. It is instead a religiously pluralistic society which has chosen to adopt a "secular humanistic" attitude in public life in order to accommodate, without rancor, numerous diverse religious interests. This attitude is reflected in court decisions and is generally accepted by all citizens.[55]

V.

The influence of the public schools, the influence of the courts and the curriculum in universities and colleges greatly contributed to secularized American life at the end of the twentieth century. This means that the philosophical, scientific and literary basis for this secularization had already been laid long before the twentieth century began and that the schools, the courts and the universities became the vehicles on which the ideas of the thinkers and writers of earlier centuries were now put into practical application.

Notably the social sciences, and in particular sociology, developed strong ties to "secular humanism," and influenced students and the general public alike to think in secular terms, to make decisions in secular terms, to view others in a secular light and to deal with daily experiences in a secular, not a supernatural, manner. In fact, Auguste Comte (1798-1857), the "father" of sociology, was born directly after the French revolution (1789) and spent his youth in the years of Napoleon I. He participated in the "enlightenment" of those years. Therefore, sociology, from its inception sought to reject, not only the old political order which the revolution had overthrown, but also sought to disestablish religion and religious authorities who were indeed the handmaidens of the repressive old order.

Progress, political and economic freedom, individualism, science and the belief in the ability of humans to solve their problems without divine intervention became the basis of social science thinking and particularly sociology. Comte had coined the word *sociology* to describe a new science which he intended would study society by scientific means, that is observation, measurement and comparison. Thus, Comte was a *positivist,* i.e. one who sought to *eliminate all bias from the observer of social life* and to deal with their work in a manner similar to mathematical studies. Comte was a mathematician and had graduated from the Polytechnical School in Paris. Harriet

Martineau (1802-1876), an English woman wrote *Society in America* even as Comte wrote *Sociology* and translated Comte into English. It was also in England that Herbert Spencer (1820-1903) published *Principles of Sociology* in 1876. These founders were accompanied by other major contributors to sociological thought, notably Karl Marx (1818-1883), Emile Durkheim (1858-1917) and Max Weber (1864-1920). All of these writers perpetuated the legacy of the enlightenment and all also assaulted the power of religion and its institutions. Marx, undoubtedly the most vehement of the critics of established religion thereby lost much of the influence he did achieve in the areas of economics and politics although that was not visible until the decline of state socialism at the end of the twentieth century. Durkheim and Weber, however, have had a major influence on our understanding of religion and it is that influence which led to the rise of the Sociology of Religion and an objective evaluation of religion ever since.[56] Thus, *positivism* entered into sociology and "*sociology originated in positivism.*" The links between positivism and sociology are the influence of positivist thought on the French and English enlightenment; the reform orientation of both early sociology and positivism and "*the scientism of the positivists, who, by extending the standards of science over all spheres of thought, were more explicit than anyone else in defending the belief that human actions can, and should, be made subject matter of scientific study.*"[57]

    It was left to the French sociologist Emile Durkheim (1858-1917) to view the collective experience of a group as the origin of ideas about the ultimate meaning of life and the ceremonies associated with those ideas. Therefore, Durkheim taught that all systems of belief have the same objective significance and fulfill the same function everywhere. Hence, according to Durkheim and sociology, there can be no false religion or false beliefs. All are true in the sense that all answer the human condition and fulfill the same functions. Durkheim said: *A religion is a unified system of belief and practices relative to sacred things, that is to say, things set apart and forbidden-beliefs and practices which unite into one single moral community .....all those who adhere to them.*" To this Durkheim added that God is society because society is more powerful than any of us and beyond our personal control. We are dependent on it and it demands our obedience to it. Therefore, taught Durkheim, religion, as a symbolic manifestation of society insures social control and is beneficial.[58]

Max Weber (1864-1920) is the fourth founding "father" of modern sociology. Unlike Comte, Marx and Durkheim, Weber was not as certain as they that rational analysis and value free research, however necessary, would have no negative consequences. A German, Weber used the word "verstehen" which means more than "to understand." The word really implies an understanding of how others see themselves and how others experience life. Weber located ethics and morality in modern society in social interaction and showed in *Science as a Vocation* and *Politics as a Vocation* the consequences of moral relativity in the work world. This was also the theme of Weber's 1904 essay *The Protestant Ethic and the Spirit of Capitalism,* which linked religious beliefs firmly to economic necessity. The issue here is that Weber showed how American Puritanism had become secular. Puritan teachings, Weber explained, encouraged wordly success which in turn undermined the "ascetic" way of life. Weber even quoted John Wesley, the founder of Methodism to the effect that wherever wealth has increased religion has decreased. Thus, Weber showed his readers "*...the massive process of secularization in the course of which utilitarian industriousness replaced the search for the kingdom of God"* even among the early Protestant settlers of seventeenth century New England.[59]

Thus, when American sociology was launched with the publication of *Dynamic Sociology* by Lester Ward (1841-1913) in 1883 this science fit excellently into the already prevailing pragmatism and secularism in the academic world of America. It is to be underscored again, that we are here speaking only of intellectuals and academics, since the vast majority of native and immigrant Americans was at that time not involved in these intellectual enterprises.[60]

Lester Ward was a social Darwinist and a reformer. This seems to be a contradiction, but is by no means unusual. Numerous thinkers have held contradictory views at one time or another in their lives and Ward was no exception. In a sense, Ward was a precursor of what was later called "the welfare state." Ward believed that the "survival of the fittest" does indeed describe human history, but that man can abolish the worst consequences of that struggle by developing a "people's government" which would eventually recast the social order.

William Graham Sumner (1840-1910) taught the first sociology course at an American university, i.e., at Yale in 1875. While Ward was a reformer, this was not true of Sumner, an extreme proponent of absolute *laissez faire* capitalism. Fifteen years later, Albion Small taught a course in sociology at Colby College and in 1892 retired from the presidency of that college to become the first chair and organizer of the Department of Sociology at the University of Chicago. There he also founded *The American Journal of Sociology* in 1895 and was principal organizer of the American Sociological Society. Shortly thereafter Franklin Giddings founded the sociology department at Columbia University.

A history of sociology would of course name many more scholars who have been and are principal contributors to that science. Among these were Keller, Veblen, Chaddock, Ogburn, and Hankins. Thomas and Znaniecki , Burgess, Thrasher, Worth and Park all taught and contributed at the University of Chicago while Ross at Wisconsin, Cooley at Michigan and Sorokin and Zimmerman at Harvard made sociology a wide spread, well known, heavily attended academic subject in every American college as the former students of these pioneers became professors of sociology everywhere in the country.[61]

At the end of this century, American sociology has changed a great deal since its inception in the 18th century and its development in the 19th. This is in part the consequence of the phenomenal growth of higher education in the U.S. since World War II. Mainly, however, the changes in sociology over the past fifty years occurred because social conditions in the United States have changed and because research methods are available in the 1990's which did not exist earlier. It is not necessary to here describe in detail the meaning of the many terms now used in sociology. It suffices to briefly summarize how sociology looks today so that it can be understood what subject matter confronts students entering American institutions of higher education at the end of the century and how that confrontation is a major influence in favor of viewing the world in secular terms.

Urban sociology as it was practiced in Chicago during the 1930's and '40's has given way to studies of race relations and poverty. However, these studies are grounded in more advanced quantitative and qualitative methods than was possible before and have therefore lost the fervor for social progress and ethics which was once part of the sociological message. Demography is studied as before, but with more sophistication. The newer interests include social stratification and political sociology, two areas not studied at all in earlier decades. Theory is today a very important aspect of sociological research including functional analysis, conflict theory, symbolic interactionism, labeling, ethnomethodology and dramaturgy.

Before the 1960's, American sociologists rejected Marxism totally. Since then, radical sociology, relying largely on the teachings of Marx, have gained some followers in the field but have provided more noise than substance.

Research funds, liberally available from the Federal government in the 1960's and less so in the '70's, have been greatly reduced in the 1990's. Nevertheless, empirical research based on relevant theory has become necessary in order to publish in major sociology journals. These journals have proliferated immensely since 1950 as narrower and narrower specialties have emerged in sociology. This has led to considerable work on trivial issues and controversies which is a sign that the science has matured and has assumed an important place in the curricula of colleges and universities.[62]

All these developments in sociology, in all its varieties, created in American higher education a major impetus for the secularization of American students who in turn staffed the public schools, the offices and laboratories of American industry and the government bureaucracies in and out of Washington. It is of course true that other social sciences contributed to secularization as well. All of them share in common the view that man himself can solve his own problems and can do so without the churches, the clergy, theology or supernatural intervention of any kind.

VI.

A poll conducted on behalf of the City University of New York on April 10-11, 1991 revealed that on that date more than 90% of Americans consider themselves as belonging to or leaning towards a religious group. That poll surveyed 113,000 American households over a one year period. Since the Census Bureau did not ask any questions concerning religion during the 1990 census this CUNY survey is the most important comprehensive religion survey yet done in this country.

Only 7% of those surveyed said they had no religion, while one half of one percent said they were Moslems, one percent said they belong to small minority religions such as Buddhism, 1.8% said they were Jewish, 26% said they were Roman Catholics and over 70% said they considered themselves Protestants.[63]

The results of this survey seem to contradict the entire discussion concerning the secularization of the United States until we remember that the survey did not ask whether, or to what extent, the respondents believed in supernatural beings, events or expectations. Such questions would have yielded different results. Therefore a study concerning the religious attitudes of members of Congress may help explain more succinctly the attitude of Americans toward religion at the end of the century. This study has merit because it is not unreasonable to assume that those who represent the American people in Washington are a cross section of believers among those whom they represent. As the authors of *Religion on Capitol Hill*, Benson and Williams, say: *".......their average citizen counterpart can likely be found in every community in the nation.*[64]

These beliefs have to do with the mind set of the believers and are not related to any denomination. Six types of religious believers were discovered by Benson and Williams among members of Congress. These were: 1. Legalistic religionists. These are people who *"place very high values on rules, boundaries, limits, guidelines, direction and purpose."* Such people submit to a set of unexamined beliefs and trust doctrines they have learned. They constituted about 15% of those studied by Benson and Williams.

Although viewed as "more religious" than the average by observers, the second group discovered by Benson and Williams are those whom the researchers called "self concerned." These are believers who are not much worried about the beliefs of others but think of themselves as having a close relationship with God. They constitute about 29% of those studied by Benson and Williams.

The Integrated religionists, constituting about 14% of the members of congress studied are those who have "tested their faith against life." They mean that they have acted and will act on the basis of their beliefs, even if such actions are not popular and contrary to public opinion.

Another 10% of believers are "people concerned" believers who worry about justice for the weak and the poor. These people think that religion is action, not dogma.

Another 10% of the believers here studied are labeled "non-traditional" believers. These are deists, often called "secular humanists" by their opponents although they are likely to believe that a God exists who, however, is not involved with humans and cannot be reached by any human means.

Finally, Benson and Williams found that 22% of those they studied are nominal religionists. Almost all of these people are church members, not because they subscribe to any church dogma, but because "it is good for the children" to belong or they have always been members and greeted some of their co-believers there for social and business reasons but who do not really believe anything.[65]

This cross section of religious attitudes in present day America clearly shows that religion is a private matter in the U.S. at the end of the century and that the "civil" religion, a term first used by the Swiss philosopher Rousseau, is now most widespread in the United States. This civil religion does not favor one particular church, any particular belief or any denomination but religion in general. According to the "civil" religion of Americans, politics and religion have merged to lead to faith in the American way of life, including belief in efficiency, freedom, democracy, equality and individualism. Herberg has noted that the American way of life is the common religion of Americans and that Protestantism, Catholicism and Judaism are its sub-faiths. "*To be Protestant, Catholic or Jew,*" said Rabbi Will Herberg in 1955 "*are today the alternative ways of being an American.*"

No doubt that is now also true of being a Moslem or a Buddhist, Hindu or member of any denomination. In the words of President Dwight Eisenhower, "*without God there could be no American form of government. Our government makes no sense unless it is founded on a deeply felt religious faith-and I don't care what it is.*"[66]

This then reveals the nature of civil religion in America. It is interfaith and it is political. Thus, the civil religion of the United States can be seen on the money issued by the U.S. government which proclaims: "*Annuit coeptis*" or "*He favors Our Undertaking,*" and *In God We Trust;*" in the hymn "*God Bless America*", reference to God in every oath of office, in courtroom procedures, at political conventions and at all formal public occasions which are invariably opened by some prayer said by clergy of any faith. The scriptures of the American secular religion are the Declaration of Independence, The Constitution and the Gettysburg Address given by the civil saint Abraham Lincoln.

Thus, Herberg recognized in the 1950's and Bellah reaffirmed in the 80's that religiousness without religion is possible and is the nature of the religious ethos in the America of the end 20th century. Religion in America does not teach theology or specific denominational content. It teaches "getting along," it teaches "belonging", it teaches sociability and "*the other directed gospel.*" Thus, Civil religion is "*a religion which validates culture and society without in any sense bringing them under judgment.*"[67] Thus, Bellah has shown that the civil religion serves the purpose of institutionalizing American values, seperate from Christian values and thereby avoiding any sectarian entaglement of government with religion without eliminating religion altogether from American life. Thus, there is no conflict between the civil religion and the state or private religion and that has served the American people well. "*The American civil religion has its own prophets, its own martyrs, its own sacred events and its own rituals and symbols.*"[68] So writes Bellah and Herberg quotes Roy Eckart, a well known theologian, who described present day American religion as *religious narcissism,* which is man centered, in which religious institutions are irrelevant while social irresponsibility is encouraged and "*the church (synagogue) becomes an ....emotional service station to relieve one's worries.*[69]

Since that was written forty years ago the secularization of America has not abated. Religion itself is now secular as we have seen. Therefore it is our next task to exhibit how American Judaism, i.e., the religion of the Jews, has become secular as well.

NOTES

[1]U.S. Department of Justice, Immigration and Naturalization Service," Immigrant and Nonimmigrant Aliens Admitted to the U.S.," in: *The 1993 Information Please Almanac,* Boston, Houghton Mifflin & Co., pp. 821-830.

[2]*Ibid.,* p.830. 1, 827,167 immigrants were admitted in 1991.

[3]Milton Plesur, *Jewish Life in Twentieth Century America,* Chicago, Nelson-Hall, 1982, Chapter 1.

[4]U.S. Department of Commerce, Bureau of the Census, *Historical Statistics of the United States,* Washington, D.C., United States Government Printing Office, 1975, p. 105.

[5]Gustavus Myers and Henry M. Christman, *History of Bigotry in the United States,* New York, Capricorn Books, 1960.

[6]Thomas A. Bailey, *The American Pageant,* Boston, D.C. Heath and Co., 1961, p. 780.

[7]Jesse D. Clarkson, *A History of Russia,* New York, Random House, 1961, p.250.

[8]Cecil Roth, *History of the Jews,* New York, Schocken Books, 1963, p. 266.

[9]Clarkson, *op.cit.* p. 251.

[10]Andrew M. Greeley, *Religious Change in America,* Cambridge, MA., Harvard University Press, 1989.

[11]Selma Berrol, "Public Schools and Immigrants: The New York City Experience," in: *American Education and the European Immigrant: 1840-1940,* Bernard J. Weiss, Ed.,Urbana, Ill., The University of Illinois Press, 1982, p. 34.

[12]Leonard Dinnerstein, "The Advancement of American Jews," in : *Ibid..,*p.46.

[13]*Ibid.,* p. 38.

[14]Gerhard Falk, *The Jew In Christian Theology,* Jefferson, N.C. and London, Mc Farland, 1992.

[15]Irving Howe, *World of Our Fathers,* New York, Simon and Schuster, 1976, p. 9.

[16]Dinnerstein, *op.cit.,* pp. 44-55.

[17] Census of the United States, 1970. Also see: Edward Fiske, *The New York Times,* February 21, 1991.

[18]John J. Appel and Selma Appel, "The Little Red School House," in ; Weiss, *op.cit.,* pp. 26 and 27.

[19]Phillip E. Hammond, *The Protestant Presence in Twentieth Century America,* Albany, State
University of New York Press, 1992, pp. 13,15, 16 and 19.

[20]Peter I. Berger, *The Sacred Canopy,* Garden City, New York, Doubleday, 1967.

[21]Talcott Parsons, "Religion in Postindustrial America," *Social Research,* Vol.41, No. 2, Summer 1974, pp. 493-525.

[22]Gerhard Falk, *The Life of the Academic Professional,* Lewiston, N.Y., Edwin Mellen Press, 1990, p.214..

[23]E. Digby Baltzell, *The Protestant Establishment,* New York, Random House, 1964, pp. 339-352.

[24]George M. Marsden, *The Soul of the American University,* New York, Oxford University Press, 1994.

[25]Violette de Mazia, "Letter of September 21, 1970,"; in : *John Dewey: Recollections,* Robert D. Williams, Editor, Washington, D.C., University Press of America, 1982, p. 9.

[26]Marguerite Block, "Letter of June 5, 1970," *Ibid.,* p. 11.

[27]Randolph S. Bourne, "John Dewey's Philosophy," *Ibid.,* p. 14.

[28]Orville G. Brim, "Letter of August 30, 1970,". *Ibid.,* p. 22.

[29]Leonard Carmichael, "Introduction," in: John Dewey, *The Child and the Curriculum,* Chicago, The University of Chicago Press, 1956, pp. vi, xi, and xii.

[30]Robert Dewey, *The Philosophy of John Dewey,* The Hague, Martinus Nijhoff, 1977, p.ix.

[31]Roy P. Fairfield, *Humanistic Frontiers in American Education,* Buffalo, N.Y. Prometheus Press, 1971.
See also: William A. Galston, "Salvation through Participation: John Dewey and the Religion of Democracy," in: *Raritan,* Winter 1993.

[32]Steven C. Rockefeller, *John Dewey,* New York, Columbia Unviersity Press, 1991, Chapter 6.

[33]John Dewey, *My Pedagogic Creed,* in: Steven C. Rockefeller, *John Dewey,* New York, Columbia University Press, 1991, p.234.

[34] Rockefeller, *op.cit.* p. 450.

[35] John Dewey, *The Humanist Manifesto,* in: Charles W. Dunn, *American Political Theology,* New York, Praeger, 1984, p. 98.

[36] John Dewey, *A Common Faith,* New Haven, Yale University Press, 1971 (1934) p.9.

[37] Rockefeller, *op.cit.,* p. 206.

[38] Leonard Carmichael, "Introduction,*"* in: John Dewey, *The Child and the Curriculum,* Chicago, The University of Chicago Press, Eleventh Printing 1971, p. vii.

[39] Shelley Burtt, "Religious Parents, Secular Schools: A Liberal Defense of an Illiberal Education," *The Review of Politics,* Vol.56, No.1, Winter 1994, pp. 51-70.

[40] *Pierce vs. Society of Sisters,* 268 U.S. 510, (1925).

[41] *Cochran vs. Louisiana State Board of Education,* 281 U.S. 913 (1930).

[42] Joel Spring, "The Courts and the Schools," in: *American Education,* New York, Longman, 1989, Chapter 10.

[43] *Ibid.,* p. 269.

[44] *Illinois ex. rel. McCollum vs. Board of Education,* 333 U.S. 202 (1948)

[45] *Engel vs. Vitale,* 370 U.S. 421, 1962.

[46] Robert F. Drinan, "The Supreme Court to Review Student Prayer Groups in High School, " *America,* vol. 162, No. 15, April 28, 1990, pp. 429-430.

[47] *Sherbert vs. Verner,* 374 U.S., 398 (1963).

[48] *Epperson vs. Arkansas,* 393 U.S. 97, (1968).

[49] *Lemon vs. Kurtzman,* 403 U.S. 602, (1971).

[50] *Edwards vs. Aguillard,* 482 U.S. 578 (1987).

[51] Drinan, *op. cit.,* pp.429-430.

[52] *Wallace vs. Jaffree,* 472 U.S. 38, (1985).

[53] Leonard W. Levy, *The Establishment Clause: Religion and the First Amendment,"* New York, Macmillan Co., Inc., 1986, p. 126.

[54] Jerry Zremski, "Supreme Court decision separating church, state has wide ramifications," *The Buffalo News,* June 28, 1994, p.4.

[55] Hammond, *op.cit.,* p.101.

[56] Beth B. Hess, Elizabeth W. Markson   Peter J. Stein, *Sociology,* New York, Macmillan, 1993, pp. 9-13.

[57]Jerzy Szacki, *History of Sociological Thought,* Westport, Conn., Greenwood Press, 1979, p.174.

[58]Emile Durkheim, *The Elementary Forms of the Religious Life,* New York, Collier Books, 1961.

[59]Reinhard Bendix, *Max Weber: An Intellectual Portrait,* Berkeley, University of California Press, 1977, pp. 66-67.

[60]Albion W. Small, *Origins of Sociology,* New York, Russell and Russell, 1924, p. 333.

[61]Lewis A. Coser, "American Trends," in: *A History of Sociological Analysis,* Tom Battamore and Robert Nisbet, Editors, New York, Basic Books, 1978, pp, 287-297. See also: Harry Elmer Barnes and Howard Becker, *Social Thought From Lore to Science,"* New York, D.C. Heath and Co., 1938, Chapter XXIV.

[62]Ralph H. Turner, "The Many Faces of American Sociology," *The American Behavioral Scientist, Vol. 33, No. 6, July/August 1990, pp. 662-684.*

[63]*Facts on File,* May 23, 1991, p. 379.

[64]Peter L. Benson and Dorothy Williams, *Religion on Capital Hill: Myths and Realities,* New York, Harper and Row, 1982, p. 107.

[65]*Ibid.,* p. pp.107-139.

[66]Will Herberg, *Protestant-Catholic-Jew,* Garden City, N.Y. , Doubleday and Co., 1955, p. 274.

[67]Robert N. Bellah, "Civil Religion in America," *Daedalus, Journal of the American Arts and Sciences,* Vol/ 96, No. 1,

[68]*Ibid., p.116.*

[69]Herberg, *op.cit..,* p. 280.

Part Three

American Jewish Institutions at the End of the Century

Chapter VIII

The Secularization of the Jewish Religion in America

I.

We have made the distinction between secularism and secularization because secularization is a process "of decline in religious activities, beliefs, ways of thinking and institutions" and "the gradual deposition of religion from almost every structure and dimension of society, except perhaps the most private and personal." Secularism is the total rejection of any kind of supernatural or transcendental view of the world, an attitude with few followers in the United States. Therefore we are here concerned with the process of secularization whereby the Jewish religion has become altered in America in this century.[1]

The best means of recognizing the secularization of Judaism in 1995 is to compare the Judaism practiced in America at the end of the twentieth century to the manner in which Judaism was practiced here one hundred years earlier. This will reveal considerable changes in the customs and ceremonies conducted by Jews in America then and now. It will also demonstrate the changes in the status and role of the American Jewish clergy. By status is here meant the sum of rights and privileges pertaining to the position of rabbi and by role is meant the sum of the duties and obligations incurred by that status.

The dominance of business competence over scholarship and learning in the American synagogue is another indication of Jewish secularization as are the changes within Judaism under these circumstances. The "circumstance" to which we refer here is best understood by considering that the *1990 National Jewish Population Study* revealed that fully 90% of American Jews define being Jewish as being a member of an ethnic or cultural group, 5% see themselves as Jewish by religion only and another 5% hold that both definitions are necessary.[2]

At least some of the consequences of these attitudes by American Jews are the changing status-role of the rabbi, the diversity of religious commitment in American Jewish congregations, the substitution of holocaust commemorations for Jewish practice, the altered meaning of the Bar/Bat Mitzvah in American Jewish life and the abandonment of Judaism as the result of the high intermarriage rate. These and many more developments were summarized by Rabbi Mordecai Kaplan in his *Judaism as a Civilization,* written in the 1930's and responsible for the rise of Jewish Reconstructionism.

II.

The Jews who came to the United States between 1881 and 1924, as well as the native Jews of Portuguese and German descent, were by no means all "Torah true". That means that many of the native Jews and some immigrants were not willing to live by the precepts of the Five Books of Moses, the Talmud (Scholarship), the Shulchan Aruch or "Set Table" and other books and mandates traditionally used to support the life style of the Eastern European Jews.

In fact, the descendants of the Portuguese Jews whose ancestors had come to the Dutch colony of New Amsterdam in 1654 and the descendants of the German Jews whose ancestors had come mainly in the early part of the nineteenth century distanced themselves from the new arrivals from Eastern Europe in many ways, just as the Jews with Spanish names had done to the German Jews generations earlier.[3]

Thus, the "Sephardic" or Spanish Jews were noted for "their haughtiness, high sense of honor and their stately manners." They were members of all of New York City's "best clubs" and one of their daughters, Emma Lazarus, was known as the writer of the poem inscribed on the Statue of Liberty and referring to immigrants as "tired, poor and huddled masses and wretched refuse." This was resented by the German Jews of the 19th century who found that while gentile society was "indifferent, they found the Spanish Jews almost unapproachable."[4]

However, when during the first World War several hundred thousand Eastern European Jews arrived in the United States, the German Jews, well established particularly in New York society, were appalled at the sight of the traditional black clothes, long beards and orthodox religious habits of the newcomers.

In addition to the religiously orthodox, there were among the immigrants some Jewish "radicals", i.e. atheists who denounced Judaism, rebelled against rabbinical authority, deliberately insulted religious Jews by holding dances on the highest Holy Day, Yom Kippur, and committed other kinds of "blasphemy" or *Loshon Harah* (Evil-speaking).

These "radical" Jews spoke the same Yiddish spoken by the great majority of Jews who adhered rather strictly to orthodox practice and attempted at first to re-create in America what had been their common heritage in Europe.[5]

The "radicals", however, were very few. Influenced by the enlightenment that had swept Europe and America for many years these Jews read not only the works of the French "philosophes" but also Karl Marx, Friedrich Engels and Vladimir Ulyanov, i.e., Lenin. Some became communists, some even returned to Russia after the revolution of 1917.

The vast majority of "Torah true" Jews however, were not radicals nor were they able to re-create Russian Jewish conditions here. They tried because that was all they knew. However, the secularization of the United States had begun in earnest by 1901 and progressed rapidly thereafter as we have seen. Furthermore, the legal, political and institutional conditions in the United States were so different from that of Eastern Europe that the vast gap between the two cultures made replication of the Yiddish culture of Europe in America extremely difficult. That is not to say that some did not succeed. In fact, there are in the United States in 1995 a few native born "Chasidic" Jews and other orthodox Jews who speak Yiddish, live by the precepts of Torah Judaism and who have thereby succeeded in perpetuating this culture within the framework of American multiculturalism.[6]

In 1901 Torah Judaism was not in the minority nor was it viewed as peculiar for a Jewish man to speak the Jewish language, wear a beard, grow earlocks, exhibit fringes hanging from a prayer shawl under his clothes or participate in three daily prayer services in one of the numerous Jewish houses of worship then found in every large American city.

Except for the established German and Portuguese synagogues, these numerous newer synagogues (Greek for assembly) were then headed by a Yiddish speaking Eastern European rabbi. Each of these congregations was usually quite small. Unlike in Europe, the American membership was entirely voluntarily and the traditional rabbi supported entirely by voluntary contributions. This was quite a shock to the newly arrived rabbis since European governments had for centuries enforced the rabbi's authority in his community and appointed him tax collector, judge and spokesman for the Jews in his town.

In eastern Europe the rabbi was a scholar-saint whose position was secure during his life time.   Some of the eastern European rabbis were deemed to perform miracles while all interpreted the religious law, known as *halacha*. Thus, these rabbis or *rebbes* had great prestige in their community and, because of their scholarship, were revered by all.

In the United States, however, all of these roles were in doubt almost from the day that the first traditional rabbi landed in New York.[7] This role conflict led to a great deal of confusion as evidenced by this story: "An orthodox Jew arrives in New York and is met at the dock by his friend from the old country. Having arrived on the Sabbath they walked from the dock to the friend's home. On the way they came by a park bench. There a man was sitting smoking a cigar on the Sabbath and reading a Yiddish newspaper. ' Well, what do you know?' said the newcomer. 'In America even the *goyim* read Yiddish.'"

The European *rebbes* were often wealthy in comparison to the abject poverty of their community. This was true because they collected fees for each interpretation or advice they were asked to give. In America, however, traditional rabbis were seldom asked anything, let alone asked to interpret *halacha* or Jewish law.

In the middle of the 20th century, traditional rabbis received a salary of about $1,200 a year and augmented that income with another $1,500 from performing various ceremonies during the year.

Some traditional rabbis earned even $4,000 a year in the 1950's at a time when average American income was about $5,200 per year and more in the professions.

At odds with his assimilationist American congregation, the traditional rabbi usually placed little emphasis on public speaking and a great deal of emphasis on study of sacred texts, particularly the Talmud, and the interpretation of The Law. That, however, did him little good in America. Instead of seeking a scholar/ saint, American Jewish congregations soon sought a performer, a public speaker and a social mixer capable of representing the Jewish community in the non-Jewish world. All that was and is impossible for the traditional rabbi alone because he will eat only *kosher* food. Such food is unknown in the general community and is not even furnished in many Jewish organized dinners and social gatherings.[8]

Thus, the traditional rabbi lost his function early in the century as secularization gripped the Jewish community. Only two functions still remain the traditional rabbi. One is to serve in a strictly orthodox congregation, Chassidic or not, and the other is to serve as a stand-in for those many Jews who will not or cannot live by the laws and regulations of talmudic Judaism but who are willing to pay so that the rabbi does so. This is particularly true of those many Jews who have no religious affiliation at all and who hire so-called "free lance" rabbis, that is, rabbis without a pulpit. These rabbis are paid for each wedding, funeral, bar/bat mitzvah or other ceremony they may perform and thereby earn somewhat more than those who are appointees of a congregation while escaping the humiliation to which almost all American rabbis are subject, whether orthodox, reform or conservative.

An excellent example of the treatment American rabbis generally suffer is the following paragraph from a longer letter published by a rabbi in a congregational bulletin.

> "I (have) described some of the activities performed by a congregational rabbi. In all of these activities the rabbi often becomes the living embodiment of the Jewish community. Because of this, his congregants must exercise great care in the way they treat him and speak to him. To criticize the Rabbi in the presence of children is to demean the only model of the Jewish heritage which many of them have. To publicly and frequently carp on his shortcomings, real and

imagined, is to jeopardize the unity and stability of the community of which he is the prime mover. To treat the rabbi as the meanest of servants rather than as the spiritual leader, is to show the Jewish and general communities our lack of regard for the tradition which he symbolized in their eyes.[9]

This letter was written in 1994 by a non-traditional rabbi, born in the U.S. and in no sense foreign. Evidently, then, it was not and is not the foreign accent, nor the unusual clothing, nor the adherence to ritual practice which led American Jews to view their clergy in so poor a light. Instead it is secularization which leads many Americans of whatever background to view all persons as utilitarian objects to be bought and used rather than as subjects to be supported and understood. Pragmatists, whose views are guided by instrumentalism, may well applaud the view that those who are employed in any capacity are therefore to be judged only on the basis of their immediate utility.

In addition to the traditional rabbi already discussed, Carlin and Mendlovitz have identified the modern orthodox rabbi; the reform rabbi in various roles and the conservative rabbi. The latter two groups also include at least two hundred women now ordained by the reform and conservative seminaries. The entrance of women into the Jewish clergy is perhaps the most immense status change yet to affect Judaism.[10]

The modern orthodox rabbi is no less concerned with the observance of Jewish law and ideology than the traditional rabbi. However, the modern orthodox rabbi is generally a native American, seldom wears the caftan, long beard and earlocks of the traditonalist and participates in the Protestantization of Judaism first introduced by the reform movement. Usually, the modern orthodox rabbi is as extensively trained in Hebrew and Jewish scholarship as the traditonalist. He knows, however, that this training is of no consequence in the congregations he must lead and that he is expected to be an organizer, fund raiser and administrator rather than a scholar. He is also expected to be a reasonable public speaker. The influence of the modern orthodox rabbi, like his conservative colleague, extends only to ritual matters. Beyond that large contributors and synagogue politicians are likely to make all decisions. Modern orthodox rabbis are generally not very much interested in dealing with the gentile world unless this is thrust upon them in small towns where they may be the only available rabbi. Education and the maintenance, if not the rebuilding, of traditonal Judaism within their own community appears to be the principal purpose of these rabbis. Their influence in the wider Jewish community is negligible precisely because these rabbis are not interested in secular matters nor viewed as "organization men or women."

Within their own congregation modern orthodox rabbis are frequently viewed as employees whose boss is every dues-paying member of the congregation. Their hours are long, they are expected to be available at all times and in particular at times when others are not working, that is, evenings and weekends.[11]

Being an organizer is however precisely the role of the reform rabbi. The reform movement, originating in 19th century Germany, is now about one hundred years old in America. Usually a member of a middle class or upper class family, the reform rabbi seldom has an extensive Jewish education comparable to that of the orthodox rabbis. However, almost all have a considerable secular education, many hold advanced degrees in history, philosophy or other secular subject matter and add to their prestige, not by Jewish learning, but by exhibiting a doctorate. Therefore, many reform rabbis prefer to be called "Dr. Cohen etc." rather than "rabbi". Reform rabbis earn upward of $100,000 per year in some of the wealthiest, big city congregations, while salaries of $80,000 are common.

In contrast to the scholar-saint image of the traditonalist who seldom preached, preaching is the most important function of the reform rabbi. The sermons given by such rabbis resemble professorial lectures and deal with matters of current interest or social issues. Reform rabbis also teach adult classes, supervise the Sunday school, conduct the synagogue service, preside over life-cycle ceremonies, visit the sick and bereaved, counsel those who seek his help, and, most important, act as ambassadors to the Gentile community. All this can be done by reform rabbis because most of the large reform synagogues, called temples by reform Jews, have a business manager who runs the mundane side of the organization.

This leaves the rabbi to participate in such organizations as the National Conference of Christians and Jews. Since reform rabbis do not restrict their diet to kosher food, they can participate in all kinds of interfaith dinners and social affairs not open to the orthodox. Many reform rabbis have undertaken the role of social reformer in their community. In that role they participate in minority concerns, sit on boards of directors of social agencies and preach a "liberal" agenda to their congregations. Reform Jews say that such attitudes stem from "prophetic" Judaism although few would be familiar with the major or minor prophets included in the Torah. It is precisely because of the general Jewish illiteracy concerning the tradition that the reform rabbi has become a minister rather than a scholar-saint as was true among traditonal Jews. The traditonal Jew is generally so well versed in the ritual and ceremony of Judaism that he does not need the rabbi to conduct these for him. American Reform Jews, conservative Jews and some orthodox Jews are for the most part ignorant of these traditions and that has led them to give the rabbi the role of priest/ parson in the Christian sense of those designations.

Reform Judaism was first practiced in the United States after 1870 when some of the German Jewish immigrants had become wealthy and established Temple Emanu-el in New York city under the tutelage of Rabbi Gustav Gottheil. At its opening *The New York Times* wrote that the new temple, as the Reform Jews like to call a synagogue, was "the first to stand forward before the world and proclaim the dominion of reason over blind and bigoted faith." Dr. Gottheil's successor, Rabbi Kaufman Kohler, wrote that German Jews were "freed from the shackles of medievalism with their minds impregnated with German sentiments no longer 'oriental.'" Thus, the wealthy German Jews who had organizaed that and other temples sought to secularize Judaism both in its practices and in its outlook. This was already true among the Reform Jews in Germany, the land of origin of that movement.[12]

The Conservative rabbinate and movement is an American development. Younger than both the orthodox and reform movements, consevatives are generally those who had an orthodox childhood but who recognize the need to adjust to present American conditions. Conservative rabbis are teachers but they are also organization men or women. Building membership, dealing with finances, planning new buildings, and increasing attendance at religious functions are all rabbinic activities. Conservative rabbis must also attend committee meetings, board meetings and community meetings. To quote one conservative rabbi: " .....he (the rabbi) becomes a drummer, a fifer, a salesman, an advertising agent" and, we can add, an entertainer.[13]

While reform rabbis view their listeners as an "audience" conservative rabbis are more likely to see their congregants as worshipers. Unlike his orthodox colleague, a conservative rabbi is unlikely to attend daily prayer services, both in the morning and at night. Reform rabbis have no such problem because reform temples do not usually conduct daily services.

A number of conservative rabbis hold positions in Jewish organizations such as the Zionist Organization of America, the United Jewish Appeal or B'nai B'rith (Sons of the Covenant), a fraternal organization. From an ideological viewpoint conservative rabbis range from the modern orthodox to the reform.

Earnings of the conservative rabbi may match those of the reform rabbi but in any case are not far behind.[14]

Undoubtedly the most radical change in the status - role of the rabbi in the past twenty years has been the entrance of women into that calling. This has been true only of the Reform and Conservative movements and has become so important that women now constitute a majority of rabbinical students in those denominations. However, the impact of women upon the Jewish religion has not yet been very great because most female rabbis are not yet senior rabbis and because those who do serve congregations have entered the education area.[15]

The sum of this discussion is easily stated: The American rabbinate is today primarily a profession and not a calling in the transcendental sense of that word. This means that rabbis now have the secular function of symbolizing the assimilation of Jews into the mainsteam of American life, interpreting the non-Jewish world to the membership and the Jewish world to non-Jews, perpetuating the ancient Jewish tradition in a thoroughly secular society by using secular means and storing the disregarded scholarship of generations in their minds and in their writings (if any), so that "the People of the Book" will not lose all they inherited from generations and generations of Jews born elsewhere and earlier and far less fortunate than their American progeny.

III.

The diversity of American Judaism is a second indication of the degree of secularization Judaism has now attained. While uniformity in any human institution, whether religious or otherwise, cannot exist and never has existed, the diversity of Judaism in America is far greater than was true in Europe from where the ancestors of most American Jews had come. Nevertheless, there was religious diversity in Judaism at all times, so that it is legitimate to see the secularization of Judaism in the 20th century not only as the outcome of the numerous influences already discussed, but also as part of the orthodox Jewish heritage. This heritage included a somewhat "this-worldly" attitude as evidenced by a study of both the Torah (Scriptures) and the Talmud (Learnings) upon which the entire edifice of Judaism rests.

Now it would seem that a rational analysis of any "Holy Writ" and belief in divine revelation are antithetical. This becomes visible if we compare the arguments of "true believers" who take the Torah literally with those who, while not rejecting the revelation at Mt. Sinai, do not. The "true believers" explain away all problems and contradictions in their sacred texts by arguing that man is of limited intellect and therefore cannot understand the meaning of the various contradictions found in the scriptures. In addition, such believers simply choose not to define such terms as "revelation," "prophecy" or "Holy Spirit" and claim that the true meaning of the sacred materials is in fact hidden from mere mortals.

There is however a humanist tradition in Judaism which has always taken a different view of the Torah. These otherwise orthodox practitioners wrote years ago that at least some sections of the Torah were composed by men and were not the transcriptions of Moses. Even among those rabbis who composed the Talmud there were many who thought that Moses was only one of several men responsible for the writing of the Torah.

They also taught that the Torah includes material that was written before Moses and that it also includes material written after his death. This is of course the only possible explanation of the last eight verses of Deuteronomy which describes how Moses died.[16]

It has for long been the opinion of the modern critical school of biblical study that the book of Deuteronomy, called Devorim in Hebrew, was written long after the other four books. This was also the view of Rabbi Joseph who is cited in the Talmud repeatedly. Furthermore, a Rabbi Jose ben Hanina is quoted as presenting Moses as the independent author of numerous biblical verses and sections.

Louis Ginzburg, a modern American scholar, has summed up the humanism of some Talmudists in this fashion: "Nothing is more characteristic of the intellectual temper of the Talmudists than their critical notes on the Bible. Some of them were more radical than many modern scholars would dare to be."[17]

The Eastern European Jewish community, consisting of all who spoke the Yiddish language, regardless of the state in which they lived, centered their lives upon the study of Torah and Talmud and accommodated the different viewpoints expounded for centuries by their scholars and rabbis. This then led to a theology which, although diverse in its interpretations, led to common practices among almost all of the eleven million Jews living in Europe before 1939.

Without discussing the theology of that now extinct community it is well to review the work of Ruth Benedict, Margaret Mead, Conrad Arensberg and their committee concerning the life of the Eastern European Jews. That committee undertook to study this now extinct culture during the second world war, not only because the war prevented the committee members to visit various far flung areas where field studies had been conducted before, but also because they, as non-Jews, thought they could develop an objective and scientifically sound description of the Jewish world as it was before 1939.[18]

Thus, Mark Zbrowsky and Elizabeth Herzog wrote the report of the Columbia University Research in Contemporary Cultures committee concerning the Eastern European Jews. The sum of their findings were these:

1. Eastern Europeans who viewed themselves as Jews and were so regarded by others thought of the universe as a designed whole planned and governed by "The Almighty" who created it from original chaos.

2. Everything in that universe was believed to have a reason, including apparent contradictions and inconsistencies.

3. In that universe, all human and divine behavior also had a reason and a purpose.

4. Since God was conceived as a reasonable being, humans too were expected to behave in a reasonable manner. Unreasonable conduct was viewed as dangerous.

5. Evil was also considered part of the reasonable universe inasmuch as joy cannot exist without sorrow, the Sabbath could not exist without the week, light could not exist without darkness.

6. God was viewed as dispensing both justice and mercy to humans.

7. Since the universe is for all men, no effort was made to proselytize non-Jews, since they too are part of God's plan.

8. Human welfare precedes all else. Therefore, even the dietary laws could be suspended in favor of health requirements.

9. The feast is as important as the fast. There were no Jewish monasteries as life is to be enjoyed.

10. Although life is hard, it is good as evidenced by the fact that nobody wants to leave it.

11. While observance of The Law was widely held to be important it was not viewed as total protection against all evils. Hence superstitions abounded, including belief in "the evil eye" and bad spirits.

12. All life is interdependent and therefore "Life Is With People", as the report by the committee is called.[19]

There was of course a great deal more to be said about the culture of the Eastern European Jew. It was, however, this culture which was brought to the United States at the end of the 19th century and which persists to this day among those Jews now generally called "chasidim" or pious ones by that majority of American Jews who live by other rules and whose world looks quite different.

That difference was first spelled out in detail when Mordecai Kaplan published *Judaism as A Civilization* in 1934. In his 1967 preface to that book's numerous editions, Kaplan argues that Judaism is more than a religion and that that view is the culmination of a thought process which began with mythology, continued with philosophy, was augmented by science and had, by 1934, reached holistic or organismic thinking.[20]

The major thesis of Kaplan's work is that following both Spinoza and Mendelssohn Judaism must adopt an attitude of religious toleration. Therefore, Kaplan would include in Judaism as a civilization, both the orthodox and the reform, the conservative as well as the non-believers because "*they share too many elements in common with the rest of Jewry - elements which are included in the term civilization -to make differences in religion a cause for aloofness.*"[21]

Nevertheless, Kaplan argues for the maintenance of religion in Jewish life and writes: "*take religion out and Judaism becomes an empty shell. Not by the furthest stretch of the imagination could a secularized life be identified with the spiritual heritage which has shaped the Jewish people into a unique entity."*

To defend that view in light of the scientific interpretation of reality which has been the mainstay of American life for a century Kaplan argues, as do so many others, that there is no way of knowing that the scientific picture of reality we now possess corresponds to the actual nature of things.

Together with Kaplan's contribution, the diversity of Judaism consists of four categories. These are the orthodox, also known as *Torah-true;* the reformists who seek to view Judaism only as a religion; the reconstructionists who hold the "Judaism As a Civilization" view and the secularists or humanists.

During the 1960's, some secularists among Jews reached the conclusion that one may be a Jew and an agnostic at the same time. Those who hold such views are not persons indifferent to Judaism. Most of these Jews were and are that eighty percent of Jews of college age who receive a higher education and are therefore subject to the philosophical, scientific and literary influences which we have shown have produced secular humanism in the Western World. The view which this "University Religion" proposes has been called "free inquiry" and refers to the attitude that nothing is sacred and that everything can and will be examined. If sacredness means untouchability, then "free inquiry" means that any idea can be rejected.

A second part of the "University Religion" is empiricism. While religion has traditionally viewed "truth" to reside in the author of an assertion, such as Moses, Isaiah or Ezekiel, empiricists at least claim that the acceptance of an idea is entirely dependent on the evidence for it and is in no way related to the author of the idea.

Thirdly, the "University Religion" refers to the indifference which most Jewish college students maintain towards traditional or even "liberal" theology. Jewish college students and that great majority of Jews who hold college degrees and others, do not argue religion. They simply ignore it. They have no interest in it. They never read about it. They give it none of their time.

Fourthly, the "University Religion" teaches that values are created by human beings and not imposed by a deity. This is what is meant by "humanism". Thus, good health habits are a value which any person can understand and may impose on himself. However, refraining from bread on Passover is a belief imposed by an unseen force, if it exists, and that is deism which the "University Religion" rejects.

In view of the development of a "University Religion," a small group of Jews formed the Birmingham Temple in the early 1960's. Birmingham, Michigan is a suburb of Detroit. This temple is devoted to Humanistic Judaism on the following principles:

1. There is no one set of intrinsic meaning which all humans share. Therefore, any variety of values and meanings may be brought to humanistic Judaism.

2. The search for meaning must be secularized. This means, that unlike the "Reconstructionist" movement founded by Mordecai Kaplan, humanist Judaism has no sancta and that includes Jewish survival.

3. Empiricism is accepted as the only means of finding "truth." Therefore there can be no "official" view of man and the universe.

4. Humanist Jews seek a meaningful language which excludes the term "God" but nevertheless accommodates "Man's Search for Meaning."[22]

That is the title of a famous book by Viktor Frankl, the Viennese Jewish psychiatrist and founder of "Logotherapy". In the first part of this astounding book Frankl describes his experiences in several Nazi concentration camps and then asks how it is possible to find meaning in life when the horrors of such experiences are possible. Says Frankl: *"Ultimately man should not ask what the meaning of life is but he must recognize that it is he who is asked. ...each man is questioned by life; and he can only answer to life by answering for his own life; to life he can only answer by being responsible. Thus, logotherapy sees in responsibleness the very essence of human existence."*[23]

Concepts such as Frankl's are used by humanist Jews to explain their needs. Thus, in Cincinnati, Ohio a Jewish congregation named "Beth Adam" (House of Man) has organized around the concept of agnosticism while retaining the view that Judaism as a civilization can be maintained without belief in anything supernatural. Its rabbi, Robert Barr, holds that Jewish prayers are "museum pieces" which are recited by few Jews and not understood by more than a handful.

The congregation has rewritten the Jewish liturgy and extols the human spirit rather than praising an intervening God. Consisting mostly of "intellectuals", the congregation still reads the Torah, that is the Jewish scriptures, but views such readings only as a historical link with the Jewish people but not a divinely inspired book. The congregation has abolished the principal recitations in all Jewish worship such as the "Shema" (Hear) prayer which is regarded as the foundation of Jewish belief in all Jewish denominations and is translated "Hear, Israel, the Lord our God, the Lord is One." The "Kaddish" in memory of the deceased has also been abolished. The word "Kaddish" means "Sanctification" and its contents extol the virtues of God, who, according to the humanist interpretation of Judaism may or may not exist, depending on the interpretation of the word "God." In the words of Rabbi Barr and William R. Jacobs, the president of Beth Adam synagogue in Cincinnati, *"The philosophy of Beth Adam does not deny the existence of God. Out of respect for the individual, the congregation does not seek to impose a concept of God, does not seek to reach agreement regarding such a concept, nor does the congregation assume that one must employ the term God to give expression to one's deeply held religious beliefs."* [24]

Instead of the traditional prayers, Rabbi Barr and his congregation have written a number of essays or paragraphs referring to various philosophical issues of concern to them. The congregation applied to become members of the Union of American Hebrew Congregations which represents the Reform movement in the United States but were not accepted on the grounds that agnosticism and Judaism are not compatible. [25]

"The Society for Humanistic Judaism" and "The Congress of Secular Jewish Organizations" have gone one step beyond congregation Beth Adam. Those who support these groups point to the more than one million Americans who, according to the National Jewish Population Study of 1990, are "born Jews with no religion." It is this group the "Society for Humanistic Judaism" would like to organize. These secular Jews wish to maintain a Jewish identity without the Jewish religion and in the absence of a Jewish language, such as Yiddish or Hebrew, languages which are seldom known to American Jews. Today, these groups seek some means of expressing their need for "essentially humanistic rituals," including life cycle events, which are distinctly Jewish and yet secular. [26]

The reason for this search is evident. Humanists, Jewish or not, want to raise their children with some set of values which pure reason cannot by itself supply. Furthermore, no one wants to live in a meaningless universe and lead a meaningless life and it is therefore very difficult, if not impossible, for many "would be" humanists to maintain their position. Even now, in 1995, severe cracks in the humanist position are visible in that many former Christians and Jews seek out esoteric religions and movements which they hope will fill the void which their traditional beliefs once filled but which the humanist movement has not been able to address.[27]

It is this problem which Rabbi Will Herberg considered when he criticized secular humanism on the grounds that it leads to "demonic idolatries." He meant totalitarianism of every kind and he claimed that failure to hold to biblical religion leads to "relativism but made humanity an absolute."[28]

Yet another means of Jewish expression has been the rise of the "Havurah" movement during the past twenty years. The "Havurah" movement stems from the counter-culture of the 1960's. Those who have resorted to this idea regarded the available Jewish institutions as *"sterile, impersonal, hierarchical and divorced from Jewish tradition."*[29]

There are independent Havurahs and synagogue related Havurahs. The independents hold their own Sabbath services, participate in a variety of traditional religious and social activities and, to some extents, observe the dietary laws. All this is done, however, on a gender egalitarian basis, without clergy and with participation from everyone. Synagogue related Havurahs generally do not sponsor Sabbath services since they do not wish to compete with the sponsoring synagogue or its rabbi. Nevertheless, they too are far more informal than is true in traditional synagogues inasmuch as they frequently meet in each other's homes and assume the leadership among themselves and are generally also independent of clergy.[30]

American Judaism, then, ranges from the strictly orthodox to the humanist and thereby allows so many interpretations of "who is a Jew" that everyone who wishes can find a place in the Jewish group. It is this immense diversity which has made a secular interpretation of Judaism very attractive to some and allows Jews of every view to belong to the Jewish community including some secular humanists.

III.

Religion does not only consist of theology. It includes visible practices as well and a number of these Jewish practices have now become secularized. An excellent example of the secularization of Jewish practice is the Bar Mitzvah or Bat Mitzvah ceremony. This ceremony is conducted for thirteen year old boys and twelve year old girls and celebrates the coming of age of the celebrants.

As we have already seen (Chapter One), this ceremony is wide spread among American Jews. Because of the diversity of Jewish practice there are those who continue to emphasize the religious, scholarly and familial significance of that ceremony as it was conducted in Europe.

In the United States, however, this ceremony has also become largely secularized so that the following story is appropriate: *"A boy was to become Bar Mitzvah shortly and his father was anxious to make a great impression upon all concerned. Therefore he hired a public relations firm and asked them to organize a Bar Mitzvah of such proportions that the ceremony would become the envy of the entire community.*

The public relations firm, anxious to please their customer, suggested that the 1,000 Bar Mitzvah guests be flown by private jets to Florida, there to parachute over Miami Beach while the Rabbi conducts the Bar Mitzvah ceremony in mid air. But the Bar Mitzvah father rejected the idea, even though the public relations firm intended to also bring each guest to shore by means of a motor boat and afterwards feast of shark. 'That,' said the Bar Mitzvah's father, 'is nothing new. Goldberg did that last year.' So the public relations firm came up with a unique and new idea. They flew the entire one thousand guests to India. They placed each on a white elephant. They hired professional hunters and they went on a Tiger safari into the jungle. A very long line formed as one thousand elephants entered the impenetrable forest. Once inside it was impossible to see more than the elephant directly ahead. Well, the bar mitzvah father sat on the last elephant. Just one half hour into the safari, the line ahead of him stopped. So the father, on the last elephant, called ahead 'what's holding up the line?' Mother, sitting on the elephant directly in front of him, shouted to the next person ' what's holding up the line?' The call went all the way up front where the Bar Mitzvah boy was sitting with the rabbi. Meanwhile the father, in the rear, was anxiously waiting for the call from the unseeable front of the line. Finally he heard something being called. The call become louder and louder.

*Now it was only two elephants away and now mother turned around
and repeated ' there is another Bar Mitzvah ahead of us! ' "*[31]
American Bar Mitzvahs are often called "affairs". The author has
seen children, dressed as adults but wearing "punk" hair styles,
participate in Bar/Bat Mitzvah dinners. Such hair styles involve
coloring the hair in two or more colors such as orange and blue etc.
Sometimes "go-go girls" are hired to enhance the party spirit. Masters
of Ceremony are not uncommon at such "affairs" as immense meals
are served and a fetish is made of the dessert. Here is a description of
such a party:

> *"He (the M.C.) gets a confirming nod from ....the Bar Mitzvah
> boy's mother and proclaims, 'Ladies and gentlemen, dessert!' The
> ballroom lights dim. In formation, the eight waitresses wearing red
> and white, parade from the Temple Beth El kitchen bearing aloft and
> ablaze Tarte aux Cerises, Flambee-flaming cherry tarts- the specialite
> de la maison from Harry Aarons Kosher Katerers, Inc. A ripple of
> applause, proper now, begins. Flames from the cognac surrounding
> the tarts lick high in the half-dark room. With the girls marching in
> perfect formation, it is spectacular. The applause grows."*

Ostentation such as this has been frequently described by observers
of the current Jewish scene. It should not be exaggerated. Only some
Bar/Bat Mitzvahs take on such foolish dimensions. Nevertheless, it is
significant that innumerable youngsters and their families agree with
the sentiment that "*The worst of it, the Hebrew, is behind him. The
good part, the 'affair ' is about to begin.*"[32] Therefore it is reasonable
to observe that the erstwhile effort to introduce children into the
religious life of Judaism by means of the Bar/Bat Mitzvah ceremony
has been reversed in secular culture. Now the ceremony signifies
closure and an end to religious involvement and an end to childhood.
The message is clear. Religion is for children, not adults.

IV.

Secularization of the American Jewish community is also
influenced by the Holocaust, by which we mean the deliberate mass
murder of the Jews of Europe between 1933 and 1945. Viktor Frankl
and many others have described the horrors of the Nazi camps in

which these mass murders took place. Nevertheless, no real understanding of those events is possible for those who did not experience them. In a sense, all human experience is limited to what the self experienced. Nevertheless, there are many life events that can be portrayed to others sufficiently to permit the listener to get some notion of the speaker's feelings, views and attitudes because a listener can usually relate to his own past the words and emotions produced by someone else. In connection with the Holocaust, however, a common sentiment is: "No explanations are needed for those who have been inside, and others will understand neither how we felt then nor how we feel now." This view is often expressed by Holocaust survivors.[33]

Nevertheless, a major effort has been made for the past thirty years to at least give some meaning to the Holocaust and in the course of this effort it has become necessary for both Jews and Christians to relate their religion to this nightmare. The question for theistic Jews is: "Where was God?" when these horrors took place. For Christians the question is: "How could this have happened among those who follow 'The Prince of Peace' and who teach or say they teach that 'God Is Love?'"

The dispute concerning this issue is indeed important. Believing Jews hate to face the fact that all their practices, all their laws, all their prayers availed them nothing in face of the killers. Believing Christians need to explain how millions of their followers could have been so brutal, so long, so often.

To escape the responsibility for the Holocaust, Christians like to blame humanists. The theory here is that the Nazi party, by embracing anti-semitism, had left the Christian fold and had espoused a purely humanist doctrine to the effect that man is everything and God does not exist. Hence, it is argued, the mass murders were the logical outgrowth of secular humanism since failure to recognize God and his laws permits humans to do anything, including mass murder.

This argument is based on the writings of Wilhelm Marr, a German publicist who coined the phrase *anti-semite* and founded the *League of Anti-Semites* in 1873 after publishing his best seller *Der Sieg des Judentums uber das Germanentum,* or, *The Victory of Judaism over Teutonism* in that year. This book went through twelve editions in six years and was undoubtedly the greatest publishing success in the German language in that century. Marr was not a Christian and said so. He also held that Jews are a race, biologically different from all other humans and that their religion had no bearing on their inherent "swinenishness." Nevertheless, Marr claimed that Jews had "become the first major power in Europe." Seeking to eliminate Jews from all participation in European life, Marr taught that Jews are "Ungeziefer" or vermin and need to be treated accordingly.[34]

Views such as these were held by large numbers of Germans in the nineteenth century and were propagated by many political parties other than the National Socialist German Workers Party represented by Adolf Hitler in the twentieth century.

In addition to his hatred of Jews, Adolf Hitler, although raised a Catholic, also had only contempt for Christianity. This has been documented repeatedly. Thus, those who knew him best held that Hitler was "a rationalist and materialist." *"The dogma of Christianity,"* he declared in one of his table conversations, *"gets worn away before the advances of science. Gradually, the myths crumble. All that is left is to prove that in nature there is no frontier between the organic and the inorganic. When understanding of the universe has become widespread, when the majority of men know that the stars are not sources of light, but worlds, perhaps inhabited worlds like ours, then the Christian doctrine will be convicted of absurdity........The man who lives in communion with nature necessarily finds himself in opposition to the Churches, and that's why they are heading for ruin-for science is bound to win."*[35]

This oft quoted passage sounds almost Spinozian and reflects a secularism which, however, cannot be called secular humanism because humanists by definition seek to improve the human condition at all times and in every manner, an attitude one can hardly attribute to Nazis.

In addition, humanists can show easily enough that *"As for the Holocaust, every uniformed German or Austrian who participated had received a conventional Christian education as a youth."*[36]

The immense involvement of Christian theology in the holocaust has by now been so well documented that Christians of all denominations have repeatedly acknowledged this relationship and have made a considerable effort to distance themselves from religious persecutions of any type but in particular from anti-Jewish conduct. This is necessary because from the writings of the early Church Fathers to Martin Luther and even to post-Holocaust theology,

Christian theologians have consistently defamed Judaism, taught that Jews were "Christ-killers," and created an atmosphere of such hostility towards Jews that the excesses of the Nazi party and their followers seemed legitimate to almost all Christians in the light of what had been taught them for nineteen hundred years.[37]

Undoubtedly, Christian involvement in the Holocaust has had an influence upon the secularization of many people who can hardly ignore that the killings and horrors of that time were perpetrated by persons raised as Christians and were tolerated by others who claimed not to know what in fact a believer in any religious system would want to know.

Upon Jews the impact of the holocaust was and is, of course, even greater. The survivors themselves have a world view which hardly anyone else can have. Thus, holocaust survivors, almost all of whom were raised orthodox Jews, have generally become agnostics because they cannot reconcile their experiences with the existence of a "loving God'" which religions generally proclaim.

Those who survived "*had every moral certainty literally beaten out of them in the Gestapo torture chamber.*" Pain, deprivation, hate and a sense that "*the injury cannot be healed; it extends through time, and the Furies, in whose existence we are forced to believe, rack not only the tormentor but the tormented.*"[38]

Primo Levi, an Italian Jewish survivor of Auschwitz, has described his torments in detail. Yet, he writes: "*In spite of all we have had to experience, I believe that even today, as in the days of the Encyclopedists, knowledge leads to recognition and recognition to morality. And I maintain that it was not the Enlightenment that failed but rather those who were appointed its guardians.*"[39]

Despite the rejection of religion which the Holocaust has caused among many American Jews (and some Christians), there are others who continue to assert the existence of God, the need for salvation, the maintenance of ritual and the efficacy of prayer. Among these is the Jewish philosopher Emil Fackenheim who continues to argue with Christians about the Holocaust, but always upon the assumption that God exists, that Judaism and Christianity are valid explanations of the relationship of God to man and man to the universe and that religion is a way of knowing.[40]

Likewise, the Jewish philosopher Martin Buber has spoken of the Nazi evil as beyond human solution or understanding. Nevertheless,

Buber, whose influence on Protestant theology is particularly great, viewed even Nazi evil as just one more evil, but not a unique and separate horror. Therefore Buber, who remained within the Jewish tradition all his life, saw the Nazi crimes as beyond human solution and held that there could be no human punishment for such deeds. This, of course, leaves only supernatural punishment in the "next world" and hence confirms, rather than rejects, traditional religious orientation.[41]

There is then no one response to the holocaust by either Jews or others. Nevertheless, that major historical tragedy, for which there is no real explanation, is at least for some good grounds for the abandonment of traditional Judaism and acceptance of secular humanism.

V.

If church attendance is a criterion of religious commitment in the Untied States then the American Jewish community lags far behind the Christian community in its commitment to religion and its institutions. Thus, about forty percent of Americans attend church every week but only 20% of American Jews do so. When asked whether religion is very important in their lives then 55% of Americans answer this affirmatively but only 30% of Jews thought so.[42]

The reasons for this wide discrepancy between the Jewish and Christian interest in religion lies in part in the double meaning of the word Jew. That is, Jewish is an ethnic as well as a religious label. Therefore, one million one hundred thousand Americans who are viewed as Jews but have no religion would have a significant impact on the answers to the questions concerning the importance of religion in their lives. This would not happen to Christians since they would not be interviewed on an ethnic basis.

A second reason for the lack of interest in Jewish religious practice by ethnic Jews is income. The median annual income of American Jews in 1989 was $39,000.- while the median income of all Americans at that time was only $30,000.- American Jews are more often college graduates than is true of Americans of any other faith and American Jews earn more than any other denomination in the United States. This means that belief in "God" and other supernatural beings is less common among Jews than others because in general belief in any god is more widespread among the poor than the rich. That is understandable in that the poor have more cause to look forward to another world than those whose present world is both satisfactory and enjoyable. In short, the wealthier classes don't need belief in other wordly personages and events as much as the poor do despite the fact that the rich are more likely to participate in Jewish organizations and "serve" on boards and committees than the poor. This latter phenomenon is of course not surprising since social honor is bought and paid for just as physical objects such as cars and coats are bought and displayed.[43]

Finally, the intermarriage pattern among American Jews has a great deal to do with the secularization of Judaism. Thus, in 1990, 68% of all married Jews then in the United States were married to a Jew by birth. Four percent were married to a Jew by choice and 28 percent were married to a non-Jew. These statistics include persons of all ages. During the years beginning with 1985, however, Jews began to marry non-Jews in much greater number. Over fifty percent of all Jewish marriages since 1985 have been with a non-Jew and twice as many mixed couples have been created among American Jews since then than is true of all Jewish couples.

The consequences of this high rate of intermarriage are that over 1.1 million Jews have no religion at all while 700,000 children of Jewish parentage are being raised in a religion other than Judaism..[44] Since this trend has been accelerating in the few years since the National Jewish Population Study was undertaken there is good reason to believe that a continued secularization of Jewish practices can be anticipated for the foreseeable future. This is true because those who are intermarried but remain within Judaism seldom opt for such stringent observances as synagogue participation, the holiday rituals and the maintenance of the food laws. Instead, intermarried persons are more likely to assume Jewish ethnicity but not Jewish religiosity.

These conditions within the Jewish religion are closely linked to Jewish family life in the United States and it is that institution which we shall therefore examine next.

NOTES

[1]Robin Attfield, *God and the Secular,* Cardiff, Wales, University College of Cardiff Press, 1978, pp211-215.

[2]Barry A. Kosmin et. al., *"The 1990 Jewish Population Survey,"* New York, The Council of Jewish Federations, 1991, p. 28.

[3]Cecil Roth, *History of the Jews,* New York, Schocken, 1963, p. 357

[4]Stephen Birmingham, *Our Crowd,* Dell Publishing Co., 1967, p. 154.

[5]Irving Howe, *World of Our Fathers,* New York, Simon and Schuster, 1976, p.140.

[6]Douglas Feiden, " Cuomo Steers Cash to Lubavitch Cronies," *Forward,* June 24, 1994, p.1.

[7]*Ibid* p. 177.

[8]Jerome E. Carlin and Saul H. Mendlovitz, "The American Rabbi, Loss of Authority," in: *Understanding American Judaism,* New York, KTAV Publishing, 1975, p. 173.

[9]Rabbi Eliot P. Marrus, "From the Rabbi" *Kol Shaarey Zedek,* July 1994, p. 1.

[10]Janet Mader, "How Women are Changing the Rabbinate," *Reform Judaism,* Summer 1991, pp.4-8.

[11]Basil Herring, *The Rabbinate as Calling and Vocation,* London, Jason Aronson, Inc., 1991, p. x.

[12]Birmingham, *op.cit.,* p. 158.

[13]Carlin and Medlovitz, *op.cit.,* p.200.

[14]*Ibid.,* pp. 212-213.

[15] Mader, *op.cit.,*pp. 4-8.

[16]Samuel Tobias Lachs, *Humanism in Talmud and Midrash,* Madison, N.J., Farleigh Dickerson University Press, 1993, pp. 126-127.

[17]Louis Ginzberg, *A Sprectrum of Jewish Learning at American Universities,* Philadelphia, Jewish Publication Society, 1906, p. 4.

[18]Margaret Mead, "Foreword,"in: Mark Zbrowsky and Elizabeth Herzog, *Life Is With People: The Culture of the Shtetl,* New York, Schocken Books, 1952, pp. 14 -15.

[19]Zbrowsky and Herzog, *op.cit.,* pp. 409-430.

[20]Mordecai M. Kaplan, *Judaism As A Civilization*, Philadelphia, The Jewish Publication Society, 1981, p.xi.

[21]*Ibid.,* p. 394.

[22]*Ibid,* p. 396.

[23]Viktor E. Frankl, *Man's Search for Meaning,* New York, Simon and Schuster, Inc., 1984, pp. 113-114; and a lecture given by Viktor Frankl in connection with a conference on "The Future of Psychotherapy" at the SAS Plaza Hotel, Hamburg, Germany, July 29,1994.

[24]William R. Jacobs and Robert B. Barr, "Many Jews Share Our Beliefs," *Forward,* Vol. LXXXXII, No.35. July 8, 1994, p. 6.

[25]Rachel Blustain, "Baruch Atah Ado....NOT!" *The Forward,* Vol. LXXXXVII, Nol.30, 978, June 3, 1994, p. 1.

[26]Seth Kulick, "The Evolution of Secular Judaism," *The Humanist,* Vol.53, No.2, March-April 1993, pp.34-35.

[27]Irving Kristol, "The Future of American Jewry," *Commentary,* Vol. 92, No.2, August 1991, pp. 21-26.

[28]Will Herberg, "Religion in Higher Education," *Journal of Higher Education,* Vol. 23, October 1952, pp. 350-358.

[29]Chava Weissler, "Coming of Age in the Havura Movement,: Bar Mitzvah in the Havurah Movement.," in: *The Jewish Family: Myths and Reality,* Steven M. Cohen and Paula C. Hyman, Eds., New York, Holmes and Meier, 1986, p. 200.

[30]*Ibid.,* p.201.

[31]Jack Rosenthal, "Bar Mitzvah Boy," in *Three Award Winning Television Plays,* New York, Penguin Books, 1978, pp. 20-25.

[32]Stanley Feldstein, *The Land that I show You,* New York, Anchor Press, 1978, pp.433-444.

[33]Frankl, *op.cit.,* p.20.

[34]Nora Levin, *The Holocaust: The Destruction of European Jewry 1933-1945,* New York, Schocken Books, 1973,p. 14 and Lucy S. Dawidowicz, *The War Against the Jews 1933-1945,* New York, Holt, Rinehart and Winston, 1975, p.34.

[35]Hermann Rauschning, *Hitler's Table Talk,* New York, G.P. Putnam's Sons, 1940, pp.59-61.

[36]Edd Doerr, "Bashing Humanists," *Church and State,* Vol. 50, No. 3, May/June 1990, p. 43.

[37]Gerhard Falk, *The Jew In Christian Theology,* Jefferson, N.C. and London, McFarland & Co., Inc., Publishers, 1992.

[38]Alexander Stille, "What the Holocaust Meant," *Dissent,* Vol. 37, No. 3, Summer 1990, p. 365.

[39]*Ibid.,* p.366.

[40]Laurie Mc. Robert, "Emil L. Fackenheim and Radical Evil," *Journal of the American Academy of Religion,* Vol., LVII, No.2, Summer 1989, p. 325.

[41]Michael L. Morgan, "Martin Buber, Cooperation and Evil," *Journal of the American Academy of Religion,* Vol. LVIII, No. 1, Spring, 1990, pp.99-109.

[42]*The Gallup Report,* No. 259, April 1987.

[43]Council of Jewish Federations, *National Jewish Population Study, p.19.* Also see: Spencer Rich, "The Rich Got Richer Again, *The Washington Post, September 20, 1992.*

[44]*Jewish Population Study, ,* p. 13.

Chapter IX

The Secularization of the American Jewish Family

I.

"The world of the east European Jews was a world in which God was a living force, a Presence, more than a name or a desire."[1]

This *Weltanschauung,* this world view, included the sacred family known to the European Jews for more than a thousand years. Such a family was patriarchial but more often matrilocal than patrilocal. This means that it was more common for a newly married couple to live with the bride's parents than to live with the groom's parents. Few had the resources to establish a home of their own.

The Jews of east Europe, whether living in the Russian Empire or the Balkans or the Baltic States, had one culture including the same language, religion and set of values. These values included the belief that "a person is part of a family and that there is no fulfillment of one's duties or one's pleasure as an isolated individual."[2] Supported by the marriage bond, the sacred family restricted sexual gratification exclusively to the spouse. Economic cooperation was a second function of the family. Traditionally, economic support for wife and children was mainly expected of the man, although in the European Jewish family it was not uncommon for a wife and mother to engage in business as well. The rearing of children is the third function of the family. In the sacred family that task is mainly that of the mother although fathers are expected to play the role of religious indoctrinator or teacher. Social solidarity is the outcome of the performance of these and other family tasks, leaving the indivdual with the impression that he needs to remain within the family all his life.[3]

Among the east European Jewish families age was not viewed as a time of decline but of expanded wisdom. Old persons were seen as "beautiful" and the fulfillments of life were accessible to the aged because age was held in high esteem.

In that culture, children were viewed as "the parents' crown" in circumstances which gave parents, and particularly the father, final authority over the conduct of youngsters who were always within sight of their elders. Both parents were treated with considerable respect although the father was viewed as a near deity.

Social control was achieved by means of public opinion but also by scolding and beatings. There was a sharp division of labor between the sexes and the roles of women, men and children were well defined. Some eastern Euorpean Jewish familes were extended families including grandparents. In that case, the oldest male was viewed as head of the household.

Above all, study of the Torah was valued so that even the poorest were encouraged to learn for the sake of learning. This study was confined to males and led to the Bar Mitzvah of thirteen year olds whose status then changed to that of an adult ready to support himself and consider marriage. Marriage was always Jewish. Marriage to a non-Jew was almost unknown and was viewed with such horror that the Jewish partner to such a "betrayal" was considered dead and the "kaddish", the prayer for the dead, was said over him. That is the thrust of the story "Chava" by theYiddish author "Sholom Aleichim" (Sholom Rabinowitz) in which the protagonist, the Jewish father, is not only shamed before his community because his daughter married a "goy'" but which also demonstrates how the Jewish father can no longer see his daughter who is now under the protection of the local priest and utterly divorced from her Jewish heritage. That story is part of the "Tevyeh" stories which have become well known around the world because they form the basis of the musical "Fiddler on the Roof."[4]

Marriage was a sacred occasion and institution as was the subsequent bearing of children. Divorce was permitted, but rare. And so, the east European Jew lived a sacred life cycle from the "cradle to the grave" presided over by the Almighty who created the world from chaos.[5] ".......it was the ferocious loyalty of the Jews to the idea of the family as they knew it, the family both as locus of expereince and as fulfillment of their obligations to perpetuate their line that enabled them to survive."[6]

Such was the culture of the vast majority of Jews who came to the United States before the 2nd World War and such was the culture of the majority of first generation immigrant Jews who lived in the United States until the middle of the 20th century.

II.

At a recent Bat Mitzvah in a "right wing" conservative synagogue, the main address to the congregation, the "dvar Torah", was given by the mother of the Bat Mitzvah girl. The mother, who has an Irish maiden name, is a Jewish woman because she converted to Judaism upon her marriage. Well educated in a secular area, she studied the traditions of the Jewish people, became familiar with Hebrew, learned Jewish history, raised her children as Jews, observes the Holy Days, attends weekly Sabbath services and involves herself so much in Jewish life that one is reminded of the following story:

"A renegade Jew who has not been seen at any synagogue in years finally marries a non-Jewish woman. No one is surprised but his parents, themselves not very attentive to the religion, are very upset about this intermarriage. However, the erstwhile *shickse* has other ideas. She becomes Jewish. Soon after her conversion her husband is seen "*in shul*" every Saturday. His relatives and friends are amazed. Here is a man who never paid attention to Judaism at all. Now he is in the synagogue at every occasion. Of course his friends ask him how this is possible. They ask him "why did you change your mind?" Exasperated, he replies that his wife has now converted and demands that he attend synagogue every week even though he doesn't like it. 'That's what you deserve for marrying a *shickse*, " says his father.

Thus, a century after the bulk of Jewish immigration came here from eastern Europe, there are 185,000 "Jews by Choice" in America, constituting about three percent of Jewishly identified persons. In addition there are 1,350,000 adult Gentiles who live in a household including a Jew. To understand that statistic better it is well to add the following: a. 700,000 children who have one or two Jewish parents are being raised in another religion. Usually these children have only one Jewish parent.   b. 210,000 persons who were born Jewish have converted to another religion. c. there are now 415,000 adults of Jewish parentage with another religion. These people were never Jewish because their parents did not pursue Judaism at the time of their birth.

These three categories together arrive at a total of 1,325,000 persons leaving yet another 25,000 who are born Jewish and are Jewish by religion but live with a gentile.[7] Evidently then, intermarriage has become the most important issue within the Jewish family in end-of-the-century America. This is the case because, as of 1995, fully 28% of all Jews by birth are married to a non-Jew while 52% of those Jews who married since 1990 married a non-Jew. In 1970 that figure was only 33%; in 1964 it was 11% and prior to that date, in 1957 it was 4%. Today, in 1995, four percent are married to a "Jew by Choice," which means that only 68% of all Jews have a spouse who was born Jewish. Furthermore it is noteworthy that the trend towards intermarriage continues unabated.[8]

Several consequences of such intermarriages are therefore in evidence. These consequences are at least "that it blurs religious boundaries between Jews and Christians; that it serves as a potential source for new Jews if the non-Jewish spouse converts; it has profound impact on the religious identity of children; and it raises serious questions of Jewish religious law and policy that bedevil the Jewish community today in an unprecedented manner."[9]

The causes of intermarriage have been debated in the Jewish community for years. Some of the studies dealing with these causes are rather limited in use because they concern only a small fraction of the Jewish population and are as unrepresentative as the study of University of Illinois faculty members made by Rabbi Henry Cohen. This showed that Jewish academics are twice as likely to be married to a non-Jew as is true of the general Jewish population. This disparity is attributed to the "academic commitment" of professors which the researcher compares to religious commitment. As we have seen throughout this book, "...................*there is the dominant philosophy of naturalism. Its method is scientific; its faith, that all being can be explained in terms of single order or efficient causation in which a supernatural Deity has no place; its morality, the ideals of humanism rooted in finite human experience; its messianic hope, that man-*

through understanding the consequences of his actions-can build a better world."[10]

These problems are illustrated by Saul Bellow in his novel, *Mr. Sammler's Planet*. *Sammler* is the German word for collector and is an appropriate name as the protagonist collects numerous Jewish experiences. He returns to his Jewish roots after making every effort to assimilate to British upper class society. Caught up in the Holocaust, Sammler survives and comes to the United States only to experience the American assimilationists, "sixties" Jewish radicals and drug users and the total break with the Jewish past which that decade represented. In the end, Saul Bellow, through Sammler, sees a Jewish future only through a relationship to Israel because the traditional Yiddish world has disappeared never to be seen again.[11]

The disappearance of that Yiddish world constitutes the core of the secularization of the Jewish family in the last fifty years. Tied to that Yiddish world was a form of traditional Judaism which reflected the east European Jewish life style now almost entirely abandoned.

This is seen by a review of the statistics cocerning the Jewish family in 1990. We have already seen that only 68% of all currently married born Jews are married to someone who was also born Jewish.

Looking now at household size the *National Jewish Population Survey* shows that "Entirely Jewish households averaged only 2.2 persons."[12] According to the United States Census, the national average household size was 2.63 persons in 1990.

Eleven percent of Jewish households contain only one person. Half of these never married, one third are widowed and one fifth are separated or divorced. Five and one half percent of the total are households including un-married couples or roommates, including homosexual unions. It is important that only 14% of all Jewish households contain a "core" Jewish couple, as defined by the National Jewish Population Survey, together with children from that union.

Household income among American Jews was reported by the National Jewish Population Survery to be slightly higher than the average household income for Americans as reported every year by the Bureau of Labor Statsitics. Contrary to various beliefs and prejudices, there is, nevertheless, a good deal of Jewish poverty. Thus, 19 percent of "core" Jewish households, including 100,000 persons, lived below the poverty line with incomes of less than $12,500.- in 1990.

Over one million American Jews, i.e., almost 1,100,000 are over 65 years old. The survey found that a plurality of Jews over 65 live in the West and that among them there is a greater number of Jews without a religion than is true in other regions of the country.[13]

Furthermore, the intermarriage rate in the West is so much greater than it is in the other regions of the country that Charles Silberman wrote in 1985: "...intermarriage rates are so far higher in the West than in the East and Mid-West ...that we almost seem to be talking about two seperate phenomena."[14]

William Toll has analyzed the meaning that may be given to intermarriage "especially in the West."[15]

To do this, Toll reviews the history of Jewish-Gentile intermarriages in Western Europe and shows that in Germany, France, Austria and Italy, these inter-marriages were very common and represented an effort on the part of the Jewish spouse to escape the stigma of being Jewish, particularly in an effort to overcome professional and business disadvantages.   That the motives for intermarriage and conversion of Jews were chiefly professional and business motives is described by Falk and Bullough in their study of 19th century German - Jewish achievers. They found that throughout the nineteenth century one third to one quarter of all German Jews were married to non-Jews and that business and professional preferment were the overwhelming reasons for the decision of Jewish men to marry a Christian and/or to convert.[16]

Whether intermarriages in the American West were as frequent as in Europe is not known. However, a search of synagogue records reveals some intermarriages in the West during the 19th century. These intermarriages were undertaken mainly by Jewish men who lived in areas where Jewish females were very scarce. Therefore Jewish men had to marry outside their faith so as to stay in the place of business they had established. "Nevertheless, the dominant theme and early twentieth-century family information in the Pacific Northwest was a localized social network in which sons and daughters of German or Polish Jewish families married one another."[17] This pattern also existed among the nineteenth century German Jews who lived in New York City during the 19th and early 20th century.[18] These networks made it possible for Jews living in isolated, small towns to neverthelss marry Jewish women living elsewhere." For example, "in a small town like Trinidad, Colorado, in 1900, it is almost impossible to detect intermarriage."[19]

This then indicates that the high rates of intermarriage found in the American Jewish community in 1995 are not caused by the dearth of potential Jewish marriage prospects, but by the abandonment of the Jewish religion. This was first discovered by Massarik in his study of California Jewish marriages. Massarik clearly demonstrated that religious identification as judged by ritual observance was the most significant factor associated with intermarriage. Thus, "observant" Jews in that 1953 study exhibited an intermarriage rate of only one percent while at that time 12% of unobservant Jews had intermarried. In addition, income was related to intermarriage so that those Western Jews whose income permitted them to live in affluent areas of California were far more likely to intermarry than was true of their older and poorer parents.[20]

We intepret these findings to mean that secularization has led to family alienation, conflict and disintegration of the Jewish family in America.

This is also the intepretation given these statistics by observers of intermarriage among the so-called "establishment Jews" who claim Jewish leadership for themselves. There has been considerable controversy among Jews concerning almost every aspect of Jewish life. However, the threat that intermarrige represents has not been denied. The core of the controversies arising over the higher intermarriage rate for Amercian Jews has been the cause of this phenomenon and the possible cure. Here the "establishment" is blamed by the Jewish "survivalists" who believe that the very same Jewish "leaders" who decry the high intermarrige rate caused this themselves.

The principal argument of the Jewish "survivalists" has been that Jews who marry non-Jews do so because they wish to escape anti-semitism and that this is hopeless. Survivalists argue that intermarriage is the outcome of "interfaith" relationships with Gentiles instigated by the so-called Jewish "leadership." Such "interfaith" efforts, say the survivalists, are instigated by Jews and lead to Jewish losses. Four kinds of Jewish-Gentile intermarriages are possible. One would be the most frequent in which the husband is Jewish but the wife is not. There are also those interfaith marriages in which the wife is Jewish and the husband is a Gentile. From the viewpoint of Jewish law, children of a Jewish mother are Jewish even if the father is not

Jewish. Then there are those interfaith marriages in which the Jewish partner accepts the religion of the non-Jewish spouse, making this at least theoretically a one religion marriage. Finally there are those interfaith marriages in which the Gentile spouse becomes Jewish, once more creating a one religion marriage.[21]

Orthodox Jews believe that interfaith marriage is the result of the abandonment of Judaism, not its cause. They see marriage of a Jew to a non-Jew as the final step in total assimilation of Jews to apostasy and view such a step as the certain outcome of the abandonment of the Jewish tradition *preceding* marriage. To the traditionalists Reform Judaism is responsible for this abandonment of the Jews through intermarriage because they consider Reform Judaism an imitation of Christianity which must inevitably lead to the conversion to Christianity of its adherents. Furthermore, traditionalists argue that any Jew married to a non-Jew cannot maintain Judaism because out-marriage makes adherence to Torah-true practice impossible.

Reform Jews counter this argument by holding that Jews who are not accomodated by Judaism in being welcomed with their non-Jewish spouse or being allowed to marry a non-Jew in a Jewish ceremony will then turn away from Judaism altogether and this threatens Jewish survival. Therefore Reform Jews are interested in sanctioning such marriages.

The evidence is that not every mixed marriage, that is a marriage between a Jew and a non-Jew, leads to the destruction of Jewish life; the evidence also indicates that sincere converts to Judaism may actually enhance the Jewish position in the next generation. Nevertheless, there are a good number of young Jews who have one converted parent, who, although Jewish, has non Jewish parents. Because the grandparents of Jewish children of such a marriage are not Jewish it seems to such Jewish young people not at all problematic to date, and therefore eventually marry, a non Jew. They themselves are in part of non-Jewish origin and therefore are often not hesitant to assert their ancestry in such a fashion.

All of this is not the uniform opinion of either the traditonalists or the reform Jews. There are some on both sides of the argument who represent the minority view in their respective religious communities.

III.

Contrary to the Eastern European Jewish family as described above, the American Jewish family at the end of the 20th century appears to be in a state of confusion and loss. The values of the religion centered family are not at all in evidence in the usual American Jewish family.

Today, Jews live almost entirely in big cities. Everyone "minds his own business," in a cold and detached fashion, a condition directly opposite the conduct of *shtetl* Jews who existed until 1940 and whose "Life Is With People" attitude was supportive and involved.

Family bonds, which were the very heart of Judaism until a century ago, have been largely destroyed. In part this is due to the high mobility of American life as seen by the migration patterns of American Jewish families. While the Northeast, and particularly New York City, was the focus of American Jewish life for the one hundred years ending in 1981, there has been a considerable change in that pattern since then. Most dramatic has been the decline in Jewish family residence in the Northeast. While over 46% of Amerian Jews were born in that area, 520,000 Jews had left the Northeast by 1990 and reduced the Jewish concentration in that region of the country to 39.6%. Meanwhile, 720,000 Jews moved into the South, increasing the share of Jews in that region to 23.5% from 14.6% two decades earlier. The Midwest saw a decline of Jews from 16.2% who were born there to 12.5% who lived there in 1990. The greatest regional change in Jewish population occurred in the West. There the Jewish population rose by more than 770,000, thus increasing from 14.9% of all American Jews to 24.4%.

The consequences of high mobility upon the Jewish family are of course the same as upon all families and have profoundly affected the level of adherence to Judaism by such families. This is best understood by contrasting the erstwhile Jewish family as it existed mainly before 1940 and as it is principally organized today. Thus, the earlier Jewish family differs from the current American Jewish family in all or most of the following characteristics:

1. All adults were expected to be married and women were expected to be married in their teens. Now, eleven percent of Jews live alone and of these one half have never married.

2. Marriage was permanent. Divorce was rare and seen as a scandal. Now, divorce is almost as common among Jews as non-Jews in America, approaching 50% of all marriages.

3. The welfare of the family was placed ahead of individual preference. This was particuarly true of the marital partner. Jews married other Jews, not only because they were more likely to meet other Jews, but also because they wished to respect the opinions of their family. In the United States the high Jewish intermarriage rate is largely the consequence of the willingness of many Jews to disregard the opinions of their family because the great mobility of Americans, Jews included, means that many are no longer living with their families and are frequently living in other towns, states and regions of the country. This in turn came about as it became fashionable to send adult children to "out-of-town" colleges.

4. Sexual relations among Jews were at one time entirely restricted to marriage. A "double standard" existed which included the expectation that Jewish women would remain virgins until marriage. Furthermore, in the European *shtetl,* many Jewish men also had no sexual experience before marriage. This is far from the case in the U.S. at the end of the 20th century.

5. Married couples were expected to have many children. Not only were children seen as an economic asset but the Jewish religion commanded the production of children as the Torah was a vital aspect of married life and the command to "be fruitful and multiply" was taken seriously. In end-of-the-century America, this commandment is not taken seriously any more as evidenced by the Jewish birthrate of 1.6 for women age 15-45.

6. Parents were expected to take care of their children and still do so in almost all American Jewish families whatever the cost. In view of the 5th Commandment, "Honor Your Father and Your Mother etc." it was also considered obligatory that children support their parents, come what may. This Commandment is still very meaningful in Jewish families but has been largely shifted to communal nursing homes and social agencies.

7. Formerly, the Jewish father was seen as the head of the household who made all important decisions and also set standards for religous obervances. Male children were more highly valued than female children. A clear pattern of patriarchal control existed in Jewish families in Europe and America. This has been radically

altered as women are today more dominant in Jewish families than was the case at any time in Jewish history before this century.

8. Jewish women seldom worked outside the home unless they ran a small business depending upon their sales ability but not upon their education. Presently Jewish women are well educated, 56% of Jewish women are college graduates, and ten percent have a post graduate degree. Among younger Jewish women the percentage is far higher.

All of these developments insure the reduction of interest in structured, formal religious institutions as evidenced by the fact that only 41% of all Jewish households are so affiliated. Thirty six percent of these affiliated households belong to the Reform movement, 43% are Conservative and 16% are Orthodox. The others are members of Chavurahs, Reconstructionist congregations and other groups.[22] However, the activities of Jewish women indicate that the Jewish family has shifted its religious impulses from the support of the synagogue and Jewish law to involvement in "Mitzvahs" or good deeds.

IV.

Are Jewish women in end-of-the-century America very different from their *shtetl* ancestors? It would seem almost heretical to so much as ask such a question if we were to compare income, secular education, mobility and influence between the European group who came here one hundred years ago and the current American Jewish woman. Yet, the difference is not nearly as great if we compare the level of Jewish knowledge and Jewish involvement between the generations.

The current, 1995, American Jewish woman is most likely to be a member of *Hadassah,* participate in Jewish committees of all kinds, is socially active as a club woman and is probably as ignorant of Jewish history, philosophy and religious thought as was her counterpart in Russia four generations ago.[23]

There are, however, numerous Jewish women whose education permits them to enter the professions, take the lead in business, attain considerable incomes in the corporate world and become successful in the political arena. These are a minority of about ten percent, yet, a significant minority. Jewish women, like many other American women and men, are generally convinced that education is important if not vital in their lives. There are many who find housework and child rearing insufficient in their need for "self-fulfillment" and feel compelled by that need to gain advanced degrees and/or to work in their chosen profession.

This issue was first explored in detail in the now famous book *The Feminine Mytique* by Betty Friedan in 1963 which insisted that housewives should not resign themselves to the traditional roles of maid, chauffeur and bedmate.[24] It is not surprising that Mrs. Friedan is Jewish since American Jewish women, more than any others, have been unwilling to stay bored at home for very long and have been most active in communal enterprises, education and business.

In 1990 just over one half of all Jewish women were employed.[25] Many Jewish women are involved either professionally or voluntarily in occupations which "solve humanity's ills." This need to be involved in "liberal causes" or to teach in minority schools or to be concerned with social work issues has been described in numerous publications concerning Jews. It is claimed by some that prophetic Judaism and the need to promote a just society are the root of this Jewish "liberalism." Unlike other American ethnic groups with high incomes, Jews have traditionally voted for the Democratic Party and have been elected on "liberal" issues. That is as true in 1995 as it was true in the days of Franklin Roosevelt except that Jews can now be elected and hold appointed office as well in far greater numbers than was true in the 1930's. Thus, both Senators from California are Jewish women while a disproportionate number of Jewish men serve in the House and the Senate of the United States.

Liberal issues have been mostly concerned with the plight of minorities in this country. That has led Jewish men and women to make considerable efforts over many years on behalf of the American black population only to be told that their efforts are not welcome. In fact, anti-Jewish sentiment is so common in the Afro-American community that one can only wonder what motivates Jewish women and men to insist on dealing with Afro-American issues when they are not welcome there and are maligned in the Afro-American community in a manner reminiscent of Ku Klax Klan language.

In a study called "The Image of the Good Jew in Lakeville," the sociologist Marshall Sklare explored this question. "Lakeville" is a Chicago suburb which houses a good sized Jewish population. The answers given by Jewish citizens there can be taken as typical of answers any American Jewish community would have given to the questions presented by Sklare. The answers to these questions, more than anything else, demonstrate the weakness of the American Jewish community and the delusions the American Jewish community has institutionalized. It is our contention that these answers exhibit the secularization of the Jewish community in America most decidedly and also demonstrate the reasons for the decline in Jewish adherence and loyalty.[26]

The question asked by Sklare was this: "In your opinion, for a Jew to be considered a good Jew, which of the following must he do? Which are desirable but not essential that he do? Which have no bearing on whether or not you consider him a good Jew? Which must he not do?"

The results are these: 93% of respondents find it essential that a "good Jew" lead an ethical and moral life. Since the phrase "ethical and moral" can be interpreted in any manner whatever, and since non Jews are certainly ethical and moral, no distinction between Jews and non-Jews can be discerned on those grounds. Nevertheless, 85% of Jews thought it essential that a Jew accepts being a Jew and not hide it. 67% thought it essential that a "good Jew" support all humanitarian causes and promote civic betterment and improvement in the community; 59% thought it essential and 32% desirable to "gain respect of Christian neighbors;" 58% thought that a "good Jew" helps the underpivileged to improve their lot, only 48% believed that it is essential to know the fundamentals of Judaism but 44% held it essential and 39% desirable to work for the equality of the black population.

The lowest ratings of all choices offered by the questionnarie was given to observation of the dietary laws which only 1% held essential. Attendance at weekly synagogue services was viewed essential by only 4%.

Answers such as these demonstrate that American Jews emphasize conduct which is open to anyone and therefore does not distinguish Jews from non-Jews. Thus, anyone can suppport humanitarian causes, participate in "civic" betterment or help the black population. This is the reason then for the high intermarriage rate in the U.S. at the end of the 20th century, namely, that Jews who marry non-Jews have generally discarded Judaism and do not differ from those whom they marry in religion, in attitude and in outlook. In fact, they are not Jews although of Jewish parentage even before they marry a non-Jew not of Jewish parentage.

The results of every survey indicated that the vast majority of Jews take a purely secular attitude towards Judaism as they see it, never noticing however, that anyone not Jewish could do the same. This means that Jews in America see no difference between Jewish and non-Jewish observance and attitude and that this is the core of the disaffection from which the Jewish group suffers.

Thus, Jewish women are extra-ordarily involved in fund raising activities, volunteers in hospital activities, charities and public "causes" from air-pollution to the election of politicians but are rarely involved in the promotion of the Jewish religion, *per se*.

This then is an example of the "civic religion" discussed earlier. It is this homogenation of Jewish and general American values which supports the indifference of so many Jews to their heritage and their tradition so that the outcome, the "vanishing" of American Jews into the mainstream of American life, is consequently greatly enhanced.

V.

This Jewish activism and need for involvement in socially useful activities has been seen as an effort to continue the Jewish tradition in the form of participation rather than its prior form, that of religious cult practitioner. There are those, particularly among Reform Jews, who hold that the foremost concern of Judaism is with good deeds, not ritual, and that the over representation of Jews in current American volunteer work is a form of religious expression more valuable than participation in any cult behavior such as the eating of only kosher foods, the observance of the Sabbath laws or the use of prayer and ceremony.

The fifth commandment to "honor your father and your mother" not only demands such treatment of parents but also promises long life to those who do so. Therefore, during the many centuries in which the "sacred" Jewish family dominated such honor was accorded fathers and mothers because the law was carried by the mores in the "shtetl" community. There can be no doubt that fathers and mothers then as now disappointed their children, or were too forceful, or "interfered" or made demands children preferred not to fulfill. However, in a "sacred" family, dominated by religious strictures, the entire community enforces the honorific position of a parent because the culture has hardly room for any other conduct.

In the United States this is by no means the case. There are, of course, innumerable Americans, Jewish or not, who do indeed honor their father and their mother. No doubt these are in the majority. However, the definition of what constitutes such honor has changed, and the number of those who have no interest in their elders has increased rapidly.[27]

In the Jewish "sacred" family the honoring of parents was defined as the willingness to anticipate the wishes of parents and to please unexpressed desires. "We honor them," says Klein, " by our efforts to live up to their expectations."[28] While this may still be the case in innumerable Jewish and non-Jewish families and in all societies, the great problem for Americans, including Jewish Americans, is for children to know what parents expect. In an anomic society such expectations are in conflict. Conflict also dominates many families inlcuding those which have experienced divorce. In such cases how does a child honor its mother and/or father? If parents are not living together and have widely different views which view should a child adopt? How can one honor two parents who agree on nothing? These and many other obstacles to the fulfillment of the 5th Commandment did not exist in the "sacred" family. Neverthless, the tradition of closeness with family continues in many Jewish homes despite mobility, despite divorce and despite intermarriage.

One means of dealing with the old is the American nursing home. Jewish sponsored nursing homes are found in most communities in the U.S. which have a sizable Jewish community. This means that there are Jewish activists in most Jewish communities who gain access to Federal funds and by means of contributions build and maintain such nursing homes.

Commonly, nursing home operators, owners and the adult children of nursing home patients like to insist that *their* nursing home is different from all other nursing homes in that it is a panacea for all that ails the old and is run by a collection of humanitarians whose concerns and deeds border on the angelic.

In truth, "........the aged are mistreated, even in the best of nursing homes."[29] Because nursing homes are bureaucratic organizations they cannot meet the emotional needs of the patients they are intended to serve. Nursing homes reduce the "life space" of their patients and force them into an institutionalized routine which deprives the patient of his independence, his freedom and his decison making powers. This incarceration is particularly painful for Americans because so much emphasis is placed on personal rights and liberties here that the contrast between nursing home living and living on the outside is particularly crass in this country. There are of course some "senior citizens" who are so impaired as to be deprived of their mobility for physical reasons. The social reason for the storage of the "old" in the warehouses called "nursing homes" is of course the increase in age and the economic condition of the American Jewish family. The old need care and there is no one in the family to give it. Not only has high mobility removed large numbers of adult children from the vicintiy of their retired parents, but, almost all of these adult chidren work or are so busy with volunteer activities that the attention the old need cannot be given. Furthermore, many middle aged, educated Jewish adults find the care and aid given to the old at home a demeaning task out of step with the image of the successful business or professional woman or man which the majority of American Jews want to protray.

The daily care given nursing home patients in Jewish homes is generally in the hands of "nurse's aids'" who are not Jewish while the administration of the Jewish homes is normally in the hands of Jewish administrators, physicians, nurses and social workers. Administrators of such homes may be lawyers, social workers or pyschologists. Such specialists seldom have more than a bureaucratic interest in the patients in their care since their prime concern is raising funds. Salaries for Jewish nursing home administrators range upward of $200,000. Therefore, those who seek to earn such incomes need to impress wealthy members of the board of directors, not nursing home patients. It is not unreasonable to observe, therefore, that the true function of the Jewish nursing home in America is to relieve families of the "burden" of caring for the old while furnishing careerists with a lucrative income.

In contrast to this end of the century American practice, in the European Jewish family, including the immigrants who came to the U.S. between 1881 and 1924, the old stayed in their homes. In fact, it was customary for newly married couples in the Eastern European Jewish family to live with parents. Usually this meant the parents of the wife but it was not unknown for "insolvent" younger people to live with the husband's family. Such arrangements always involved friction between the generations. This friction generally centered upon the "mother -in law" relationship. "It is commonly assumed that the groom's mother will be hard to please. ....The mother ...feels it a righteous duty to be critical."[30]

The Yiddish speaking Jews institutionized the role of the mother-in-law by conducting a "quarreling dance" during the wedding feast. The two mothers engaged in this display of mock anger which concludes with an embrace thus exhibiting the demands of the group for a peaceful resolution of the friction the family union inevitably produces. Since families are emotional centers designed to dispense emotional gratification and solidarity not available elsewhere the need to limit quarrels and disagreements was always a social issue and its consequences were always well controlled in all cultures.[31] However, with the exception of the small *hasidic* community among American Jews, family quarrels are no longer limited by such institutionlized safeguards in the Jewish community. As we have already seen, high mobility, a great emphasis on economic and educational success and the substituion of personal interests over family values have weakened the community so much that neither public opinion nor dependence on community values can prevent dissent in American life, including Jewish life. There is simply nothing that can stop anyone from moving thousands of miles away from family while rejecting the values of parents, sibling and erstwhile friends. In fact, this is so common that four observations can be made concerning family quarrels in American Jewish families, four observations which may very well fit non-Jewish middle class families as well. These are:

1. Conflict is frequent and severe. The quarrels concern dominance and are commonly described as "who is the boss" struggles.

2. Despite this, there are many Jewish and non-Jewish families who are concerned with each other, the welfare and state of health of family members and the need to be of financial assistance.

3. The quarrels serve the function of establishing an optimal distance between the generations. Thus, many mothers, but by no means all, seek to lessen the distance between themselves and the younger generation while the younger generation usually seeks to increase that distance. After several years of experience with the conflict which arises from these different interpretations of how to live together a *modus vivandi* is reached and the conflict ceases or is at least reduced.

4. In the event that the older generation is much poorer or far less educated than the younger generation the conflict is much more severe than when the "in-laws" are native born, well educated and financially well off. Since the latter scenario is increasingly common among American Jews the quarreling should have lessened as compared to the relationships in the Yiddish speaking group before the Second World War. At the end of the century differences between generations are commonly resolved by mobility in that one or both families live at some distance from each other.

VI.

Because reason and objectivity are the common intellectual and verbal fare of most Americans and in particular are matter of course arguments of the semi-educated middle class it is not surprising that Jewish Americans are almost entirely in agreement concerning their view of religious practice. This despite the fact that there is a good deal of divisiveness between Jewish organizations.

What is meant here is that Jews are generally unwilling to live in the orthodox tradition and that even among those who attend orthodox synagogues there are many who cannot believe in the traditional Jewish way of life. One common observation is that almost all who are unable to perform Jewish ritual or live by the rules of the Talmud would like to see their children participate in Jewish activities more than they ever did. In short, many Jews want freedom from religion but they also want the benefits which the education of their children in the Jewish religion of their choice will confer on them.

It is evident to anyone who knows something about the Jewish family as it existed one hundred and fifty years ago that the principal change that has come to the Jewish family is the removal of authority and the institution of individual choice. This means that father dominated families among Jews seldom exist in America unless they are very orthodox or *chasidic* in their outlook. "Authority and tradition are closely related to each other," and it is for that reason that tradition has been largely relinqished in the American Jewish family as each family member, seeking autonomy, "asserts him(self) or herself with impunity."[32]

Until the 1990's there was still some doubt as to the direction into which the American Jewish family would move. That is, whether tradition would be continued at the cost of failure to enter into the mainstream of American life or, in reverse, whether tradition would be entirely discarded so as to blend into the principal aspects of American existence without indicating any Jewish traits whatever.

Now, in the 90's it has become evident that some Jews will cling to the tradition no matter what the cost. Therefore there are several hundred thousand *chasidim* and other orthodox Jews to whom the tradition is the full meaning of life. Much more important in numbers are orthodox Jews who do not belong to any *Chasidic* sect but who observe the *halacha,* the Jewish law, in detail.

Nevertheless, the overwhelming number of American Jews are "revolving door" Jews, i.e. "in on Rosh Hashonah out on Yom Kippur." That vast majority who hold these attitudes see no need to be more involved with the Jewish religion than they now are and are unlikely to maintain the authority oriented traditions of Judaism. "The American Jewish family is not receptive to religious instruction on what is permissible and what is not."[33]

This is the essence of secularization. Surely, religion rests on authority. Yet, authority is in ill repute in America, whose citizens pride themselves on their autonomy and their right to chose their own life style.

Thus, one of the principal reasons the *halachic* approach to Judaism has had so few followers in the United States is that any authority runs counter to the American point of view. Autonomy, individualism, self-determination and the right to make any choice are the hallmarks of the American life style. Therefore, the Jewish tradition has been largely discarded in America and a superficial recital of random verses from random Jewish souces has been susbtituted during the minimal "service" found in the vast majority of reform and many conservative synagogues. It is of necessity that this minimalist approach be used because there is no alternative. It is, at this writing in 1995, inconceivable that any substantial number of Amerian Jews would be willing to accept any authority whatever, least of all the authority of a rabbi.

Therefore, Jewish education needs now to instill the wish to study and live according to *halacha.* This cannot be done by families alone. A study - group network should be established to serve as adjunct faculty with a view of transmitting the Jewish law informally to those who seek such instruction. This is of course the purpose of the *Chavurah* movement already discussed.

There are Jewish families who have found the answer to a simultaneous emphasis on Jewish tradition and a present day American life style in the "Young Israel" movement. Those who participate in "Young Israel" are orthodox, observant Jews who nevertheless are open to secular interests and almost always have a secular education. This permits such Jews to hold on to traditional Jewish values in an American life style and with a view to raising their children as English speaking Americans. This manner of adjustment differs from the *Chasidic* orthodoxy based on Yiddish, the wearing of medieval European clothing, the exclusion of women from the main stream of community life and the segregation of the group from most Jewish community affairs by reason of *halachic* intepretations which view almost the entire Jewish community as ignorant apostates (*Am haaratzim*).

VI.

One of the latest social phenomena which some think threatens the American family and therefore the American Jewish family as well is the ever increasing number of single people in this country and the low rate of reproduction which is in part related to the single state and largely related to birth control used by the married.

Beginning in the 1950's Americans have married at a later age although even in the 1960's three quarters of the Christian population of the United States aged 18-24 had married, reaching 90% in the age category 25-34. Among Jews only 37% were married at age 24 and 87% were married at age 34. Hence Jews fell behind both Protestants and Catholics in these age categories. This considerable difference between the Jewish and non - Jewish marriage rates at various ages was caused by the high proportion of Jews who live in cities and the great number of Jews who seek a higher education. Both urbanization and entry into professions delays marriage and declines birth rates.

The most important reason for the decline in Jewish birth rates, however, is the increasing secularization of Jews. Religiously active Jews are more inclined to have children because of their pro-natalist heritage and subculture. In so far as Jewish involvement in the traditional religious subculture wanes, Jews may be expected to bear fewer children owing in part to their increasing remoteness from their pro-natalist religious tradition.[34]

In both the 1960's and the 1970's married Jews had fewer children than did married Christians. Thus, in the 1960's married Jews aged 25-34 had averages of 2.1 to 1.5 children depending on which study one reads. In the 1970's these averages had dropped to 1.2 and 0.7.[35]

In 1981, Paul Ritterband and Steve Cohen found that about two thirds of Jewish men in their early twenties have never married although 95% of Jews aged thirty four to forty five have married. This was one of the findings of the Greater New York Jewish Population Study. This was followed by the National Jewish Population Study of 1990. The outcome of both these studies concerning Jewish fertility and child rearing is this:

In 1981 a study encompassing about one third of all the Jews in the United States showed that children ever born for women aged thirty five to forty was 2.2 thereby meeting the replacement level.[36] In 1990 however, the fertility of women who were Jews by religion was 1.57 in the age group thirty five to forty four, a fertility considerably less than the replacement level. Among Jews with no religion the fertility rate for women aged 35-44 was 1.43.[37]

In 1981 these developments were very much visible but were viewed as less of a threat than the "pessimists" in the Jewish community allegedly predicted. Yet, ten years later, in 1991, it turns out that the "pessimists" were right. The birth rate has remained low, divorce is increasing and intermarriage is far greater than was expected ten years earlier.

Jewish divorce had also been on the increase in the two decades of the '70's and eighties. Compared to the Christian divorce rate there was and is a Jewish "divorce deficit." Nevertheless, the popularity of divorce in American life has influenced Jews as well, as the increase in Jewish divorce since 1970 demonstrates.[38]

There are many observers of the Jewish community who view all of these changes in the Jewish family from a traditonal "sacred" institution to a current "secular" institution as inevitable. Many Jews are convinced that intermarriage, loss of authority, divorce and a low birth rate are here to stay and that nothing can alter these conditions. Therefore they, and many others, believe that Jewish education must be the institution which will make Jewish survival certain. The argument here is that a child, and an adult, who is well versed in his tradition, will not abandon the Jewish people no matter whom he marries.

Therefore we will next consider Jewish education and describe the secularization of that erstwhile sacred institution as it developed in America these past 75 years.

NOTES

[1]Irving Howe, *World of Our Fathers,* New York, Simon and Schuster, 1976, p. 11.

[2]Mark Zbrowski and Elizabeth Herzog, *Life Is With People,* New York, Schocken Books, 1952, p. 291.

[3]John J. Honigmann, *Understanding Culture,* New York, Harper Row and Co., 1963, pp. 86-87.

[4]Sholom Aleichem, *The Tevye Stories,* New York, Pocket Books, Inc., 1965, pp. 126-142.

[5]Zbrowski, *op.cit.,* p.409.

[6]*Ibid.,* p.20.

[7]Barry A. Kosmin et. al., *Highlights of the CJF 1990 Jewish Population Study,* New York, Council of Jewish Federations, 1991, p. 6.

[8]Judith Zimmerman and Barbara Trainin, Eds., *Renascence or Oblivion,* New York, The Federation of Jewish Philanthropies, 1979, pp.6-7.

[9]Jack Wertheimer, *A People Divided: Judaism In Contemporary America,* New York, Basic Books, 1993, p. 59.

[10]Marshall Sklare, "Intermarriage and the Jewish Future," in: *Observing America's Jews,* Waltham, Mass. The Brandeis University Press, 1993, p. 234.

[11]Saul Bellow, *Mr. Sammler's Planet,* New York, The Viking Press, 1970.

[12]Barry Kosmin, *NationalJewish Populatin Survey,* op.cit., p. 17. (See also Jack Wertheimer, *op.cit.)*

[13]*Ibid., pp.* 17-20.

[14]Charles Silberman, *A Certain People: American Jews and their Lives Today,* New York, Summit Publishing Co., 1985, p. 294.

[15]William Toll, "intermarriage In the Urban West," in: *Jews of the American West,* Moses Rischin and John Livingston, Eds., Detroit, Wayne State University Press, 1991, p. 168.

[16]Gerhard Falk and Vern Bullough, "Achievement Among German Jews Born During the Years 1785-1885," *The Mankind Quarterly,* Vol. XXVII, No.3, Spring 1987, p.357.

[17]Toll, *op.cit.,* p. 173.

[18]Stephen Birmingham, *Our Crowd,* New York, Dell Publishing Co., Inc., 1967.

[19]Toll, *op.cit.,* p.173.

[20]Fred Massarik, "A Report on the Jewish Population of Los Angeles," *Western Jewish History,* Vol. 49, 1953, p. 11.

[21]S. David Breslauer, "Intermarriage as Punishment and Folly, " in: *Meir Kahane,* Lewiston, N.Y., The Edwin Mellen Press, 1986, p. 114.

[22]*Ibid.,* p.37.

[23]Sol Gittleman, *From Shtetl to Suburbia,* Boston, Beacon Press, 1978, p. 168.

[24]Betty Friedan, *The Feminine Mystique,* New York, Dell, 1963.

[25]Kosmin, *op.cit.,* p.12.

[26]Marshall Sklare, "The Image of the Good Jew in Lakeville," in: *Observing American Jews,* Waltham, Mass., Brandeis University Press, 1993, pp. 205-214.

[27]Isaac Klein, *The Ten Commandments In a Changin World,* Jerusalem, Citadel Press, 1963, p. 63.

[28]*Ibid.,* p.65.

[29]Robert E. Burger, " Commercializing the Aged," *Annual Editions: Readings In Social Problems,* Guilford, Conn., The Dushkin Publishing Group, Inc., 1993, pp.207-209.

[30]Zbrowski, *op.cit.,* p. 276.

[31]John J. Honigmann, *Understanding Culture,* New York, Harper and Row, 1993, p. 86.

[32]Norman Linzer, *The Jewish Family:Authority and Tradition in Modern Perspective,* New York, Human Sciences Press, Inc., 1983,p.195.,

[33]*Ibid.,* p. 198.

[34]Steven M. Cohen, *American Modernity and Jewish Identity,* New York, Tavistock Publications, 1983, p. 118.

[35] Cohen, , op.cit., p. 116.

[36]Steven M. Cohen "Vitality and Resilience in the American Jewish Family," in *The Jewish Family: Myths and Reality.* Steven M. Cohen and Paula Hyman, Eds., , New York, Homes and Meier, 1986, p. 221.
[37] Barry A. Kosmin, et.al. *The National Jewish Population Survey,* New York, The Council of Jewish Federations, 1991, p. 15.
[38]Cohen, *American Modernity etc., op.cit.,* p.120.

Chapter X

The Secularization of American Jewish Education

I.

In 1937 there appeared a small book by Franz Rosenzweig (1886-1929), the Jewish philosopher who had lived and died in Germany. This book included his famous essay "Renaissance of Jewish Learning" in which Rosenzweig wrote: "Jewish study and teaching, Jewish learning and education- they are dying out among us."[1]

Rosenzweig discussed how in Germany, and in the Western world generally, Jewish learning "runs a respectful distance behind the learning of the 'others'." This meant secular studies. The same is of course still true as we can readily see by listing the great American Jewish achievers of the past fifty years. Among these are Oppenheimer in physics, Bernstein in music, Javits and Kissinger in government, Hook in philosophy, Kallen in history, Rickover in military science and a host of others too numerous to present here. However, there is no one in Jewish education among these "greats."[2]

Rosenzweig actually outlined a possible curriculum for Jewish schools which he thought should include three years of Hebrew study, also the study of the Bible in the original Hebrew because he believed that no translation could possibly convey the true Jewish meaning of Scripture. He proposed that synagogue attendance should be part of religious instruction for pre-Bar Mitzvah boys and he opposed "youth services" for he believed that young and old should pray together. Rosenzweig proposed that Torah with Rashi should be studied by children 13 years old and that the Babylonian Talmud should be introduced before a boy ended his Jewish education upon becoming Bar Mitzvah. Those who stayed past Bar Mitzvah were to learn Talmud and Midrashim, the Jewish literature up to Zunz and Mendelssohn, and Jewish philosophers such as Maimonides.[3]

Rosenzweig claimed then (1924), that the trend toward conversion "which every year takes away the best from among us," could be blamed on the poor religious instruction received by western Jews. Rosenzweig rightly recognized the contribution of Moses Mendelssohn (1729-1786) to this state of Jewish education, to Jewish apostasy and to the conversion to other religions by many German Jews.

This conversion trend among the Jewish intellectuals of the nineteenth and early twentieth century in Germany was fueled by the high intermarriage rate between German Jews and non-Jews amounting to about 30% between 1870 and 1933.[4] It was however also furthered by ambition. Since German universities would not appoint Jewish professors, hospitals would not appoint Jewish physicians and the civil service was closed to Jews as well, numerous Jews had themselves baptized for the sake of convenience and advancement. In retrospect this kind of "baptism" is frequently criticized, although Rosenzweig wrote that the "individual is guiltless." He believed that the anti-Jewish attitude of the nineteenth century Germans was responsible for this behavior among Jews and not those who wanted to satisfy their ambitions. It is interesting that among those who were so baptized was the great Jewish German poet Heinrich Heine (1797-1856) who wrote in his *Lamentationen* or *Lamentations: "Keine Messe wird man singen keinen Kadosh wird man sagen, nichts gesagt und nichts gesungen, wird an meinen Sterbetagen,"* or *"No Mass will anyone sing, no Kaddish will anyone say, nothing said and nothing sung will mark the days of my death."* Evidently Heine, who had also nominally converted to Christianity, recognized the futility of his apostasy as he was neither accepted by his former nor his new co-religionists.

Rosenzweig continues his discussion of the decline of Jewish learning and teaching by additionally seeking the cause of Jewish decline in the reduction of the Jewish home from its dominant position over so many centuries to the dominance of outside influences. "Life comes from outside," says Rosenzweig and, like the sociologist Ferdinand Tönnies, laments the separation of the home from the work world, which is governed by different laws and different requirements than the Jewish home or for that matter, the non-Jewish home.[5]

Finally, Rosenzweig refers to the "desertion of our scholars to realms of alien knowledge," by which he meant the interest shown by so many Jews in studying at modern European universities and abandoning the erstwhile study of *Talmud* which was the central interest of all European Jews until the middle of the nineteenth century. Thereafter, Western Jews, living in Germany, France, the Low Countries and England and certainly the United States abandoned Talmud study in favor of secular studies. This does not mean that no one studies Talmud or has studied Talmud since then. Certainly, in Eastern Europe, Talmud study continued to occupy a primary place in the lives of the 11 million Jews living there before Hitler. Since then, the Eastern European Jewish community has not only suffered the loss of ninety percent of its people through murder, but has also been decimated by the assimilation of Soviet Jews leading to their almost total ignorance of things Jewish.

In the United States there are few Jews today (1995) who can or want to study Talmud. However, there are some American Jews who do so and who can be found in the "Yeshivas" of the United States where about 55 such theological schools operate on a full time basis enrolling about 5,000 students. This is indeed a very small percentage of American Jews who send about 400,000 children to some type of Jewish education in the 1990's. Nevertheless, Talmud study continues to this day (1995) and will undoubtedly continue into the indefinite future.

This does not mean that Jewish education is a great success in America. On the contrary. The tiny fraction of Jews who study Talmud today tells us more than anything else one can say about the American Jewish community, that the sacred is out and the secular is "in". Among America's Jews there are only 500,000 today who view the 613 commandments of the Torah or, in non-Jewish terms, the "Old Testament" as divinely inspired and as worthy of being followed "without question."[6]

If failure to study Talmud were the sole criterion of the secularization of Judaism in present America, then Jewish education could still be rated a great success. However, there is a good deal of discrepancy between the educational opportunities available to American Jews and the number who take advantage of these opportunities to attain a Jewish education.

Several reasons for this discrepancy exist and all of them are an aspect of the secularization of the American Jewish community.

The first of these is the pragmatism with which Americans approach almost everything, including education. Not only Jews, but all Americans wish to know what contribution an education or the study of any subject matter can make to their principal aim, i.e., the earning of money and the attainment of the "American Dream." That dream includes conscpicuous consumption of goods and services, financial independence, the development of a business or the holding of a good job. It includes "prestige" to be derived from all of these prerequisites and it includes a secular education and secular college degrees.

An education in Talmud contradicts all of these values and removes the Talmud student/scholar from active participation in the social and economic life of any American community. This is true because Talmud scholars believe that "Torah is to be studied for its own sake", not to make a living. Therefore, American Torah and Talmud students will attain a high school and often a college education in order to earn a livelihood while studying Torah and Talmud part time. Such students will also wear modern American clothes if it is necessary to hold their job and they will also "date" in order to find a spouse but not because they view "dating" as fun. In short, secularization has affected even the most orthodox of American Jews and has made inroads into their edcuational commitments.[7]

For that overwhelming majority of Amerian Jews who do not study Talmud the intrusion of the secular upon the sacred is of course far greater. Since evidently Talmudic study is not a money maker and has no immediate, physical consequences it is almost unheard of for even a Talmud student to become a Talmud scholar. This is even more true for those who were not Talmud students in their youth and hardly necessary for an American rabbi as we have already seen.

II.

That the Talmud students are motivated by a belief in God and in supernatural events surprises no one. It is however suprising that Jewish educators, devoted to the perpetuation of Judaism and the Jewish people, are embarrassed by references to the supernatural and to God.

This is not to say that those who seek the rabbinate or who are involved in Jewish education or the Jewish communal service are agnostics. Normally, they are theists. However, discussion of the role of God in Jewish life appears foolish to them not only because Americans live in a secular environment which hardly allows for such a discussion but also because money and political pressure or "cash and clout" get things done while God has neither.[8]

Samuel Schafler has made a list of reasons for this failure of Jewish educators to so much as mention God in the classroom, at meetings and in their conversation. These reasons are:

1. Fear and unsureness. Schafler believes that Jewish "sophisticates" fear being accused of holding on to old, outdated "anthropomorphisms."

2. Others fear that they will repeat old theological errors or

3. that they are so influenced by "childhood experts" that they do not want to give children a notion of the existence of God either too early or too late or in the wrong context etc.

4. Finally Schafler belives that it is in any event helpful to teach children about God, heroes and miracles.

It is the view of this author that the dominance of the secular in American life, and in particular among American Jews, has made those Jews committed to a theological view of the world ashamed of their beliefs lest they be seen as lunatics, "hasidim, cultists and kooks."

Schafler also recognized that many Israelis are agnostics and secularists thus making it entirely possible to study the Hebrew language and Jewish culture without reference to God. An entirely secular Jewish education is now possible. Thus, while in pre-Zionist days Jewish education meant education in Judaism, Jewish education in 1995 need not mean a religious education at all.

Finally it is evident that among Jews any effort to teach God in the classroom or to mention Him at all will inevitably lead to the question: "Where was God during the Holocaust?" That is of course an unanswerable question and therefore many teachers find it far easier not to mention God at all than to have to say that no-one knows.

Since Jewish identity is dependent on the Jewish religion much more than on an interest in Israel or in Jewish communal affairs failure to place emphasis on God both in the classroom and at all Jewish gatherings contributes to the decline in Jewish continuity in the United States.[9]

Furtheremore, the excessive emphasis on the secular in the American Jewish community has created a paradox for Jewish families which they themselves usually encourage and which has contributed greatly to Jewish losses. That paradox is the wish to give children a Jewish education without teaching them Judaism, that is, the Jewish religion and its concomitant, the belief in a supernatural God.

Traditionally, Jewish moral education was dependant on the study of *The Holy Scriptures*, a phrase which in English does not quite convey the meaning of its Hebrew equivalent, *Torah,* but can be understood to mean that the study was to lead to the observance of the commandments, known as *mitzvahs,* and the development of commitment and motivation known as *kavanah.*[10]

This point of view has been reinforced by numerous stories, legends and proverbs. These are to the effect that deeds, not mere belief, are the final object of Torah study. Therefore it was traditionally believed among Jews that moral and ethical conduct could only be derived from Torah study. It was said among the traditonal Jews that "If a man learns the law without the intention of fulfilling it, it were better for him had he never been born."[11]

In addition to thought and feeling, then, action was always emphasized among Jews as a necessary component of morality. When this is contrasted to the current approach to moral education from the rationalistic, cognitive viewpoint or the transmission of values or the effort to transmit emotional and interpersonal experiences then it can be seen that none of these forms of moral education conform to the traditional Jewish attitude. One question which all Jewish schools must therefore answer is whether or not these schools can transmit the Jewish view of moral conduct by means of their curriculum and their structure. This question is particularly important in light of the poor effort made by American public schools in teaching ethics. This poverty is undoubtedly influenced by the fear of running afoul of the "wall of separation between church and state" which has always been important for Jews lest the teaching of morality or ethics be translated into the teaching of the majority religion. Jews therefore have two reasons for sending their children to a day school. One is the probability that Jewish children will feel harrassed into participating in the majority religon against their will and the other that no ethics whatever are taught precisely because an effort must be made by public schools to avoid the overt teaching of religion.

Of course, one of the great weaknesses of Jewish concern with morality has always been the failure of Jews to defend their own interests on the grounds that to do so is somehow "immoral." It was this attitude which led the European Jews to conclude that it is "not Jewish to fight" and ended in Hitler's gas ovens. In short, there are many interpretations of what constitutes morality, including the view that even Jews have the right to defend their lives as evidenced by Israeli success in four major wars.

It is reasonable and accurate to say that in 1995 the majority of Jewish children do not remain in Jewish schools long enough for any significant learning to take place; that Jewish schools cannot attract or hold a sufficient number of competent teachers; that school budgets can hardly meet the ever increasing costs; that the curriculum is frequently a haphazard effort and not well planned and that "the climate in which Jewish education functions remains essentially unsupportive."

This was true in 1985, in 1975 and before that and before that and before that. So far, nothing has changed as this century is nearing its end.

It has been estimated that about 80% of those Jewish children who obtain any Jewish education are asked to do so in the "supplementary" schools which meet four to six hours a week in the late afternoon and Sundays. Ninety percent of these schools are supported by synagogues. Nevertheless, almost all of these schools face a dilemma that has not been resolved and will not be resolved. That is the wish of most of the parents who send their children to such schools to have these children identify with Judaism and to relate their children to the Jewish heritage without sacrificing any of the time needed to be involved in other, secular, activities such as music lessons, sports and other after school activities. That dilemma is in turn the consequence of the wish of most Jewish parents and children to educate children in a minimal Judaism in the synagogue school which will nevertheless insure that

Jewish children maintain a secular attitude and lifestyle. The dilemma lies in the fact that synagogues are established to teach religion. This dilemma is best understood if we remember that for centuries education of children in Judaism was considered a form of religious worship and a religous commandment as found in Deuteronomy 6:6,7 which may be translated as: "Take to heart these words with which I charge you this day. Impress them upon your children." This is still the major motive for the education of orthodox Jewish children. However, the ninety percent of Jewish children who are not orthodox are expected to learn only enough about Jewish history to know something about the Holocaust and Israel; have a minimal knowledge of the Hebrew language, know some Jewish customs and ceremonies and be given some instruction in Jewish ethics. No theological frame of reference is required by the overwhelming number of Jewish parents who send their children to the synagogue Sunday schools or afternoon schools.[12]

Friedman has written an ethnography of one such Reform Jewish Sunday school. This illustrates that the limited Jewish education available there serves to give some of the children in attendance a Jewish identity, even if Jewish learning is hardly possible in that setting. Not only the limited time available for instruction but also the extremely limited knowledge of the teachers prohibits in-depth learning of a Jewish curriculum. Therefore the subject matter is structured around holidays, games, songs, dances and some knowledge of Israel and the Holocaust. The major deficiency of such a school lies not only in the limited time available but also in the failure of most parents who send their children to these Sunday schools to reinforce affiliation with Jewish values at home. This is due not only to the secular attitude of most of the Jewish parents but also to the frequency of religious intermarriage among the families of Reform Sunday School children. Numerous children from such homes are both Jewish and Christian and celebrate holy days derived from both traditions. In an overhwelmingly Christian country this means *ipso facto* that children from such backgrounds will probably not be Jewish because they will hardly be inclined to marry Jews.[13]

Somewhat more time is given to students in the Jewish supplemental schools meeting in the afternoon on school days. Mostly attended by children from "conservative" Jewish families, these afternoon schools have been well described by Samuel Heilman, professor of sociology and an ethnographer. In an excellent study of two Jewish afternoon schools, one reform and one conservative, professor Heilman found this in 1992: In the afternoon schools as much as a third of the time is taken up in "structuring and maintaining student involvement." The need for this is the great temptation to "flood out" or remove oneself entirely from participation in the lesson taught by numerous forms of disruption such as conversation with other students, leaving the room for various reasons such as "a drink of water" or loud and gross conduct of many kinds, even during an effort by the teacher to involve children in prayer.[14]

The oberservations of Heilman in the schools and classes he visited have also been seen and experienced by numerous informants in other schools and other cities. Examples abound. In one class, about to study *Lamentations,* students chose to ask and talk about the possibility of receiving snacks from the teacher while others make "off color" jokes. In another class students ignore the lesson and the teacher so as to laugh about the use of foul language. Heilman also found that there is a good deal of pressure on students who do wish to learn, not to show too much involvement and not to know too much.

The meaning of this deliberate effort by Jewish students to disrupt and "flood out" in Jewish schools, according to Heilman, is to resolve the dilemma of living in both the Jewish and the secular society at the same time. "Flooding out," that is, disregarding the lessons being taught, permits the student to live in the secular American world even while attending the Jewish school as a sign of his adherence to the tradition. In short, "flooding out" has the function of permitting its practitioners to live in both worlds at once.[15]

A structure which has no function will soon disappear. Therefore it is reasonable to view the Jewish afternoon or supplementary school as a functioning organization, one that "works" in the sense that it permits its participants to be secular and committed Jews at the same time. Principally, the part time Jewish school serves to insure Jewish identity rather than Jewish learning. London has listed five "conventional qualities" which he regards as essential criteria of Jewish identity. These are: 1. Theology and belief - the belief in the unity of God as opposed to the Christian trinity, for example. If that is the case, then numerous Jews do not qualify because of the widespread agnosticism in the Jewish community. 2. Ritual practice - is also widely ignored by large number of Jews as shown by the National

Jewish Population Survey. 3. Ethnic or "tribal" family membership in an extended Jewish family. This too, is in doubt in many Jewish families in the U.S.A. as the intermarriage rate between Jews and non-Jews has risen to 52% in 1994. 4. Community affiliation and 5. Self definition, i.e., seeing one self as Jewish. This last criterion may be the most common even among those who have reliquished all connection to Jewish institutions and individuals. There are indeed many persons in the U.S. whose relationsip to anything Jewish is only their name but who nevertheless view themselves as Jewish. In consideration of all of these criteria the Jewish school has been assigned the task of preserving Jewish identity.[16]

This means that those who have attended the afternoon Jewish schools may not know very much about the vast body of Jewish knowledge and civilization which could not have been imparted to them in the time available. However, even the afternoon school permits its students to "learn ..... what it means to be Jewish."[17]

One principal of a supplementary Jewish school has revealed her observations in that position and the condition of such schools as they are found all over the United States. "Confessions of a Supplementary School Principal," written anonymously by a "Dr. Sue", discusses a supplementary school whose children are mainly drawn from families whose parents also received their Jewish education in such a school. "Our families have lost their way, and their Jewish values as well," says Dr. Sue. The "shocking examples" supporting that statement are these: only five students out of 23 have a "Tanach" or Bible in their home; twenty out of 23 students in an ethics class were prepared to save a pet dog from drowning rather than a stranger; in a class of 13 none lit candles on Friday night although one had seen this in his grandmother's house; only six out of 18 students in another class had ever seen a Seder and these six believed that *charoset,* a mixture of apples, nuts and honey also includes blood. With such Jews "who needs anti-semites?" asks Dr. Sue. To top it off, a student attending a Sabbath morning service asked why there would be a service when no Bar Mitzvah was taking place.

Since 73% of Jewish children who receive any Jewish education at all attend the supplementary schools "Dr.Sue" and many others are justified in asking "What will be the future for......Jewish children remaining in our supplememtary schools?"[18]

In view of the fact that only 41% of Jewish households have a synagogue affiliation and the vast majority of Jewish children cease to receive a Jewish education of any kind after reaching "Bar Mitzvah" age, it is evident that the supplementary afternoon school cannot insure Jewish survival.

The afternoon schools are plagued not only by the lack of interest and discipline illustrated above, but also by a perpetual personnel problem. Since congregational schools, meeting only 10-12 hours a week, can hardly offer full time employment to its teachers, this means that teachers must either work in a day school until 3 p.m. and then work an exhausting additional schedule or live on the minimal wages a congregational school can pay.

Since the American Jewish community has never been able to recruit a sufficient number of native teachers it has become necessary to appoint numerous Israeli teachers. While these teachers have the ability to speak the Hebrew language and are undoubtedly competent in mastering the curriculum, many are not acquainted with the American ethos and hence tend to isolate the Jewish school from the mainstream of American life.

In addition to these problems the teacher in a Jewish school faces the further difficulty which the lack of dignity accorded such teachers in the Jewish community imposes. It is no exaggeration to observe that teachers in Jewish schools, and in particular in part time schools, are held in contempt by the Jewish community and the parents who send their children there. This atmosphere of disdain contributes a great deal to the manner in which children in turn treat teachers in the so-called "Hebrew Schools" and make teaching there so difficult that a very high turn over in teaching staff is assured..

Principals and other adminstrators, including the Directors of Bureaus of Jewish Education, are equally confronted with this contemptuous attitude so that it takes a considerable emotional expenditure to endure the assault upon the self respect of personnel in Jewish schools. "People get worn down by the personal and professional indignities one must endure" in Jewish education and that is one of the prime reasons for the "Great Exodus" of Jewish educators.[19]

Traditonally, teachers and rabbis were seen as honorific persons in the European Jewish community. This was true because it was believed that such teachers were transmitting the word of God i.e. the

Torah, and that therefore they as well as their message were viewed as important and greatly esteemed.

Secularization has changed all that. Since the principal purpose of Sunday school and afternoon school is the promotion of a Jewish identity while the religious substance of Judaism is hardly accorded any attention, the messenger is as irrelevant as the message. Thus, Jewish teachers suffer from a lack of authority, prestige and dignity not only because a secular society measures the worth of its members according to financial crieteria, but also because the dispensation of every occupation forms the foundation upon which the perception of its worth must rest. Thus, physicians are highly regarded in the United States not only because of their high income and length of schooling but also because they reputedly dispense good health to their patients. Even professors have a high prestige rating in America and elsewhere, not because of their evidently moderate income, but because they dispense an important commodity, i.e., a college education.

The part time teacher in a part time Jewish school, however, dispenses nothing that is viewed so important as to be given much attention or effort. The evidence for this is the immense absenteeism in Jewish part time schools. Sports, plays, meetings of every kind, music lessons and parties all take precedence. Thus an atmosphere of disdain for Jewish education is promoted in each generation of students in these schools which insure that Jewish education at the level of congregational schools can have no future.

The curriculum of the Jewish part time schools is indeed ambitious. So ambitious in fact that few, if any, of the part time afternoon or Sunday school students learn anything at all. In part that was, and still is in some cases, the consequence of attempting to teach "more and more about less and less" thus insuring that students will remember nothing about everything. More recently, numerous groups interested in Jewish education have tried to restructure the curriculum in Jewish schools in such a manner as to master six areas only. These are to be: 1. The ability to converse in Hebrew 2. the ability to understand the major concepts in Jewish history 3. knowledge of major Biblical texts 4. knowledge of some Jewish literature 5. the ability to know the prayers and lead weekly and Sabbath services 6. the ability to read any Haftarah, the Torah and know home rituals.

Such a curriculum is of course very large and hard to achieve. It is highly dubious that any part time school can come close to attaining even one of these objectives.[20]

Therefore, these schools are viewed as inadequate by some Jews who want their chidlren to have a more substantial Jewish education. Furtheremore, Jews have found over many years of fighting the battle concerning the separation of church and state in the public schools that it is nearly impossible for public schools not to become Christian schools at least during the Christmas season. This means that Jewish children, particularly in neighborhoods where Jews are a small minority, are forced into Christian beliefs no matter the various court decisons in that area. Furthermore, Jewish children in public schools inevitably become the victims of anti-Jewish discrimination which will range from exclusion to overt, physical persecution. Therefore Jews are forced to live in areas with heavy Jewish concentration so that they will have the protection of numbers in the public schools or to send their children to Jewish day schools.

For all these reasons and because the vast majority of American Jews are native born and feel free to live their lives as they see fit and feel entitled to reject the Christianization of their children in public schools, the Jewish day school has become more popular in the 1990's than ever before. This trend began in the 1970's and has continued since so that one quarter of all Jewish women under age 45 who have received any type of Jewish education have received it in a day school. Since about one third of the 400,000 students in Jewish schools are enrolled in a day school it is evident that these day schools now form the back bone of Jewish education in the United States, having advanced from a Yiddish speaking European *milieu* to a native American form in the past forty years.[21]

This occurred despite the vehement opposition to the Jewish day schools in the early years of the American phase of that movement. This is of course a well known event in ethnic succession as American born grandchildren of immigrants are always more willing to acknowedge their ancestry than is true of the first generation or even the second.

Jewish day schools, like all schools which introduce religious material into their curriculum, must be financed privately. This is one of the cardinal principles of the Jeffersonian dictum concerning the "wall of separation between church and state" although the numerous cases decided by the Supreme Court of the United States in connection with this "wall" have not always beeen without ambiguities. A few of these cases, briefly listed, are : *Pierce vs. Society of Sisters* (1925) which permitted parents to decide whether to send their children to a public or private school; *State of Wisconsin vs. Jonas Yoder* (1972) which permitted parents to remove their children from school after completing the eighth grade; *Zorach vs. Clausen* (1952) permitting parents to withdraw their children from public school under "release time" provisions so they could attend religious school elsewhere; *Engel vs. Vitale* (1962) prohibiting the conduct of prayer in a public school during school hours; *Everson vs. Board of Education* (1983) permitting Boards of Education to distribute textbooks to children in religion controlled schools and also permitting such children to be transported to school at public expense.[22]

There are many more such decisions which we need not list here. Suffice it to say that the Jewish day school must be financed by parents who are already paying taxes for the support of public schools so that the day school is not always accessible for those who are financially limited and/or cannot get sufficient help to pay the tuition which can reach $5,000 per student per year.

III.

The considerable decline in the number of Jewish children enrolled in Jewish supplementary schools over the past thirty years has been accompanied by an increase in the number and proportion who are now attending a Jewish day school.

Thus, in 1962, "the peak enrollment year in Jewish schooling on the North American continent, about 540,000 children were enrolled in *Jewish supplementary schools.*"

In 1986 a 55% decline in that enrollment had been experienced, not only because of a decline in Jewish birth rates but also because of the high Jewish intermarriage rate and because the day schools had grown from an enrollment of 60,000 to an enrollment of 130,000 full time students. Thus, both the reduction in the supplemental school enrollment and the high birth rates among orthodox Jews who send their children to day schools have influenced these trends.[23]

Until the beginning of the second half of this century Jewish day schools were entirely Orthodox and devoted to European style Talmud study. It was in 1957 that the Conservative movement began the establishement of "Solomon Schechter" schools and thereby contributed immensely to the devlopment of nearly 900 Jewish day schools in America of which even the Reform now enroll 2%. Nevertheless, 80% of all students in Jewish day schools are under orthodox supervision.

Both the decrease in the enrollment in the supplemental afternoon Jewish schools and the increase in the enrollment in day schools are related to the birth rate. The part time schools, almost entirely dependent on Conservative and Reform children, exhibit the consequences of the declining Jewish birth rate. However, the day schools mainly enroll othodox children who come from homes who are opposed to birth control and have many children. This has also influenced the ever increasing enrollments in Yeshivas.

There was a time, prior to the second World War, when almost all Jews in the United States lived in Jewish neighborhoods in America's large cities. These neighborhoods were so overwhelmingly Jewish that Jewish children attending public school were generally in the majority in those schools. Consequently, these schools were closed on important Jewish Holy Days, anti-Jewish conduct was hardly known since the non-Jewish minority would not or could not display such behavior and courses of interest to Jewish students were taught in public schools. This is still true in some Long Island, N.Y. communities. However, the dispersal of the native born Jewish population over most of the fifty States and the consequent weakening of the Jewish aggregates in formerly all Jewish areas has contributed to the need to attend Jewish Day schools in order to escape anti-Jewish hostility and to capture the advantages of the Jewish Day school.[24]

A number of additional reasons for the growth of the day school after the second World War have been advanced. These are the effect of the Holocaust; establishment of Israel, the entry of Eastern European Jews into the United States and dissatisfaction with the public schools. Almost all orthodox Jews send their children to day schools. A good number of orthodox Jews have moved from communities which do not have such schools to communities which do have them since the very existence of Jewish orthodoxy depends on an adequate education in an orthodox school.

The day school enterprise is very expensive. It has been estimated that at the beginning of the next century the cost of such education will reach the $1 billion level. Day schools, although mainly attended by orthodox children, nevertheless attract some children from a diverse religious background. In communities with large Jewish populations it is undoubtedly possible for each Jewish religious movement to establish a day school reflecting the religious preferences of the sponsors. In smaller communities this is not possible. In communities with less than 30,000 Jews more than one day school cannot operate so that a "middle of the road" conservative attitude is likely to predominate in the schools.

One consequence of the Day school movement has been the increase of those who study Talmud. As we have already seen, about 5,000 American Jews do so full time. Another 5,000 do this part time and are associated in the *kollel* movement.[25]

In 1990, Alvin I. Schiff, Executive Vice President of the Board of Jewish Education of Greater New York, summarized the needs and hopes for American Jewish education in the ensuing decade. This important summary lead him to the conclusion that the "crucial objective" of American Jewish education must be to "learn to compete."

Schiff lists several possible responses to the condition of American Jewish education at the end of the 20th century. The first of these is the *transformationists* response whose supporters view the changes now taking place in American Judaism with equanimity because they believe that American Jews have become and are becoming more and more integrated into American life and that the alterations in life style and attitude among American Jews as compared to their immigrant ancestors help in promoting Jewish continuity in the United States.

There are also, according to Schiff, the *survivalists*, those who view acculturation in the form of intermarriage, ignorance of Jewish civilization and traditions and alienation from the Jewish people as a great threat to the survival of Judaism in the United States.

Finally, Schiff points to the *realists*, who, he says, undertand the inevitablity of change, and therefore recommend that the Jewish community *learn to compete effectively* with all those forces in American life which threaten Jewish survival. To compete effectively Schiff recommends a number of actions by the Jewish community of which the principal recommendations are:[26]

1. Strengthen the Jewish day schools.
2. Promote Israel experiences and Jewish camping.

3. Support Jewish studies on the college campuses.
4. Further the careers of young people in Jewish education.

In view of the increasing number of Jewish college students who reject Jewish life, the high rate of intermarriage, failure of Jewish children to receive a Jewish education of any kind, failure of Jewish supplemental schools to equip Jews to lead Jewish lives, shortage of Jewish teachers and underfunding of Jewish schools it may be very difficult if not impossible to reach the goals outlined by Schiff. Thus, secularization has indeed overtaken Jewish education with the exception of a few who attend Jewish day schools and Jewish institutions of higher education. Yet, as we shall see, even there secularization has made great inroads.

IV.

Yeshivah University, located in New York City, is not the only Jewish secular unversity in the U.S. It is, however, the oldest, having been founded in 1886. This does not mean that Yeshivah university is only secular. On the contrary, orthodox religious beliefs are the basis for education at the University. However, the university, according to its president, Rabbi Norman Lamm, seeks to influence the whole Jewish community. Therefore, said Dr. Lamm, "we are committed to secular studies, including all the risks that this implies, not only because of social and vocational reasons, but because we consider that it is the will of God that there would be a world in which Torah is effective; that all wisdom issues ultimately from the Creator and therefore it is the Almighty who legitimizes all knowledge."[27]

In view of the considerable emphasis on religious beliefs in these remarks it is doubtful that anyone not committed to a supernatural view of the world would want to enroll at Yeshivah unversity. This raises the question of influence. While Yeshivah unversity no doubt has some influence upon the orthodox Jewish community this is hardly possible among the vast majority of America's secular Jews. The problem of influence goes further, however.

It concerns the non-Jewish world as well and refers to the influence or lack of influence of academicians upon the decision making process in the American community. Such influence is limited if it exists at all. This is also true for American Jewish education. As we shall see, the American Jewish community is business oriented and business men govern it. Therefore Jewish educators, rabbis and administrators place a great deal of emphasis on labels to the exclusion of the vast majority of the Jewish people in America. Labels, such as "Doctor", are compensations for the failure of Jews engaged in education, the rabbinate or communal work to gain decision making power in the Jewish community. Consequently all those who have no college degree and even those who do but do not hold advanced degrees must be repelled by the endless recital of doctorates and professorial insignia of all kinds. In short, that vast majority of Jews who are arrogantly referred to as "the Jewish masses" feel repelled by the exhibitionism so common in the academic community.

"How many Jews will want to gain a Jewish education or teach in a Jewish school?" This question must be answered in face of the hostility of the Jewish community to Jewish education and in view of the excessive emphasis placed upon advanced degrees or the possession of material goods. Thus, academics in Jewish life are hardly noticed unless they are among the "large contributors" who are lauded at every communal dinner, in all Jewish publications and among the general media as well. In short, in a community of "conscipicuous consumption" who will want to play the poor relation if there is no need to do so? This becomes visible if we look at the background of students at Yeshivah University in New York. From this we learn that evidently Jewish education attracts principally those who are committed to Judaism and who are financially well off. There is no room at the Jewish sponsored universities, such as Yeshivah University in New York and Brandeis University in Waltham, Mass., for those whose financial resources are limited.

The graduating classes at Yeshivah University, an all male institution, were surveyed in 1986 and in 1987 concerning their social background and their reasons for attending there. This revealed that almost all students were born and raised in a suburb of New York City or come from another large urban area in the United States; hardly any of them work part time during their college carreer; many are the sons of Yeshivah graduates and all come from "affluent" homes. Almost all seek to become lawyers or physicians; only 7 percent wish to become rabbis and an even smaller percentage would consider entering Jewish education or communal work.[28]

It is remarkable that the number of students at an orthodox Jewish unversity wishing to enter Jewish communal employment is so low.

Yet, this is in line with the description of the rabbinate and Jewish education as already discussed here.

In fact this rejection of the "sacred" as compared to the "secular" is already embodied in the catalogue statement of "Purpose and History" of Yeshivah University. Here we read that the "University's thousands of graduates (includes) "judges, university professors.....business executives, government officials, artists, writers, doctors and scientists."[29] There is no doubt that this statement is true. However, these educational results of a Jewish university do not differ from the outcome of any other institution of higher learning in the Untied States. Anyone who reads the catalog of any unversity in America will find a similar statement. Thus, even Yeshivah University is today in part a secular institution although related to Jewish tradition.

We find then, that even those charged with promoting the welfare of a Jewish university find it necessary to elevate the secular attainments of their alumni and not their contributions, if any, to the study of Torah.

Brandeis University, named after Supreme Court Justice Louis Brandeis, is also a Jewish sponsored University. Unlike Yeshiva University, Brandeis Unversity is called "non-sectarian". It therefore "offers no theological instruction." However, the university offers a degree in the Jewish communal service. In short, Brandeis is a secular unversity and does not differ from any other private, secular university in the United States.[30]

Significantly, then, Jewish Higher education is also secular. This leaves the Jewish Theological Seminary, an institution devoted to the study of Jewish theology and the training of conservative Rabbis. Yet, even this institution, devoted to theology, found it necessary to support "a nonsectarian graduate school" known as "The Institute for Advanced Studies in the Humanities." Similar views can be found in the publications of the Hebrew Union College which trains Reform Rabbis.[31]

An excellent illustration of the manner in which even Yeshiva University had become a secular instituion by 1966 is a statement by Rabbi Irving Greenberg, professor of history at Yeshiva University, who said that at that time Yeshiva was "turning out secularly oriented students." He furthermore claimed that many of those who left Yeshiva without graduating are those who "are ethically and religiously more sensitive than those who stay."[32]

The dilemma faced by Jewish orthodoxy is therefore the need to remain true to the Torah tradition while living in the present, technological world as well. This dilemma has been solved for the majority of orthodox rabbis and their followers by studying in both secular and sacred areas. Thus, like so many other Talmudic scholars, Rabbi Joseph B. Soloveitchick, who was regarded as "the towering ideologue" of American Orthodoxy and was professor at Yeshiva University for many years, earned a Ph.D. in philosophy from the University of Berlin in 1931.[33]

Similarly, many of the graduates of Yeshiva University seek to combine orthodox Jewish living with an adjustment to the surrounding secular world. A survey of Yeshiva graduates has shown that the majority of Yeshiva alumni chose spouses with Orthodox values; attend modern Orthodox synagogues; participate in traditional Jewish practices; contribute to charities associated with Orthodox causes and "support institutions which strengthen Orthodoxy." These Yeshiva alumni live in predominantly Jewish neighborhoods whose citizens share their beliefs and they send their children to Jewish schools which teach similar views.[34] This then indicates that Yeshiva University succeeds to some extent in preserving orthodox practices among its alumni.

It ought to be understood, however, that this life stlyle is open to only those American Jews who live in New York City or similar Jewish communities. Thus, as the dispersion of American Jews continues and the centers of Jewish life become more diffuse, it will be more and more difficult for Jews to participate in an orthodox Jewish life style which is simply not available outside New York or a few of the larger American cities.

Nevertheless, even Yeshiva University has become secularized. The secularization of Yeshiva can be contrasted to the founding of the Orthodox Rabbinical Seminary of New Haven, Conn. in the 1920's which offered no secular studies and to the founding of the Telshe Yeshiva in a Cleveland, Ohio suburb in the 1940's. That Yeshiva is devoted to the perpetuation of the European tradition in the recreation "almost intact, of both the methodology of talmudic study and the insulated spirit of their old-country home." This comment refers not only to the Telshe Yeshiva but also to the founding of a Yeshiva in rural New Jersey equally devoted to the study of Talmud for its own sake and without a secular curriculum.[35] Evidently, the total enrollment at such traditional institutions of Jewish learning is small and far overshadowed by the secular forms of Jewish higher education elsewhere.

One example of a secular Jewish college is The Spertus College of Judaica, located in Chicago, Illinois. This college was founded in 1924 as part of the Board of Jewish Education of Chicago, founded that same year. Twenty years later, "the College was incorporated as a legal entity unto itself " with these purposes:[36]

1. "To maintain and operate a college in which youth and adults may receive an education, on a college and post-graduate level, in Jewish history, literature, philosophy, religion and in any other subject relating to Jews and Judaism."

2. to train Jewish teachers; club leaders in various Jewish organizations and those who seek to learn the Hebrew language.

3. to establish standards of higher Jewish education

4. to offer guidance and advice to Jewish institutions and organizations seeking to promote programs in Jewish education.

Added to this list is the hope that the college can carry out scholarly research, writing and publication.

The college confers the bachelor's and the master's degree in several areas. This college, and a number of others throughout the United States, are secular institutions which will undoubtedly continue to serve the small number of Jews willing to gain an advanced Jewish education. While such colleges as Spertus were at one time seen as the answer to the massive defections from Jewish learning and scholarship which had occurred in the United States after the First World War, a far different and unanticipated solution to the problem of giving Jewish youths an opportunity to learn about their heritage developed in the 1960's . That was the entrance of Judaic Studies upon the campuses of numerous American universities.

V.

Judaic Studies at American Colleges and universities is undoubtedly one of the truly great success stories in Jewish education. There are now more than 300 American Colleges and universities which offer courses in Judaic studies of which 40 have Judaic studies majors and 27 offer graduate degrees.

In addition publications of a Jewish nature have increased in the thirty years since 1965 and include such diverse publishers as the Unversity of Alabama Press, Indiana University Press and more traditionally interested publishers and just about every academic press in America. All of this is a tremendous change from the days when there were only two full time professors of Jewish history in all of the United States, Harry W. Wolfson at Harvard and Salo Baron at Columbia.[37]

These Judaic studies programs were mainly introduced in the 1960's. The author participated in the organization of such a program at the State Unversity of New York at Buffalo which then proceeded to appoint two professors of Judaic studies, one at its Elmwood campus and one at its Amherst campus. The impetus for doing so in Buffalo as well as so many other secular and Christian institutions of higher learning came largely from the civil rights movement of the 1960's. True enough, that movement had nothing to do with Jewish concerns. On the contrary. Many who led that movement, and particuarly the Rev. Jesse Jackson, were and are hostile to Jews. However, the idea that a racial minority had rights became legitimized in America. Therefore, when Jewish leaders took it upon themselves to encourage the development of Jewish Higher Education in secular universities there was suddenly little opposition to this idea because it had become popular to permit the expression of minority views and minority culture in public. In short, "what is good for the goose is good for the gander," or, what is justifiable for the black community is justifiable for the Jewish community. Black studies became all the rage in the 60's as well and hence, Jewish studies, a far older and more established concern, although usually outside unversities, seemed acceptable.

"One of the axioms of academic life in Europe and the United States was that although Jews had a religion and a set of laws, they had no culture-at least none that any educated person needed to know anything about."[38] All this suddenly changed as courses in Jewish history, sociology, philosophy and language became of interest to non-Jewish students as well as Jewish students. In fact, Jewish students who had utterly neglected their Jewish education and had at best attended some indifferent Sunday school have been taking courses in Judaica for the past twenty five years precisely because these courses are now secularized, that is "cleansed" and presented within the walls of academe, the one institution which secular Jews respect as the source of upper middle class status, prestige and occupation.

Thus, when in the 1960's and 70's Judaic studies "exploded" on American campuses the rationale and justification for teaching these courses changed from the earlier, feeble effort to view Jewish courses only as a background to Christian civilization to "the particularistic nature of the Jewish experience." Rather than being oriented toward non-Jews, the study of Judaica was now directed toward Jews. The underlying goal, reflecting the American Jewish communal agenda, was now 'Jewish survival' rather than 'Jewish acceptance'."[39]

Thus, students who enroll in Judaica programs in higher education find that these programs include the social, religious, historical, philosophical, literary and cultural aspects of Jewish civilization. "Core" courses are offered in all areas taught in all colleges and therefore that practice is also followed in Judaica. Students will enroll in a one year, or two semester sequence in Jewish history; in "survey courses"; in "independent study" courses allowing students to write a term paper under the supervision of a professor; in sociology courses and in archeology.[40]

Christian colleges and universities also proceeded to teach Judaica beginning in the '60's. This was largely the result of the revision of attitudes towards Jews and Judaism among Christians as a consequence of both the declaration concerning Jews by the non-Catholic Christian World Council of Churches in 1961 and the famous Catholic Declaration *"Nostra Aetate etc."* or *"In Our Age etc."* of 1965.[41]

These developments in Jewish education reveal then that the "vanishing" American Jew is not vanishing at all. "The end in *not* at hand," says Charles Silberman. Instead, a great change has come to American Judaism. Judaism and Jewish life in America have become secular, American and hence acceptable to Americans who are Jewish and who are not Jewish. It may be said that American Jewishness has become homogenized and part of the fabric of American culture as a whole. America, as we have shown, is a secular country. Therefore, that which is secular survives. That which is not secular is questionable and questioned, particularly among America's Jews. Therefore Jewish culture as part of a university curriculum can survive. But can Judaism, as an other - wordly, sacred, religious community also survive?

The most orthodox, Torah true believers among Jews, the Chasidim or Pious, believe that it can and have taken measures to insure that they too will be accomodated within the walls of the secular unversities of the United States. Particularly the Lubavitch movement with its great zeal to teach has provided secular unversities with courses on Talmud, Jewish history, religion and other subjects. Whenever such courses are not taught as part of a regular department offering Lubavitch scholars have taught them in the universites as auxiliary courses and even without pay for the professors if necessary. This indicates again that not only Jewishness, but Judaism, are not vanishing as Jews have learned that in America "if the mountain won't come to Mohammed, then Mohammed must come to the mountain." That has been accomplished and it is a success. Thus, the Association for Jewish Studies has over 700 members which means that there are that many professors of Jewish Studies employed at colleges and universities in North America.

Cooperman has summarized several of the principal advantages the Jewish community has derived from these developments. For those teaching and researching in the area of Judaica as recognized, secular university professors the advantages are immense as compared to the status of so-called Hebrew teachers a generation ago. Not only the financial and material benefits accruing to any professor but also the social standing of a professor devolve upon those who teach Judaica at universities. It is remarkable that the Jewish community holds those in contempt who teach Judaica in a Jewish setting but enhances the status of those who teach the same subject matter in a secular, non-Jewish university.[42]

Considerable financial savings for the Jewish community are a second advantage of the entrance of these pursuits into the secular universities. The university, not the community, now pays the salaries, pensions, expenses, books and office supplies of the professor of Judiaca. Finally, and most important, because Jewish studies are a secular subject in a secular university the courses taught there are attended by some Jewish students who had long ago given up all interest in Jewish education, viewing that as a childish Sunday school activity. Secularization of Judaica has thus made it acceptable to that vast majority of Jewish students at secular universities whose interest in Jewish civilization had disappeared two generations ago.

The negative aspects of this secularization, according to Cooperman, are that the college students who take Judaica courses are almost only taking introductory survey courses because very few will make Judaica their "major."

Furthermore, "the rise of Jewish Studies at secular universities has been accompanied by the demise ....of many Jewish sponsored colleges....."

That, however, is only a material loss. The real loss that the secularization of Jewish education inside the secular unviersity provides is the loss of Jewish values. Universities do not teach values, they teach objectivity and analysis. Thus, it is even possible, in fact certain, that some can gain a good deal of knowledge about Jewish civilization in a secular university even as they become more and more alienated from Judaism by reason of such study. This is recognized by Cooperman who points out that professors of Jewish studies, not rabbis, are now asked by Jews to interpret Judaism for them. Yet, professors are not necessarily devoted to the values Judaism has taught the world for centuries. "These academics," says Cooperman, "owe neither institutional nor intellectual loyalty to any part of the Jewish community."

The outcome of this development therefore is that Judaism as understood in the academic world is a Judaism which defines "Jewish identity in purely secular terms."[43]

It is of course not clear whether or not the secularization of Judaism by means of the educational process will insure the survival of Judaism into the unseen and not foreseeable future. It is however certain, that as of 1995, the vast majority of American Jews will not permit its survival in any other way. The immense defections from the Jewish cause and the great number who have relinquished their membership in the community of Israel through negligence and ignorance or even hostility have mandated that secularization of Judaism be one of the means adopted by those who continue to have an interest in Jewish survival.

Another means of hopefully securing that goal is Jewish secular community organization which is the direct consequence of the secularization of the Jewish religion, the Jewish family and Jewish education. That then is the focus of our next chapter.

NOTES

[1]Franz Rosenzweig, *On Jewish Learning,* N.N. Glatzer, editor; New York, Schocken Books, 1955, p. 59.

[2]Meir Ben-Horin, *Common Faith-Uncommon People,* New York, The Reconstructionist Press, 1970, p. 171.

[3]Zvi E. Kurzweil, *Modern Trends In Jewish Education,* New York, Thomas Yoseloff, 1964. pp.212-213.

[4]Gerhard Falk and Vern Bullough, "Achievement among German Jews Born During the Years,1785-1885," *The Mankind Quarterly,* Vol. XXVII, No.3, Spring 1987, pp.355-357.

[5]Heinrich Heine, *Heines Werke,* Berlin, Deutsches Verlagshaus Bong & Co., no year, vol. 1, p. 207.

[6]William D. Helmreich, *The World of the Yeshivah: An Intimate Portrait of Orthodox Jewry,* New Haven and London, Yale University Press, 1982 p.ix-xi.

[7]*Ibid.,* p. 318.

[8]Samuel Schafler, "God and the Jewish School," *Jewish Education,* Vol. 57, No. 1, Spring 1989, p. 41.

[9]*Ibid.,* p. 42.

[10]Sara G. Efron, " Old Wine, New Bottles: Traditional Moral Education in the Contemporary Jewish Classroom," *Religious Education,* Vol. 85, No., 1, Winter 1994, p. 52.

[11]The Talmud, Lev.Rabbah 35:7. In Efron, *op.cit.* p. 55.

[12]Walter I. Ackerman, "Jewish Education," in: Bernard Martin, *Movements and Issues in American Judaism,* Westport, Con., Greenwood Press, 1978, p. 184.

[13]Norman L. Friedman, "Reform Jewish Sunday School Primary Grades Department: An Ethnography," *Jewish Education,* Vol. 55, No. 2, Summer 1987, pp. 18-25.

[14]Samuel Heilman, "Inside the Jewish School," *What We Know About Jewish Education,* Los Angeles, Torah Aura Productions, 1992, p. 306.

[15]*Ibid.* p. 311.

[16]Perry London, "The Goals of Jewish Education: Jewish Idenity Must be Primary," *Agenda* , Vol.1, No.1, Fall, 1992, p. 8.

[17]*Ibid., p. 314.*

[18]"Dr. Sue." Confessions of a Supplementary School Principal," *Jewish Education,* V. 57, No. 1, Spring 1989, p.39.

[19]Saundra Sterling Epstein, "The Great Exodus of Jewish Educators: Why Is It Happening?" *The Pedagogic Reporter,* Vol.XXXIX, No.2, May 1989, p. 33.

[20]Ackerman, *op.cit.,* p. 196.

[21]Barry A. Kosmin, Sidney Goldstein, Joseph Waksberg, Nava Lerer, Ariella Keysar and Jeffrey Scheckner, *The 1990 CJF National Jewish Population Survey,* New York, Council of Jewish Federations, 1991, pp. 31-33.

[22]Gerhard Falk, *A Study of Social Change,* Lewiston, N.Y. The Edwin Mellen Press, 1993, pp. 151-155.

[23]Alvin I. Schiff, "The American Jewish Day School: Retrospect and Prospect," *ThePedagogic Review,* Vol.XXXVIII, No. 3, November 1987, pp.1-3.

[24]Lloyd P. Gartner, *Jewish Education in the United States, : A Documentary History,* New York, Teachers College Press, 1969, p. 218.

[25]*Ibid.* p. 3.

[26]Alvin I. Schiff, "Toward the Year 2000 - Condition of Jewish Life: Implications for Jewish Education," *Jewish Education,* V. 58, No. 1, Spring 1990, pp. 3-9.

[27]Jeffrey S. Gurock, *The Men and Women of Yeshivah: Higher Education, Othodoxy and American Judaism,* New York, Columbia University Press, 1988, p. 247.

[28]*Ibid.* pp.1-7.

[29]Yeshivah University Undergraduate Catalog, 1991-93, p.12.

[30]Brandeis University Bulletin, 1993-1994, p.2.

[31]Academic Bulletin of The Jewish Theological Seminary of America, 1993-1994, p. 3.

[32]Gurock, *op.cit.,* p. 221.

[33]Jeffrey S. Gurock, "Resisters and Accomodators," in: *The American Rabbinate: A Century of Continuity and Change, 1883-1983, "* Jacob

R. Marcus and Abraham J. Peck, Editors, Hoboken N.J., KTAV Publishing House, Inc., 1985, p. 54.

[34]Bernhard H. Rosenberg, "A Study of the Alumni of the James Striar School at Yeshiva University," *Jewish Education,* Vol. 61, Spring 1994, p. 10.

[35]*Ibid., p. 60.*

[36]Byron L. Sherwin, *Contexts and Content: Higher Jewish Education In the United States,* Chicago, Spertus College of Judaica Press, 1987, pp. 225-278.

[37]Charles E. Silberman, *A Certain People: American Jews and Their Lives Today,* New York, Summit Books, 1985, p.227.

[38]*Ibid.,* p. 227.

[39]Sherwin, *op.cit.,* p.173.

[40]Sandra R. Shimoff, " Judaic Studies: An Interdsiciplinary Model," *Jewish Education,* Vol.57, No.2, Summer 1989, p. 13.

[41]Gerhard Falk, *The Jew In Christian Theology,* Jefferson, N.C., McFarland & Co., 1992. pp.144-149.

[42]Bernard D. Cooperman, "Jewish Studies and Jewish Identity: Some Implications of Secularizing Torah," *Judaism,* Vol.42, Spring 1993, pp.229-243.

[43]*Ibid.,*pp.233-237.

Chapter XI

Organized American Jewishness at the End of the 20th Century

I.

There are a large number of Jewish organizations which have proliferated in the United States during the twentieth century. Some of these organizations are entirely secular organizations, in the main devoted to fund raising and civil rights causes but not to Jewish issues, while others are of a religious or Zionist nature or seek to further Jewish education. A review of these organizations reminds us that despite the secularization here reviewed there remains a group of Jews who are willing to participate in Jewish life in a variety of ways and for a large number of reasons.

Thus, the Encyclopedia of Associations lists 25 Jewish organizations concerned with Jewish education with a combined membership of less than 30,000. In addition, the ultra-orthodox Lubavitch movement claims a membership of 600,000 persons in their *Central Organization for Jewish Education.* It is likely that this organization, unlike any other, includes all members of the world-wide Lubavitch movement and even more.[1]

While some of the organizations dealing with Jewish education have a religious bent, there are also such groups as *The American Association of Professors of Yiddish* and *The Association for the*

Sociological Study of Judaism, which have no religious significance and list only three hundred members each.

In addition, the Encyclopedia of Associations lists 147 other Jewish organizations ranging in announced memberships from the very large to the minuscule. Thus, the World Union for Progressive Judaism claims to have 1,500,000 members employing a staff of six. Active in 29 countries this immense group "arranges for the training of rabbis, and teachers; represents progressive Jewry at the United Nations" and publishes a biannual and a quarterly journal every year. The Lubavitch Movement claims 1,000,000 members and is devoted to "proclaiming Judaism and the observance of the Torah world wide. The Torah is the body of law and wisdom contained in Jewish scripture and other sacred literature and oral tradition." Various publications and meetings, conferences and auxiliary groups help in this effort.

B'nai B'rith reports 500,000 members and employs 280 people. This organization, headquartered in Washington, D.C., sponsors the B'nai B'rith Hillel Foundation which is active on 450 American University and College campuses. This organization employs rabbis on each campus who conduct religious and other Jewish services, offer programs to Jewish students and assist in promoting introductions between Jewish female and male students during their college years. B'nai B'rith also sponsors the B'nai B'rith Anti-Defamation League which actively defends Jews against anti-Jewish hate attacks and is otherwise active in efforts to promote inter-religious harmony and fellowship. Hadassah, The Women's Zionist Organization, lists 385,000 members and a staff of 150. This organization of Jewish women is well known for the maintenance of the Hadassah Hospitals in Israel, the Hadassah College of Technology in Jerusalem; the Career Counseling Center for high school students and a variety of Zionist activities. There are numerous other large organizations promoted and funded by American Jews.

Meanwhile, the American Congregation of Jews from Austria have only 300 members and the Association of Humanistic Rabbis appears to have only one member, Rabbi Sherwin Wine of Michigan.

The purposes and aims of these many organizations vary immensely. Thus there is the Neturei Karta of the U.S.A. located in Brooklyn, N.Y. who "conducts research into.......Zionist collaboration with Nazis, directly or indirectly during the Holocaust years." Also known as "Guardians of the Holy City," this organization which does not list the size of its membership publishes a journal called *The Jewish Guardian* which is devoted to "the real orthodox Talmudic view on Judaism."

In Culver City, Cal., there is a National Jewish Hospitality Committee whose purpose is to "welcome and assist converts to Judaism and serve non-Jews who for marital or personal reasons have an interest in Judaism."

Even smaller is the "Committee for the Implementation of the Standardized Yiddish Orthography." Founded in 1958 the committee has no meetings and no conventions but restricts its activities to correspondence concerning Yiddish spelling and the publication of a "Guide to Yiddish Orthography." Its membership is not listed in the Encyclopedia of Associations.

Two thousand German speaking people of the Jewish faith are members of the New World Club which issues a German newspaper called "Aufbau" or "Reconstruction" with a a world wide circulation of 30,000.

The American Society of Sephardic Studies with 117 members "exchanges historical, cultural and linguistic material about Sephardim or Spanish, Portuguese and Oriental Jews."

Some of the organizations listed have as members other organizations. Thus, The United Synagogue of Conservative Judaism has as its members 800 Conservative congregations with a membership of 1,500,000 while the Union of Orthodox Jewish Congregations of America is represented by 1,200 congregations including 600,000 members and employs a staff of 160.[2]

The largest Jewish organization of all is the Council of Jewish Federations of which the United Jewish Appeal is the principal beneficiary. This organization, which collects about $840 million from American Jews each year, is perhaps the best example of a fund raising effort anywhere and is today, in 1995, "the real religion" of many American Jews. Thus, while the United Way campaign raises about $3 billion each year from all Americans, including Jews, Jewish Americans constituting only 2.8% of the American population give the UJA $840 million annually. How is that done?[3]

Marc Lee Raphael has described the methods used by the United Jewish Appeal to bring about such immense contributions. These methods rest in small part on the impulse to charity and good deeds traditional in the Jewish community. The principal method for collecting money for the Jewish Appeal is however force. This means that "The Jew no more gives *tzdakah* (charity) than the citizen gives income taxes to the government. You pay your taxes because you must."[4]

This fact is best illustrated by these statistics. There are about 3,186,000 Jewish households in the U.S. The median annual income of these Jewish households was $39,000.- in 1990. Of these households, 1,811,000 or 57% were entirely Jewish.[5]

Yet, only 45% of these households contribute to the United Jewish Fund campaign, a percentage which slips to 20% in New York City where 30% of all American Jews reside. The reason for the lower rate of contribution in New York is that the force of public opinion cannot be applied as successfully in New York as in smaller communities like Des Moines, Iowa where 85% of all Jews contribute or Richmond, Va., where the contribution rate is 60 percent because Jews in these communities all know one another, depend on one another and feel the pressure of communal approval or disapproval a great deal.

Twelve percent of the 867,000 mixed Jewish-non-Jewish households contribute to the UJA and only 4% of those who contain "no core Jews" do so. These 4% are persons who are not Jewish now but were born as Jews.

Because participation in the efforts of the United Jewish Fund is so low, it becomes evident that the money raised by that organization has to come from a small group of large contributors.

These contributors are solicited in a manner that was invented in the 1920's by Joseph Willen, director of the New York fund raising drive for many years. Says Silberman: "Since, Willen believed, lawyers were more likely to respond to an appeal from their fellow lawyers, jewelry manufacturers from their fellow jewelry manufacturers, and so on, he began to organize a separate fund raising campaign for each industry."[6]

This works very well not only because those who know each other or, in sociological terms, belong to the same "reference group" are more likely to contribute to someone with whom they have some affinity, but also because Willen introduced a second method of collecting funds. This second method is the "card-calling" luncheon. At these luncheons large contributors are honored with bronze plaques. Speeches are made describing the lives of the honoree-contributors. The honoree-contributors find their picture in a local Jewish or other newspaper particularly as annual Jewish Federation dinners and meetings are dedicated to them.[7]

Other methods of fund raising include inviting potential donors to the homes of prestigious business "leaders," appointing wealthy persons to so-called Young Leadership Cabinets and organizing "Super Sunday," on which volunteers telephone potential donors concerning contributions the week after the Super Bowl football game.

It has been claimed that the most successful campaign for funds for the Jewish Federation-United Jewish Appeal campaign has come from Cleveland, Ohio. That is undoubtedly true as the Jewish community of about 70,000 Jews has involved as many as 3,000 Jews in the annual Federation Fund campaign. It is also in that community that the executive of the Federation made the remark that "involvement with federation is the real religion here." That remark could well be extended to all of the United States and exhibits more than any other statement that "checkbook Judaism" has captured the Jewish psyche almost entirely at the end of the 20th century. Irving Bernstein, formerly executive vice-chairman of the United Jewish Appeal, remarked that "the UJA is, through Israel, America's Jewish religion." Secular Jewishness has replaced sacred Judaism among many Jews who practice "checkbook Judaism" exclusively. "Not prayer, but philanthropy," said Bernstein.[8]

The number of Jewish organizations seeking funds is far greater than the 172 Jewish organizations listed in the Encyclopedia of Organizations. All of these groups seek to increase their income beyond what is allocated them by the so-called "United" Jewish Appeal. Consequently there is no end to the solicitation of the same individuals in the Jewish community. These are generally people who have been known to give money before and who are then mercilessly accosted in the mail, at home and at work, and on the telephone by additional organizations who have been given the names of such contributors by previous fund recipients. Thus, the same person will receive upward of three contacts per day from solicitors for money. These indifferent solicitors will mispronounce the name of their prospect, become aggressive during telephone contacts and create the impression, both in writing and in person, that the solicitor is doing the candidate a "favor" by demanding money from him. Many people are so angered by this unending demand for their money coupled with an utter lack of accountability for the money collected that more than half of all American Jews give nothing whatever to any Jewish "cause."

It ought to be understood by Jewish contributors that the clients of Jewish agencies are not necessarily Jewish. Thus, about one half of residents of Jewish Homes for the Aged are not Jewish and up to 85% of people serviced by the Jewish Family Service are not Jewish. The reasons for this are, first, that Jews are serviced at non-Jewish agencies if they want this. Further, that some of the money collected comes from non-Jewish sources. Finally, many Jewish agencies, particularly Homes for the Aged, are too large and too expensive to be financed only by the Jewish communities in most American cities outside of New York. Therefore it is necessary to include non-Jews in the funding and in the clientele. Now many non-Jews do not want to eat Kosher food. Thus, in Jewish nursing homes there is often no kosher food, or food that may be interpreted to be non-kosher, even if there are some residents who sought out a Jewish nursing home precisely because they meant to eat only kosher. However, the need to support a large establishment usually means that kosher and other religious requirements are sacrificed on the altar of expediency, that is, non-Jewish money. If these Jewish sponsored agencies and nursing homes were not too large for the Jewish communities in many smaller places, then these issues would not arise. However, Jewish communities usually pride themselves on their modernity and inclusion of all possible devices and programs in Jewish agencies. Furthermore, the salaries of executives of Jewish agencies would be far smaller if the agencies they head served only Jewish needs. Therefore, it is in the interest of such executives to increase the size of their domain even if this means the sacrifice of religious Jewish interests. *No better example of the secularization of the Jewish community can be found.*

One may ask: "Would it perhaps be better to build a small home, organize a smaller agency, pay lower salaries and keep the entire establishment Jewish?" In any event, these decisions indicate that religious belief is easily discarded when income is involved. The secular need easily defeats the religious strictures at the end of a century of American Judaism.[9]

Whatever their merits, the demands of all these "agencies" have led to a rejection of fund raisers and their clientele by those who have heard it all before, over and over and over, day in and day out. This then is "checkbook Judaism" whose main beneficiary has been Israel.

There can be no doubt that this "checkbook Judaism" of giving large sums of money to the Council of Jewish Federations Fund Campaign came from the anxiety American Jews have felt for many years over the security of Israel. It is for that reason that collections increased a great deal during and after each of Israel's wars. What remains to be seen is whether the enthusiasm for giving provoked by those wars will continue to fund the many projects of the Untied Jewish Federation Fund Campaign once Israel lives at peace with its neighbors, a prospect now very much at hand. It is therefore not surprising that it is now proposed that $3.- of every $10.- contributed to the United Jewish Appeal should be spent on Jewish domestic needs in the United States. This revision of the relationship between Israel and American Jews has been furthered by Yossi Beilin, the deputy foreign minister in the cabinet of Yitzchak Rabin, and other Israelis who feel the need to escape the dominant position of American Jews in the relationship between the two communities.

Furthermore, Israel has made great economic gains in the past three years so that its "$60 billion annual gross domestic product equals that of Egypt, Jordan, Syria and the territories combined'" while "Israel's $20 billion export market is growing at about a 10 percent annual clip.."[10] These developments make the new, more independent relationship between Israel and the American Jewish community possible.

There are of course two sides to money collection. One side is the solicitation of funds. The other side the spending of the collected money. This second side, the spending side, is not visible to most of the contributors because it is only visible to board members and to those employed in various executive positions. These people are usually labeled "leaders" in the Jewish community thus identifying "leadership" with conspicuous consumption, not only of material objects but also with the buying of social honors such as offices in organizations, memberships on boards, opportunities to at least claim to speak for the Jewish community and the obsequious theatrics of community organization employees.

II.

In November 1994 *The Forward,* a Jewish newspaper founded in 1897, published a list of fifty American Jewish "leaders" and added a description of each to the list.

This list is very significant in explaining the secularization of the American Jewish community at the end of the 20th century precisely because it illustrates how far American Judaism has come from the days when Rabbis, scholars and Talmudic giants were the leaders of the Jews.

Of the fifty "leaders" depicted by the *Forward,* ten are rabbis. This would at first glance indicate that the Jewish clergy, known for their scholarship, are still very much in charge of the Jewish community. However, a closer look shows that is not the case at all. Instead, these rabbis are quite far removed from the tradition since only three of the rabbis are scholars in any sense of that word and the others are political activists concerned with managing large organizations, lobbying for black or lesbian rather than Jewish causes or seeking tax credits for non-public schools.

Even the three "scholar" rabbis include Rabbi Menachem Mendel Schneerson who died in June of 1994 and Rabbi Norman Lamm, who, despite his undoubted scholarship, is best known for his fund raising activities on behalf of Yeshiva University whose president he is. He was also instrumental in bringing about the so-called "Yeshivah" decision of the United States Supreme Court in 1980 which ruled that a private university does not have to recognize a professor's union on the grounds that professors are themselves management and hence cannot also be labor.

Rabbi Schneerson was the "Lubavitcher Rebbe", and in that capacity also served as head of a $100 million organization encompassing 200,000 followers world wide. Regarded by some of his followers as "The Moshiach" or Messia, he too was an "organization man." Only Rabbi Aaron Soloveitchik among the fifty "leaders" in American Judaism can be regarded as a "great talmudic scholar."

The other women and men who were listed as "Jewish leaders" in November of 1994 are all either professional practitioners in the Jewish Communal Service, elected officials of numerous Jewish organizations or publicists and writers such as Elie Wiesel, Norman Podhoretz, Irving Kristol, Cynthia Ozick and Letty Pogrebin.

These writers are of course known to that tiny group of "intellectuals" who read *Commentary* or similar journals. Such reading is however far from the average American Jew who is normally ignorant of the existence of such material as well as Jewish history. That ignorance is so pervasive that Leslie Wexner, called "billionaire benefactor" by *Forward,* contributed "a huge chunk of his fortune" to the Jewish education of "aspiring young Jewish leaders (and) the next generation of Jewish communal stewards."[11]

The extent of secularization within the Jewish community is thus illustrated by this array of ambitious politicians whose efforts to reach leading positions within Jewish community organizations are well rewarded. For example, the executive vice president of the American Joint Distribution Committee "earns" $310,805 per year and receives additional benefits of $7,750.- The executive vice-president of the New York UJA-Fedaration, Stephen Solender, receives $ 301,000.- per year. The executive director of the Jewish Federation Employment and Guidance Service, Alfred Miller, received a salary of $237,737 in 1992. The budget of that service was $87 million that year. Other 1992 salaries were: John Heimersdinger, director of the Jewish Guild for the Blind with a budget of $30 million received $183,101; Oskar Rabinowitz, executive of Jewish Community Services of Long Island with a budget of $10 million received $163,850; Alan Siskind of the Jewish Board of Family and Children's Services with a budget of $75 million received $157,500; The Brooklyn Hebrew School for Special Children paid Rabbi Morris J. Block, executive director $137,077 on a budget of $10 million; the Jewish Association of the Aged with a budget of $14 million paid Ron Guardia $115,000 and Paul Gitelson, director of the Jewish Child Care Association of NY received $115,000 with a budget of $8 million.[12] Executives of Jewish nursing homes and other organizations earn upward of $200,000.-[13]

There are those who say that the employees of Jewish organizations are "worth it." Since the President of the United States earns $200,000 plus $50,000 in taxable expenses, it is difficult to understand how these salaries, derived from charitable contributions, can be defended.[14]

Salaries of other executives of Jewish organizations are equally large thus making the Jewish Communal Service a lucrative profession whose practitioners need not necessarily have any zest for the Jewish cause but a good deal of political skill needed to satisfy the rich and the super-rich who employ them.

The employers are of course the board presidents and board members who pay considerable sums in order to hold a chairmanship on either a local or a national level. Consequently it is visible that almost all elected and employed officials of Jewish organizations are members of the upper class, earn immense salaries and are mainly unable to comprehend the needs of poor or disadvantaged Jews because their own financial position makes it almost certain that they have neither experienced nor seen poverty or need.

Another great disadvantage resulting from these excessive salaries is the unwillingness of many Jews to contribute to the United Jewish Appeal or other charitable groups because they feel that their contribution will not help those intended but will be entirely absorbed by the salaries, expense accounts and "benefits" of the "in-crowd." It is significant that only 910,000 Jewish households out of a total of 3,186,000 Jewish households contribute anything to the United Jewish Appeal.[15]

It is remarkable that among the "leaders" of the Jewish community as defined by *Forward* are such persons as Jack Sheinkman, President of the Amalgamated Clothing and Textile Workers of America. Sheinkman's "contribution" to the Jewish cause is his association with Jesse Jackson, the black leader who denounced Jews repeatedly and called New York City "Hymietown."

Similarly the former President of the American Jewish Committee, Morris Abram, is known as a "Jewish fighter for black equality", an effort which the black community has recognized by screaming "Kill the Jews" in the Crown Heights Pogrom in 1991. The truth is that the so-called "leadership" of the Jewish community did nothing to help the Jewish victims of that pogrom. It was only that the Australian brother of the murdered Yankel Rosenbaum, Norman Rosenbaum, activated the Justice Department in a minimal manner to prosecute the killers.

This despite the fact that the "leader" Morris Abram was also at one time President of the American Jewish Committee, president of Brandeis University, chairman of the Conference of Presidents (of various Jewish organizations) and numerous other groups. How is it, one may ask, that all these organizations would not lift a finger to help the victims of the Crown Heights Riots in 1991 or the victims of the bombing of the Jewish Community center in Buenos Aires, Argentina by Iranian terrorists?

Failure of the Jewish "leadership" to help Jews in need is an old tradition in this country as well documented by Arthur D. Morse in his book *While Six Million Died: A Chronicle of American Apathy.* In addition there are innumerable other sources illustrating this failure.[16]

Yet, a far more recent reaction to the inability of the American Jewish community to develop true leaders with followers who trust in them is contained in this letter, published in November of 1994. The author has heard such comments in all parts of the United States although few can express in writing what many say in less grammatical terms.

"...........*Many baby boomers are put off by the financial corruption, non-accountability, luxurious salary structures, hierarchical control and old-boy male centricity of most Jewish organizations.*"[17]

Even if the perceptions contained in the above letter excerpt were altogether untrue, it is nevertheless significant that such attitudes are prevalent in the American Jewish community because perceptions are reality and have real consequences.

III.

The *American Jewish Committee* with about 45,000 members has a budget of $18 million and a staff of 200. The *American Jewish Congress* with about 50,000 members has a budget of $6.5 million and a staff of 75. That organization appeals mostly to a wealthy group of Jewish elitists. Both groups are organized to combat anti-Semitism as is the Anti-Defamation League of *B'nai B'rith (The Sons of the Covenant).* The ADL has a budget of $31 million and a staff of 400. Recently, Edgar Bronfman, perhaps the largest contributor to Jewish organizations in America, suggested that these three groups be merged and that the savings resulting from such a merger be used to deal with Jewish/non-Jewish intermarriage instead of anti-Semitism which, according to Bronfman, is declining so much that three organizations are wasting money. Needless to say, the executives of these groups found that suggestion obnoxious, banal and insidious.[18]

B'nai B'rith is the largest Jewish fraternal organization in the United States and elsewhere, claiming a membership of over 500,000.

It is worthwhile for our purposes to briefly review that organization's efforts and attainments because of its large scale appeal to Jews of every economic status, both male and female, old and young.

Deborah Dash Moore has described the origins of *B'nai B'rith,* which was founded by German immigrants in 1843, and called it a "secular synagogue."   She writes that; "B'nai B'rith founders recognized the necessity of moving outside of the sphere of the synagogue to reach all Jews on common ground."[19]

This is precisely the role of B'nai B'rith as that organization led in promoting Jewish survival and Jewish causes outside the religious establishment. Thus, the *Anti-Defamation League of B'nai B'rith* was founded in 1913 in an effort to combat anti-Jewish bigotry, an effort in which the A.D.L., as it is commonly known, has been immensely successful.

Prior to the 1990's this effort was never enough because the wide spread anti-Jewish attitude on the part of much of the American public made A.D.L. an almost indispensible support for many a Jew who could not fight his battles alone. With the decline of anti-Jewish conduct and the almost total Americanization of Jews in the U.S. the fight against anti-semitism or anti-Judaism seemed less important than before. However, the A.D.L. has more recently entered the political arena in order to combat *The Religious Right: The Assault on Tolerance and Pluralism in America.* That is the name of a book published in 1994 by A.D.L. The purpose of publishing such books is to resist Christian fundamentalists who seek to "return faith to the public schools, subsidize private religious education, roll back civil rights protection, oppose all abortions, etc." In view of the outcome of the 1994 Congressional elections this agenda is a real threat and is taken as such by A.D.L.. It remains to be seen whether the A.D.L. view is accurate or whether it is alarmist as some would claim.[20]

Yet more dramatic and at least as important has been the success of the Hillel Foundation, also sponsored by *B'nai B'rith.* This foundation, which supports Jewish student activities on the campuses of American colleges and universities, was founded in 1923 at the instigation of a Christian professor of Bible at the University of Illinois. In 1924, Rabbi Benjamin Frankel, who had named the organization after the great first century Rabbi Hillel, succeeded in convincing B'nai B'rith to sponsor this enterprise. More recently, lack of money has caused Hillel to distance themselves once more from B'nai B'rith as that organization is no longer able to support Hillel as heretofore. Therefore, Hillel has changed its name to: *Hillel, The Foundation of Jewish Campus Life.*[21] Today, in 1995, Hillel is the recognized Jewish student representative on almost all campuses in the United States, Canada, Israel and other countries. It is generally administered by a rabbi of any persuasion, but sometimes has as its director someone who is not a rabbi. It is secular, yet it sponsors religious services. *Hillel* remains neutral relative to religion but has succeeded in representing Jews and Judaism in the academic community. Indeed a remarkable achievement.

Ahava or Love, *Zedaka* or Justice, and *Achdut* or Unity are the three Hebrew words from which the letters A.Z.A. are derived. That organization is yet another B'nai B'rith project adopted at the 1924 convention of B'nai B'rith when A.Z.A. had already been established in a number of Western American cities. That organization is designed to bring together young Jewish boys for sports and sociability. Together with B'nai B'rith Girls, organized by B'nai B'rith Women in 1940, these two groups have become the B'nai B'rith Youth Organization.

B'nai B'rith also established an Adult Jewish Education Committee, a United Nations Liaison Committee, sponsors numerous publications and many more programs. Undoubtedly, a Jew who wishes to participate in Jewish activities without ever setting foot inside a synagogue and without participating in any religious activities whatever could easily find enough to do within secular B'nai B'rith alone. In addition, as we have described, there are so many other Jewish organizations demanding time and money that secular Jewishness easily outdistances Judaism and its religious demands in the lives of American Jews.[22]

Almost every Jewish community of any size has a Jewish Community Center. In New York City these "Centers" are generally called Young Men's and Young Women's Hebrew Association and stem from the first of these organized in Baltimore, Md. in 1854. These associations had been literary societies at their inception in Cleveland, Buffalo, Syracuse and Louisville, becoming a national association in the 1860's. The programs of the Philadelphia and New York City YMHA's became varied and extensive in the 1860's and included physical education as well as Sunday Schools and Schools of Religion.

In at least thirty American communities, settlement houses were formed to help the recent immigrants who came in great numbers at the end of the 19th and beginning of the 20th century. These settlement houses also evolved into Jewish Community Centers once immigration lessened.

One of the functions of these centers was to permit the immigrants to learn more about American life even while retaining the Jewish identity of the immigrant and his native contemporaries.

While these community centers operated on a voluntary basis before 1900 full time "superintendents" or "executive directors" were first appointed in 1900. It was also around the turn of the century that these centers, by any name, associated in a nation wide association called League of Young Men's Hebrew Associations and grew considerably into the 1920's. At that time most of these organizations began to use the name Jewish Community Center as they increased and diversified their program. This program included then and still includes physical education, recreational activities, "intellectual" events such as book fairs, speeches and study groups and social events such as dances, dinners and "singles" affairs.

Since these centers include so many clubs and sub-groups they permit many people to learn the art of politics as they seek election to the innumerable offices such clubs provide. Therefore it is not surprising that many of the officers of national Jewish organizations learned the skill and art of political maneuvering in Jewish Community Center Clubs. This is not to say that the rich and the super-rich are not given the most important positions in Jewish life even if they did not participate in these clubs or the Jewish Center. Money will buy the presidency of a large social service organization whether Jewish, Christian or otherwise. Nevertheless, political skills are very important for those who seek to assume "leadership" positions in social service organizations because even among the wealthy there is a good deal of competition for such assignments. In the Jewish community the presidency of an organization, particularly on the national level, is so highly prized because many Jews see in such prominent positions an opportunity to deal with the top elected officials of the U.S. or the state government. Thus, the chair of the Conference of Presidents of Major American Jewish Organizations is regarded by some to be the spokesperson for all American Jews and therefore is frequently invited to visit with the President of the United

States or other government officials. One unfortunate consequence of such ambitions is that the politicians seeking or holding visible offices within the Jewish community may forget the need to address Jewish concerns in their anxiety to please and be received by political office holders.

The Jewish Center movement grew as secularization increased in American Jewish life. Thus, the Jewish Centers around the country assumed an educational function in the 1930's when the Jewish Welfare Board organized a lecture bureau designed to present speakers on various Jewish topics to the membership. These were principally secular speakers dealing with secular topics. Added to these educational efforts were the annual Book Fairs now (1995) held in all Jewish communities which have a Jewish Community Center. These book fairs not only exhibit and sell books by Jewish authors and on Jewish topics but present speaker/authors to the Jewish community. The extent of secularization which has encompassed the Jewish community can be measured by the kinds of speakers recruited.

Thus, in November of 1994 a medium sized Jewish community in the Mid-West invited as the principal speaker at the Jewish book fair the lawyer William Kunstler. Kunstler has never been known to favor Jewish causes or contribute anything to the Jewish community. On the contrary. Devoted to the "civil rights" of various minorities, he has incessantly defended those who have vehemently and obscenely denounced the Jewish people.

He has defended Spike Lee, a movie producer, who makes anti-Jewish movies and gives anti-Jewish speeches. In fact, Kunstler actually supplied Lee with materials with which to make a movie called "Malcolm X" which is grossly anti-Jewish.

Kunstler also defended El Sayyid Nossair, an Egyptian, for killing Rabbi Meir Kahane. Nossair was not convicted as Kunstler prided himself on his defense, saying that Kahane deserved to be murdered.

In addition, Kunstler, although born to Jewish parents, has said that he is no longer a Jew and has declared himself outside of the Jewish community. Thus, on July 6, 1993, Kunstler told the New York Times that he attended Seder every year but goes to other ceremonies as well. "I go to Catholic churches and Sikh temples and native American ceremonies," he said. Further, Mr. Kunstler told the times that; "he married two Jewish women and at least some of his four grandchildren - he is not sure how many- consider themselves Jews.

His two youngest daughters, aged 15 and 16, do not. "They are more interested in ACT Up and AIDS causes."[23]

Now there will be those who will uphold an invitation to Kunstler as being open minded. There will be those who will say that Kunstler has every right to defend anyone he chooses and that is true.

However, the Jewish Community Center is not obliged to give such a man a platform for his views. This is done, however, because Kunstler is controversial and because he is an "ambassador to the goyim," and looks good in public. His disdain for things Jewish and his controversial views certainly improved the attendance figures at his speech. In fact, it drew a large crowd because it generated considerable publicity.

Yet, neither Kunstler nor his message advanced the cause of Judaism one bit. Instead, such an invitation reveals most of all how far Jewish "professionals" have come in traversing from Jewish values and concerns to purely commercial and secular interests.

These Jewish "professionals" are today mostly social workers who hold the M.S.W. degree and/or have graduated from Brandeis University with a background in Jewish communal work. Some have an interest in Jewish philosophy, in Judaism and in Jewish concerns. Others do not. Such an interest is not a criterion for membership in the National Association of Jewish Center Workers founded in 1918.[24]

While the secularization of the Jewish Centers in this country has kept pace with the secularization of the Jewish community as a whole, this was not the announced purpose of the Jewish Center movement when Oscar Janowsky wrote his survey of the Jewish Center movement in 1945-1947. Adopted as the "principles for the future," the so-called Janowsky report held that "*The religious and cultural differentiation of the Jewish group....is sanctioned by American democracy.*" Therefore the report, as adopted by the delegates to the convention of the Jewish Welfare Board in 1947, demanded that "*the program of the Jewish Center should devote primary attention to Jewish content*" and "*should be permeated by the spiritual-cultural factors which constitute the Jewish way of life.*"[25]

This may well have been the case at the time such a goal was adopted. Today (1995) it is distinctly not the practice, even if it is the intent. Jewish content is hardly visible in the Jewish Center movement at the end of the century. There are several reasons for this, some of which are already in evidence in the pages of this book.

One reason is the high intermarriage rate. Large numbers of those who are now members of the Jewish Center have no Jewish background and no interest in including Jewish content in the program of the Jewish Center. Furthermore, many members of the Jewish Center are not Jewish because of the dispersal of Jews across the United States and the consequent decline in Jewish concentration in a few urban areas. This has meant that the Centers became dependent on including large numbers of non-Jews in their membership, thus adding to the number of members who have no interest in the Jewish content of the program. In addition, many center workers who are Jewish are secularists and see no need for a specific Jewish content in the Jewish Center program. In addition, there are numerous Jewish center employees who are not Jewish.

Hence it is entirely possible and frequently practiced that a Jewish person can participate in the Jewish Center program to a considerable extent without having any commitment to Judaism, to Jewish values or to any Jewish cause. In short, there is nothing Jewish in the Jewish Center swimming pool nor is Judaism located in a Jewish Center punching bag. Therefore, it is not without justification to hold that the Jewish Center movement may at best be able to give some members a sense of Jewish identification but that it is otherwise so secular that this movement contributes very little to the survival of the Jewish people.

Despite the diversity in program which most Jewish Centers provide at least 50% of the attendance at such programs is devoted to physical education and recreation with a heavy emphasis on child serving and the needs of the retired members.[26]

These needs must be served and are well taken care of by Jewish Centers. Yet, there is nothing particularly Jewish in the programs for these age groups nor is that possible now (1995). Were a particularly Jewish content attempted it would run contrary to the interests of the intermarried, the non-Jews and the secularized Jews already mentioned.

IV.

The phrase "leadership" is commonly used to label Jews who voluntarily contribute large sums of money to Jewish causes. Whether or not the word "voluntarily" is appropriate here may well depend on the business interests of such contributors rather than their commitment to Jewish survival. In any event, such persons are normally invited to join the self-perpetuating boards of directors in the Jewish agencies already mentioned. They direct the fortunes of the numerous Jewish organizations from B'nai B'rith, the Hillel Foundation, and the Jewish Welfare Board to the Jewish Community Centers, the synagogues and that great host of other organizations constituting the American Jewish community.

Since board members are not chosen for their commitment to Jewish values or their knowledge of Jewish culture but solely because of their willingness and ability to contribute money it can be said that board memberships are for sale both in the Jewish and the non Jewish community agencies promoting one cause or another.

Nevertheless, it is commonly claimed by professionals who staff the Jewish agencies that such board membership leads those so chosen to devote themselves to Jewish values and Jewish attitudes, that such board members and officers of Jewish organizations embody the *mitzvot (good deeds)* of *tzdakah (charity)* and that this involvement in Jewish causes has such an impact on the children of such board members that it contributes to the survival of the Jewish people.

This would mean that the children of lay leaders in the Jewish community would have similar interests and would be more likely to continue the Jewish tradition than is commonly the case among those Jews not so involved.

Two studies of the intermarriage rate of children of 8,000 American Jewish "leaders" indicate however that the intermarriage rate of the children of such contributors exceeds 50% and therefore resembles the overall Jewish intermarriage rate. Similarly, synagogue affiliation, ritual practice and devotion to Jewish education are equally lacking among the children of such board members. In fact, a 1991 study has shown that there is considerable hostility toward what is perceived as "the Jewish establishment" among financially successful younger Jews.[27]

The ignorance of children of Jewish "leaders" concerning Judaism and Jewish civilization is of course shared by their elders. The evidence for this is the effort of Leslie Wexner, a billionaire contributor to Jewish causes, who "Pumped a huge chunk of his fortune......into sponsorship of courses, seminars, retreats etc." for lay leaders of the Jewish communities across the United States. He did so because "he was dismayed by the minimal level of their Jewish knowledge" and therefore endowed Jewish education for such "leaders." It should be added that Jewish professionals are generally also ignorant of Jewish history, civilization and culture and could benefit equally from such an endowment.[28]

Further evidence that lay "leaders" and many Jewish professionals have little knowledge concerning Jewish culture and civilization is the meager support given Jewish day schools by such "leaders." Our review of Jewish education has revealed that Jewish day schools are the only probable source of Jewish survival in America. Yet, few of the "leaders" of the Jewish community send their own children to such schools or support them with more than "lip service."

The reason for all this is "check-book" Judaism which prescribes that financial contributions are the only criterion of Jewish involvement. That belief is in turn dependent on the common American notion that all things, particularly social honor, can be bought. Thus, Jewish "leaders" buy positions of honor in the Jewish community without needing to participate in anything Jewish other than in the positions thus sold. Consequently an utter ignoramus concerning Jewish affairs, history or civilization can be and has often been president or chair of this or that Jewish group solely because of his ability to finance the salaries of the professionals involved. Thus, a cycle of need dictates that ignorance and even rejection of Jewish values shall be enthroned in Jewish communal affairs as the professionals, eager to secure their emoluments, elevate anyone with money to positions of influence and power. Those who accept such positions do so in the certainty that they will be the objects of the obsequious fawning of the professional employees of Jewish agencies, receive a good deal of publicity in the Jewish and even the general media and simultaneously enhance their business image. None of these benefits, however, secure Jewish survival nor enhance the Jewish cause.

It has been suggested that Jewish professionals urge Jewish "leaders" to send their children to day schools and that Jewish professionals urge Jewish study groups upon such "leaders." Such efforts can hardly succeed however, because the dependence of Jewish professionals on the wealthy "leaders" is such that the professionals would hardly risk making unpopular suggestions to those whose largesse is the source of their sustenance.[29]

V.

There are however American Jews who are now (1995) changing their emphasis from integration into the main stream of American Jewish life to an emphasis on the survival of the Jewish people in America. This is more likely to occur at the end of the twentieth century than ever before because more than one hundred years have now passed since the principal immigration of European Jews to the United States began. Therefore American Jews are generally native Americans of native parents and feel secure in the knowledge that their American credentials are unquestioned. Furthermore, the events of the nineteen sixties promoted the view, now commonly accepted, that ethnicity can be celebrated alongside Americanism and that which is good for the Irish or the Poles is also good for the Jews. Hence, public displays of Jewish symbols, such as the Menorah, are no longer unheard of in many American cities. Jews march in public on Israel Independence Day and rabbis pray at graduation ceremonies. The orthodox, displaying beard, black clothes and earlocks are willing to portray their beliefs in the media and are often supported in their fundamentalist views by Christians with similar agendas.

Zionism continues to be popular in the United States and Israel continues to receive the support of the American people. Interfaith study groups visit Israel as Jews join with others in enhancing common causes and non-Jews have taken up the most emotional of all Jewish causes as their own, i.e., the Holocaust. There are holocaust events in Christian establishments every year as churches invite guest speakers to lecture to their congregations on that heinous crime.

Ecumenism (the inclusion of 'the world') is commonplace in almost all American communities today and Jewish Americans are indeed included. It is unfashionable to be a religious bigot and the label "anti-Semite" is studiously avoided and rejected with vehemence by anyone seeking public office or influencing the media. Passover and Chanuka greetings are broadcast on Television, even in communities with small Jewish populations, college courses on Jewish history are taught by rabbis in innumerable non-denominational and Christian schools.

Most important in giving Jews a sense of security and belonging in America is the phenomenal economic achievement of American Jews. Thus, it has been estimated that about one fourth of the most wealthy

Americans are Jewish even though only 1.8% of the American population is Jewish. If the over age forty population is considered, then eight percent of college educated Americans are Jewish while 20 percent of "the most elite sectors of American society" are Jews. In fact, at the end of the twentieth century Jews have entered into areas of power and prestige in America which were once entirely reserved for white Anglo-Saxon Protestants. This is visible in government as two recent additions to the United States Supreme Court are Jewish while two Jewish women were elected as Senators from California.[30]

Jews have entered the American academy in unprecedented numbers and American Jewish Nobel prize winners abound. There are and have been American Jews prominent in sports, in the arts and in communications.

Thus, Jewish influence upon American life is far greater than Jewish numbers would warrant. Furthermore, hostility to Jews is at an all time low in the United States of 1995.

From all this one should be able to abstract attitudes of Jewish elites, not only towards Jews and Judaism, but also towards social and political issues generally. This is worth discussing because Jewish survival depends largely on the opinions and behavior of Jews who are able and/or willing to promote the Jewish cause and keep it alive. I mean that in view of the widespread secularization of Jews in America, Jewish survival will finally depend of the "Weltanschauung" (view of the world) adopted by Jewish "elites" whether in finance or education, in the arts or in politics. For as we have seen, these are the people who are recruited into the boards and decision making positions of Jewish organizations, and Jewish organizations are the representatives of the Jewish people in every phase of life and will decide in microcosm where the larger group will go and where it will be in the future.

"Jews are generally wealthier, better educated, and hold higher status jobs than the average American."[31] Since Republicans are generally wealthier, more educated and have higher status jobs than Democrats it would therefore be reasonable to expect that American Jews would normally vote for the Republican party. That, however, is not the case and has again failed to materialize even in the election of 1994. Once more the overwhelming number of Jewish voters chose Democrats. This is best illustrated by the results of the election in New York State which has a large Jewish population. There 61% of all

Jewish voters voted for Mario Cuomo, the Democrat Governor and loser, while 37% voted for the winner, Republican Gov.- elect George Pataki. Likewise, 87% of Jewish voters chose incumbent Sen. Patrick Moynihan, a Democrat over his Republican rival. In the same election, 62% of white Protestant voters chose Pataki over Democrat Cuomo who received only 31% of their votes. Comparing the Jewish vote to New Yorkers who earn $50,000 to $74,999 it turns out that only 43% voted for Cuomo and 52% for Republican Pataki. Evidently, Jews do not vote their pocketbook.[32]

This peculiar voting pattern is a political anomaly and tells us a great deal about the Jewish elite and American Jews generally. This is not to say that there are no Jewish conservatives. Thus, *Commentary*, a Jewish sponsored and edited magazine with intellectual pretensions, is distinctly conservative in its outlook and publishes articles reflecting a conservative point of view. There are also some Republican politicians who are Jewish such as Senator Spector of Pennsylvania and the former Senator Rudman of Connecticut. Nevertheless, the overwhelming number of Jewish voters and politicians adhere to the Democratic party despite the evidence that Democratic attitudes and platforms are not always in Jewish interests.

Lerner, Nagai and Rothman have made an effort to explain this discrepancy by administering a detailed questionnaire to 1,340 persons they identified as elites among the American military; corporate business leaders; law partners in major law firms; high ranking civil servants; principal journalists; prime time television producers and directors; major movie producers and leaders in public interest groups.

The outcome of their study was this: Twenty eight percent of those interviewed labeled themselves as Jewish. Three out of four of these self-styled Jews considered themselves "liberal." This is extremely high, not only because only 37% of non-Jewish elites called themselves "liberal" but also because only one third of the Jewish public held that view. This political orientation is not related to religious views of the respondent except that Jews who converted to another religion are as conservative as those whose religion they have adopted.

Voting behavior of Jewish "elites" also follows the Democrat and liberal point-of-view. So-called "elite" Jews have consistently preferred the Democrats regardless of religious denomination although the

Orthodox are more likely to vote Republican than either the Conservatives or the Reform.[33]

Even more surprising is the disproportionate number of "elites" who view themselves as liberal if compared to the majority of Jews. Thus, one third of the Jewish public call themselves liberal but three out of four "elite" Jews carry that label. Similarly, Jewish "elites" are less favorable toward laissez-faire capitalism than are non-Jews. More than two thirds of Jewish elites believe that government should reduce the income gap between rich and poor while less than half of non-Jews in similar circumstances believe that.

While a large number of Jewish elites are quite liberal in connection with foreign policy issues, support for Israel is almost unanimous among them, although that is not the case among non-Jews.

Three "dimensions" of liberalism have been identified and in all three there is a "significant ideological gap between Jewish elites and non-Jewish elites." The first, called "expressive individualism", refers to abortion, gays teaching in the schools, the environment, adultery.

The second "dimension" of liberalism is called "system alienation" and refers to the view Jewish elites have of the legal system, private enterprise, public ownership of corporations, foreign policy and other aspects of "the system." In each instance, Jewish elites are more ready to criticize "the system" and to believe that the rich take unfair advantage of the poor or that the rich have too much control of these institutions. "Collective liberalism" is the third "dimension" of liberalism. This refers to such items as collective ownership of big corporations, government guaranteed jobs, fairness of private enterprise and others.

In all three of these "dimensions" Jewish elites are more "liberal" than is true of non-Jews except that the orthodox are more conservative than are other Jews. Lerner et. al. have tested a number of hypotheses to explain this "liberalism" among Jewish elites which contradicts their status and even their self interest and come to the conclusion that family tradition and marginality explain this attitude. This means that culture lag is also involved in that Jewish elites vote and act according to "liberal" standards because their parents did so and raised them in these traditions. In addition, Jews, even those who have achieved a high social position, feel uncertain of their status and seek a "universal" explanation for anti-Jewish experiences (anti-semitism) rather than a particularistic one. This is true because most Jews have rejected orthodoxy and conformity to Jewish law and substituted general "ethics" as the focus of their concerns. It is thus more convenient for Jews to work for a universally "better" world in the hope of benefiting from it rather than work for specifically Jewish solutions to discrimination and bigotry which would probably not attain as much support as the "universalist" approach.[34]

In view of the Holocaust these attitudes of Jewish "elites" are understandable. Although a half century has passed since the end of that hideous phase in Jewish history, the Holocaust is by no means forgotten. On the contrary. The Holocaust museum in Washington, D.C. opened only recently. Holocaust events have become part of some Christian observers also. Commemorations of the "Kristallnacht" destruction of German synagogues are not uncommon and support for commemorating such events is widespread. This support has become the religion of some Jews now so that many Jews who never attend a synagogue and have no interest in perpetuating Judaism will nevertheless attend the annual Holocaust memorials in their community and will financially and personally participate in such efforts. This is true because "Holocausting" is popular, because it is secular and because it lends an aura of martyrdom to American Jews whose connection to these events is only remote and anecdotal.

VI.

The major Jewish organizations already mentioned were founded early in the twentieth century with the express purpose of fighting anti-Jewish bigotry. While such bigotry still exists it is evident that there are some who believe this is no longer a major issue in the American Jewish community. For example, a controversy erupted in November of 1994 between leaders of the World Jewish Congress and the executive director of the Conference of Presidents of Major American Jewish Organizations over the statement by WJC president Edgar Bronfman that "there is just too much cost, too much overhead, too much counting swastikas in bathrooms."[35]

The reason for this fixation upon anti-Jewish bigotry lies of course in the entire "liberal" agenda of the principal Jewish agencies in the United States. As Ku Klux Klan style white anti-Jewish hatred declined and Jews became more and more accepted into the American "main stream", the large Jewish organizations needed to justify their continued existence and therefore took up the cause of other minorities. This was done, not only because of the decline in anti-Jewish attitudes in America, but also because of the aforementioned "universalism" upon which Jewish liberalism rests. That "universalism" is wedded to the proposition that if *all* injustices can be eliminated then anti-Jewish hatred will also be eliminated. This view is an heir-loom of nineteenth century and early twentieth century European Jewish attitudes which had disastrous results. It was precisely this attitude which permitted the German and other Western Jews to ignore the danger to their position *before* the Nazi rise to power. The Jews of Germany in particular thought that they could save themselves by supporting the German socialist party while in Russia some Jews believed that Communism would be their salvation.

It has never been necessary for American Jews to make such choices or to seek escape from government persecution in the support of socialist or communist parties. However, Jewish organizations have gone out of their way to support the aspirations of black Americans, not only because of the much touted interest of Jews in social justice, but also because of the "universalist" illusion so common among American Jews.

The black community, however, saw the support of the Jewish establishment otherwise. As early as 1932 Marcus Garvey, at that time the most prominent black leader in America, sent a message to his followers praising Hitler and the Nazi treatment of the German Jews. In 1935 riots against the Jews of Harlem were organized by Sufi Hammed and in 1943 another riot followed in New York city in which blacks burned Jewish stores and property. In 1946, Kenneth Clark, then the most famous of black professors, wrote that Jews only pretend to be the friends of the black minority in order to exploit them and in 1966 Horace Bond, president of the African- American Institute, claimed that "Jews control the media and seek to stab all minorities in the back."

During the 1960's Malcolm X, H. Rap Brown and Stokeley Carmichael, all black leaders, raged against Jews incessantly while the black New York radio station WBAI broadcasts this poem even in the 1990's: "Hey, Jew boy with that yarmulke on your head, you pale faced Jew boy, I wish you were dead."

Black professors have been notoriously anti-Jewish. For example, John F. Hatchett of New York University claimed that Jewish teachers in the New York schools commit "genocide" against Afro-American students, black revisionist "scholars" write that the holocaust never happened while Leonard Jeffries, professor of "black studies" at the City College of New York teaches that Jews were responsible for the slave trade and that "Jews are dogs."

Despite all this, and numerous other indications of black disdain and hatred for Jews, numerous Jews traveled to the rural South during the 1960's voter registration drives and went far beyond anything ever done for the victims of Nazi terror in the '30's, to help black Americans obtain "their" civil rights.

Michael Schwerner and Andrew Goodman, two Jewish students from New York, were murdered in Mississippi in the cause of civil rights. Yet, Leroi Jones, a.k.a., Imu Baraka, calls these two martyrs in *his* cause "artifacts" and "paintings on the wall," while the civil rights leader Archie Shepp said in a Greenwich Village speech that Schwerner and Goodman "acted only to satisfy their conscience."

Louis Farrakhan, the most notorious Jew baiter of the 1990's, is also black but has hardly been condemned for his fascist bigotry.

Added to this sorry record is the pogrom staged by the black community of Crown Heights against the Hasidic Jews in 1991 and the murder of Yankel Rosenbaum on that occasion.

All of this plainly demonstrates that universalist, secular liberalism is a failure and a Jewish illusion.[36] Furthermore, this attack upon Jews by the black community indicates at least that Jews cannot expect to survive in America or anywhere else unless the "universalism" so far represented by the Jewish organizations is replaced by particularism in the sense that Jews seek to secure their survival by means of Jewish education and the alleviation of Jewish discomforts.

One source of these discomforts is the proposition that prayer be returned to the public schools by means of a constitutional amendment. This idea is supported by many black leaders even if it is anathema to Jewish groups. However, the Jewish effort to support the black community has not led to a reciprocal effort to guard against the introduction of prayer into the public schools. On the contrary. Many black clergy are happy to see such a constitutional amendment pass.

Thus, white and black Christian conservatives are in the ascendancy in 1995, leaving the majority of Jews, not interested in religion, isolated as the last and only secular humanists in America.

All of this must be seen against the backdrop of an ever increasing Christian conservatism which is leaving the large secular Jewish organizations to fend for themselves with an antiquated agenda and no allies.

The entrenched Jewish "leaders" and organizations have been unwilling to recognize these black attitudes because a direct confrontation with black anti-semitism would have to lead to an admission of failure for secular liberalism and a change in the Jewish agenda to specific Jewish causes.

The truth is that the Jewish agenda must be changed and concentrate much more on Jewish issues foremost among which is the great rate of Jewish attrition which is due both to the rate of Jewish intermarriage and the willingness of American Jews to relinquish their cultural heritage which so many view as irrelevant.

Because Judaism, the religion, and Jewishness, the secular Jewish culture, have so few followers, the proportion of Jews in the world today (1995) is exceedingly small. Thus, the Israeli demographer Sergio Della Pergola has calculated that Jews are only 0.25 percent of the world population now (1993).[37]

Therefore, the Jewish condition in the United States and in the world today confronts a paradox. For the first time in centuries Jews are not persecuted anywhere. Israel has proved its worth to those who needed a place to go as the Jews of Yemen, of Ethiopia and of the former Soviet Union have been able to find asylum there and did not have to beg others for admission when they needed to leave their native lands. American Jews are better off than any Jewish community has ever been in the entire history of the Jewish people. Far from persecution, Jews in America have reached the very pinnacles of success. Yet, even as this is true, the threat to Jewish survival is now the very acceptance Jews are enjoying . *Secularization is now the greatest threat to Jewish survival* because that attitude must lead to the assimilation of Jews into the mainstream of non-Jewish culture and the disappearance of Jewish life from the United States.

Except for the orthodox Jewish community in Israel, where they number about 350,000 and in the United States and Western Europe where they have altogether an equal number of followers, Jews are nearly indistinguishable from the surrounding peoples among whom they live.

Thus, while Jewish organizations abound and Jewish "leaders" write checks and collect money from others, a singular and effective strategy for Jewish survival into the next century is yet to be developed both in the United States and in Israel where the peace initiative of 1993 and 1994 has removed the threat of possible annihilation of that Jewish community and confronted Israel with the need to live with those many contradictions which large scale immigration from various cultures must inevitably bring to all immigrant countries.

This need is however much more urgent in the United States. Therefore it is necessary to once more review the rate of secularization in America today before concluding with some predictions concerning the American Jewish community in the foreseeable future.

NOTES

[1]Carol Schwartz and Rebecca Turner, Eds., *The Encyclopedia of Association,* 29th Edition, Vol. 1, Part 1, Detroit, Gale Research Inc., 1994, pp. 1012-1015.

[2]*Ibid.,*p. 2337-2341.

[3]No author, "Charitable seductions," *Time,* Vol.144, October 3, 1994, p.51.

[4]Marc Lee Raphael, *A History of the United Jewish Appeal, 1939-1982,* Scholars Press, Brown Judaica Studies 34, Providence, R.I., 1982.

[5]Barry A Kosmin, et. al., *Highlights of the CJF 1990 Jewish Population Survey,* New York, Council of Jewish Federations, 1991, p. 17.

[6]Charles E. Silberman, *A Certain People: American Jews and their Lives Today.,*New York, Summit Books, 1985, pp. 189-235.

[7]No author, "Federation meeting to honor Nathan Benderson, Harry Kosansky for leadership, achievements." *Buffalo Jewish Review,* Vol. 87, No. 11, November 18, 1994, p. 1.

[8]Raphael, *op.cit.,* p. 115.

[9]Bob Curran, The Buffalo News, Sunday, Janury 22, 1995,p. B-2.

[10]David Makovsky, "The Business of Peace,", U.S. News and World Report, Vol. 117, No.18, November 7, 1994.

[11] No author, "The Forward Fifty," *Forward,* Vol. 98, No.31, November 18, 1994, p. 14.

[12]"Captains of Charity," *Forward,* Vol.97, No. 30,963, February 18,1994, p.1.

[13]"The Forward Fifty," *op.cit.,* pp.11-14; and *The Forward,* Vol. 98, No. 31,021, March 31, 1995, p. 2.

[14]*1993 Information Please Almanac,* 46th Edition, p. 41.

[15]Kosmin, *op.cit.,* p. 36.

[16]Arthur D. Morse, *While Six Million Died: A Chronicle of American Apathy,* New York, Random House, 1967.

[17]Sally Jacoby, "The Mystery of Organizational Malaise," *Forward,* Vol. 98, No.31,002, November 18, 1994, p. 6.

[18]*Forward,* op.cit., p.1.

[19]Deborah Dash Moore, *B'nai B'rith and the Challenge of Ethnic Leadership,* Albany, State University of New York Press, 1981, p. 11.

[20]Midge Decter, "The ADL vs. the Religious Right," *Commentary,* Vol. 98, No.3, September 1994, p. 45.

[21]Told to the author by Rabbi Shay Mintz, Hillel Director at the University of Buffalo,.December 16, 1994.

[22]Moore, op.cit., p. 161.

[23]Ron Rosenbaum, "The Most Hated Lawyer in America," *Vanity Fair,* Vol.31, March 1992, p. 88.

The New York Times, July 6, 1993.

[24]Louis Kraft, *A Century of the Jewish Community Center Movement,* New York, National Jewish Welfare Board, 1953, p. 28.

[25]*Ibid.,* p. 40.

[26]Morris Levin, "An Analysis of Study Material on the Image of the Jewish Community Center Held by Membership and the Jewish Community," in Irving Canter, Ed., *Research Readings in Jewish Communal Service,* New York, National Association of Jewish Center Workers, 1967, pp. 190-191.

[27]David Dubin, "Lay Leadership and Jewish Identity," *Journal of Jewish Communal Service,* Vol. 68, No.   4, Summer 1992, p. 357.

27. *"The Forward Fifty,* op.cit., p. 14.

28. Dubin, *op.cit.,* p. 361.

29. Steven M. Cohen and Leonard Fein, "From Integration to Survival: American Jewish Anxieties in Transition," *The Annals of the American Academy,* Vol. 480, No. 1, July 1985, p. 80.

30. Robert Lerner, Althea K. Nagai and Stanely Rothman, "Marginality and Liberalism Among Jewish Elties," *Public Opinion Quarterly,* Vol. 53, No. 3, Fall, 1989, p. 330.

31. "The Vote In New York State" *The New York Times,* November 10, 1994, p. B 14.

32. Lerner, el.al., *op.cit.,* pp.345-347.

32 *Ibid.* p. 348.

34. Rachel Blustain, "Jewish Leaders Striking Back at WJC Brass," *Forward,* Vol.98, No. 31,005, December 9, 1994, p. 1.

35. Irving Kristol, "Why Religion Is Good for the Jews," *Commentary,* Vol. 98, No. 2, August 1994, pp. 19-21. See also: Paul Gurevitch, "The Jeffries Affair," *Commentary,* Vol.93, March, 1992, pp. 34-38; Charles Horowitz, "The New Anti-Semitism," *New York,* Vol. 26, July 11, 1993, pp. 20-27; Thomas W. Hazlett, "The Wrath of Farrakhan," *Reason,* Vol.26, No.66, May, 1994.
36. Robert S. Wistrich, "Do the Jews Have a Future?" *Commentary,* Vol. 98, No. 1, July, 1994, p. 23.

Part Four

Jewish Continuity In a
Secular Society

Chapter XII

The Secular Life in America

I.

If the Jewish community is to survive in America it will have to provide its followers with answers to those needs which secular society has created for all who live in it at the end of the 20th century and at the beginning of the twenty first century.

There can be no doubt that secularization is the dominant mode of thinking in America at the end of the Twentieth Century and that the belief in *Progress* as taught by Herbert Spencer is still a part of that thinking. We have defined secularization as "the gradual deposition of religion from almost every structure and dimension of society, except perhaps the most private and personal."[1]

This is certainly the case within the American Jewish community as it is in the American community as a whole. As we have seen, secularization has had a long history in the United States so that the American Jewish community could hardly escape its influence. Obviously, American Jewish institutions have become largely secularized and the Jewish religion has become marginalized in the process.

In 1950, in the middle of the century, Henry Steele Commager, already then one of the most influential historians in America, published *The American Mind* and assured his readers that the

American mind is pragmatic, optimistic and secular. Commager summarized the condition of America at that time in a manner which is still valid. Said he:

"They (Americans) had created an economy of abundance; ....they had become the richest people on the globe;.........they were democratic in law......they were equalitarian by conviction.........they had solved the ancient problem of liberty and order..........*they had all but banished God from their affairs: who or what would they put in His place?*"

The church, said Commager, was no longer able to satisfy the spiritual needs of the community and had therefore assumed the secular function of serving as a social organization while moral instruction had been relegated to the media.[2] That this was and is also true of the synagogue has already been shown. Furthermore, it is evident forty five years after Commager published these words that the trend has continued unabated. Thus, the historian Arthur Schlesinger Jr. asserted in 1993 that "secularity is the leading characteristic of Americans."[3]

Secularity has two perimeters, two borders. On the one side it borders on a society free of all inhibitions and permitting the most dastardly atrocities. That is the world of Auschwitz and the Holocaust, a world of dictators and totalitarian government. On the other side is religious fundamentalism which, in the U.S.A. at the end of the twentieth century, is best seen on television where Bible thumping believers demand the establishment of orthodox Christianity as the "official" religion of the country. Both totalitarianism and fundamentalism relieve the individual of personal responsibility. It is therefore to be expected that neither secularism nor fundamentalism will win substantial support for their position in the United States and that the middle ground of moderation will be maintained in the foreseeable future. Thus, as we have shown repeatedly, secularization but not secularism has prevailed in this country and continues to hold the allegiance of most Americans. Nevertheless, the idea of *Progress* which has always been so much a part of secularization may not survive much longer, precisely since it is absurd to argue that the Holocaust, and Hiroshima which came much later than the enlightenment, are indications of progress over the nineteenth century.

There are those who would dispute that secularity is the principal American characteristic and who believe that it is merely the major emphasis and opinion of the "eastern establishment". In view of the election results of November 1994 it is possible that the religious "right" may yet be able to gain some ascendancy in America and assert itself once more in a manner not foreseen by the "intellectuals" who have for so long dominated the media and the political agenda in the United States.[4]

This is possible because those who hold the conservative, Republican and fundamentalist point of view are by no means uneducated or backwards. On the contrary. Several leading members of the Republican delegation to the House and the Senate are former college professors who hold advanced degrees and have authored books and scholarly papers.[5]

Secularization, however, does not derive merely from the personal preferences of this or that writer or politician. It derives principally from the lack of social solidarity, an ever increasing social and physical mobility and mainly the depersonalization of social relations.[6]

All of these features of secularization are abundantly visible in American society at the end of the twentieth century. Therefore, men seek to deal with these threats by finding some means of overcoming anomie, overcoming a world in which nothing is permanent and dealing with the consequences of impersonal, calculated and mechanized human relations.

The truth is that while the enlightenment and the rise of scientific humanism liberated millions from the enslavement of superstition and dogma, it also permitted other men to substitute the dogmas of the totalitarians for the dogmas of the religious. Precisely because nothing is permanent and millions crave social solidarity and a sense of personal relationships Auschwitz became as much the consequence of the enlightenment as is Jeffersonian democracy. This is evident to anyone who recognized that the Holocaust was possible only because those who perpetrated these horrors had rejected the possibility of God in history and had become convinced that man is "the measure of all things."

No one understood this better than Adolf Hitler. Innumerable conversations with Hitler by his table companions, political allies, military associates and friends revealed his contempt for Christianity which he viewed as a "religion fit only for slaves." He saw religion as a systematic cultivation of human failure. "Hitler was a rationalist and a materialist," says his biographer, Bullock. In one of his conversations Hitler reputedly said: "....Gradually the myths crumble. All that is left is to prove that in nature there is no frontier between the organic and the inorganic. ....(Religion) is heading for ruin - for science is bound to win." Hitler, and his followers, evidently felt no need to understand more than that. They were interested in power for its own sake and were willing to do anything to gain and hold it, in particular to use science for their purposes.[7]

There is therefore the danger that secularization, carried to the point of secularism, can, but must not, end in destruction and mass murder. We have shown that secularism is the assertion that there is no God and no supernatural condition whatever. Those who believe this are therefore free to do whatever they can, including destruction, since such conduct has no consequences for them. Nevertheless, many humanists do not behave in a destructive fashion since secularism and humanism need not have such an outcome. In the case of the Nazi mass murders, it did. In short, what can occur does not have to occur.

Therefore it is of interest to discover how the Holocaust can be explained in theological terms. If it cannot be so explained, then that hideous event would at least preclude the continuation of Judaism and seriously damage Christianity. It is the author's contention that the Holocaust has already damaged both religions although theological explanations do exist.

Thus, the Jewish theologian Ignaz Maybaum argues that the victims of Treblinka, Auschwitz and other extermination centers "....died innocently so that others might live." The major contention here is that "....*the Jew, ...stands for justice, mercy and truth. He stood for everything which made every word of Hitler a lie.*" The further argument is that Jews are chosen by God and are therefore unable to choose for themselves whether or not to become victims. God had already designated them victims, according to Maybaum, and therefore the Holocaust once more demonstrated that "*Their election was still valid. ...The Jewish people was again chosen not to be like the gentiles.*"[8]

A similar view is held by the Christian theologian Clemens Thoma who writes:

> "*For a believing Christian the meaning of the victimization of the Jews under the Nazi terror.......is not too difficult to establish. The six million who were killed in Auschwitz and elsewhere direct their*

thought first of all to Christ, whom the Jewish masses in their suffering and death are like. Auschwitz is the most monumental modern sign for the most intimate bonding and unity of Jewish martyrs -representing all Judaism- with the crucified Christ, although this could not have been conscious for the Jews concerned. The Holocaust is for believing Christians, therefore, an important sign of the unbreakable unity, grounded in the crucified Christ, of Judaism and Christianity despite all divisions, individual paths and misunderstandings."[9]

The outer periphery of secularization or secularism is the introduction of a tyranny founded on the view that man may do whatever he can do. This is so remote from American reality that it receives no consideration.

The other side of secularization is fundamentalism which can also end in tyranny. Fundamentalism seeks to impose religion upon unwilling populations and in the name of God is allowed most anything, including the destruction of democracy. There is little chance that fundamentalists will become the dominant force in America despite the fact that those who oppose all abortions, seek to impose prayers upon school children and mean to weaken if not eradicate the first amendment to the U.S. constitution have a considerable following among the members of Congress most recently elected (1995).

All indications are that the spirit of moderation will prevail and that neither the abandonment of democratic institutions nor the imposition of fundamentalism will destroy American democracy.

For example, a recent report by *Public Agenda,* a non-partisan research organization, found that 95% of Americans believe that schools should teach "respect for others regardless of their racial or ethnic background." Additional findings were that among the values Americans want their children to learn are such important features as these: 84% of Americans think that students should have friends from different religious and racial backgrounds and that it is good to live in an integrated neighborhood. Even respect for homosexuals is rated as important by 61% of the American population.[10]

II.

Although we have every reason to believe that democratic institutions and hence the "wall of separation between church and state" and other guarantees of American freedom will prevail, it is important to consider why it is that so many Americans have recently elected conservative Christians to political office or are at least siding with the views concerning moral issues espoused by them.

This is important because the Jewish community in the United States constitutes less than two percent of the American population and must therefore live in a world dominated by Christians or at least those with a Christian heritage.

It is significant that Jews, as we have seen, are far more often identified with "liberal" causes than their proportion to the population warrants and that this is even more true of Jewish intellectuals, business leaders and government officials than of the bulk of the Jewish population.

Since a secular attitude towards public issues and moral conditions in the United States is therefore supported by most Jews but is not necessarily supported by non-Jews and if so not to the same extent, it is entirely possible that the American Jewish population is now (1995) out of step with the views of most Americans concerning such issues as crime, sexual conduct and deviant behavior in general.

The prolific historian Gertrude Himmelfarb has summarized this issue in an excellent manner. In addition, the facts concerning deviance in America are visible in various government publications and are not to be denied. A review of these conditions will lend credence to the complaints by many Americans that the country is far too "liberal". "Liberal" is a stance with which most American Jews are identified. Secular humanism, also a proclivity of Jewish Americans, is believed to be responsible for this "liberal" ideology.[11]

The statistical picture of American morals in 1994 as compared to earlier years was this: In 1920 the illegitimacy ratio was about 3% of all live births in the United States. In 1960, the illegitimacy ratio was 5%; in 1970 it had risen to 11%, in 1980 it was 18% and by 1991 it had risen to 30%. Since then it has gained another 3% so that in 1995 about one third of all American children are born to single mothers.

For whites alone the illegitimacy rate was over 22 percent in 1991 and for blacks it had at that time reached 68 percent. The United States was first among all industrialized nations in the rate of teen age illegitimacy in 1991, "the rate having tripled between 1960 and 1991." Even the proportion of youngsters engaging in sex had increased so that by 1988 one quarter of all fifteen year old girls had engaged in sexual intercourse.[12]

Crime has been the principal focus of American fears for a least the decade 1984-1994. The reasons are evident. In 1960 somewhat under 1900 crimes were reported by the F.B.I. Uniform Crime Report for every 100,000 Americans. In 1970 this figure had doubled and by 1980 it had tripled. In 1993 it was 5,482.9 and in 1992 it was 5,660.2 per 100,000 inhabitants of the United States. Consequently, violence is commonplace in the United States of the '90's. Thus, about 24,000 Americans are murdered every year as suicide takes an equal number of lives.[13]

All of this is augmented by very high rape, assault and robbery rates; by a huge amount of white collar crime and by a divorce rate of 50%. In addition there are innumerable welfare recipients who stay on the rolls for as long as eight to ten years. All this has led Senator Daniel Patrick Moynihan to describe the downward curve of deviance to the effect that many things which were once abnormal or deviant are now considered normal and expected. Thus, deviance had been redefined so that illegitimacy is renamed "non-marital child bearing," single parent families are commonplace and violent crime is so ordinary that the St. Valentine's Day Massacre in Chicago, which claimed seven lives and became part of crime history, would hardly be noticed in 1995 Los Angeles where many more than that are murdered every weekend.

Even if one were to ignore whether "liberals" or others are at fault, the evidence is that the decline in American morality has been perceived to be related to the secularist trends with which we have here been concerned. The plain truth is that personal failure to conduct one's life in a manner once called "moral" has led, and must lead, to the wide spread difficulties besetting American life at the end of the century. Therefore, secularization is threatened in the United States as a large number of voters want to return to the view that personal responsibility is important and that all difficulties are not the responsibility of an ill defined "society" but never the perpetrators.

Fundamentalism, best understood by its electronic message, has increased its followers because the ethos of "value free" and "non-judgmentalism" has failed. This does not mean that 18th Century and 19th Century Puritanism is about to become popular. It does mean that more and more Americans want to find a hold on some moral guide so that they can avoid drugs, and premarital sex, and violence and self-destruction. Moreover, the belief that *progress* is inevitably tied to secular, scientific living has become questionable in view of the crime problem, the decline of the family and the persistence of poverty in the United States. It is obvious that one hundred years after Herbert Spencer, progress is only an opinion, not a natural condition, and that which comes later is not necessarily better.

Therefore secularization is being challenged in the United States at the end of the twentieth century, not only by religious fanatics, but by generally liberal minded people who have come to the conclusion that "non-judgmental" attitudes are not always helpful and that personal accountability is an important means of securing one's life goals and the future of social life.

Many years ago Herbert Spencer (1820-1903), the British philosopher-sociologist, taught that it was natural law, not divine revelation, that ordered the universe. Further, that mankind (humankind) could uncover these natural laws by means of the scientific method and that these laws, once uncovered, would result in *progress* for all men, a progress called civilization. Spencer lived into the Twentieth Century and was a very popular writer enjoying a great deal of recognition in America. His influence on secularization was extraordinary. Spencer published a multi-volume *Principles of Biology,* promoted evolution before Darwin, wrote and published *Principles of Psychology* and *Principles of Sociology.* Consequently, Spencer who had no university degree and no official position but lived on his patrimony, was not only taught at American universities but was widely read by the educated American public.[14]

The belief in Progress as the certain outcome of secularization and science was largely due to his influence. Yet, at the end of the twentieth century belief in the doctrine of Progress is challenged by experience and history.

III.

When, in 1933, Franklin D. Roosevelt became President of the United States, Spencer was enthroned in America. This means that the ideas of Spencer had become part of the rhetoric of the business oriented Republican party of Herbert Hoover whose principal promoters, the American Liberty League, represented the rich.

After the election of Roosevelt it became customary among his followers to view Spencer and his American mouthpiece, William Graham Sumner, as antiquated and removed from reality forever. The truth is, however, that both the Roosevelt *New Deal* and subsequently Lyndon Johnson's *Great Society* were based on the view that progress is inevitable and that these programs were *progressive*. Additionally government programs relieved the individual of sole responsibility for his fate and shared that responsibility with government. Government in turn leaned heavily on physical science and on the social sciences for decision making because it was believed until recently that "science could save us."

At the end of the twentieth century that view is in doubt. In addition it is evident that government programs, however well meant and constructed, cannot solve all problems. On the contrary. Many problems are the outcome of the very programs designed to alleviate poverty, dependency and crime. It is obvious now (1995) that much that happens or does not happen to men is related to that inner will and conviction which is addressed by the Biblical sentence "man does not live by bread alone." Nor by government programs nor by science, as Spinoza predicted. Thus, secularization stands accused of depriving men of initiative and the driving force which Weber called "The Protestant Ethic," but which may also be found among non-Protestants. Others have called the same force "the will". Whatever it is which motivates men to do their best and to make every effort to succeed and overcome obstacles has been weakened by government programs and the attendant secular attitudes which support such programs. Let us see what programs are meant and what has happened to Americans in the twentieth century to bring on the reaction experienced in the 1990's.

When Franklin D. Roosevelt was inaugurated President of the United States on March 4, 1933, one quarter of the American labor force, or thirteen million workers, were unemployed. On that same day every bank in America had shut down. In view of the desperation then gripping the American population the programs and efforts of the Roosevelt Administration were not only fully justified to deal at once with the immediate needs of the poor but also justified in order to save both democracy and capitalism. The unprecedented suffering of the American people could not be alleviated by the methods previously in use by the United States government or by the private charities seeking to deal with the crisis now commonly called "The Great Depression." Therefore the Roosevelt Administration and Congress, acting with unaccustomed speed, passed the following legislation between March 9 and June 16 of 1933: The Emergency Banking Act; The Economy Act; the Civilian Conservation Corps; The Federal Emergency Relief Act; The Agricultural Adjustment Act; the Emergency Farm Mortgage Act; The Tennessee Valley Authority Act; The Truth In Security Act; the Home Owners Loan Act; the National Industrial Recovery Act; the Glass-Steagall Banking Act; the Farm Credit Act and the Railroad Coordination Act. In addition, congress abolished the gold clause in private and public contracts and abandoned the gold standard.[15]

This list serves to indicate the size of government involvement in aiding citizens to recover from the Great Depression. It is not necessary to discuss what each Act proposed and did. It is only necessary to recognize that government spending based on secular and scientific approaches was viewed as the solution to most problems as of 1933 when these programs were both popular and necessary and when their eventual negative outcomes could not have been foreseen.

In addition to the programs just listed, the Public Works Administration had been established in June of 1933 and served the purpose of putting innumerable Americans to work who otherwise would have had no chance of employment.

By 1935, however, Congress had passed the most revolutionary legislation in the history of the country with the passage of the Social Security Act. This act includes old age insurance, unemployment compensation, aid to the jobless, the sick, the blind, mothers and children. "....*it still meant a tremendous break with the inhibitions of the past. The federal government was at last charged with the obligation to provide its citizens a measure of protection from the hazards and vicissitudes of life..........With the Social Security Act, the*

*constitutional dedication of federal power to the general welfare
began a new phase of national history.*"[16]

These programs were continued by every Administration after
Franklin Roosevelt and were then further enhanced by Roosevelt's
protege, President Lyndon Johnson.

In 1964 that President succeeded in having Congress establish the
Office of Economic Opportunity with the purpose of empowering the
poor. That office launched "Head Start", a program permitting
disadvantaged children to gain a pre-school education, the
Neighborhood Youth Corps designed to provide job skills and college
work-study programs, the Community Action Program which
organized the poor to help themselves and Volunteers In Service to
America (VISTA).

In 1966 Congress also passed the Demonstration Cities Act, later
called the Model Cities Act. Yet, only one year later, in 1967, several
American cities were burning as the result of riots sparked by those
who were the principal targets of these help-measures. The first of
these riots occurred in Newark, N.J. and the second in Detroit.
Subsequently other riots occurred in such cities as Miami and Los
Angeles. Added to all these racially motivated riots was the disastrous
Democratic Convention of 1968 in Chicago which produced large
scale riots and violent police action, injuring 20 and arresting 140.[17]

The consequences of all this were that large numbers of Americans
viewed President Lyndon Johnson as a failure, thus forcing him not to
run for another term, which he announced on March 31, 1968.[18] In
addition, many voters also viewed Johnson's programs with suspicion
because the successes these programs brought were obscured by the
noise of the protests and burnings and riots in the streets.

These riots, together with the ever rising crime rate and the vastly
expanded number of illegitimate children, ever lasting poor on welfare
and additionally the wide spread drug problem led many Americans to
believe that "nothing works" and that a return to the spiritual, the
super-natural, the religious will be much more helpful than all the
programs on earth.

Thus the belief that religion can do what other efforts could not do
was enhanced together with the view that a mere "scientific" approach
to America's deficiencies would not work. Thus, nothing gave
secularization more of a bad name than the inability of the Roosevelt-
Johnson years to "fix" our society. As many of these programs failed,

as government intervention failed science could not help these programs succeed. Instead a general mistrust of scientific oriented society has become commonplace even as scientific developments affect everyone. In the age of the computer and the word processor there is no stopping new inventions and discoveries almost every day. Yet, those who seek to gain more from life than electronics can deliver seek once more to explain their problems in super natural terms. Therefore Judaism can be one of those explanations but Jewishness can not.

IV.

Science has no conscience. It is rational, it functions technically but because it is morally indifferent it has been unable to satisfy the needs of millions whose faith in "progress" is hard to maintain in view of the ever increasing personal difficulties secular society has imposed on so many. Ferraroti has identified several such personal difficulties as have other sociologists.[19]

Among these are: Lack of personal control over one's own life. It is clear to millions that secular/scientific decision making has made them impotent to decide what they want to do with their lives. Democratic rhetoric persists in teaching that each American has the power to make his own decisions and to conduct his life as he pleases. The truth is that economic need prevents almost everyone from making very many decisions as the market place decides who is employed, technology requires a long education and the individual actor on the stage of business or industry must conform to the whims of the electorate, the customer or the boss. It appears to many that they have no control over their lives and that everyone else, anonymous of course, makes decisions for them.

Large organizations have taken the place of the individual in a science oriented secular world. These large organizations, in business or in government or in professional associations, have no interest in showing friendship to an individual or one another. Instead, these organizations represent special interests and seek to gain their own ends "in the guise of the general interest."

Because of the failure of secular society to take responsibility for individual human needs "the individual in difficulty does not know to whom to turn; he looks for a face, someone's helping hand ......and forms to be filled in are presented."

Technical means are out of the control of democratic institutions and of the individual who loses his rights. For example, invasion of privacy is easy and done without the knowledge of the (subject) victim. Electronics guarantee that this development will go much further than it is already.[20]

Thus, alienation rules. As Tönnies observed over one hundred years ago:

> "In the middle ages there was unity, now there is atomization; then the hierarchy of authority was solicitous paternalism, now it its compulsory exploitation; then there was relative peace, now wars are wholesale slaughter; then there were sympathetic relationships among kinfolk and old acquaintances, now <u>there are strangers and aliens everywhere.</u> The society was made up chiefly of home and land loving peasants, now the attitude of the businessman prevails; then, the man's simple needs were met by home production and barter, now we have world trade and capitalist production; then there was permanency of abode, now great mobility; then there were folk art, music and handicrafts now there is science - and the scientific method applied, as in the case of the cool calculations of the businessman, <u>leads to the point of view which deprives one's fellow men and one's society of their personality, leaving only a framework of dead symbols and generalizations.</u>"[21]

The difference between traditional and rational societies is here at hand.[22] Thus, sociology teaches that traditional societies pass sentiments and beliefs from generation to generation so that social patterns in such societies are guided by the past. This was certainly true of Judaism and other religions, as we have seen. Thus, behavior was considered right because it had been accepted for a long time. In rational societies, however, behavior is expected to be deliberate, matter of fact and calculated to achieve a certain goal. The rational, secular world has no room for sentiment. Because technical competence takes precedence over close relationships in a secular society, the whole world becomes impersonal. Modern society increasingly amounts to the interplay of specialists concerned with particular tasks, rather than people sensitive to human feelings.[23]

One major reason for this insensitivity to human needs are the large-scale organizations arranged into bureaucracies which treat people as a series of cases rather than as unique individuals. This is true of Jewish organizations as well as any other. Furthermore, the American Jewish community as well as the entire American community needs to accommodate itself to the exigencies of its individual members which stem from the rapid change from traditional modes of life to so-called modern or secular life styles. Unless a structure can fulfill the functions assigned to it, it will disappear. Therefore the Jewish community is confronted with the same list of changes in life style which confronts all American society and which must be dealt with now if American democracy and Jewish life in America seek to survive. These exegencies are related to both culture patterns and social structure and are mainly concerned with the maintenance of values.

V.

A value is a preference for a line of action. As this book has shown, the traditional Jewish and non-Jewish life styles in America and elsewhere were based on sacred values derived, in the Jewish case, from the study of Talmud and Torah and ritual practice and supported by the agreement of even the hostile Christian environment in which European and sometimes American Jews lived.

American values at the end of the twentieth century differ a good deal from the traditional values of the Jewish community. One difference is that American values are heterogeneous, that is, they are derived from many sources and many ethnic groups and many sub-cultures. Traditional Jewish values were derived from only one source, the orthodox Jewish tradition. That tradition included a few sub-cultures such as the Chasidim, but even these sub-cultures did not differ in basic assumption about the aim of life and its content. American values today are secular in character while Jewish values, by their very name, are derived from religion. There are many conflicting sub-cultures in America each holding a different view of what is important and what is not. For that reason norms, that is expected behavior, also differ a great deal in the end-of-the-century United States. There is much tolerance of diverse conduct, including homosexuality and even criminal behavior. This was never true in the sacred, traditional Jewish community. Behavior was seen in moral terms and diversity was hardly tolerated. It is for that reason that the well known play "Fiddler on the Roof" is based on an explanation of Jewish tradition. Tradition, that is past orientation, governed Jewish life for centuries. American life, including Jewish American attitudes, are future oriented. Jews send their children to college in exceptionally high numbers because they worry about their children's future, not their people's past. In fact, American Jews, like many Americans, know very little about their past and have not much interest in discovering much about it because the future is of interest, the past is viewed as negligible and unimportant. "History is bunk," said Henry Ford.

The Social Structure of American life has a great deal of bearing on Jewish social structure in the United States. Traditionally, status and role in the Jewish community was gender oriented and gave men innumerable privileges.

That is by no means the case in the United States in 1995. On the contrary. While European Jews and immigrant Jews to the United States had a decidedly patriarchal family organization, that point of view has long been abandoned by American Jews. Here, Jewish men are at best equals, but often less than that in their homes and in their families. Jewish women are decidedly dominant in the American Jewish family and are the decision makers in almost all family matters.[24] In view of the ever increasing number of female college graduates in the Jewish community and by reason of their earnings, occupations and political power, Jewish women and middle class women in general, have achieved ascendancy over men as of 1990.

This means that the patriarchal family exists only in Chasidic Jewish homes, governed as they are, by reference to the sacred traditions of Judaism. In that vast majority of Jewish homes which are governed by secular consideration alone, women are clearly the boss, the decision makers and the final authority in case of dispute.

This is particularly the case among the numerous American Jewish women who are employed outside the home, run their own business or hold a professional position. Independent of their husbands' income or good will they can and do "throw their weight around."

We have seen that in the Eastern European "shtetl" the Jewish population lived a highly primary life. "Life Is With People" is therefore not only the title of a book but it is a description of how the

Eastern European Jew lived and survived.[25] Such a life continued in the United States during the first third of the 20th century but is almost unknown in the American Jewish community today (1995).[26]

It is therefore not the family, but the economy which dominates American life at the end of the twentieth century. Based on industrial mass production and involving a great deal of white collar employment, material goods, money, purchasing power and social advantages dominate the thinking of Jewish Americans. As we have seen, the American Jewish community is largely dominated by "check book" Judaism so that the wealthy determine the direction and organization of American Jewish life almost to the exclusion of all other considerations. This is also true in the non-Jewish American community. Traditionally, Jewish life was family oriented and involved little if any "white collar" work. Trade and agriculture dominated in Europe, handicrafts and trade dominated in early 20th century America. At the end of the century the professions and large business interests are dominant in the American Jewish community. Both of these occupational patterns are governed by secular reason and by goal oriented behavior with sentiment bringing up a distant second place, if that.

Among the immigrants who came to the United States in the first part of the century, the extended family was very important. Such a family involved parents, children, grandchildren, cousins and a host of more distant relatives. That family served not only a socialization function but also was a productive unit working together to survive.

In view of the great mobility of the American family at the end of the century (1995) the nuclear family dominates now. Consisting only of a married couple and their offspring, the nuclear family socialized its children but is not a unit of production but of consumption. Frequent moves from place to place make such families dependent on "friends" not relatives and create an impersonal environment which has at its consequences all the vicissitudes of anomie. A high divorce rate (50%); excessive alcoholism and drug addiction levels; mental illness; aggressive criminality; white collar crime and above all a sense of isolation and loneliness are the consequence of the great change from a sense of obligation and honor dominating traditional societies to emphasis on individual rights, equality and dignity which has become important today. Self determination, not honor, has become the measuring rod of interpersonal relations in modern America.

However, self determination is accompanied by loneliness and isolation and a level of estrangement best illustrated by George Tooker's painting *Landscape.*

Religious pluralism has been the mainstay of Jewish acceptance in the United States since the days of George Washington and has also been the principal social device undermining Jewish continuity. Religion guided the world view of Jews and others for centuries. It still guides many Jews, whatever their denomination. Nevertheless, religious pluralism has meant the right to dissent and become indifferent to the Jewish heritage altogether so that American Jews need to discover a means of survival other than the traditions which have so far and so long permitted survival under tragic and painful circumstances.

In the secular society of the 1990's education has become the very key to the economic success craved by most Americans. In a society dominated by "conspicuous consumption" it is economic power and occupational prestige which motivates Americans. Therefore advanced secular education is highly prized in American society. Jewish Americans lead all other ethnic groups in that respect. Traditionally, only a limited number of "elites" received a secular education while the Jewish population instilled religion in their children by operating schools designed to teach only Torah and Talmud. The Jewish "aristocracy" in end-of-the-century America is the doctor, meaning the physician. Closely followed by lawyers and other professionals, Jewish men and women pursue these occupations relentlessly, not only because of the income derived from such work but also because of the "prestige" or psychic income yielded by these professions. Thus, physicians led all other occupations in "prestige" in a National Opinion Research Center survey made in 1993 while lawyers came in second and professors third.[27]

Traditionally, Jewish scholars had been the most prestigious leaders of the Jewish community. Even in the early years of Jewish immigration to the United States that was still the case, although at the end of the nineteenth century these Jewish scholars were mainly German born or Americans of German ancestry who had placed Jewish scholarship on a scientific basis. The early German Jewish scholars in America founded the Hebrew Union College in 1875, the Jewish Publication Society in 1888, the American Jewish Historical Society in 1892 and the Jewish Theological Seminary in 1887. Thus, while these efforts to secularize Jewish learning were highly successful and yielded much new knowledge, the outcome was nevertheless the almost universal abandonment of Jewish scholarship by the Jewish community with the exception of the few who entered upon such scholarship as their life profession. It is certain that at the end of the century very few Jews have an extensive Jewish education and that Jewish scholarship is now in the hands of a tiny minority whereas in the traditional Jewish community almost everyone could at least study the Talmud and the Mishna without becoming great interpreters thereof.[28]

These then are some of the changes in American Jewish life which Judaism must now confront and with which it must now deal successfully if the tradition is to continue to hold its followers and offer them solutions to those needs which a crass materialism cannot satisfy.

VI.

Two explanations for the rapid changes briefly outlined above have been developed by sociologists. One of these explanations is the overly familiar Marxist approach also known as a conflict theory based on class and the demands of capitalism.

The second of these explanations is called *structural-functional analysis.* According to that point of view, now largely accepted by almost all American sociologists, the United States is now a Mass Society. Mass society refers to a society in which industry and bureaucracy have eroded traditional social ties and in which kinship and relationships have become weak. Impersonal neighborhoods lead to a sense of isolation by each individual and a sense of personal powerlessness and moral uncertainty prevails.[29]

Tönnies called the traditional village community, or the *shtetl,* as it was called in Yiddish, a *Gemeinschaft.* This word is derived from the German word *gemein* or common, and refers to the small communities in which almost all human beings lived before the Industrial Revolution. Everyone, in such communities, was surrounded by relatives and life long friends. Community standards were enforced by gossip and not the law while differences were hardly known within the community. There was no separation of "church and state." Christians, as well as Jews in Europe, were compelled to participate in the rituals of their religion. This does not mean that everyone was forced into ritual practices he wanted to avoid. Far from it. It did not occur to the Jews or Christians who lived in Europe before the Industrial Revolution that any other life style was possible. No one had yet heard of Jefferson's famous dictum nor would it have received much support if anyone had heard of it.

People were close to one another physically but also socially. Everyone in a village knew everyone else, not by what they did for a living, but who they were and who their ancestors had been. All that has changed since the Industrial Revolution and with ever increasing velocity has reduced individuals to their functions. Thus, people know of one another as "bakers", "doctors", "bank clerks" without ever knowing the person so delimited.

Instead of direct, face to face communication the mass media now present information to masses of people who are utterly atomized as computer networks complete the destruction of face to face relationships.

Large, impersonal, secondary organizations are now expected to fulfill the many functions once assumed by family, by friends and by a benevolent upper class. Even the charitable agencies appear to consist of faceless, mindless bureaucrats who work for large organizations utterly unresponsive to individual needs.

In view of all this, traditional values, whatever their origin, disappear altogether or are seriously diminished. Differences of opinion abound until it becomes hard to know what one believes or should believe. As this depersonalization progresses more and more people insist that race, religion, gender or sexual orientation should play no part in how they are treated. It is believed that it is unjust, undemocratic and even illegal to give these categories any validity. This may seem like progress to some but it is evident also that if people cannot be evaluated by reason of such obvious features as their age, sex, race, religion etc., than they can only be differentiated according to occupation and income. This dehumanizes everyone. This means that if it is wrong to consider race, gender, religion and sexual preference in dealing with others, than there is hardly anything left which can be used to differentiate between individuals. All become a homogenized mass. No one is seen as a person.

Thus, uniformity of treatment, which ignores differences based on race, religion etc., creates a new problem. Faceless bureaucrats govern the population of the United States at a distance. Individual needs, nor even names, mean anything. Everyone appears to be only a number dealt with by a computer on the telephone. No interpersonal relations can arise in such a society.

Most important for an understanding of the condition of American society in the 1990's is however the problem of personal identity. It is in this area that the greatest challenge to the Jewish community arises. For Jewish Americans, like all Americans, are no longer living in the small, face-to-face communities of the past. Instead, the price of liberation from the narrow mindedness of these past communities has been and is both freedom and loneliness, tremendous diversity and liberty but also atomization and an inability to form a social identity amidst very fast social change.[30]

Because the Jewish community is relatively affluent, the immense choices given an upper middle class American strike at Jewish identity as hard as at any person in that social class. This means that it is not necessary to be Jewish because one has a Jewish name or a Jewish family. All options are open to those with money, education and influence. Devoid of beliefs which help some to set a course or a direction and follow that course throughout their life time, many Americans, and Jews among them, rush from one life style to another but never find satisfaction in any mode of existence. Such people move from one relationship to another, experience several divorces, discard children, remove themselves from their parental family, experiment with drugs, change religions or try this or that social movement in an anxious effort to belong and establish an identity. Many of those who have cast off their anchors to a stable life become extremely angry at any reminder of their inherited identity and blame their early upbringing, their familial religion or ethnicity for all their problems.

They fail to see that their real difficulty is "relativism," the belief that all life styles are equally acceptable and worthy in a democratic society and that therefore those who adhere to one mode of living are "narrow minded" or "undemocratic." The great difficulty with that belief is not that it is not true, but that it does not work. Even if it can be shown that all life styles are equal or of similar worth it is nevertheless evident that few, if any, individuals can tolerate the constant changes and insecurities which the practice of "relativism" imposes on them. In short, it is one thing to truly accept all diversity as just, right and equal, it is another to live in numerous different sub-cultures and maintain one's emotional equilibrium. David Riesman has explained this situation by calling persons with pre-industrial society characters "tradition directed." By this he means people who rigidly conform to time honored ways of living. *"The tradition directed character hardly thinks of himself as an individual."*[31] According to Riesman, the tradition directed person is expected by his reference group to behave in a certain way, no matter who he is or what he thinks. Social control is therefore imposed by the use of shame. That segment of American Jews who adhere to the Chasidic way of life may be seen as examples of the tradition directed person. Many of the Chasidim (Pious Ones) continue to speak Yiddish. Their clothes resemble the clothes of the ghetto Jews of Europe as they model their lives on the past. It is important to understand in this connection that Chasidim have so many traits in common, not because they imitate each other, but because they come to the same conclusions by drawing upon the same traditions. Such persons are often viewed as deviant by the great majority who do not participate in the same rituals. They are viewed as rigid.

Riesman also distinguished those whom he calls "inner directed." Such persons, Riesman says, are controlled by a sense of guilt implanted by parents. Such persons, unlike the tradition directed individual, are stable and certain of their conduct even if their behavior is not approved by others because they learned early in life to internalize principles. They then act upon these principles no matter what others may think. Orthodox Jews, not identified with Chasidism, are most likely to exhibit this type of personality. Many orthodox Jews will wear skullcaps (Yarmulkes) and beards while conservative Jews will often exhibit the Star of David on a chain or in their lapel, unconcerned about the possible disapproval of others.

Those who lead a more flexible life and adapt easily to others are called "other directed" by Riesman. These are the imitators who seek to live according to the latest fashions and trends and whose life is superficial and dependent on the views of others. No longer tied closely to his family, the "other directed" American cannot go it alone. *"The other -directed person is, in a sense, at home everywhere and nowhere, capable of superficial intimacy with and response to everyone."* Such people are controlled by anxiety, says Riesman, which works like radar in that they are always in need of knowing what everyone else is thinking, doing and saying. Innumerable Jews in

America and elsewhere have surrendered to this mode of living even as all of American society militates in favor of "other direction."[32]

"Other direction" is more characteristic of Reform Jews than of other Jews as the Reform group are much more worried about the views of others concerning their religion than is true of Chasidim, Orthodox or Conservative Jews. Many Reform congregations have built and maintained large synagogues, called Temples, in downtown areas of big cities despite the fact that their membership lives miles away in the suburbs. These Temples are kept in the city because the Reform Jews wish to maintain a Jewish presence in the city. Hence many of these Temples are elaborate and architectural masterpieces. This is done to impress the general public and the "leading" clergy in the city. Reform and some Conservatives Jews are also much more interested in ecumenical alliances with non-Jewish clergy than is true of the orthodox or the Chasidim.

VII.

Alienation is a condition commonly defined as the inability to deal with any person or event unless that person or event satisfies one's immediate needs at that moment. Alienated persons are not otherwise interested in anyone else. The root of alienation is competition for goods, services, social honor and private satisfaction. Alienation leads one to create strangers everywhere so that others come to be seen as objects, not subjects, or as commodities to be used and exploited.[33] The great Jewish philosophers, Martin Buber, has dealt extensively with this dilemma of modern man. His principal contribution to our understanding of that dilemma is his discussion of what he calls the "I and Thou" relationship. This is a necessary but poor translation of the German concepts "Ich und Du" and refers to the two ways in which we can relate to others. One is exploitative in that we deal only with others to the extent that we can get something from them. That is the "I".

The other, the "Thou," is the understanding we achieve through love. It is the understanding of the needs of others. A "Thou" relationship is one which gives consideration to the needs of our fellow men. Buber describes how many of us have been so trained to deal only with our needs and our wishes that we no longer see the needs of others and therefore cannot gain the satisfaction of human companionship which depends precisely on the ability to understand the "Thou" relationship.[34] In fact, those who need others the most, those who are most lonely and anxious to gain companionship, often create the very loneliness from which they suffer by unendingly talking only about themselves because their need drives them to such conduct. Thus, the most lonely and isolated people in American society, often old people, create the social distance they seek to overcome. It is in this area that religion can make a contribution.

Traditionally, religion was a means of combating alienation. As the great French-Jewish sociologist Emile Durkheim showed, religion was, and still is a means of bringing its followers in touch with one another. Religion is social and therefore serves the purpose of permitting the individual to face inevitable dangers and fears with the help of the community. This refers to death, to natural disasters, to illness, to losses of all kinds and even to the unfortunate consequences of success, such as excesses in the use of alcohol, sex and the acquisition of material goods and most certainly to loneliness. In Durkheim's own words, religion serves "to strengthen the bonds attaching the individual to the society of which he is a member."[35]

Munch has described one of the most remote "primary" communities, the people of Tristan da Cunha, an island in the South Atlantic. Descendants of British sailors and Asian and African women, these islanders were forced to move to England in 1961 because their island suffered a volcanic eruption.

In England, the Tristaners were received with great sympathy. All 264 of them were given homes, worked good jobs, had television sets and other amenities they had never known before and earned far more money than they had ever believed possible. Yet, as soon as they could, most of the Tristaners returned to their lonely island, 1500 miles from the nearest human habitation. Lonely amidst the millions of Englishmen who surrounded them, they felt that nothing in their lives was personal any more. Since their native tongue was English, the Tristaners had no language barrier. The barrier they felt was that they had not grown up with their new neighbors. "They lacked the warmth, the involvement, the commitment and concern that can only be found in a small community ....where all know each other from childhood."[36]

The secularization of American society, however, has robbed even religion of the function of bonding people to one another. This is best understood by observing televised religion which is directed at each viewer separately. This is of course true of all manifestations of mass society as the very phrase "mass" implies. Mass society depends on mass communication. Mass communication in turn is the projection of one stimulus upon innumerable individuals who happen to read a newspaper, listen to a radio program or watch a television performance. Each person is separate, apart from others. There is no communication between the individual viewers, listeners or readers since they do not even know who else is receiving the message they are watching, hearing or reading. As electronic communication becomes more and more sophisticated this trend of receiving messages and sending messages in isolation and privately becomes greater and greater. Thus, unseen and anonymous persons deliver messages to one another on the "Electronic Super High Way" which, despite all its benefits, cuts off human interaction more and more despite the fact that the number of people who can be reached anonymously is ever increasing. Thus, privacy is both increased as private persons can use electronic devices alone and at will, even as privacy is invaded by those who use the same devices to enter other people's homes, bank accounts and even government secrets.

Two consequences have arisen from the extensive use of electronic means of communication. One is that the network of human interaction has become bigger in that more people can be reached than ever before. This permits people who otherwise would be utterly alone to communicate without running the risk of exposing their shortcomings to others. For example, someone who is frequently rejected by reason of his age, appearance, physical condition or emotional message can now communicate with others without being seen. This reduces the risk of rejection within the limits of the electronic network.

The second consequence however is, that many people will never learn how to deal directly with other people. Sociologists speak of "primary" groups as those who have direct, physical contact with one anther. A "primary group" is one which permits the individual to see, touch, hear and feel the other person. An example is the traditional family which permits the individual to form long lasting relationships of a personal and enduring kind. Among these *primary* groups is and was religion, which can lead to the feeling of belonging and causes the believer to speak of others within the group as "we."[37]

Electronics avoids this. Electronic communication removes all human relationship into the realm of the "secondary", remote, programmed and institutionalized condition. Evidently, a believer who receives a religious message on his television set cannot very well identify with others who also receive such a message, no matter how forceful the preachers, how beautiful the singing or the background. Televised religion is devoid of interaction and lends itself to exploitation as well illustrated by such "evangelists" (good messengers) as Jim Bakker and Jimmy Swaggart.

The problem religion, including Judaism, must therefore confront is whether religion can deal with human isolation, loneliness, lack of solidarity, depersonalization, impermanence and alienation.

There is a large body of literature seeking to predict the Jewish future. Almost every book, journal article and newspaper column concerning present day Judaism in the United States seeks to predict what will happen to the Jewish community in the twenty-first century. These predictions are concerned with the future of large Jewish organizations and discuss at length whether orthodoxy, conservatism or reform will survive or will merge or will disappear altogether. Others deal with the issue of whether the relationship between the American Jewish community and Israel will be the same if and when the peace process succeeds. Yet others discuss at length the future of the large Jewish organizations. All of these speculations are of course incapable of foreseeing events any better than the fall of the Soviet Union could have been foreseen.

What is certain however, and not a matter of speculation, is the necessity to address the human needs outlined in this chapter. It is assumed by the author that Judaism will survive, even if in altered form. This is certain because Judaism has always altered its form but never its message. That message is that no Jew is alone; that no Jew is isolated; that each Jew is a person, not an object; that Judaism is permanent, not a fad and that the Jewish people constitute a "moral community." These assertions are based on the Covenant between God and Israel which binds all Jews together and which is affirmed by the Torah.

If that is so, then Judaism will survive in America. It is therefore the task of the next chapter to examine the extent to which American Judaism has met the needs just outlined. An honest and objective discussion of the present state of Jewish theology is therefore in order.

NOTES

[1]Lawrence Barman, "Confronting Secularization: Origins of the London Society for the Study of Religion," *Church History,* Vol. 62, No. 1, March 1993, p.22.

[2]Henry Steele Commager, *The American Mind,* New Haven, Yale University Press, 1950 pp. 426-443.

[3]Arthur Schlesinger, Jr., "The Future Outwits Us Again," *The Wall Stree Journal,* September 28, 1993, Sec. A, page 14, column 3.

[4]Garry Wills, "The Secularist Prejudice," *Christian Century,* Vol. 107, No. 30, October 24, 1990, pp. 969-973.

[5]No author, "Sea Change," *U.S. News & World Report,* Vol. 117, No.20, November 21, 1994, p. 39.

[6]Franco Ferrarotti, *Faith Without Dogma: The Place of Religion in Post Modern Societies,* Transaction Publishers, New Brunswick, 1993, p. 90.

[7]Alan Bullock, *Hitler, A Study In Tyranny,* New York, Harper Torchbooks, 1962, p. 390.

[8]Steven T. Katz, *Post-Holocaust Dialogues: Critical Studies In Modern Jewish Thought,* New York New York University Press , *1983, p. 156.*

[9]Clemens Thoma in: Franz Mussner, *Tractate on the Jews,* Philadelphia, Fortress, 1984, p. 44.

[10]Jean Johnson and John Immerwahr, "What Americans Expect from their Public Schools," New York, Public Agenda, 1994 and *American Educator,* Vol. 18, No. 4, Winter, 1994-95, p. 4.

[11]Gertrude Himmelfarb, "A De-moralized Society: The British-American Experience," *American Educator,* Vol. 18, No. 4, Winter 1994-95, p 14.

[12]*Ibid.* p.16 and U.S. Department of Health and Human Services, National Center for Health Statistics, *Illegtimacy in the United States, 1920-1991.*

[13]United States Department of Justice, Federal Bureau of Investigation, *Uniform Crime Reports, 1992 and 1993,* Washington, D.C., United States Government Printing Office, 1993 and 1994.

[14]Lewis A. Coser, *Masters of Sociological Thought,* New York, Harcourt Brace Jovanovitch, Inc, 1971, p. 106.

[15]Arthur M. Schlesinger, Jr., *The Coming of the New Deal,* Cambridge, The Riverside Press, 1958, p. 5 and pp. 20-21.

[16]*Ibid.,* p.315.

[17]Joseph A. Califano, *The Triumph & Tragedy of Lyndon Johnson: The White House Years,* New York, Simon and Schuster, 1991, pp.75-85 and 122-148.

[18]*Ibid.,* p. 270.

[19]Franco Ferraroti, *Five Scenarios for the Year 2000,* New York, The Greenwood Press, 1986, pp.5-6.

[20]*Ibid,*p. 8.

[21]Ferdinand Tönnies, *Geist der Neuzeit,* Leipzig, Hans Buske Verlag, 1935 and *Gemeinschaft und Gesellschaft,* 1887. The latter work is available in English. Translated as *Community and Society* by Charles P. Loomis it was published by American Book Co., in 1940.

[22]This discussion is based on a similar discussion in: *Sociology* by John Macionis, Englewood, N.J.,Prentice Hall, 1995.

[23] Reinhard Bendix, *Max Weber: An Intellectual Portrait,* Berkely, The University of California Press, 1962,pp. 423-430.

[24]Gwen Gibson Schwartz and Barbara Wyden, *The Jewish Wife,* New York, Peter H. Wyden, Inc., 1969.

[25]Mark Zborowski and Elizabeth Herzog, *Life Is With People,* New York, Schocken Books, 1952.

[26]Irving Howe, *World of Our Fathers,* New York, Simon and Schuster, 1977.

[27]No author, *General Social Surveys:Cumulative Codebook,* Chicago, National Opinion Research Center, 1993, pp. 937-945.

[28]Irving Howe, *World of Our Fathers,* New York, Simon and Schuster, 1976, p.498.

[29]David E. Pearson, "Post-Mass Culture," *Society,* Vol.30, No.5, July-August 1993, pp.17-22.

[30]David Riesman, *The Lonely Crowd: A Study of the Changing American Character,* New Haven, Conn., Yales University Press, 1970.

[31]*Ibid.,* p.17

[32]*Ibid.,* p.99.

[33]Gerhard Falk, *Murder: An Analysis of Its Forms, Conditions and Causes,* Jefferson, N.C. and London,
Mc Farland, 1990, p. 190.

[34]Martin Buber, *I and Thou,* Walter Kaufman, Translator, New York, Scribners, 1971.

[35] Emile Durkheim, *The Elementary Forms of the Religious Life: A Study In Religious Sociology,* J.W. Swain, Translator, New York, Macmillan, 1912, p. 226.

[36]Peter A. Munch, *Crisis In Utopia,* New York, Crowell, 1971.

[37]Charles Horton Cooley, *Human Nature and the Social Order,* New York, Schocken Books, 1964.(Originally 1902.)

Chapter XIII

Jewish Survival in America

I.

There are in the United States and elsewhere Jews who seek to be Christians as well. Some belong to a group called "Jews for Jesus," others are called Messianic Jews while the so-called Hebrew Christians are the oldest of these groups.

It has been argued that anyone who believes that Jesus was the Messia is therefore not a Jew. This issue is important in Israel where citizenship may depend on being Jewish. In the United States that is of course not an issue. What is at issue here is however why some become Christians and who is participating in this fast growing movement which now encompasses about 200 congregations and about 15,000 members. Some estimates are higher. While the members of these congregations, who observe Jewish ritual but include a belief in "Yoshua", as they call the Christian's savior, insist on being Jews, they are seen as converts by mainstream Jews.

Interviews reveal that some of these Judeo-Christians are people who seek a sense of stability in a world that has not satisfied them "spiritually." Whatever religionists may mean by that word, the fact is that the established synagogues have lost these Jews because they feel that the establishment's synagogues are cold, unfeeling, disinterested and unkind. This is often felt by people who survived a crisis in their lives, including divorce or immigration. Thus, Russian Jews who have come recently have been led to these "synagogues" by friends. Others were converted to Christianity by reason of marriage and feel they do not fit into the Christian environment at all. By joining a "Jews for Jesus" group or coming to a Messianic Jewish group they feel accepted and included. This is true because Jewish converts to Christianity are still seen as Jews by their new-found brethren and, additionally, seek to speak in the accents and phrases of Jews. They need to be at home and find that very difficult, if not impossible, in a Christian Church. Then there are intermarried couples who both feel that in a Messianic synagogue they can live with their marginality.

There are now in New York City three full time, private Messianic day schools. Although not accepted by the mainstream Jewish community, these Judo-Christians view themselves as Jews fulfilled by the inclusion of the "New Testament" in their lives.

These are of course not secularized Jews. Instead they are religiously affiliated but seek to target other Jews for their movement. These "other Jews." can be found among that vast number of secularists who are an easy mark for the promises of Christianity clothed in a Jewish garb.[1]

The first chapter of this book began with a quotation from Rabbi Robert Gordis' *Judaism In a Christian World.* "It cannot be denied," wrote Rabbi Gordis in 1966, "that there are major ills in the Jewish community which often serve to alienate from Judaism many young people, not to speak of their elders."[2]

The principal ill of which Rabbi Gordis spoke has been excessive secularization. We have seen how that came about and what its consequences have been for Jewish institutions in the United States. Therefore it is not surprising that some Jews now seek the comforts of another religion in their reaction to "check book" Judaism and total reliance on a humanistic approach to Jewish needs.

There is of course a Jewish theology, or rather, there are several Jewish theologies depending on denominational preference. These theological and philosophical contributions to Judaism are hardly known to observant Jews or to Jewish secularists. Nevertheless, these theologies have a great deal of influence upon the Jewish clergy and in turn become the background upon which such clergy preach to their congregants. Thus, the views and writings of theologians and philosophers become much more important than is commonly recognized. Therefore we will examine these views now and see what interpreters of Jewish law can say about satisfying the spiritual needs of Jewish Americans a the end of the century.

II.

Solomon Freehof (1892-1990), Joseph B. Soloveitchick (1903-1993), Abraham Joshua Heschel (1907-1972) and Mordecai M. Kaplan (1881-1983) were all rabbis. Their teachings have influenced millions of Jews in America and elsewhere, and, in the case of Heschel, have been important to non-Jews as well. An examination of the writings of these scholars is one means by which the differences and the similarities between the various branches of American Judaism can be discerned. This is not to say that other writers and other means of learning about these differences are not available. It is however fruitful to review briefly some of the views held by these theologians because they justify the position taken by the followers of each of the Jewish movements now extant in America.

Solomon Freehof was undoubtedly the most prolific, if not the principal interpreter of Jewish Law within the Reform Movement in 20th Century America. Contrary to frequently voiced opinions, Reform Judaism does relate to *Halacha* or Jewish Law and it was the life time effort of Rabbi Freehof to interpret that Law in the light of the basic Reform convictions which that movement has espoused since its founding in 1818 in Hamburg, Germany.

While the Reform movement was erstwhile unwilling to permit the expression of Judaism through the traditional forms and rituals of orthodoxy, this has now changed. Today, at the end of the 20th century that movement has changed into two directions at once. "The guiding principle of Reform today is the autonomy of every individual to choose a Jewish religious expression that is personally meaningful."[3]

This position represents a considerable change because, on the one hand, it permits customs that were literally banned from Reform usage while at the same time it insists on being innovative. Thus, in recent years some Reform "Temples" have re-introduced the Hebrew language, the office of cantor, and emphasis on Jewish tradition and an acceptance of Zionism, previously rejected, and now universally assumed. Thus, while modern Reform does not prescribe specific beliefs and practices it does wish to derive its practices and belief from tradition.

This attitude is evident both in the *Centenary Perspective* issued one hundred years after the *Pittsburgh Platform* of 1885 which constituted the first American ideological statement of Reform beliefs and practices and the *Responsa* of Rabbi Solomon Freehof. The Pittsburgh platform sought to recognize "only its moral laws," referring to Mosaic legislation. One hundred years later Solomon B. Freehof suggested that "individuals, rather than the Conference (Central Conference of American Rabbis), write codes, responsa, as well as theoretical articles on Jewish law. In this way, an ongoing debate would create a consensus and thus a link with the *Halacha* would be created."[4]

Freehof also believed that the earlier "prophetic" approach to Judaism which had been the cornerstone of Reform had faded and that a new path was needed. He believed that to be a modern approach to Jewish law. This does not mean that Freehof wanted to return to orthodoxy. He showed, however, that even among the orthodox, *Halacha* had changed and that no Jewish group, whatever its claims, was or is living by the unchanged laws of earlier years. This, Freehof argued, could be seen by studying the *Responsa* of the orthodox, the conservative and the reform. The number of questions asked and answered were to Freehof an indication where the Jewish people stood with reference to *Halacha*. Thus, Freehof claims in several essays that questions concerning business practices and ritual cleanliness of women were hardly ever asked of any responsa committees. This means to Freehof that these issues were of little importance today and are being settled in secular courts, even among the orthodox.

Freehof also argues that tradition can be consulted today because the period of revolt against orthodox strictures is over and interpretations based on the law can be accepted more readily on their own merits today. "We can approach *Halacha* openly because we are not controlled by it." The essence of this approach is popularity. Reform Judaism today will include what the Jewish people want to observe and will reserve to another time those laws which are now in disuse.

The individual, not the group, is the focus of the Reform Jewish movement and it is in this approach that diversity lies and becomes inevitable.[5]

The consequence of the new approach to Judaism now taken by Reform is that traditions long abandoned have returned to the Reform movement. For example, Reform rabbis may now wear the *tallit* or prayer shawl as will some congregants. The *kippah* or skull cap has been reintroduced by Reform Jews although it is optional. Bar and Mat Mitzvah are celebrated regularly and a cantor or *Chasan* leads the prayers in almost all the large Reform temples today. Often, the cantor is female and in that respect Reform has been the first to include women in ceremonial and religious leadership roles. Significant is that these customs have been returned to Reform despite the earlier, nineteenth century attitude that ritual is not rational. The need for tradition and the willingness of congregants to participate in these ancient customs is seen by Rabbi Arthur Lelyveld of Cleveland as "..the need for a warmer, more affirmative expression of Judaism." He meant that rationalism alone is unsatisfactory and that, in the words of Rabbi Alexander Schindler, former president of the Union of American Hebrew Congregations: "The movement that used to be hyper rational now recognized that it is important to feel, nor just to think."[6]

This recognition may well be the saving grace of Judaism in the 21st century. Evidently, the need for fellowship, relationships and a need for emotional warmth is great. Secularization has served Jews well as we have seen. Now, three generations after the Holocaust and five generations after the mass migrations from Eastern Europe Judaism has reached the outer limits of secularization and therefore must return to tradition if it is to survive. It is the contention of this author that American Jews are doing just that now and that the Reform movement is one example of this shift in emphasis. It is therefore entirely possible that once this trend has been well recognized and experienced by that great army of secular Jews who do not attend any synagogue ever, who do not participate in the life of the Jewish people in any way but who still see themselves as Jews because of their memories, that great number will yet return to Judaism and its ancestral roots.

There are those who argue that Reform Judaism is a way out of Judaism altogether. That argument holds that Reform is less structured than Orthodoxy or Conservatism, that therefore it is easier to live in the Reform tradition and that Reform resembles non-Jewish worship and customs so much that the "next" step after Reform is conversion or secularization. It appeared at one time that there were no limits to Reform and that therefore Reform would simply eradicate itself by accepting any and all behavior.

That, however, did not come true. Despite the fact that Reform has returned to a number of Jewish traditions while simultaneously making radical innovations such as accepting the child of a Jewish father and a non-Jewish mother as Jewish and permitting homosexuals membership, the Reform refused to admit a Humanist Jewish congregation to membership into the Union of American Hebrew Congregations lest "atheism is a legitimate Reform option."[7]

Although Reform is growing rapidly in the United States at the end of the 20th century because of its diversity and permissiveness, it is highly doubtful that this trend will long continue. Reform Jews as all humans need some structure in their lives as Durkheim has shown. Therefore, at the risk of losing everything, Reform justifiably refused to embrace atheism. If Reform can stay at least within the limits of that belief, then it can be and is, not only a gate out of Judaism but also a gate *into* Judaism by non-Jews and by secularists who need to maintain their individuality and yet belong to the Jewish people.

III.

Orthodox Judaism is far more structured than Reform. In fact, the very word *orthodox means "straight belief"* and so it is. Orthodox life is structured around the concept of *Halacha* which Reform and Conservative Jews also embrace but which is far more pronounced among the Orthodox.

The great scholar Rabbi Joseph B. Soloveitchik has written a book entitled *Halakhic Man*. This book reveals the attitude of Orthodox Jews towards that body of law which Jews call *Halacha*. "He (the orthodox Jew) orients himself to the world by means of fixed statutes and firm principles," writes Soloveitchik.[8]

The final outcome of living a life according to Halacha is the actualization of reality. This means, according to Soloveitchik, that "we hope for and eagerly await the day of Israel's redemption when the ideal world will triumph over the profane reality."

This belief is far from that of the secularist who sees only what science will show him. Halakhic man believes that he can reach and manage his own salvation. Judaism has not had priests for over 1900 years. Hence intercession is not known in Judaism. This attitude eliminates not only the need for clergy in this world but also the need for angels and other supernatural beings in the next world.

Another feature of the life of "halakhic man", according to Soloveitchik, is the maintenance of emotional equilibrium achieved by those who observe the commandments. Neither excessive melancholy or depression nor excessive joy or euphoria is permitted "halakhic" man. Both extremes of emotional excesses are forbidden those who follow the law. *"Neither modesty nor humility characterizes the image of halakhic man......His most characteristic feature is strength of mind."*

The most fundamental principle of all in the life of the orthodox is the Study of Torah. This is so important that all other considerations fall away in comparison. Therefore, "Halakhic Man" is not talkative but seeks to speak only sparingly and only when necessary. Such men do not seek approval from others, do not tremble before others, do not seek public recognition and avoid "idlers, wastrels and loafers."[9] This attitude resembles that of Socrates who, according to Plato, not only taught that virtue is knowledge but also refused to beg for mercy from the crowd which had condemned him to death.

"Halakhic Man" lives his life in accordance with Torah or Halacha and does not merely "enclose (it) within the confines of cult sanctuaries."[10]

Finally, "Halakhic Man" is creative in the sense that he is self fulfilling, individualistic and free. He is not tied to the group or the direction of the crowd. He makes his own decisions within the Torah or Halakha and therefore has true liberty.

Surely there will be those who see it otherwise. Certainly there are those who believe that precisely the adherence to the innumerable Laws of Halakha reduce the believer to a slave of legalistic interpretations and customs and ceremonies.

It is not our purpose to discuss the dispute of the orthodox and the Reform around this issue. Instead it is my view that Judaism has so many facets and sub-groups; has so many different interpreters and interpretations and is so wide ranging in its practices and beliefs that there is room for everyone but the atheist in its denominations. Even the atheist who says nothing about his views will not be rejected because Judaism does not ask anyone to list his beliefs or to subscribe to a set of dogma. Reform, orthodox and conservative Jews all live under the same roof, whatever their differences.

Indeed these differences sometimes seem immense and insurmountable. The strength of Judaism is, however, its diversity. This is most visible among the conservatives and is exemplified by the foremost thinker and philosopher in 20th century Judaism, Abraham Joshua Heschel.

Heschel was identified with the Conservative movement in Judaism although he had also taught at the Reform Hebrew Union College in Cincinnati. His principle teaching was and is that man is not concerned only with himself but with others. The needs of others and the wish to be useful in this world are the cornerstones of man's existence, says Heschel. Therefore freedom, according to Heschel, is *"liberation from the tyranny of the self centered ego."*[11]

As Spinoza had predicted and Heschel affirmed, reason alone could not satisfy the human mind nor explain man's situation in this world. Heschel therefore tried to synthesize the Jewish tradition with the problems of the present world. Heschel taught that God takes a direct hand in dealing with his creatures, man, and that Judaism constitutes the response to God's call to man. Heschel taught that there is a "holy dimension" to life which cannot be reached by cool analysis and scientific measurements.

Perhaps one of the most astonishing theological propositions made by Heschel was his teaching of "God's participation in human history...finds its deepest expression in the fact that God can actually suffer."

These teachings and much more led to the active involvement of Rabbi Heschel in the issues of his day. He participated in the Christian-Jewish dialogue surrounding Vatican II and also marched in the Civil Rights movement in the U.S. alongside Martin Luther King. Thus, unlike the orthodox, he did not detach himself from public discussion and immerse himself only in religious teachings. Nor did he abandon the tradition and seek to allow almost anyone into Judaism as is true of Reform. By taking the middle ground he became *ipso facto* conservative although his influence goes far beyond that movement.

It is not the purpose of this book to teach or discuss theology. What we have shown, however, is that there is room for anyone and everyone in the canopy of Jewish religious life. Reconstruction and Chasidism widen that canopy even more and lead us to the conclusion that the failure of so many Jews to participate in Jewish life is not to be attributed to a lack of theological substance within Judaism. In short, anyone who wishes to do so can find so much in the writings and teachings of Jewish theologians and philosophers that all can be satisfied. The difficulty is evidently not lack of Jewish substance but lack of interest.

IV.

Although there has been a resurgence of participation in religion in America in the years beginning with the Reagan presidency, that is, 1981, there has also been an increase of conflict concerning religion and issues of public policy in which religion is involved.

The most strident and even violent of these issues has been abortion although arguments concerning the influence of religion on education have not been far behind. There are also disputes concerning intermarriage, the role of women in religion, TV evangelism, the influence of "secular humanism," and others. While there are undoubtedly American Jews who have participated in all of these disputes these issues have never ranked very high on the agendas of Jewish organizations or Jewish individuals.

Instead, Jews have confined their arguments to issues within the Jewish community and not in the public arena. This is in part due to the influence of Jewish history which has taught European Jews not to be too involved in public issues lest the Jewish community become the target of attacks by all parties to the dispute while weakening the Jewish community at the same time. There are innumerable examples of this attitude in Jewish history.

For example, during the Russian Revolution and the subsequent civil war in that country, both sides pretended to know that the Jews were siding with the other side and therefore attacked Jews under their control.

In Austria, even during the benign reign of the Emperor Francis Joseph just before the First World War, both conservatives and liberals blamed Jews for all their ills.

In Germany, during all of the nineteenth century, both the friends and the enemies of the Kaiser railed against the Jews as had earlier generations of German Protestants and Catholics who, at the time of Martin Luther (1485-1546), called each other "Judaizers" and blamed the Jews for all the malaise of Christianity on either side.[12]

Although there is no objective reason to transfer these Jewish attitudes to the United States, there is the subjective reason for such a transfer, i.e., tradition. Much of what people believe and do is determined by what is traditional even if it no longer applies to present circumstances. Sociologists call this "culture lag", meaning that a part of the culture, in this case ideological culture, lags behind changed circumstances.

Another reason for the failure of Jews to become too much interested in public disputes concerning some of these issues is that the orthodox Jewish community lives a rather isolated life entrenched within the walls of Torah and other orthodox Jewish concerns. Many orthodox Jews know little and wish to know less about public issues. This means that those Jews most interested in religion are least interested in dealing with public matters.

Furthermore, liberal Jews who do participate in public discussion have traditionally not called for the use of violence or even public stridency but have been much more interested in "quiet diplomacy" in order to gain their aims. Hence it appears that Jewish Americans are less involved in fights and arguments concerning religion than other Americans.

However, if we are to believe Rabbi Jack Wertheimer, this public stance is deceiving. His book *A People Divided* tells a different story and indicates that there are deep and threatening divisions in American Judaism at the end of this century.[13]

Wertheimer writes that a Jewish culture war has erupted between Jewish religious groups as different answers are proposed to the problems secular society has imposed upon Jews and Judaism in America. Among these problems are: *"the rising rate of intermarriage and the resulting question of how to integrate the children of such marriages into the Jewish community; the feminist revolution and the demands of Jewish women for equality in religious life; and the declining levels of synagogue affiliation and involvement of third and fourth generation American Jews, which has forced all Jewish institutions to compete for members."*

Wertheimer goes on to show that orthodox Jews are so isolated from other Jews that they consider non-orthodox Jews irrelevant, an attitude matched by Reform Jews or at least their rabbis, who believe that orthodoxy is a fossil with no hope of resurrection. While Reconstructionists generally share most of the Reform concerns and Conservatives often side with orthodoxy, these groups are by no means at peace or unified.

One of the most divisive issues in American Judaism has been the question of "Who Is a Jew?" That question is answered differently by the different denominations as Reform hold a Jew to be anyone who has either a Jewish mother or a Jewish father even if the other parent is not Jewish. Traditionally, only those born of a Jewish mother were considered Jews. Obviously then, some will hold that marriage between a person having a Jewish father and a non-Jewish mother to a persons having two Jewish parents will be considered an intra-Jewish marriage by some and an inter-marriage by others.

There are many other disagreements between Jewish denominations, all of which leads Wertheimer to the conclusions that: *"Social barriers between the Orthodox and non-Orthodox worlds are growing higher as the religious conflict intensifies."*

There are a number of other issues which divide the Jewish community at the end of the 20th century. These are not always issues of religion but political matters. For example, a Jewish organization which calls itself *Toward Tradition* advertised in the December 16, 1994 issue of the New York Times that: "Judaism is a conservative and traditional religion." The advertisement goes on to support capital punishment, respect for parents and teachers, responsibility for individual actions, the necessity of war and respect for the military, private property and wealth and local charity together with an effort to avoid dependency. All of this is capped by the statement: *"Thus Judaism and its eternal values have little in common with modern American liberalism whose policies have failed......"*

That viewpoint runs counter to the liberalism of the great majority of American Jews but may well attract an ever increasing number of Jewish voters as black anti-semitism fuels the disillusionment of many Jews with the ways of their political past.

Another issue threatening to divide the Jewish world is the relationship between Israel and the American Jewish community. There are those who see these two communities drifting apart, each with its own interests. This issue has come before the Jewish public as the United Jewish Appeal is under pressure to spend more money on American Jewish affairs and less on Israel even as some Israelis argue that they would be better off accepting less American money and therefore less dependency of American Jews. The American Israel Public Affairs Committee, for years the principal lobbyist for American support of Israel on Capitol Hill, is now the focus of a great deal of controversy over the peace initiative of the Rabin government.

There is dispute in Crown Heights, a New York City neighborhood housing orthodox Jews and many Afro-Americans, not only over interracial relations but also over the political power of some orthodox rabbis to the exclusion of others.

The status of Jerusalem is another divisive issue among Jews, both in America and in Israel. This is the consequence of the influx of large numbers of orthodox Jews into Jerusalem, their high birth rate and the acrimonious debate over whether the orthodox are attempting to impose their agenda on the entire city, orthodox or not.

Even memory of the Holocaust is a matter of dispute among Jews as such writers as Leonard Fine call for the abandonment of Holocaust commemorations and the assertion by Fine and others that "*Zionism is not about the survival of the Jewish people.*"[14]

That attitude is bitterly resented by Holocaust survivors who view such comments as an abandonment and a betrayal of those who died there. The dispute concerning the role of American Jews during the Second World War and immediately thereafter has become an issue only in recent years as historians have shown that the American Jewish community was at best complacent about the mass murders of Jews in Europe between 1933 and 1945. Even after the war was over Jewish organizations sought to return the survivors to Poland and other hotbeds of anti-Jewish hatred as "Jewish leaders in the U.S.A. were not prepared to cope with the needs of the survivors."[15]

It was not until the middle of the 1970's that the Holocaust became institutionalized in the American Jewish community so that since that time Holocaust commemorations have become annual events all over the United States.

V.

This is indeed a short and abbreviated list of disputes among American Jews. If there were nothing more to Judaism than these arguments, then one might indeed conclude that *Commentary* and *Look* were indeed right in labeling the American Jews as *"vanishing"* as early as the 1950's.

As we have seen, however, the disputes between Jews affect only a minority because a large number of Jews do not affiliate and are therefore utterly immune to the divisiveness which so much worries Rabbi Wertheimer. The fact is, that indifference is a much greater threat to the American Jewish community than differences of opinion. At least, the disputants are interested in the Jewish cause. This is not so among the 66% who are not affiliated.[16] Therefore there are several scenarios which could explain the Jewish future in America, although no such explanation may prove to be accurate.

Intermarriage is no doubt of greatest concern to all Jews because it has been traditional to believe that intermarriage leads eventually to the destruction of the Jewish people.

That, however, is no longer a matter of choice. We have seen that individualism in religion is now (1995) of greatest importance to Americans. Not only Jews, but Christians and others believe that they have a right to make their own decisions concerning their religion and their religious behavior. Catholics have expressed this view innumerable times with particular reference to disputes within the Church concerning the teachings of the Pope and the conduct of American Catholics in opposition and in disregard of these teachings.

Thus, Jewish Americans are not alone in failing to respond to tradition. Therefore it must be assumed that intermarriage of Jews and non-Jews is here to stay and that the erstwhile belief that Jewishness is an ascribed condition inherited at birth is not so. There are now and will be ever more Jews in America who were not born Jewish or who were born of one Jewish parent. This cannot be altered. The Jewish community must deal with this fact and is doing so. Therefore Jewish life in America will be enhanced by the influx of people whose abilities, productivity, contributions and insights were previously excluded. The truth is that Jews have not proselytized for so long because it was forbidden them by Christian law, but not because it was prohibited by Jewish law. For example, the Synod of Vienna in 1267 repeated the prohibition forbidding Jews to convert Christians to Judaism, a prohibition which had been in effect for centuries.[17] That prohibition therefore became a Jewish attitude even after it was no longer required nor effective in the United States and elsewhere.

Similarly, Jews were at one time prohibited from saying in the Kaddish prayer that the Messiah was yet to come. Therefore that sentence was dropped from the Kaddish prayer. It is hardly used today, except by Chassidim. Here is another example of how Christian prohibition became Jewish custom.

Therefore the tradition of viewing as Jews only those born into Judaism or having a Jewish mother is antiquated and dysfunctional. Judaism is not a biological condition. Were this so, then the first Jew, Abraham, born a Chaldean, could never have become a Jew. Evidently, then, Judaism and Jewishness are both dependent on the process of socialization which has also been called enculturation.

The agents of socialization are the family, education, religion, peers, the workplace and the mass media. Evidently, a person raised in a religion other than Judaism will therefore be socialized in a non-Jewish family to be emotionally attached to the religious preference of his family. We have seen, however, that large numbers of Americans are raised without a religion and have no such attachments. Judaism can therefore become the religion and the sub-culture to which an otherwise secular person can attach herself and feel comfortable. Socialization can take place among adults as well as children. An adult, however, who has married a Jewish person although he is not Jewish himself, can certainly learn Judaism and Jewishness in a family he founded himself. Here the socialization process has a good chance of succeeding as the symbols of the Jewish faith are used to attach the newcomer to the ancient House of Israel. Strong ties to a group one has met as an adult are also found among those who become Americans in later life or those who remarry after divorce. Thus, naturalized citizens can and are re-socialized to accept American symbols such as the flag as their own, to sing patriotic songs and to observe national holidays such as Thanksgiving and Independence Day with as much fervor as is true of native born Americans. There is therefore no reason to believe that a person who has become a "Jew by Choice" in adult life cannot do the same.

Since the majority of those who convert to Judaism do so because they have married a Jew, the family can be the most powerful instrument of socializing the non-Jew into Judaism and Jewishness. This has succeeded in at least 385,000 instances of conversion into Judaism and will continue.

Education is another powerful agent of socialization. This is obvious to everyone and is the prime focus of almost any conversion effort made in the United States. Every synagogue which offers conversion gives the potential convert a long reading list, instructs potential converts in Jewish history, customs and ceremony and at least a reading knowledge of the Hebrew language. More than that, the potential convert learns to know Jews and makes those emotional adaptations necessary to identify with the group he intends to enter.

Most important, however, is the introduction of a new *life theme* to the person intending to become Jewish. Even after formal conversion, a "Jew by choice" will be confronted with that overriding way of viewing and interpreting the world. Thus, Judaism, and hence the Jewish person, is most likely to be concerned with the issue of justice in this world, and not so much with anticipating conditions in "the next world." There are of course innumerable Biblical reminders that justice is of great concern to those who follow the Jewish tradition. For example, the prophet Amos wrote: "Seek the Lord that you may live, seek good and not evil, that you may live; and that the Lord, the God of hosts, may be truly with you as you think he is; hate evil and love good and establish *justice* in the gates of the land."[18]

The Bible quotes Jeremiah: "If one practices *justice* and righteousness, if one champions the cause of the poor, then it is well with one-this indeed is to know Me, says God."[19]

To Micah is attributed: "He has told you man, what is good; and what the Lord requires from you; but to do *justice* and to love mercy and to walk humbly with your God"[20] and in Isaiah we read that famous passage: "Seek *justice*, relieve the oppressed, judge the fatherless, plead for the widow."[21]

These, and a host of other admonitions to do that which is just has been the core of Jewish existence. The whole concept of *halacha*, the law, rests on the concept of justice so that, as we have seen, Jews ranging in observance from Reform to Orthodox consult *halacha*. To be a Jew depends therefore first, and foremost, on absorbing into one's personality a concern with social justice *in this world*. That, however, is not unique to Jews and can be learned by someone who converts to Judaism.

An outgrowth of a concern with justice is social action. Because Jews have been taught concern for creating a just society, many Jews, far out of proportion to their number, have taken an active part in promoting social agendas of all kinds. The overwhelming number of these agendas have been of the kind that are called "liberal" by the American media. Concern for the civil rights of minorities is a leading agenda of American Jews. This has of course become a pitfall for those who believed that their promotion of minority causes would be reciprocated by the recipients of Jewish largesse. When the opposite occurred in the persons of Louis Farrakhan and other hate filled black leaders many Jews were utterly shocked because they attributed to others their own concern for justice. Jews felt betrayed and in fact were betrayed, by those who benefitted by Jewish efforts on their behalf.

This sense of betrayal came about mostly because Jews, and everyone else as well, attribute to others their own concerns and their own viewpoint. But others are not necessarily obsessed with justice. Other considerations, such as racial pride, or a sense of independence, leads some minorities to reject *ex post facto* their benefactors, the Jews.

Self reliance is another important Jewish trait as already discussed with reference to Leo Pinsker and his pamphlet, "Auto - emancipation." This is also an important American value so that many Americans who are not Jewish would find that vital Jewish attitude appealing and understandable.

This leads us to a consideration of yet another very much Jewish trait. That is the need to perform the role of victim. Although there has never been an active, government sponsored persecution of the Jewish people in America, American Jews nevertheless display a need to resort to victim status and to make victimization the master status of Jewishness.

This is seen in particular with reference to the annual Holocaust commemorations held in all American Jewish communities. Innumerable wealthy contributors to Jewish causes who were born in the United States and know nothing of the erstwhile Nazi persecutions other than what they have read, nevertheless rush to perform at such commemorations. They speak there. They appear in the media and pontificate upon Holocaust experiences they never had. They shove aside the usually poor and socially rejected actual Holocaust survivors in order to gain publicity for themselves. Professors, who never saw one Nazi, let alone experience Nazi persecution, lead discussions on such topics as "The Psychoanalytic Explanations of the Jewish Catastrophe In Europe" or "Hitler Analyzed."

In fact, "holocausting" has become the secular religion of some American Jews so that we repeatedly see the spectacle of having American born Jews chair Holocaust Centers or direct such Centers while survivors have no part in the activities these "experts" chair and/or direct.

A third, secular aspect of being Jewish is a great concern with education and its trappings. The doctorate has been called the sign of Jewish nobility in the sense that the title *von* was and continues to be the sign of German nobility. Jewish occupational distribution easily proves this great need to be educated. As we saw in earlier pages of this book, an exceptional number of American Jews hold college degrees or graduate degrees. This does not indicate that Jews are more intelligent than other people. Instead it indicates that Jewish insecurity, even in America, is so great that Jews are not willing to risk holding a low social status and/or being poor. There are of course poor Jews. For them, poverty is even more painful than for non-Jews because the Jewish community, by reason of its considerable educational attainment, is economically better off than any American denomination and share with Presbyterians and Episcopalians "the highest overall social standing in the United States."[22]

These attainments, both in education and in economics, are requirements in the Jewish community. Public opinion, the demands of the opposite sex before marriage, the expectations of relatives, and the preservation of a sound self image all militate among Jews to make every effort to secure an education and to rise economically.

These attributes are thus essentially Jewish. All of them can be learned, of course, and therefore these attributes can and are diffused to "Jews by Choice."

It ought to be in the interest of American Jews to proselytize other Americans. Since there are large numbers of Americans who have no religion either because they were not raised in one or have relinquished the religion they once had, Jews should and will augment their numbers by actively seeking converts.

Religion creates differences in life style, in beliefs, in attitudes and in behavior. Therefore those who learn and become socialized around Jewish life styles, beliefs, attitudes and conduct are Jews particularly if they have formally converted to Judaism and participate in the Jewish community and in all those actions which matter to American Jews.

Peers are very important in the socialization process. Therefore, as more and more "Jews by choice'" are accepted into American Judaism the help of other "Jews by Choice" will be very important in giving the newcomers an opportunity to assimilate to their new status on more than just a behavioral level. That means that peers can help a new Jew to do more than only observe rituals. A feeling that one is Jewish, derived from long association, is very important in bringing about a true conversion. This can be and has been achieved. There are "Jews by Choice" among all Jewish groups, including Chasidim, including Orthodox, Conservative and Reform Jews. These groups are under an obligation to give the new "Jew by Choice" a sense of belonging and integration into the group. This has evidently been achieved much more readily by the orthodox and the chasidim because these groups make more demands on the convert than is true of Reform and Reconstructionist congregations. The latter alter the religion to suit the convert, the orthodox seek to change the convert so as to fit the religion.

Self esteem is vital if one is to carry out a conversion and live with a new religion. For non-Jews who convert to Judaism this may create more problems in the work place than elsewhere. Nevertheless, Judaism is usually legitimized in the U.S. and is accepted by almost anyone as part of the triumvirate, "Protestant, Catholic, Jew."

This does not mean that Jews and Judaism are given the prestige and the honorific position in American society attributed to Christianity. It does mean, however, that unlike any other society anywhere outside of Israel, Judaism is normative in America. It is expected that some Americans are Jewish. It is socially understandable, supported by public opinion and included in the American main-stream of thinking and behaving. That, despite some anti-Judaism and anti-semitism.

Therefore one can and many do act the role of Jew in the work place. Since most Jews work among educated Americans, the level of anti-Jewish hostility which undoubtedly still exists among some Americans is muted by the requirements of the educated community. Direct, confrontational bigotry is hardly known in the professional, college level work environment of most American Jews even if latent bigotry is expressed in some situations in which Jews are not present.

The media have contributed a great deal to this favorable reception of Jews and Judaism in the last twenty five years in the United States. By portraying the sins of the Holocaust for a quarter of a century in the most graphic terms it is very unpopular to call for religious persecution in the United States. Those who spread hate and bigotry are confined to "free access" radio talk shows and do in fact surface sometimes when their diabolic diatribe becomes a matter of law suits, public outcries or Jewish protest.

The large, establishment television and radio networks and newspapers, however, publish and broadcast supportive material concerning Jews and Judaism all the time. At Jewish Holy Days, Jewish citizens are publicly congratulated. Bar Mitzvahs are celebrated in the presence of non-Jews and the ceremony is widely known. Rabbis pray at public events and public graduations and are shown doing so in the media. Events within the Jewish group receive favorable comment in the media such as the ordination of women to the Rabbinate. Jewish "leaders" are quoted in the media concerning issues which are not necessarily only of Jewish interest and Jews are routinely appointed to high offices in government, industry and education in the United States without comment concerning their religion. In short, the media have created an atmosphere of acceptance for the Jewish community in the United States which make it "normal" to be a Jew in the America of the last part of the 20th century.

How normal is best seen by the willingness of Jews to now attack other Jews in public and to side with non-Jews against other Jews. Erstwhile, and particularly in Europe, it was anathema for a Jew to denounce another Jew in a non-Jewish place such as a court of law or to side with a *goy* against another Jew no matter how grievous the offense. In the United States this is no longer the case. As long ago as 1952 when the Rosenbergs were prosecuted, convicted and sentenced to death for spying for the Soviet Union by a Jewish prosecutor and a Jewish judge, Jews have felt they could treat other Jews without reference to group solidarity. Undoubtedly, the United States government deliberately appointed Jewish prosecutors and a Jewish judge in the infamous Rosenberg case precisely to avoid the charge of bigotry. It is however significant that Jews could and did prosecute and convict these alleged spies. The case did not arouse wide spread anti-semitism. No public denunciation of the Jewish community followed as was the case in the Dreyfus prosecution in France in the previous century.

Similarly, Jonathan Pollard was convicted as a Jewish spy for Israel without repercussions for the Jewish community as a whole. Whatever one may think of that conviction, it is significant that Pollard was not brought before a Jewish judge, no special effort was made to avoid the charge of bigotry and no anti-Jewish movements, let alone pogroms, ever developed in the United States because of it. That Jews can fail, that Jews can be criminal, that Jews can be publicly exposed as un-American is taken as normal in the United States just as these failings are also the attributes of some non-Jews.

The issue here is that the media have created this normalization which benefits the Jewish community so much so that conversion to Judaism by a non-Jewish American no longer constitutes a sensation, is not seen as deviance and occurs within the expectations, the norms, of American society.

VI.

Those who predict the future are bound to be wrong. Too many human emotions, actions and unexpected consequences obscure even the most soundly based predictions. That does not mean, however, that all predictions are always wrong. It only means that some predictions will be wrong and others will be quite accurate.

For example, Will Durant, writing in *Our Oriental Heritage,* predicted in 1934 that Japan would go to war with the United States. Said Durant: "*Usually in history, when two nations have contested for the same markets, the nation that has lost in the economic competition, if it is stronger in resources and armaments, has made war upon its enemy.*"[23] Seven years later, that prediction came true. There are other authors, public speakers and observers who have made predictions with moderate success.

Presently, in 1995, numerous authors and speakers on Jewish life in America agree with Rabbi Jack Wertheimer that Jews are *A People Divided* and that the rift between Jews on the issues of religion, feminization, boundaries, Jewish descent and relationship to Israel are ever increasing and are threatening the perpetuation of the Jewish people as such.

This is indeed a frightening and sad assessment from the view point of those who wish for the perpetuation of Judaism and Jewishness in America and in the world. It is also a limited assessment which overlooks much that can be said in favor of Jewish vitality and resurgence.

First, it is evident that Jewish unity existed only in the European *shtetl* before the 2nd World War because it was forced upon the European Jews by the unrelenting hostility of the Christian world in which they lived. In short, the price of that unity was brutal anti-semitism culminating in the Hitlerite mass murders. That unity was bought at so high a price that it was not worth it so that those who are sometimes heard to say that Jews "need" some anti-semitism in order to hold together are not only wrong but limited in their understanding of the nature of European bigotry.

Jews are of course not the only religious or ethnic group who display tensions and disagreements among each other. Catholics are engaged in a tremendous dispute concerning the issues of feminization, birth control, abortion, authority and lay participation. Protestantism by its very name indicates dispute and splintering into innumerable denominations. Moslems have literally killed each other over religious disputes as have Christians. The list goes on and on. There is no evidence that a religious or moral community cannot persist even amidst disputes and disagreements.

Judaism and Jewishness both have something to offer that attracts and will always attract followers, believers and participants. We have already seen that Reform and Reconstruction allow individuals to make their own decision concerning the nature of their Jewish beliefs and practices. We have seen that orthodoxy encapsulates the individual in the *halacha*, in the law and provides a sense of belonging and security otherwise seldom achieved in American life. Conservatives stress historical Judaism and permit their followers to be connected to the tradition within the framework of American needs and circumstances.

These variations within the Jewish world permit almost everyone to come in and participate. Instead of seeing these differences as divisive they can also be seen as inclusive, as ubiquitous.

In addition to the religious groupings in Judaism there are of course also the numerous secular organizations already mentioned. These organizations and the entire Jewish secular establishment arises in part from the high economic status of American Jews. Religion has always been less popular among the wealthy than the poor because the "next world" is far more attractive to someone who has little comfort and honor in this world than to someone who has "heaven on earth" by reason of his income, prestige, social honor, dominance, consumption level and freedom. All of these are attributes of the wealthy and all of them devolve upon the Jewish community in greater proportion than upon the non-Jewish community. Hence the greater secularization of the Jewish community.

Within the secular Jewish community there are those who give no heed to Jewish matters whatever but there are also those who involve themselves in secular Jewish organizations. The preponderance of these organizations are fund raising groups who finance, or say they finance, innumerable Jewish causes such as Israel, homes for the aged, the Jewish Community Centers, Jewish education and much more.

These organizations are voluntary and have all the attributes of voluntary organizations. Among these attributes are first availability. This means that those who volunteer and those who "serve" on boards of directors and those who participate in innumerable committee meetings can do so because they need not work at menial tasks and for long hours each day. Evidently, Jewish participation in so many voluntary activities in America is not only the product of beliefs in justice, equality and ethical conduct but is also promoted by the chances which a good income gives many Jews to find the time and the money needed to engage themselves in voluntary causes. Therefore, one function of voluntary groups is to give its activists an opportunity to spend the time that less affluent persons spend at work. Voluntary activism is too time consuming and risky to be undertaken by the poor. It must therefore be undertaken by the financially secure.

It is of course an axiom of common sense that even those who have time and money would not spend either on causes in which they do not believe. Therefore, Jews who volunteer to work for Jewish causes must believe something that would lead them to participate.

Hence, it can be safely assumed that even the most secular Jews who volunteer to participate in one manner or another in Jewish activities feel some affinity for the Jewish people and seek to ensure Jewish survival. Such volunteers are generally optimists. A pessimist, in this case someone who believes that Judaism and Jewishness or the Jewish people are vanishing anyway or have no future, would hardly spend his money or time on a lost cause. This optimism is very much visible among all volunteers for all causes and always for the reasons just mentioned.[24]

Jewish volunteers are not only optimists, they also believe that they can make a difference. Therefore one function of voluntary organizations, Jewish or not, is to give the individual who volunteers a sense of potency and personal power. Volunteers think that what they do will have consequences and that history is not inevitable as taught by Marx and others. This sense of personal power is further enhanced among those volunteers who give large sums of money because they not only see the fruits of their contributions in the buildings named after them, but also because they hold such titles as "Chairman" or "President" of this board and that. Furthermore they collect the obsequious symbols and "servile compliance" of the employees of the various organizations for which they volunteer. Therefore, one additional function of voluntary participation is the promotion of a social hierarchy dependent on conspicuous consumption, not only of material objects such as large cars and fur coats, but also on charitable giving.

Activism on the part of Jewish and other causes has been traditional in the Jewish community. Therefore many Jewish volunteers are the children of Jewish volunteers of the previous generation. Therefore, another function of secular Jewish voluntarism is the collection of parental approval and intergenerational harmony.

Now volunteers generally act in concert with others and are motivated by the personal ties they have with those already volunteering. Hence, Jewish volunteerism is also motivated by a need to associate with other Jews and to perpetuate the Jewish group through these contacts. Such groupings, outside the synagogue environment and in the absence of religious symbols, nevertheless help to perpetuate the Jewish people. It can even be said that the framework of secular Jewish organizations may serve some to buoy their Judaism to the same degree as do ritual and ceremony within the synagogue. Since, however, the secular organizations do not suffer from denominational wrangling and disagreements but seek to work toward a common cause, it can be argued in conclusion *that secularization is the very strength of American Jewishness and Judaism* and that its perpetuation is assured precisely because American Jews have become largely secular.

This point of view does not negate the importance of the Jewish religion in Jewish life. It only holds that the secular aspects of Jewish life are not as remote from the religious aspects as may appear on the surface and that the Jewish people are far healthier, far more resilient than some pessimists would want us to believe.

VII.

We have seen in this book how Judaism in America has become secularized and how at the end of the 20th century American Jews and non-Jews have segregated religion from their daily lives, made it very individualistic, substituted "check book" Judaism for traditional Jewish scholarship and ritual observance.

We have then demonstrated how the secularization of Judaism began with Spinoza in the 17th century and continued in the works of Mendelssohn, the enlightenment philosophers, the Zionists and such modern Jewish philosophers as Mordecai Kaplan. Because Jewish philosophers and the Jewish people lived almost entirely in non-Jewish surroundings, philosophers who were not Jewish also influenced the secularization of Judaism as they influenced the secularization of other religions. Among these philosophers were the ancient Roman thinkers, some medieval scholars and in more modern times Kant, Goethe and Voltaire.

In the United States, deism became popular in the eighteenth century through the writings of Paine and Jefferson. But the German philosopher Marx and the French writers Comte and Durkheim also had a great influence upon the secularization of the United States.

In addition, the rise of science influenced secularization in America and the European world. Bacon, Hobbes, Newton, Faraday, Gauss , Darwin and a host of other scientists all the way to Einstein secularized the Western world in an irrevocable manner. Yet, scientists and philosophers were generally not atheists, but deists as had been true of Spinoza.

Added to this barrage of secularization from philosophers and scientists was the literary output of such famous writers in Europe as Voltaire and Pope, Gibbon, Blake, Shelley and Housman. This was matched by such secularizers as Hawthorne, Ingersoll and Lewis in the United States. In addition, the United States produced numerous secular Jewish writers who sought to denude Judaism of its supernaturalism. Among these were Kaplan, Roth and Kosinski.

Thus, when the great waves of Jewish immigrants came to the United States at the end of the 19th and the beginning of the 20th century they found here a society, still imbued with Protestantism, but on the verge of secularization not only because of the influences brought to America by the immigrants themselves but also because of the long history of hostility to religion present in the New World since the days of the Revolution. All this was summarized and injected into American education by John Dewey, no doubt the most influential American philosopher of both the 19th end 20th century. Thus, the schools which Jews attended in such large numbers were and are secular; teach subject matter which is at least neutral if not hostile to religion and created a new American Jew, separated, but not divorced from European Jewish tradition and steeped in American secularization.

These new American Jewish attitudes then led to the secularization of the Jewish religion, the secularization of the Jewish family and the secularization of Jewish education. Therefore, secular, not religious Jewish organizations predominate in American Jewish life today, i.e., in 1995.

Yet, despite all the victories of secularization during the past three hundred years, it is now evident that secularization alone is not satisfactory to many Americans. This dissatisfaction has come about because it has become evident to many Americans that science and government programs and rational answers for every problem are not good enough and contribute nothing to the permanent needs of millions who once thought that "science could save us."

Therefore many Americans have sought to become connected to religion once more albeit in a new and American form. This is true of Jews as well as non - Jews. Among American Jews new forms of theology have arisen. These theologies, whether Reform, Orthodox or Conservative, seek to answer the needs of end of the century American Jews. Disillusioned with crass materialism, unwilling to live a purely secular life some Jews have returned to more traditional Judaism than was of interest to them or their parents. Others have turned to non-Jewish religions. Most have used secular organizations to express their need to make a contribution to the good of mankind and the perpetuation of the Jewish people.

The conclusion of our study therefore is that American Judaism is in transition from those traditions which served a now almost extinct immigrant generation to a new and vibrant American Judaism which will yet equal if not surpass the Judaism of the past.

NOTES

[1]Vince Beiser, "For the Love of Jesus," *The Jerusalem Report,* Vol. 5, No.19, January 26, 1995, pp. 26-31.

[2]Robert Gordis, *Judaism In a Christian World,* New York, McGraw - Hill, 1966, p.193.

[3]Jack Wertheimer, *A People Divided,* New York, Basic Books, 1993, p. 96.

[4]Walter Jacob, "Solomon B. Freehof and the Halacha," in: Solomon B. Freehof, *Reform Responsa for Our Time,* Cincinnati, Ohio, The Hebrew Union College-Jewish Institute of Religion, 1977, p. xiv-xv.

[5]Solomon B. Freehof, *New Reform Responsa,* Cincinnati, The Hebrew Union College Press, 1980, pp. 1-5.

[6]Charles E. Silberman, *A Certain People: American Jews and their Lives Today,* New York, Summit Books, 1985, p.258.

[7]Jack Wertheimer, *op.cit.,* p.110.

[8]Joseph B. Soloveitchick, *Halakhic Man,* Philadelphia, The Jewish Publication Society, 1983, p. 19.

[9]*Ibid,* p. 88.

[10]*Ibid,* p.94.

[11]Abraham J. Heschel, *Between God and Man: An Interpretation of Judaism,* Fritz A. Rothschild, Editor,
New York, The Free Press, 1959, p. 28.

[12]Gerhard Falk, *The Jew In Christian Theology,* Jefferson, N.C. and London, McFarland, 1992.

[13]Jack Wertheimer, *op.cit pp. 170-190.* .

[14]Forward Staff, "The Featherman File," *The Forward,* Vol.98, No. 31, 011, January 20, 1995, p. 2.

[15]Alfred Lipson, "The Liberation and Its Aftermath-A Personal Viewpoint," *Together,* Vol. 9, No. 1, December 1994, p. 3.

[16]George Gallup, Jr. and Jim Castelli, *The People's Religion:American Faith In the 90's,"* New York, Macmillan, 1989, p. 116.

[17] Falk, *op.cit.*, p. 43.
[18] Amos, 5:4, 14-15.
[19] Jeremiah, 22:15-16.
[20] Micah, 6:8.
[21] Isaiah 1:11.
[22] Wade C. Roof, *A Generation of Seekers: The Spiritual Journeys of the Baby-Boom Generation,* New York, Harper Collins, 1992.
[23] Will Durant, *Our Oriental Heritage,* Simon and Schuster, New York, 1954, p. 933.
[24] A good discussion of these motives is found in :Doug McAdam, *Freedom Summer,* New York, Oxford University Press, 1988.

Bibliography

Books

Adams, James T., *Jeffersonian Principles,* Boston, Little Brown & Co., 1928.

Adamson, Fulton Henry, *The Philosophy of Francis Bacon,* Chicago, The University of Chicago Press, 1948.

Aleichim, Sholom, *The Tevye Stories,* New York, Pocket Books, Inc., 1965.

Allen, Harvey, ed., *The Works of Edgar Allan Poe,* New York, P. F. Collier and Son, 1927.

Alpert, Harry, *Emile Durkheim and His Sociology,* New York, Columbia University Press, 1939.

Altmann, Alexander, *Moses Mendelssohn - A Biographical Study,* University, Ala., The University of Alabama Press, 1973.

Amacher, John, *Benjamin Franklin,* New York, Twayne Publishers, Inc., 1962.

Amos, 5:4, 14-15.

Anthony, H.D., *Sir Isaac Newton,* New York, Abelard-Schuman, 1960.

Aptheker, Herbert, *Marxism and Christianity,* New York, The Humanities Press, 1968.

Aries, Phillippe, *Centuries of Childhood,* Robert Baldick, Trans., New York, Alfred A. Knopf, 1962.

Armitage, Angus, *William Herschel,* Garden City, N.Y., Doubleday & Co., 1963.

Ashforth, Albert, *Thomas Henry Huxley,* N.Y., Twayne Publishers Inc., 1969.

Attfield, Robin, *God and the Secular,* Cardiff, Wales, University College of Cardiff Press, 1978.

Badt-Strauss, Bertha, *Moses Mendelssohn, Der Mensch und das Werk,* Berlin, Welt Verlag, 1929.

Bailey, Thomas A., *The American Pageant,* Boston, D.C. Heath and Co., 1961.

Baltzell, E. Digby, *The Protestant Establishment,* New York, Random House, 1964.

Barnes, Harry Elmer and Howard Becker, *Social Thought From Lore To Science,* New York, D.C.Heath, & Co., 1938.

Battamore, Tom and Robert Nisbet, Editors, *A History of Sociological Analysis,* New York, Basic Books, 1978.

Beik, Paul H., and Laurence LaFore, *Modern Europe,* New York, Henry Holt and Co., 1959.

Beiser, Frederich C., *The Fate of Reason: German Philosophy from Kant to Fichte,* Cambridge, The Harvard University Press, 1987.

Bellow, Saul , *Mr. Sammler's Planet,* New York, The Viking Press, 1970.

Ben-Horin, Meir, *Common Faith-Uncommon People,* New York, The Reconstructionist Press, 1970.

Bendix, Reinhard, *Max Weber: An Intellectual Portrait,* Berkely, The University of California Press, 1977.

Benson, Peter L. and Dorothy Williams, *Religion on Capitol Hill: Myths and Realities,* New York, Harper and Row, 1982.

Berger, Peter I., *The Sacred Canopy, Garden City,* N.Y. , Doubleday, 1967.

Birmingham, Stephen, *Our Crowd,* New York, Dell Publishing Co., Inc., 1967.

Boorstin, Daniel , *The Lost World of Thomas Jefferson,* New York, Holt, 1948.

Brandeis University Bulletin, 1993-1994.

Brasch, Moritz , Editor, *Moses Mendelssohn's Schriften zur Metaphysik und Ethik sowie zur Religionsphilosophie,* Leipzig, Leopold Voss Verlag, 1880.

Braswell,William, *Melville's Religious Thought: An Essay In Interpretation,* New York, Pageant Books, 1959.

Breslauer, S. David, *Meir Kahane,* Lewiston, N.Y., The Edwin Mellen Press, 1986.

Brooke, John, *Let Newton Be!*, New York, The Oxford University Press, 1988.

Brown, Marshall G. and Gordon Stein, *Freethought In the United States: A Descriptive Bibliography*, Westport, Conn., The Greenwood Press, 1963

Buber, Martin, *I and Thou*, Walter Kaufman, Translator, New York, Scribners, 1971.

Bucco, Martin, Ed., *Critical Essays on Sinclair Lewis*, Boston, G.K. Hall & Co., 1986.

Bullock, Alan , *Hitler, A Study In Tyranny*, New York, Harper Torchbooks, 1962.

Bynum, Jack E. and William E. Thompson, *Juvenile Delinquency: A Sociological Approach*, Boston, Allyn and Bacon, 1992.

Califano, Joseph A., *The Triumph & Tragedy of Lyndon Johnson: The White House Years*, New York, Simon and Schuster, 1991.

Canter, Irving , Ed., *Research Readings in Jewish Communal Service*, New York, National Association of Jewish Center Workers, 1967.

Carlebach, Joseph , *Das Buch Koheleth*, Frankfurt, a.M., Hermon Verlag, 1936.

Carlebach, Julius, *Karl Marx and the Radical Critique of Judaism*, London, Routledge & Keegan Paul 1978..

Carroll, John A. and Mary W. Ashworth, *George Washington*, *vol.7*, New York, Scribner's Sons, 1957.

Census of the United States, 1970.

Chadwick, Owen, *The Secularization of the European Mind in the Nineteenth Century*, New York, Cambridge University Press, 1977.

Cicero, Marcus Tullius, *De Natura Deorum and De Divinatione* , Cambridge, Harvard University, 1961.

Clark, Gordon H., *Hellenistic Philosophy*, New York, Appleton - Century Crofts, 1940.

Clarkson, Jesse D., *A History of Russia*, New York, Random House, 1961.

Cohen, Steven M., and Paula C. Hyman, Eds., *The Jewish Family: Myths and Reality*, New York, Holmes and Meier, 1986.

Cohen, Steven M., *American Modernity and Jewish Identity*, New York, Tavistock Publications, 1983.

Coleman, William, *George Cuvier: Zoologist*, Cambridge, Mass., Harvard University Press, 1964.

Commager, Henry Steele, *The American Mind*, New Haven, Yale University Press, 1950.

Commins, Saxe and Robert N. Linscott, *The Social Philosophers*, New York, Random House, 1947.

Commins, Saxe and Robert N. Linscott, *The Philosophers of Science*, New York, Random House, 1947.

Comte, Auguste, *Catechisme Positiviste*, Paris, Delmont, 1852.

Cooley, Charles Horton, *Human Nature and the Social Order*, New York, Schocken Books, 1964 (Originally 1902).

Coser, Lewis A., *Masters of Sociological Thought*, New York, Harcourt Brace Jovanovitch, Inc., 1971.

Cramer, C.H., *Royal Bob: The Life of Robert G. Ingersoll*, New York, The Bob Merrill Co., 1952.

Cross, R. Nicol, *Socrates, The Man and His Mission*, Freeport, N.Y. Books for Libraries Press, 1970.

Crowther, J.G., *Francis Bacon*, London, The Cresset Press, 1960.

Cuzzort , Ray P. and Edith W. King, *20th Century Social Thought*, New York, Holt, Rinehart and Winston, 1980.

Danby, Herbert, *The Mishnah*, Oxford, The Clarendon Press, 1933.

Darrow, Clarence and Wallace Rice, *Infidels and Heretics*, Boston, Mass., The Stratford Co., Publishers, 1929.

Darwin, Charles, *The Origin of Species by Means of Natural Selection* or *The Preservation of Favored Races in the Struggle for Life*, New York, Macmillan, 1927.

Dawidowicz, Lucy S., *The War Against the Jews 1933-1945*, New York, Holt, Rinehart and Winston, 1975.

Deuteronomy 31: 6,7,23.

Dewey, Robert, *The Philosophy of John Dewey*, The Hague, Martinus Nijhoff, 1977.

Dewey, John, *A Common Faith*, New Haven, Yale University Press, 1971 (1934).

Dewey, John , *The Child and the Curriculum*, Chicago, The University of Chicago Press, Eleventh Printing 1971.

Dreiser, Theodore, *Notes on Life*, University, Alabama, The University of Alabama Press, 1974.

Dubos, Rene, *Louis Pasteur: Free Lance of Science*, Boston, Little, Brown and Co., 1950.

Dubos, Rene, *Louis Pasteur*, Boston, Little, Brown and Co., 1976.

Dunn, Charles W., *American Political Theology*, New York, Praeger, 1984.

Dunnington, G. Waldo, *Carl Friedrich Gauss: Titan of Science*, New York, Expository Press, 1955.

Durant, Will and Ariel, *The Age of Louis the XIV*, New York, Simon and Schuster, 1961.

Durant, Will and Ariel, *The Age of Voltaire*, New York, Simon and Schuster, 1965.

Durant, Will and Ariel, *Rousseau and Revolution*, New York, Simon and Schuster, 1967.

Durant, Will, *Our Oriental Heritage*, Simon and Schuster, New York, 1954.

Durant, Will, *The Life of Greece*, New York, Simon and Schuster, 1939.

Durant, Will, *The Renaissance*, New York, Simon and Schuster, 1953.

Durant, Will, *The Reformation*, New York, Simon and Schuster, 1957.

Durant, Will and Ariel, *The Age of Reason Begins*, New York, Simon and Schuster, 1961.

Durkheim, Emile, *The Elementary Forms of the Religious Life*, New York, Collier Books, 1961.

Durkheim, Emile, *The Elementary Forms of the Religious Life: A Study In Religious Sociology*, J.W. Swain, Translator, New York, Macmillan, 1912.

Dushkin Publishing Group, Inc., *Annual Editions: Readings In Social Problems*, Guilford, Conn., 1993.

Eisenberg, Azriel, *Modern Jewish Life In Literature*, New York, The United Synagogue of America, 1957.

Elder, Dominic, *The Life of Thomas Paine*, Notre Dame, Ind., The University of Notre Dame, 1951.

Eliades, Mircea, Ed., *The Encyclopedia of Religion, Vol. 13*, New York, Macmillan Publishing Co., 1987.

Elwes, R.H.M., *The Chief Works of Benedict Spinoza*, New York, Dover Publications Inc., 1955.

Encyclopedia Judaica, Vol. 2, The Macmillan Co., New York, 1971.

Encylcopedia Judaica, Vol. 13, New York, The Macmillan Co., 1971.

Facts on File, May 23, 1991.

Fairfield, Roy P., *Humanistic Frontiers in American Education,* Buffalo, N.Y., Prometheus Press, 1971.

Falk, Gerhard, *The Life of the Academic Professional,* Lewiston, N.Y., Edwin Mellen Press, 1990.

Falk, Gerhard, *The Jew In Christian Theology,* Jefferson, N.C. and London, McFarland & Co., Inc., 1992.

Falk , Gerhard , *A Study of Social Change,* Lewiston, N.Y., The Edwin Mellen Press, 1993.

Falk, Gerhard , *Murder: An Analysis of Its Forms, Conditions and Causes,* Jefferson, N.C. and London, McFarland & Co, Inc., 1990.

Feldstein, Stanley, *The Land That I Show You,* New York, Anchor Press, 1978.

Ferrarotti, Franco, *Five Scenarios for the Year 2000,* New York, The Greenwood Press, 1986.

Ferrarotti, Franco, *Faith Without Dogma: The Place of Religion in Post Modern Societies,* Transaction Publishers, New Brunswick, 1993.

Frankl, Viktor E., *Man's Search for Meaning,* New York, Simon and Schuster, Inc., 1984.

Freehof, Solomon B., *Reform Responsa for Our Time,* Cincinnati, Ohio, The Hebrew Union College-Jewish Institute of Religion, 1977.

Freehof, Solomon B., *New Reform Responsa,* Cincinnati,The Hebrew Union College Press, 1980.

Freeman, Douglas S., *George Washington: A Biography,* New York, Scribner's, 1957.

Fried, Lewis, *Handbook of American-Jewish Literature,* New York, Greenwood Press, 1988.

Friedan, Betty, *The Feminine Mystique,* New York, Dell, 1963.

Gallup, George Jr. and Jim Castelli, *The People's Religion: American Faith In the 90's,* New York, Macmillan, 1989.

Gallup Report #259, The, April 1987.

Gartner, Lloyd P. , *Jewish Education in the United States: A Documentary History,* New York, Teachers College Press, 1969.

Gay, Ruth, *The Jews of Germany,* New Haven, Yale University Press, 1992.

Gelpi, Donald L, *Endless Seeker: The Religious Quest of Ralph Waldo Emerson,* New York, University Press of America, 1991.

General Social Surveys:Cumulative Codebook, Chicago, National Opinion Research Center, 1993.

Gerould, Gordon H., Richard Foster Jones and Ernest Bernbaum, eds., *Romantic Literature,* New York, The Ronald Press Co., 1943.

Gibbon, Edward, *The History of the Decline and Fall of the Roman Empire,* London, Methuen & Co., 1896-1902.

Gilbert, Martin , *The Holocaust,* New York, Hill and Wang, 1979.

Ginzberg, Louis, *A Sprectrum of Jewish Learning at American Universities,* Philadelphia, Jewish Publication Society, 1906.

Gittleman, Sol , *From Shtetl to Suburbia,* Boston, Beacon Press, 1978.

Glazer, Nathan, *American Judaism,* Chicago, The University of Chicago Press, 1972.

Goethe, Johann Wolfgang, *Faust Part I,* R.M.S. Heffner, Helmut Rehder and W.F. Twaddell, eds., Madison, Wis., The University of Wisconsin Press, 1956.

Gordis, Robert, *Judaism in a Christian World,* New York, McGraw Hill, 1966.

Gordis, Robert, *Koheleth-The Man and His World: A Study of Ecclesiastes,* Schocken Books, N.Y. 1968.

Graetz, Heinrich, *History of the Jews, Vol 5,* Philadelphia, The Jewish Publication Society, 1895.

Grayzel, Solomon, *A History of the Jews,* Philadelphia, The Jewish Publication Society of America, 1947.

Greeley, Andrew M., *Religious Change in America,* Cambridge, MA., Harvard University Press, 1989.

Gurock, Jeffrey S., *The Men and Women of Yeshivah: Higher Education, Orthodoxy and American Judaism,* New York, Columbia University Press, 1988.

Hadden, Jeffrey K. and Anson Shupe, eds., *Secularization and Fundamentalism Reconsidered,* N.Y., Paragon House, 1989.

Halpern, Ben, *The Idea of the Jewish State,* Cambridge, The Harvard University Press, 1961.

Hammond, Phillip E., *The Protestant Presence in Twentieth Century America,* Albany, State University of New York Press, 1992.

Harkness, Georgia, *The Modern Rival of the Christian Faith,* N.Y., Abbingdon-Cokesbury, 1952.

Harlow, Ralph V., *The United States,* New York, Henry Holt and Co., 1959.

Harnack, Adolf, *Outlines of the History of Dogma,* Ed Knox Mitchell, Translator, London, Hodder and Stoughton, 1893.

Haynes, Charles C., *Religion In American History,* Alexandria , Va., Association for Supervision and Curriculum Development, 1990.

Hegel, Georg, W. F., *On Christianity,* New York, Harper, Row, Inc., 1948.

Heilman, Samuel, *What We Know About Jewish Education,* Los Angeles, Torah Aura Productions, 1992.

Heine, Heinrich, *Heines Werke,* Berlin, Deutsches Verlagshaus Bong & Co., Vol.1, no year.

Helmreich, William D. , *The World of the Yeshivah: An Intimate Portrait of Orthodox Jewry,* New Haven and London, Yale University Press, 1982.

Herberg, Will, *Protestant-Catholic-Jew,* Garden City, N.Y. , Doubleday and Co., 1955.

Herrick, Jim, *Against the Faith: Essays on Deists, Skeptics and Atheists,* Buffalo, N.Y., Prometheus Press, 1985.

Herring, Basil, *The Rabbinate as Calling and Vocation,* Northvale, N.J., Jason Aronson, Inc., 1991.

Heschel, Abraham J., *Between God and Man: An Interpretation of Judaism,* Fritz A. Rothschild, ed.

Hess, Beth B., Elizabeth W. Markson   Peter J. Stein, *Sociology,* New York, Macmillan, 1993.

Hobbes, Thomas, *Leviathan,* Richard Tuck, Ed., New York, Cambridge University Press, 1991.

Holborn, Hajo, *A History of Modern Germany,* New York, Alfred A. Knopf, 1969.

Holt, Anne, *A Life of Joseph Priestley,* Westport , Conn., Greenwood Press, 1970 (Originally published by Oxford University Press in 1931).

Honigmann, S. J., *Understanding Culture,* New York, Harper Row and Co., 1963.

Howe, Irving, *World of Our Fathers,* New York, Simon and Schuster, 1976.

Howells, William Dean, *Literary Friends and Acquaintance,* Bloomington and London, Indiana University Press, 1968.

Hutcheson, Harold R., *Lord Herbert of Cherbury's "De Religione Laici"* , New Haven, Yale University Press, 1944..

Information Please Almanac, Boston, Houghton Mifflin & Co., 1993.

Isaiah, 1:11,.52: 1 and 2.

Jacob, Margaret, *The Newtonians and the English Revolution, 1689-1720*, Ithaca, N.Y., Cornell Univeristy Press, 1976.

Jennings, B. Sanders, *The United States*, Evanston, Ill., Row, Peterson, 1962.

Jeremiah, 22:15-16.

Joshuah 1: 6.

Kant, Immanuel, *Die Religion Innerhalb der Grenzen der Blossen Vernunft*, Hamburg, Felix Meiner Verlag, 1956.

Kaplan, Mordecai M., *Judaism As A Civilization*, Philadelphia, The Jewish Publication Society, 1981.

Katz, Steven T., *Post-Holocaust Dialogues: Critical Studies In Modern Jewish Thought*, New York, New York University Press, 1983.

Katz, Jacob, *Forerunners of Zionism*, Jerusalem, Keter Books, 1973.

Klein, Isaac, *The Ten Commandments In a Changing World*, Jerusalem, Citadel Press, 1963.

Koch, G. Alfred, *Republican Religion*, New York, Henry Holt and Co., 1933, p. 250.

Kosmin, Barry A., Sidney Goldstein, Joseph Weksberg, Nava Lehrer, Ariella Keysar and Jeffrey Scheckner, *Highlights of the CJF 1990 Jewish Population Survey*, New York, Council of Jewish Federations, 1991.

Kraft, Louis, *A Century of the Jewish Community Center Movement*, New York, National Jewish Welfare Board, 1953.

Kunitz, Stanley J.and Howard Haycraft, *British Authors of the Nineteenth Century*, New York, The H. W. Wilson Co., 1936.

Kurzweil, Zvi E., *Modern Trends In Jewish Education*, New York, Thomas Yoseloff, 1964.

Lachs, Samuel Tobias, *Humanism in Talmud and Midrash*, Madison, N.J., Farleigh Dickerson University Press, 1993.

Lamberti, Marjorie, *Jewish Activism In Imperial Germany*, New Haven, Yale Univrsity Press, 1978.

Lanczos, Cornelius, *Albert Einstein and the Cosmic World Order*, New York, Interscience Publishers, 1965.

Lathrope, George P., Ed., *The Complete Works of Nathaniel Hawthorne*, Boston, Riverside Edition, 1893.

Lazare, Bernard, *L' Antisemitisme: Son Histoire et Ses Causes*, Paris, Le Puits et le Pendule, 1982.

Lemay, J. A. Leo, ed., *Deism, Masonry, and the Enlightenment,* Newark , The University of Delaware Press, 1987.

Lemay, J.A. Leo, *The Oldest Revolutionary,* Philadelphia, The University of Pennsylvania Press, 1976.

Lenski, Gerhard, *The Religious Factor,* Doubleday, Garden City, N.Y., 1961.

Levin, Nora, *The Holocaust: The Destruction of European Jewry 1933-1945,* New York, Schocken Books, 1973.

Levy, Leonard W., *The Establishment Clause: Religion and the First Amendment,* New York, Macmillan Co., Inc., 1986.

Lewis, Sinclair, *Babbitt,* New York, Harcourt, Brace & World, Inc., 1950.

Lewis, Sinclair, *Elmer Gantry,* New York, Harcourt, Brace and Co., 1927.

Lewissohn, Ludwig, *Theodore Herzl,* New York, The World Publishing Co., 1955.

Linzer, Norman, *The Jewish Family: Authority and Tradition in Modern Perspective,* New York, Human Sciences Press, Inc., 1983.

Locke, John, *A Letter Concerning Toleration,* Mario Muntori, Ed., The Hague, Martinus Nijhoff, 1963.

Lukes, Steven, *Emile Durkheim, His Life and Work: A Historical and Critical Study,* New York, Penguin Books, 1973.

Madaule, Madeleine Barthelemy, *Lamarck, The Mythical Precursor,* Cambridge, The MIT Press, 1982.

Mahler, Raphael, *Jewish Emancipation*, New York, The American Jewish Committee, 1941.

Maimonides, Moses, *The Commentary to Mishnah Abbot,* Arthur David, Translator, New York, Bloch Publishing Co., 1968.

Major Writers of America, New York, Harcourt, Brace aend World, 1962.

Manuel, Frank E., *The Prophets of Paris,* New York, Torch Books, 1962.

Manuel, Frank , *The Religion of Isaac Newton,* Oxford, Clarendon Press, 1974.

Marcus, Jacob R. amd Abraham J. Peck, *The American Rabbinate: A Century of Continuity and Change, 1883-1983,* Editors, Hoboken N.J., KTAV Publishing House, Inc., 1985.

Margolis, Max L. and Alexander Marx, *A History of the Jewish People,* New York, Mediridan Books, Inc., 1960.

Marsden, George M., *The Soul of the American University,* New York, Oxford University Press, 1994.

Martin, Bernard, *Movements and Issues in American Judaism,* Westport, Conn., Greenwood Press, 1978.

Masani, P. R., *Norbert Wiener,* Basel, Birhauser Verlag, 1990.

Maslow, Will , *The Structure and Functioning of the American Jewish Community,* New York, American Jewish Congress, 1974.

Mauthner, Fritz, *Der Atheismus und seine Geschichte im Abendlande, Vol.3,* Stuttgart, Deutsche Verlags Anstalt, 1923.

McAdam, Doug, *Freedom Summer,* New York, Oxford University Press, 1988.

McClellan, David, *Marxism and Religion,* London, The Macmillan Press, Ltd., 1987.

McCloy, Shelley T., *Gibbon's Antagonism to Christianity,* Chapel Hill, The University of North Carolina Press, 1933.

McMaster, John Bach, *Benjamin Franklin as a Man of Letters,* Boston, Houghton, Mifflin & Co., 1887.

Melville, Herman, *Typee: A Peep at Polynesian Life,* Evanston, Ill., Northwestern University Press, 1968 (1846).

Melville, Herman, *Omoo: A Narrative of Adventures in the South Sea,* Evanston, Ill., Northwestern University Press, 1971 (1847).

Melville, Herman, *Pierre, or The Ambiguities,* Evanston, Ill, Northwestern University Press, 1971 (1853).

Melville, Herman, *Moby Dick or The Whale,* New York, The Heritage Press, 1943 (1851).

Micah, 6:8.

Mitchell, Stephen, *The Book of Job,* San Francisco, North Point Press, 1987.

Mitchell, James and Jess Stein, Eds., *The Random House Encyclopedia,* New York, Random House, 1990.

Moore, Deborah Dash, *B'nai B'rith and the Challenge of Ethnic Leadership,* Albany, State University of New York Press, 1981.

Morais, Herbert M., *Deism in Eighteenth Century America,* New York, Russell and Russell, 1960.

More, Louis T., *Isaac Newton: A Biography,* New York, Dover Publishing Inc, 1934.

Morse, Arthur D., *While Six Million Died: A Chronicle of American Apathy,* New York, Random House, 1967.

Mott, Frank L. and Chester E. Jorgenson, *Benjamin Franklin,* New York, American Book Co., 1936.

Munch, Peter A., *Crisis In Utopia,* New York, Crowell, 1971.

Mussner, Franz, *Tractate on the Jews,* Philadelphia, Fortress, 1984.

Myers, Gustavus and Henry M. Christman, *History of Bigotry in the United States,* New York, Capricorn Books, 1960.

Neusner, Jacob, *Understanding American Judaism,* New York, KTAV Publishing House, 1975.

1993 Information Please Almanac,The, Boston, Houghton Mifflin & Co. 1994.

Olby, R. C., G.N. Cantor, J.R.R. Christie and M.J.S. Hodge, eds., *Companion to the History of Modern Science,* London, Routledge, 1990.

Owen,.John, *Skeptics of the Italian Renaissance,* New York, The Macmillan Co, 1908.

Packard, Alpheus S., *Lamarck,* New York, Arno Press, 1980 .

Pessin, Deborah , *The Jewish People*, New York, The United Synagogue, 1952.

Pinsker, Leon , *Auto-emancipation,* New York, Masada, 1935.

Pinsker, Sanford, *Critical Essays on Phillip Roth,* Boston, G.K. Hall & Co., 1982.

Pizer, Donald , *The Novels of Theodore Dreiser: A Critical Study,* Minneapolis, The University of Minnesota Press, 1976.

Plamenatz, John P., *Man and Society,* London, Longmans, 1963.

Plesur, Milton, J*ewish Life in Twentieth Century America,* Chicago, Nelson-Hall, 1982.

Pope, Alexander, *Collected Poems, Epistles and Satires,* New York, Everyman's Library, 1959.

Quinn, Arthur Hobson, *The Literature of the American People,* New York, Appleton- Century- Crofts, 1951.

Raisin, Jacob S. *The Haskalah Movement in Russia,* Philadelphia, The Jewish Publication Society of America, 1913.

Raphael, Marc Lee, *A History of the United Jewish Appeal, 1939-1982,* Scholars Press, Brown Judaica Studies 34, Providence, R.I., 1982.

Rauschning, Hermann, *Hitler's Table Talk,* New York, G.P. Putnam's Sons, 1940.

Rhodes, John E., *Germany: A History*, New York, Holt, Rienhart and Winston, 1964.

Riesman, David, *The Lonely Crowd: A Study of the Changing American Character*, New Haven, Conn., Yales University Press, 1970.

Rischin, Moses, Livingston, Eds., Jews *of the American West*, M Detroit, Wayne State University Press, 1991.

Robertson, John M., *A Short History of Free Thought*, New York, Russell and Russell, 1957.

Rockefeller, Steven C., *John Dewey*, New York, Columbia Unviersity Press, 1991.

Romier, Lucien, *A History of France*, London, Macmillan & Co., 1962.

Roof, Wade C., *A Generation of Seekers: The Spiritual Journeys of the Baby-Boom Generation*, New York, Harper Collins, 1992.

Rose, Peter I., Ed., *Esssays on Jewish Life in America: The Ghetto and Beyond*, New York, Random House, 1969.

Rosenthal, Jack, *Three Award Winning Television Plays*, New York, Penguin Books, 1978.

Rosenzweig, Franz , *On Jewish Learning*, N.N. Glatzer, editor; New York, Schocken Books, 1955.

Rosten, Leo, *The Religions of America*, N.Y., Simon and Schuster, 1955.

Roth, Cecil, *History of the Jews*, New York, Schocken Books, 1963.

Roth, Cecil, *History of the Jews*, New York, Schocken Books, (1st Paperback Edition), 1963.

Russell, Bertrand, *Why I am Not a Christian*, London, Allen & Unwin, 1957.

Sanderson, Stephen K., *Macrosociology*, New York, Harper & Row, 1988.

Sayen, Janice, *Einstein In America*, New York, Crown Publishing, 1985.

Schauss, Hayim, *The Lifetime of a Jew*, New York, Union of American Hebrew Congregations, 1976..

Schlesinger, Arthur M., Jr., *The Coming of the New Deal*, Cambridge, The Riverside Press, 1958.

Schlipp, Paul A., Ed., *Albert Einstein*, London, Cambridge Unversity Press, 1970.

Schwartz, Carol and Rebecca Turner, Eds., *The Encyclopedia of Association,* 29th Edition,Vol.1, Part 1, Detroit, Gale Research Inc., 1994.

Schwartz, Gwen Gibson and Barbara Wyden, *The Jewish Wife,* New York, Peter H. Wyden, Inc., 1969.

Sears, Paul R., *Charles Darwin,* Charles Scribner's Sons, New York, 1950.

Segreff, Klaus Werner, *Moses Mendelssohn und die Aufklarungasthetik im 18ten Jahrhundert,* Bonn, Bovier Verlag, 1984.

Shelley, Percy Bysshe, *The Necessity of Atheism,* Buffalo, Prometheus Books, 1993.

Sherwin, Byron L., *Contexts and Content: Higher Jewish Education in the United States,* Chicago, Spertus College of Judaica Press, 1987.

Silberman, Charles, *A Certain People: American Jews and their Lives Today,* New York, Summit Publishing Co., 1985.

Sklare, Marshall, *Observing America's Jews,* Waltham, Mass., The Brandeis University Press, 1993.

Small, Albion W., *Origins of Sociology,* New York, Russell and Russell, 1924.

Sokolow, Nachum, *History of Zionism, v. 1,* London, Longmans, Green and Co., 1919.

Soloveitchick, Joseph B., *Halakhic Man,* Philadelphia, The Jewish Publication Society, 1983.

Spiller, Robert E., ed., *Literary History of the United States,* New York, The Macmillan Co., 1963.

Spinoza, Baruch, *Tractatus Theologico-Politicus,* in: *The Chief Works of Benedict de Spinoza,* Translated from the Latin by R.H.M. Elwes, New York, Dover Publications, Inc., 1951.

Spinoza, Benedict de, *The Political Works,* A.G. Wernham, Translator, Oxford, The Clarendon Press, 1965.

Spring, Joel, *American Education,* New York, Longman, 1989.

Stark, Rodney, and William S. Bainbridge, *The Future of Religion: Secularization, Revival and Cult Formation,* Berkeley, University of California Press, 1985.

Stephens, William, *An Account of the Growth of Deism in England,* Los Angeles, The University of California , 1990 (This is a reprint of the original which was published in 1696).

Stonequist, Everett V. , *The Marginal Man,* New York, Scribner, 1937.

Straus, Leo, S*pinoza's Critique of Religion,* New York, Schocken Books, 1965.

Szacki, Jerzy, *History of Sociological Thought,* Westport, Conn., Greenwood Press, 1979.

Taylor, A.E., *Philosophy, Its Scope and Method,* Vol. XIII, London, A. Constable & Co., 1908.

Thio, Alex, *Sociology: An Introduction,* New York, Harper & Row, 1989.

Thompson, James W. and Edgar N. Johnson, *An Introduction to Medieval Europe 300-1500,* New York, W.W. Norton & Co., Inc., 1937.

Tonnies, Ferdinand, *Geist der Neuzeit,* Leipzig, Hans Buske Verlag, 1935

Tonnies, Ferdinand, *Gemeinschaft und Gesellschaft,* Hans Buske Verlag, 1887. American Book Co., 1940.

Tyler, Moses Coit, *The Literary History of the American Revolution, 1763-1783,* New York, G.P. Putnam and Sons, 1897.

Ueberweg, Friedrich, *The History of Philosophy from Thales to the Present Time,* George S. Morris, Translator.,New York, Charles Scribner's Sons, 1890.

United States Department of Commerce, Bureau of the Census, *Historical Statistics of the United States,* Washington, D.C., United States Government Printing Office, 1975.

United States Department of Health and Human Services, National Center for Health Statistics, *Illegtimacy in the United States, 1920-1991.*

United States Department of Justice, Federal Bureau of Investigation, *Uniform Crime Reports, 1992 and 1993,* Washington, D.C., United States Government Printing Office, 1993 and 1994.

van Gennep, Arnold, *Les Rite de Passage,* Paris, No publisher, 1909.

Warren, Sidney, *American Freethought 1860-1914,* New York, Gordian Press, Inc., 1966.

Waxman, Chaim I., *America's Jews In Transition,* Philadelphia, Temple University Press, 1983.

Weiss, Bernard J., Ed., *American Education and the European Immigrant: 1840-1940*, Urbana, Ill., The University of Illinois Press, 1982.

Wertheimer, Jack, *A People Divided: Judaism In Contemporary America*, New York, Basic Books, 1993.

West, J. F. , *The Great Intellectual Revolution*, London, Cox and Wyman Ltd., 1965.

West, Geoffrey, *Charles Darwin*, New Haven, Yale University Press, 1938.

Wheeler, Daniel E., *The Life and Writings of Thomas Paine*, New York, Vincent Parke & Co., 1908.

White, Andrew Dickson, *A History of the Warfare of Science with Theology in Christendom*, New York, The Free Press, 1965.

Whitehead, Alfred N., *Process and Reality: An Essay in Cosmology*, New York, Harper Torchbooks, 1960 (Macmillan 1929).

Whiteny, Charles, *Francis Bacon and Modernity*, New Haven, The Yale University Press, 1986.

Wiesel, Elie, *Night*, New York, Hill and Wang, 1960.

Williams, Robert D., ed., *John Dewey: Recollections*, Washington, D.C., University Press of America, 1982.

Wilmot, Lawrence T., *Whitehead and God: Prologomena to Theological Reconstruction*, Waterloo, Ontario, The Wilfred Laurier University Press, 1979.

Wolf, Abraham, *A History of Science, Technology and Philosophy in the 16th and 17th Century*, New York, Harper, 1959.

Woocher, Jonathan S., *Sacred Survival: The Civil Religion of American Jews*, Bloomington, Indiana University Press, 1986.

Wood, Paul S. and Evelyn M. Boyd, *Masters of English Literature*, New York, The Macmillan Co., 1942.

Wood, Alan, *Bertrand Russell: The Passionate Skeptic, A Biography*, New York, Simon and Schuster, 1958.

Wundt, Wilhelm, *Einleitung in die Philosophie*, Leipzig, Verlag von Wilhelm Engelmann, 1901.

Yeshivah University Undergraduate Catalog, 1991-93.

Yovel, Yirmiyahu, *Spinoza and Other Heretics: The Marrano of Reason and The Adventures of Immanence (2 vols.)* Princeton, N.J., Princeton University Press, 1989.

Zbrowsky, Mark and Elizabeth Herzog, *Life Is With People: The Culture of the Shtetl*, New York, Schocken Books, 1952.

Zimmerman, Judith A. and Barbara Trainin, Eds., *Jewish Population, Renascence or Oblivion*, New York, Commission on Synagogue Relations, Federation of Jewish Philanthropies, 1979.

Journals

Austin, William H., "Isaac Newton on Science and Religion," *Journal of the History of Ideas*, vol. 31, No. 1, 1970.

Barman, Lawrence, "Confronting Secularization: Origins of the London Society for the Study of Religion," *Church History*, Vol. 62, No. 1, March 1993.

Beiser, Vince, "For the Love of Jesus," *The Jerusalem Report*, Vol. 5, No.19, January 26, 1995.

Bellah, Robert N., "Civil Religion in America," *Daedalus, Journal of the American Arts and Sciences*, Vol. 96, No. 1, in Childress and Harnard, eds., *Secularization and the Protestant Prospect*, Philadelphia, Westminster Press, 1970.

Breuer, Edward, "Politics, Tradition, History: Rabbinic Judaism and the Eighteenth Century Struggle for Civil Equality, " *Harvard Theological Review*, Vol. 85, No. 3, July 1992.

Burtt, Shelley, "Religious Parents, Secular Schools: A Liberal Defense of an Illiberal Education," *The Review of Politics*, Vol. 56, No. 1, Winter 1994.

"Charitable seductions," *Time*, Vol. 144, October 3, 1994.

Chaves, Mark, "Interorganizational Power and Internal Secularization in Protestant Denominations," *The American Journal of Sociology*, Vol. 99, No.1, July, 1993.

Cohen, Steven and Leonard Fein, "From Integration to Survival: American Jewish Anxieties in Transition," *The Annals of the American Academy*, Vol. 480, No. 1, July 1985.

Cooperman, Bernard D., "Jewish Studies and Jewish Identity: Some Implications of Secularizing Torah," *Judaism*, Vol.42, Spring 1993.

Decter, Midge, "The ADL vs. the Religious Right," *Commentary*, Vol. 98, No.3, September 1994.

Doerr, Edd, "Bashing Humanists," *Church and State*, Vol. 50, No. 3, May/June 1990.

"Dr. Sue," Confessions of a Supplementary School Principal," *Jewish Education*, V. 57, No. 1, Spring 1989 .

Drinan, Robert F, "The Supreme Court to Review Student Prayer Groups in High School, " *America*, vol. 162, No. 15, April 28, 1990.

Dubin, David, "Lay Leadership and Jewish Identity," *Journal of Jewish Communal Service*, Vol. 68, No. 4, Summer 1992.

Efron, Sara G., " Old Wine, New Bottles: Traditional Moral Education in the Contemporary Jewish Classroom," *Religious Education*, Vol. 85, No., 1, Winter 1994.

Epstein, Saundra Sterling, "The Great Exodus of Jewish Educators: Why Is It Happening?" *The Pedagogic Reporter*, Vol.XXXIX, No.2, May 1989.

Falk , Gerhard and Vern Bullough, "Achievement Among German Jews Born During the Years 1785-1885. *Mankind Quarterly*, Vol. XXVII, No 3., Spring 1987.

Falk, Robert, "Thomas Paine: Deist or Quaker?" *Pennsylvania Magazine of History and Biography,*Vol. 62, 1938.

Foster, Claude R., "Historical Antecedents: Why the Holocaust?" *The Annals of the American Academy of Political and Social Science*, Vol. 40, No. 7, 1980.

Friedman, Norman L., "Reform Jewish Sunday School Primary Grades Department: An Ethnography," *Jewish Education*, Vol. 55, No. 2, Summer 1987.

Galston, William A., "Salvation through Participation: John Dewey and the Religion of Democracy," *Raritan*, Winter 1993.

Gans, Herbert J., "American Jewry: Present and Future," *Commentary*, Vol.21, No.5, May, 1956. Gans,Herbert J., "The Future of American Jewry," *Commentary*, Vol. 21, No.6, June, 1956.

Gurevitch, Paul, "The Jeffries Affair," *Commentary*, Vol.93, March, 1992.

Hazlett, Thomas W. , "The Wrath of Farrakhan," *Reason*, Vol.26, No.66, May, 1994.

Herberg, Will, "Religion in Higher Education," *Journal of Higher Education*, Vol. 23, October 1952.

Himmelfarb, Gertrude, "A De-moralized Society: The British-American Experience," *American Educator*, Vol. 18, No. 4, Winter , 1994-95.

Horowitz, Charles, "The New Anti-Semitism," *New York*, Vol. 26, July 11, 1993.

Johnson, Jean and John Immerwahr, "What Americans Expect from their Public Schools," New York, Public Agenda, 1994 and *American Educator,* Vol. 18, No. 4, Winter, 1994-95.

Kristol, Irving, "The Future of American Jewry," *Commentary,* Vol. 92, No.2, August 1991.

Kristol, .Irving, "Why Religion Is Good for the Jews," *Commentary,* Vol. 98, No. 2, August 1994.

Kulick, Seth, "The Evolution of Secular Judaism," *The Humanist,* Vol. 53, March/April, 1993.

Lerner, Robert, Althea K. Nagai and Stanely Rothman, "Marginality and Liberalism Among Jewish Elties," *Public Opinion Quarterly,* Vol. 53, No. 3, Fall, 1989.

Lipson, Alfred, "The Liberation and its Aftermath-A Personal Viewpoint," *Together,* Vol. 9, No. 1, December 1994.

London, Perry, "The Goals of Jewish Education: Jewih Identity Must be Primary," *Agenda,* Vol.1, No.1.Fall, 1992.

Mader, Janet, "How Women are Changing the Rabbinate," *Reform Judaism,* Summer 1991.

Makovsky, David, "The Business of Peace,", U.S. News and World Report, Vol. 117, No.18, November 7, 1994.

Massarik, Fred, "Knowledge About U.S. Jewish Populations," *Journal of Jewish Communal Service,* Vol.68, No.4, Summer 1992.

Massarik, Fred, "A Report on the Jewish Population of Los Angeles," *Western Jewish History,* Vol. 49, 1953.

McRobert, Laurie, "Emil L. Fackenheim and Radical Evil," *Journal of the American Academy of Religion,* Vol., LVII, No.2, Summer 1989.

Morgan, Michael L., "Spinoza In History," *Judaism, Vol.40, No.2,* Spring 1991.

Morgan, Michael L., "Mendelssohn's Defense of Reason in 'Jerusalem', *Judaism,* Vol. 38, No.4, Fall, 1989.

Morgan, Michael L., "Martin Buber, Cooperation and Evil," *Journal of the American Academy of Religion,* Vol. LVIII, No. 1, Spring, 1990.

Norden, Edward, "Counting the Jews," *Commentary,* Vol. 92, No.4, October 1991.

Park, Robert E., "Human Migration and the Marginal Man," *American Journal of Sociology,* Vol. 33, May, 1928.

Parsons, Talcott, "Religion in Postindustrial America," *Social Research,* Vol. 41, No. 2, Summer 1974.

Pearson, David E., "Post-Mass Culture," *Society,* Vol.30, No.5, July-August, 1993.

Plaut, W. Gunther, "Emancipation: The Challenge of Living In Two Worlds," *Judaism,* Vol., 38, No., 4.

Rosenbaum, Ron, "The Most Hated Lawyer in America," *Vanity Fair,* Vol.31, March 1992.

Rosenberg, Bernhard H, "A Study of the Alumni of the James Striar School at Yeshiva University," *Jewish Education,* Vol. 61, Spring 1994.

Rosenthal, Erich, "Five Million American Jews," *Commentary,* Vol. 26, No.6, December 1958.

Schafler, Samuel, "God and the Jewish School," *Jewish Education,* Vol. 57, No. 1, Spring 1989.

Schiff, Alvin I., "Toward the Year 2000 - Condition of Jewish Life: Implications for Jewish Education,"*Jewish Education,* Vol.58, No.1, Spring, 1990.

Schiff, Alvin I., "The American Jewish Day School: Retrospect and Prospect," *The Pedagogic Review,* Vol.XXXVIII, No. 3, November 1987.

"Sea Change," *U.S. News & Woirld Report,*Vol. 117, No.20, November 21, 1994.

Sharot, Stephen, "Judaism and the Secularization Debate," *Sociological Analysis,* Vol. 52, No. 1, Spring 1991.

Shimoff, Sandra R., "Judaic Studies: An Interdsiciplinary Model," *Jewish Education,* Vol.57, No.2, Summer,1989.

Stille, Alexander "What the Holocaust Meant," *Dissent,* Vol. 37, No. 3, Summer 1990.

Turner, Ralph H., "The Many Faces of American Sociology," *The American Behavioral Scientist, Vol. 33, No. 6, July/August 1990.*

"The Vanishing American Jew," *Look,* Vol.22, May 13, 1958.

Wills, Garry, "The Secularist Prejudice," *Christian Century,* Vol. 107, No. 30, October 24, 1990.

Wine, Sherwin T., "Humanistic Judaism and the 'God Is Dead' Theology", *Religious Humanism,* Vol.1,Winter 1967.

Wistrich,Robert S., "Do the Jews Have a Future?" *Commentary,* Vol. 98, No. 1, July, 1994.

Newspapers

Blustain, Rachel, "Baruch Atah Ado....NOT!" *The Forward,* Vol. 97, No. 30, 978, June 3, 1994.

Blustain, Rachel, "Jewish Leaders Striking Back at WJC Brass," *Forward,* Vol. 98, No. 31,005, December 9, 1994.

"Captains of Charity," *Forward,* Vol.97, No. 30,963, February 18, 1994.

Curran, Bob, *The Buffalo News,* Sunday, January 22, 1995.

"Federation meeting to honor Nathan Benderson, Harry Kosansky for leadership, Achievements.", *Buffalo Jewish Review,* Vol. 87, No. 11, November 18, 1994.

Feiden, Douglas, "Cuomo Steers Cash to Lubavitch Cronies," *Forward,* June 24, 1994.

"The Featherman File," *The Forward,* Vol.98, No. 31, 011, January 20, 1995.

Fiske, Edward, *The New York Times,* February 21, 1991.

"The Forward Fifty," *Forward,* Vol. 98, No.31, November 18, 1994.

Jacobs, William R. and Robert B. Barr, "Many Jews Share Our Beliefs," *Forward,* Vol. LXXXXII, No.35. July 8, 1994.

Jacoby, Sally, "The Mystery of Organizational Malaise," *Forward,* Vol. 98, No.31,002, November 18, 1994.

Rich, Spencer, "The Rich Got Richer Again, *The Washington Post,* September 20, 1992.

Steinfels, Peter, "Picture of Faith Worries Catholic Leaders," *The New York Times,* June 1, 1994, pp. A 1 and B 8.

The New York Times, April 25, 1929, p.60, column 4.

The Wall Street Journal.

Zremski, Jerry, "Supreme Court decision separating church, state has wide ramifications," *The Buffalo News,* June 28, 1994.

Legal cases

Cochran vs. Louisiana State Board of Education, 281 U.S. 913 (1930).

Edwards vs. Aguillard, 482 U.S. 578 (1987).
Engel vs. Vitale, 370 U.S. 421 (1962).
Epperson vs. Arkansas, 393 U.S. 97 (1968).
Illinois ex. rel. McCollum vs. Board of Education, 333 U.S. 202 (1948).
Lemon vs. Kurtzman, 403 U.S. 602 (1971).
Pierce vs. Society of Sisters, 268 U.S. 510 (1925).
Sherbert vs. Verner, 374 U.S., 398 (1963).
Wallace vs. Jaffree, 472 U.S. 38 (1985).

Bulletins

Academic Bulletin of The Jewish Theological Seminary of America, 1993-1994.
Bulletin of Temple Shaarey Zedek, Buffalo, N.Y. July, 1994.

INDEX

About the Author

Gerhard Falk is the author of *The Jew in Christian Theology* (McFarland, 1992) and over fifty other publications, including *Murder* (McFarland, 1990); *Aging in America;* and *A Study in Social Change.* A popular lecturer and speaker, Dr. Falk holds the State University of New York Chancellor's Award for Excellence in Teaching. He is Professor of Sociology at the State University of New York College at Buffalo.